PRIVATE INTEREST, PUBLIC SPENDING

Balanced-Budget Conservatism and the Fiscal Crisis

Sidney Plotkin and William E. Scheuerman

South End Press
Boston, MA

Cover design by Nancy Adams
Text design and production by the South End Press collective
Printed in the U.S.A.

Library of Congress Cataloging-in-Publication Data
Scheuerman, Williams
    Private Interest, public spending: balanced-budget conservatism and the fiscal crisis/ William E. Scheuerman and Sidney Plotkin.
    p. cm.
Includes Index.
ISBN 0-89608-464-7: $16.00.– ISBN 0-89608-465-5: $40.00
    1. Finance, Public–United States–1933- 2. Government spending policy–United States. 3. Budget–United States. I. Plotkin, Sidney. II. Title
HJ25.2.S33 1993
336.73–dc20
                            93-14852
                            CIP

South End Press, 116 Saint Botolph St, Boston, MA 02115
99 98 97 96 95 94   1 2 3 4 5 6 7 8 9

CONTENTS

ACKNOWLEDGEMENTS

The authors received welcome support for this project from several sources. The Henry J. Kaiser Family Foundation, Menlo Park, California, provided a grant to Bill Scheuerman so that he could complete research at the Walter E. Reuther Archives in labor history at Wayne State University. At Vassar College, two wonderful students, Alfredo López and Susan Smith, helped Sid Plotkin greatly by tracking down sources and doing a host of research-related tasks. Karin Aguilar-San Juan, our editor at South End Press for most of this project, proved to be a stern but supportive critic, and Carlos Suarez patiently steered the manuscript through its final stages. Finally, a valued coterie of colleagues and friends—Ray Broyczka, Jim and Sondra Farganis, Obika Gray, Rodolfo Rosales, and Sue Nissman—aided and strengthened this study, sometimes unknowingly, by their willingness to talk through and debate ideas. Of course, for any errors or imperfections of analysis in the book the authors alone bear full responsibility.

This book is dedicated to our parents, wives, and children.

INTRODUCTION

The story of the U.S. political economy in the years between 1973 and 1992 is the tale of three dismal trends and one big effort to paper them over with propaganda. Stagnation, growing inequality, and ballooning federal debt are the dominant economic hallmarks of the last generation. Devastating as they are to the vast majority of the population, the economic hallmarks of the recent past are not without a strong ideological veneer. Two decades of economic decline have triggered a deliberate political effort to deflect attention from the private causes and social consequences of stagnation, inequality, and mushrooming federal debt. Out of the structured disconnection between material trend and public ideology reverberate the familiar patterns of the 1980s and 1990s: tax resistance; dog-eat-dog competition for public spending; expanding federal debt; the irrelevance of political debate; governmental paralysis at all levels; and, perhaps the weirdest phenomenon, the tremendous growth of national government spending even as state and local governments feel the big fiscal squeeze.

Cumulatively, such developments have fractured and crippled the U.S. political economy. The unified and abundant political economy of the post-New Deal era is gone, finished. Elites have collaborated to lessen the central government's responsibilities in virtually every sphere of economy and society, blaming it only for stagnation. Nowadays the overarching symbol of U.S. decline is not the tottering corporate giant, but the giant government deficit. Of course, despite Rightwing attempts to completely dismantle government social programs, government continues to pay millions of non-working people to consume. Bill Clinton will spend even more to provide national health insurance, a long-needed expansion of the welfare state. But entitlements apart, national government activism and social planning are pretty much dead letters.

Government at all levels stands bowed before the discipline of market economics. Even the once pro-government Democrats call for a more competitive economy and a leaner state. Neither economic stagnation nor jobless recovery—not even the threat of urban explosion—motivates substantial federal activism. Hamstrung by deficits, Washington grows more distant from the states. Down at the end of the line, in the cities, meanwhile, thrive the forces of social dissolution and misery. Yet as federal government abdicates its responsibilities, the economy itself becomes ever less capable of directing resources toward the needs of society as a whole.

This study examines the political and economic dynamics behind conflicts between public spending and private power. Ours is at once an analysis of material trends, ideological obfuscation, and political responses. We seek to explain the roots of economic derangement, the strategies by which private economic irrationality is transformed into public fiscal crisis, and the ways these developments shape the context for political action. Ultimately, though, our concern here is with action, with what people can to do change the situation in democratic ways and with democratic results. Though we devote much attention here to what is and why it is that way, we do so in order to probe for points of vulnerability in the system of injustice, and for democratic possibility in an otherwise formidable ideological charade.

This work began with a more limited focus. We started by focusing on how private stagnation and conservative priorities affected the "shop floor" conditions of public-sector workers, how public employees answered the attack, and how they might better do so, particularly on behalf of a broader Left response to the conservatism prevalent in both major parties. One of the authors, Bill Scheuerman, is a leader in a major public-employee union in New York State, with much experience in the bitter fight to defend public employees and the quality of public services against the onslaught of what we call "balanced-budget conservatism." The other, Sid Plotkin, has worked with several community-based organizations and studied the private preoccupations of suburbia.

The original plan of this work was to focus exclusively on conflicts between public spending and private interests in New York State. There, the nation's most liberal governor, Mario Cuomo, achieved his first real political success in a primary-election struggle with New York City's conservative Democratic Mayor Ed Koch, a victory that depended heavily on Cuomo's ties to public-sector unions. How did this strong liberal governor behave in an era of balanced-budget conservatism? A major contender for the Democratic nomination for president in 1992, with obligations to working-class voters and organizations, Cuomo had to contend with the multiple pressures of fiscal crisis, especially the colliding forces of tax-cut demands from business and the suburbs and demands to preserve the public sector from unions and community-based organizations. How did Cuomo respond? What did public labor do? What concessions did Cuomo have to make to corporate and propertied interests as the price for his re-election? How, if at all, did state employees answer Cuomo's strategic and tactical gambits with progressive political strategies of their own? What lessons might progressives, especially public-employee unionists and community activists, learn from these varied experiences? What difference did it all make to the people of New York State?

The more we studied the New York experience, the clearer it became that Cuomo prevailed by going back on most of his liberal promises and by giving New York's well-organized business lobby the income and business tax cuts that it wanted. To pay for this corporate-directed largess, Cuomo forced public employees to accept speed-ups, layoffs, benefit cuts, attrition, and even payless furloughs, while asking ordinary taxpayers to ante up the difference in lost business taxes.

In New York, during the Cuomo years, as in the nation during the Reagan-Bush years, balanced-budget conservatism proved to be an ideological veneer for tax policies designed to redistribute income from ordinary workers to the rich—while reducing the scope of public benefits for working people. Yet, curiously, while New York's Cuomo mimicked the pro-upper-class policies of the Reagan era, it was also true that Cuomo managed to maintain his reputation as a compassionate liberal. More important, Cuomo avoided reactionary anti-tax movements. California and New Jersey, also led by activist liberal governors, were not so lucky. In these states, middle-class tax revolts produced big tax cuts and more. As a result of embittered tax politics, public policy in California and New Jersey turned sharply right, notably more so than in New York. Yet these states also had liberal Democratic governors, Jerry Brown in California and James Florio in New Jersey. What was different about these cases? Was it within the power of Brown and Florio to stem the tide of tax revolt? Were the economic forces within their jurisdictions so overwhelming that reaction was inevitable? Was New York under Cuomo fortunate to be spared more vicious reactions? Or did Cuomo better understand the intricate fiscal politics that requires two parts social retrenchment and two parts compliance with corporate demand?

To develop a richer grasp of Cuomo's New York, we decided to broaden our analysis to include the tax-rebel states of California and New Jersey. These studies gave useful perspective to the questions we studied in New York. Most important, the comparisons helped illustrate how politics shaped the outcomes of retrenchment. Indeed, as we developed the analysis that follows, we focused on more than the politics of fiscal conflict in the states or the impacts on public employees and the public sector. This book is, in fact, a broad examination of the way a very conservative brand of politics and political strategy now affects the balance and conflict of social classes in key states and in the nation as a whole.

Again and again, as we looked at political-economic circumstances in the various states, we were impressed by the fact that economic factors did not dictate or determine political outcomes in any simple or direct way. If anything, the economic circumstances of the last two decades seemed propitious for radicals. Jobs disappeared, corporations went on the attack against labor, ordinary people found it ever harder to make ends meet, consumer confidence sagged. Old-fashioned radical warnings of stagnation and impoverishment were widely validated by the evidence of economic malfunction. If there was ever a situation ready-made for progressive groups, the recent stagnant, slow-growth economy would have seemed to be it.

The main focus of recent U.S. politics has obviously not been on jobs, enhancing the economic rights of working people, or meeting social needs. Instead, the focus has been on deficits, taxes, and the irrationality of public spending. Mainstream politicians have aimed at reducing popular economic rights, dismantling social programs, weakening domestic government, and empowering business. *The erosion of capitalist performance has given rise to conservative solutions rather than radical movements.* Business, helped by popular conservative politicians such as Ronald Reagan, used politics to shift blame for economic failure onto the public sector. This ideological displacement has been extremely effective for recent business purposes. But it remains to be seen whether an ideology of displaced responsibility can hold the system together for longer-range purposes.

For now, the more pressing issue is to realize that, even *within* the predominant conservative framework, conservative definitions of the economic context, as well as its reliance on market forces and the need to reduce public spending, have not yielded uniform class responses. A main theme that emerges from the study is that even when we look at conventional politics in the states from within, people of all classes have choices to make about their political responses. Within the parameters of capitalist democracy meaningful change is possible. Our analysis suggests that throughout the recent decades elected officials, interest-group leaders from the business and working classes, and middle-class tax protestors all faced delicate and complex situations. They reacted not according to a predetermined set of economic causes and effects, but out of a complicated brew of power, ideology, interest, strategy, and emotion, with consequences just as disparate and complicated for the people living in New York, New Jersey, and California. In other words, we came away from this study as convinced as ever about the power of capitalist wealth in U.S. politics; but perhaps also more convinced than when we began about the power of politics and political choice, of the possibility of human agency and freedom in shaping, limiting, and reinforcing the power of property. For ill as well as good, we learned new lessons about how ordinary people can affect politics and government, and through such influence, the broader course of the economy. Most important, we saw that the task for working people is not only to influence what happens in government, but to do so in a constructive and on-going fashion. The book was written on the assumption that the Left—that scattered and disconnected amalgam of labor unions, community-action and social-rights groups—can and should contribute to the creation of a more democratic, socially responsible economy. The corporate economy, after all, is not serving many of the most important needs of working people; the predominant ideology masks the real causes of material disarray, and each major party is engaged in perpetuating that ideology through the politics of evasion. The public has little confidence in conventional politicians and politics. On the other hand, the task for the Left is extremely difficult, perhaps insurmountable. Inasmuch as balanced-budget conservatism has successfully identified state fiscal mismanagement as the predominant public issue, Left groups must wage two simultaneous but quite different struggles. On the one hand, unions and community groups have to use all their scarce political muscle just to protect public jobs and the programs and constituents they serve. On the other hand, in order to achieve democratic social change, Left groups must find ways to isolate corporate power and irresponsibility as the root of the problem to redirect the political economy so that it will serve general interests. The complexities here are daunting.

When unions and community activists get caught up in the trials of securing their most immediate interests, they understandably have little time or patience for broader ideological concerns. Holding on is hard enough. As the politics and economics of retrenchment beat down on people, it is all they can do to fight just to stay above water, even if such limited triumph comes at the expense of other communities or unions. Yet if the Left forgoes larger considerations centering on corporate power and the abdication of social responsibilities by Washington, Leftists inevitably play into the hands of the political Right. Unless unions and community groups find ways to coalesce behind national challenges to the orthodoxy of balanced-budget conservatism, what the political system has in store for ordinary people is an interminable series of demands to take less. Many individuals will just give up, having no viable alternatives. Indeed, many have already stopped voting, indifferent to electoral politics. The only reasonable strategy in today's two-front struggle is, as we suggest in the Conclusion, for Left activists to organize individual battles in ways that broaden alliances and enlarge public understanding of government responsibility. Otherwise, individual struggles for economic self-preservation will never become class acts.

In the broadest sense, then, this study assumes that clearer understanding of the links between economic and political power and between public policy and political action is crucial to more effective change and less counterproductive pressure from below. Our book is an example of applied, politically focused, and value-guided political science. We make no apologies for declaring our commitment to the use of social science for the cause of ordinary working people.

Here's a roadmap for the book: Chapter One offers a conceptual framework of the fractured political economy and its disguise: the omnipresent political focus on deficits, spending cuts, and tax avoidance that we call balanced-budget conservatism. Chapter Two is a review of the main causes and effects of the slow-growth economy: private corporate stagnation, growing class inequality, and ballooning federal debt. Challenging the conventional wisdom that sees deficits as fundamentally a problem of excessive government spending, this chapter offers a critical review of the material conditions and forces within the corporate-led economy that lead to big government spending. Chapter Three reveals the real economic situation by correcting the distortions of balanced-budget conservatism. Here we describe the main principles of balanced-budget conservatism and discuss how conservatives use it to justify and celebrate meat-axe approaches to public employees, public spending, and public needs. Most important, we stress the divisive consequences of balanced-budget conservatism, which, as often as not, masquerades as a celebration of grassroots democracy, community control, and states' rights.

The remaining chapters trace the mixture of political and economic forces, Rightwing ideology, and collective action as they are reflected in the suburbs, in the precincts of organized corporate power, and among unionized public employees. Chapter Four brings into focus how modern-day Fortress Suburbia grows out of historic patterns of divide and rule in U.S. politics. This chapter suggests how balanced-budget conservatism flourishes in the suburbs because it flows out of this divisive political tradition. Especially by means of the tax question, we argue, this tradition sustains divisions between urban and suburban working people, helping to keep suburbanites linked in key ways to the causes of capital. In essence, this chapter examines how U.S. politics has worked to pit segments of the economic majority against each other, weakening the social basis of the Left, and giving disproportionate voice and power to upper-income, anti-tax interests. Chapter Five considers the effects of such divisions in the context of the California and New Jersey tax revolts. It reveals how failures of liberal leadership, especially weaknesses rooted in the ambivalence of the Democratic Party toward suburbanization, helped to propel local tax revolts forward and ultimately to swing state and national political debates to the Right. Chapters Seven and Eight take detailed looks at New York State under Cuomo. These chapters consider the price Cuomo had to pay to keep business happy and the suburbs from exploding. Chapter Seven documents the reorganization of business in New York and its effect on Cuomo's budget and tax policies. In Chapter Eight, we look at the reactions of public-employee unions and their rocky, uneven record of response to the Cuomo-business alliance. Chapter Nine concludes the study with a summary of the broad political implications of the analysis. We focus here on the implications for progressive strategies in the Clinton era, an era that we think has much more in common with the Reagan-Bush years than many excited liberal observers would like to believe.

Chapter One

THE FRACTURED POLITICAL ECONOMY

I have no interest in raising taxes until spending is cut—no tax increases without the spending cuts.

President Bill Clinton

Let us now face the fact that for many a recession is a tolerable, even a pleasant thing. And let us say so. This will not be popular. There could be indignant denial. That is often the response to unwelcome truth.

Economist John Kenneth Galbraith[1]

U.S. workers currently face what is arguably the most difficult situation in labor history. Three big trends now move against the interest of labor. First, U.S. corporations, preoccupied with global competition, international stagnation, and continuous pressure to lower costs, are rapidly displacing human labor with automatic machine technology. This is true not only in manufacturing, but in service industries as well. Throughout the private economy, secure full-time jobs are harder to come by. Ominously, the fully automated fast-food stop will soon join automatic tellers and the charge-card gasoline pumps as labor-saving devices of the automated service sector. Even low-paying service-sector jobs are on the verge of extinction.

Second, despite slow growth and jobless recovery, the federal government is frozen by the deficit question. Fearing conservative reactions on Wall Street and Main Street, Washington refuses to add significant new doses of spending, known as a stimulus, to energize the economy or to create new jobs. Riding the crest of his 1992 victory, and after just four months in office, President Clinton could not move even a small jobs package through Congress. No more spending, no more taxes, said the Republican Senate minority. In a remarkable display of majoritarian concession to minority influence, Clinton tossed in the towel. Forget the stimulus approach; to pay down the deficit he would have "no tax increases without the spending cuts."[2]

Finally, crunched by slow growth in employment and a decade of reductions in federal aid, state and local governments are fortunate to stay just one step ahead of tax increases and spending cuts themselves, not to mention layoffs of public employees, tax revolts, and community protests over threatened programs. These governments, which together employ seven times as many workers as the federal government, compete hungrily for new business investment by offering competitive tax abatements and other benefits, which local tax payers must then make up through higher tax rates or reduced services. But states and cities have little choice. They need business to generate jobs, wages, and taxes. Desperate for scarce labor-intensive capital, many jurisdictions steal existing businesses from one another. Among the states and cities, economic policy has become a war of each against all.

The system is disintegrating, and no economic grouping has the economic vitality to energize the whole. Slow corporate growth worsens the federal deficit, reinforces political preoccupations with capping the debt, and restricts government's power to enliven the corporate economy. The economic squeeze exacerbates pressures on state and local jurisdictions, which fiercely struggle for jobs-creating investment within a production system that is steadily jettisoning its need for permanent, full-time workers.

Toward a Post-Labor Economy?

The declining supply of well-paying, secure, full-time jobs is one of the worst threats to labor. The U.S. economy is less capable than ever before of supplying such jobs. As one sign of the broader trend, for the first time in U.S. history, workers must now comprehend the bizarre reality of a jobless recovery. The very terminology suggests how insensitive to human needs current economic thought has become. In other words, economists look for signs of health and disease in the requirements of systems, not people. Systems recover; people remain ill. A little history can illuminate the shift. Typically, recoveries from recession in the post-World War II era have led to job growth in the range of 5% to 7%; between March 1991 and February 1993, the most recent recession, the number of new jobs grew by less than 1%. And in some places, such as New York City, the number of jobs actually fell despite recovery.[3] Coming on the heels of a decade during which most newly created jobs were in low-wage services, the number of two-earner families leapt upward, and temporary, part-time jobs became the best opportunity many workers could get (see Chapter Two). The theme of "jobless recovery" only hammers home the insight that relationships between economic growth and individual access to paid work have already changed in fundamental ways.[4]

These days, pressured by competition originating from production sites across the planet, the U.S. mega-corporations rely disproportionately on capital and technology rather than labor to reap their profits. Between 1988 and 1990, for example, as companies such as IBM, Sears, and GM laid off workers in droves, employment in the big corporate sector dropped by 500,000 jobs. All told, the Fortune 500 companies, the solid core of the once mighty U.S. corporate economy, now employ only about one in ten workers, down from 21% in 1970. More and more, the big firms rely on automated machines and cheap, Third-World labor to produce their wares. Many business executives, and President Clinton himself, like to argue that such trends result from the poor education and skills of U.S. workers. Automated machines are seen as a last resort for businesses that cannot find employees capable of handling complex production processes. If we had a better trained workforce, so the conventional wisdom goes, we would have more jobs. To further this end, Clinton proposed during his campaign to require that all firms employing fifty or more people invest 1.5% of their capital in worker training.

The exclusion of smaller businesses from the trend toward job retrenchment is crucial, as we shall see in a moment, but the key point for now is that even government data show that education is not the main logjam when it comes to job creation. The government's own Commission on the Skills of the American Workforce recently reported that 80% of U.S. employers are satisfied with the skills of their workers and only 5% expect future increases in skill requirements. Numerous college graduates find it hard to get jobs that demand much more than minimal skills. A fifth of today's college graduates now work in low-skill jobs, up from 11% in 1968. In 1992, for example, 1.3 million college graduates held blue-collar jobs; 664,000 worked as retail sales clerks; 83,000 as maids or janitors; and another 166,000 drove trucks and buses. And even before the 1990 recession, 440,000 college graduates were simply unemployed.[5]

The real driving force behind corporate replacement of humans by machines is not poor education; it is cost. New automated machines are simply cheaper than new workers. Since 1987, the cost of an average worker, including wages and benefits, has risen by more than 17% compared with the average price of new business equipment. Taking falling interest rates into account, the gap has widened by almost 40%. As TV business commentator Adam Smith cheerily notes, "A computer

doesn't charge for overtime and doesn't get health-care benefits."[6]
Jeremy Rifkin graphically depicts labor's future as the prevalent logic of
capital accumulation unfolds:

> One does not need to look far to get a glimpse of things to
> come. The Postal Service plans to cut 47,000 workers by
> 1995, predicting that computers will be able to read letters
> and sort mail far more efficiently than humans. Similarly,
> AT&T intends to replace up to 6,000 operators with robotic
> operators that can distinguish key words of speech. Postal
> service and AT&T workers are not alone. Most American
> workers are employed in tasks that can be done by comput-
> ers, automated machinery and robots.[7]

In effect, through heightened automation, U.S. Big Business is not
only producing commodities, it has begun to relieve large segments of
the workforce from the economic market. More and more workers have
become surplus people for whom job markets no longer exist. In a real
sense, people have now been discharged from what Marx called
capital's reserve army of labor. Indeed, the whole concept of the reserve
army becomes suspect in a world economy bent on shattering the very
need for labor. The fact is corporate capital is now generating a surplus
of unwanted free time for tens of millions of workers. It is forcing labor
into a status of terrifying freedom from work—and wages. Because jobs
are the only legitimate way to gain an income in this society, indeed,
because jobs are the very anchor of social status in this society, invol-
untarily "liberated" workers stand to lose not only their economic
security, but their very dignity and rank as contributing citizens. Without alternative means of earning a living, without access to the key
economic role that confers standing as full-fledged citizens, without
alternative outlets for absorbing their energy and creativity in socially
useful activity, superfluous workers face life as economic refuse. Their
new levels of free time are enjoyed not as "freedom," but as a soul-numb-
ing threat to economic security and psychic self-worth. Andre Gorz,
perhaps the Left's most acute observer of these developments, concludes that labor currently faces nothing less than a profound, revolu-
tionary change. Absent a political-economic movement to reorganize
the way work and income are distributed, labor's challenge is somehow
to locate itself in an economy in which its role grows superfluous. As
Gorz writes, labor's chances can only be glum within "a social system
which is unable to redistribute, manage or employ this new-found
free-time; a system fearful of the expansion of this time, yet which does

its utmost to increase it, and which, in the end, can find no purpose for it other than seeking all possible means of turning it into money."[8]

Of course we would be exaggerating to say that the U.S. economy has lost *all* its capacity to generate new jobs for ordinary workers. In today's economy, however, such jobs are created mainly, if at all, in the ruthlessly competitive small-business sector. While jobs were fast disappearing inside the corporate sector during the late 1980s, jobs in companies employing less than twenty workers grew by more than four million. Today, more than thirty-six million U.S. citizens work in places with less than 100 employees. This is one major reason why, when President Bill Clinton recently signed legislation granting workers unpaid family leave (itself a small sign of the looming redistribution of work), he raised no objections to exemptions for firms employing less than fifty workers. With this critical loophole, Clinton hoped to keep small businesses hiring. But by excluding the smallest employers, Clinton also effectively ensured that this vital right to unpaid leave covered only 39% of the workforce.[9]

The sad fact is that jobs are growing fastest in that sector of the economy—small business—which is least organized by unions and which pays the lowest wages and benefits. In 1991 companies employing less than 100 workers paid about $4.25 less per hour than firms employing 500 or more workers, while the benefits paid by small firms were about $3.00 per hour less than their large corporate counterparts. Similarly, half of U.S. adults without health insurance labored in companies with less than twenty-five workers.[10] As small, competitive-sector businesses become the last refuge of labor in the U.S. economy, workers face a future of intensifying pressures to accept lower wages and smaller benefits. Some in the labor movement hope the Clinton Administration will back reforms to help labor unions bring many of these workers into the fold. But organizing small shops is notoriously difficult. And business makes no bones about the fact that it will fight tooth and nail against such moves. "That's business' nightmare," declares one trade journal, warning that "even with a Democrat in the White House, unions probably can't win against all-out business opposition."[11]

The Deficit and Economic Evasion

Since the 1930s, of course, the government has tried to pick up the slack when corporate investment sags. Through spending programs and tax cuts, Washington "primed the pump." Not any more. The national government, which once stood as employer and economic booster of last resort, is nowadays so preoccupied with cutting the deficit that it seems unwilling, if not downright incapable, of developing a master plan for economic renewal. To his credit, Clinton's 1992 campaign for president hammered away at the economic insecurity theme, and Clinton did promise plans to create millions of well-paying, high-skilled jobs. What he did not explain is how his program would reverse the technical logic of dis-employment. As economics writer Robert Kuttner has observed, "In circles where experts earnestly call for additional high-skilled workers, the dirty little secret is the scarcity of jobs that require more skills."[12]

In a crucial political sense, however, the jobs-technology-training debate is quite beside the point. When he took power in January 1993, Clinton placed his economic emphasis elsewhere than on jobs and industrial restructuring. Instead, his economic plan foretold of higher taxes on the rich and a call to bring down the federal budget deficit by as much as $500 billion over five years. Toward the same end he actually promised to boost unemployment by cutting more than 100,000 federal jobs. Clinton did vow to counteract this trend somewhat by spending $10.9 billion over five years on job training and employment programs. But the 50-to-1 ratio of deficit reduction to jobs spending suggests where Clinton's real priorities lie.[13] For Clinton, no less than for H. Ross Perot and other segments of the U.S. power elite, the Number One economic problem is not the jobs deficit or forced free time, it is the budget deficit. In this crucial respect, Clinton's Democratic Administration promised more a change in the means of dealing with fiscal imbalance than a decided shift away from Republican preoccupations with deficits. Unlike Republicans, who insist that spending cuts must come before tax increases, Clinton originally proposed to raise taxes on corporations and the rich to build up government revenues. But inasmuch as he slanted his first budget toward deficit reduction, not economic restructuring, Clinton obviously agreed with conservatives that deficits should rank at the top of the nation's political agenda. Besides, once his jobs plan went down to defeat in March 1993, Clinton explicitly endorsed the conservative terms of debate, uttering the words that head this chapter: "I have no interest in raising taxes until spending is cut—no tax increases without the spending cuts." Confirming the priority of his anti-deficit mission, Clinton even proposed the lock-up of all revenues raised under his plan in a new government "trust fund" to be used solely for deficit reduction.

Although it is sometimes difficult to locate a moving Clinton within the taxes versus spending cuts debate, the key point is that he has done little to challenge the terms of the debate itself. On Capitol Hill, politicians focus on ways to slice the deficit and to identify those who will pay. This debate is a conservative's dream, for its central focus is how to break connections between the public sector and the needs of working people. As debate over reducing public spending, raising taxes, firing government employees, and cutting back public services dominates the political agenda, a strange conservative consensus emerges. Republicans battle Democrats over whether to raise the bridge (taxes) or lower the river (spending), but both parties agree that anti-deficit considerations must frame serious discussions of contemporary political economy. In other words, both parties agree that government is too big, that it is overly responsible for social needs, and that it is insufficiently attentive to business needs. In this deficit-driven debate, the private economy is excused from any responsibility for sagging growth.

Questions involving the very dynamics of the corporate economy itself, or its dimming prospects for labor, go unexamined. Because "the huge and persistent federal deficit has become a symbol of everything wrong with our system of government," the current organization of debate lets our economy off the hook.[14] In this respect, the deepest fracture of all in the present situation may well be the ideological divide separating the private sources of our economic troubles and the public sector's preoccupations with deficits.

Origins of the Deficit Mania

Once upon a time, of course, deficit reduction was a purely Republican Party theme. Lunch-pail Democrats actively embraced federal deficit spending to achieve "full employment." It was Main Street and Wall Street Republicans who complained about high taxes, wasteful spending, and rising deficits. Under this organization of partisan debate, which lasted roughly from 1932 until 1980, Democrats won eight presidential elections and Republicans four. Though the federal government spent, taxed, and ran deficits throughout this period, voters seemed to care much more about jobs than taxes, spending, and deficits. They seemed to have few problems with deficit spending as long as deficits helped to create jobs without raising the lid on inflation.

By the time he left office, of course, President Ronald Reagan had collaborated with four largely Democratic Congresses to accumulate $1.3 trillion in new federal debt, the largest peacetime credit spree in U.S. history. Yet despite the enormous deficit numbers, it is doubtful that Reagan would have been disappointed had he enjoyed the right to run for a third term. The fact is, unemployment dropped to 5.5% in 1988, about a point and a half less than it was in Carter's last year in the White House. Reagan's deficit economy did generate more than ten million new jobs. Many of these jobs did not pay very much, many more were the direct result of exploding military investments and health costs, and millions of well-paying industrial jobs were permanently lost in the

1980s. And, the economy soon stalled again anyway. We will have more to say about these and related trends in later chapters. For now, though, the key point is that Reagan used big deficits to deliver on his promise to quicken economic growth and add jobs.

Not that policy makers had all that much room to maneuver. Had the political elite really attempted to balance the federal budget during the bad recession of 1982, they would have met with disastrous results. One business study estimates that achieving fiscal balance would have pushed unemployment rates into the 13-14% range and lost nearly $1 trillion in output.[15] It would probably also have cost the president his job in 1984.

Since the New Deal, most presidents, including Republicans such as Nixon, have tickled the economy with spending to ensure abundant jobs and public contentment during their re-election years. In this sense Reagan did, albeit at a vastly accelerated rate, only what other administrations had done. As Hegel observed, however, at some point changes in quantity can be so vast as to produce changes in the very quality or nature of things. Thus with Ronald Reagan's deficits. Reagan's political economics did more than continue old practices. With the active compliance of Democrats in Congress, Reagan drastically altered the mechanics of federal budgeting. By piling huge tax cuts on top of even larger military spending increases, and continuing to apply such increases even after the economy entered recovery, Washington self-consciously and drastically built up the deficit to mountainous heights.[16] In just three years, between 1981 and 1983, the federal deficit more than doubled as a percentage of total federal spending, jumping from 11.7% to 25.2%.

What seemed to stick in the craw of many U.S. citizens, indeed, what may well have actually frightened many analysts, was the sight of unprecedented $200 billion deficits. In the mid-1980s, deficits became the omnipresent subject of news broadcasts, talk shows, magazine articles, and books. Media reports abounded with warnings of a coming crash, "a day of reckoning." And when the New York Stock Exchange dropped more than 500 points on October 19, 1987, the public's worst fears were fulfilled. In this climate of growing budget and financial uncertainty, the more tangible problems of stagnant wages, job insecurity, and rising personal debt had a massive new symbolic target: the dizzying federal debt.

The Reagan-era deficits gave a kind of fantastic mathematical expression to the other more immediate economic troubles of ordinary working people. All the economic difficulties faced by people in their everyday lives were captured in the singular wonder and irrationality of government spending. How could a responsible government regularly spend $200 billion more than it had? One vast abstract concept, the $200 billion deficit gradually came to symbolize a deranged economic structure. Here was a uniquely understandable, singular motive force behind the nation's economic troubles.

In 1992 billionaire Ross Perot made it the central mission of his insurgent presidential campaign to focus and legitimize the notion that the federal debt should be *the* nation's top priority. "The debt is like a crazy aunt we keep down in the basement. All the neighbors know she's there, but nobody wants to talk about her," declared Perot.[17]

In truth, U.S. politicians have talked about little else since at least the mid-1980s. Once deficit-mania took hold, along with the realization that corporate-led economic growth was not nearly strong enough to help pay the bills, Congress and the president faced enormous pressures, especially from business, the media, and middle-class taxpayers, to stabilize government's rising debt and interest burden. But Republican presidents and Democratic Congresses, caught in a maze of contradictory pro-spending, anti-taxpaying interests, could not agree on where or what to cut. Three times in the 1980s Congress, unable to pass budgets on time or through normal political processes, watched pathetically as the federal government temporarily shut itself down for lack of authority to expend funds. To avoid such calamities in the future, Democratic Congresses defaulted and accepted Republican solutions.

First, Congress tried to put budget reductions on automatic pilot. It passed laws, such as the Gramm-Rudman budget reduction law of 1985 and its follow-up versions, Gramm-Rudman II and III, each of which required automatic spending cuts—half from defense, half from domestic programs—if Congress deliberately failed to reduce public spending. Gramm-Rudman threatened to take budgeting, perhaps the single most consequential political act of legislatures, out of congressional hands. Budgeting, Gramm and Rudman seemed to be saying, was now too important to be left to democratic political processes. When faced with draconian Gramm-Rudman spending cuts, Congress wriggled out of its own straight-jacket, using all manner of gimmicks and charades to produce cuts. Among other tricks, Congress took off budget the cost of the savings and loan bailout, estimated at upwards of $500 billion, but counted as part of regular government revenues the surplus in the Social Security trust fund, which may be used only for Social Security payments. After the three versions of Gramm-Rudman failed to make a dent in the deficit, Congress tied its own hands more tightly in 1990. In exchange for the tax increase that probably cost George Bush his re-election, Congress divided the federal budget into mutually exclusive categories of military, domestic, and international spending and set ceilings on expenditures for each category. Among other concessions to Bush, Congress agreed that it would not use spending reductions in one category to subsidize increases in another. In effect, Congress made it illegal for itself to capture the "peace dividend" to meet social needs. Deficits were now eating everything in sight.[18]

Congress kept spending money not because it was inherently wasteful or incapable of making priorities. As we shall see later, Congress did make "hard choices" to cut a variety of domestic social programs in areas such as the environment, housing, and mass transportation. The real problem in deficit reduction was that members knew full well the crucial impact of government spending on economic activity. Congress continued to spend more money than it raised, just as it had throughout the post-World War II boom years, because it feared the economic collapse that would come if it reduced spending. But several factors shaping the political context in the 1980s could not be more important. Under the pressure of rising deficit anxieties, the norm for measuring congressional budgeting policy was no longer the health of the economy, but whether the deficit got smaller. It was this disconnection between budget policy and economic performance that justified the estrangement of national policy from action on economic restructuring, the fracture line separating public policy and economic reorganization. The Democratic Congress knew that quick movement toward balanced budgets would be economic suicide: the lives of whole communities, of entire industries, such as agriculture and real estate, of millions of people, would be shattered if more than $300 billion were suddenly sucked out of the economy. The negative multiplier effects of such withdrawal would be economically disastrous. At the same time, however, Democrats in Congress also knew that rapidly accumulating deficits frightened millions of voters and worried the even more consequential onlookers in the bond market; the sheer magnitudes involved just plain scared people and kept interest rates high. Eagerly encouraged by their anti-spending Republican critics, Democrats regularly whipped themselves into agonies of self-recrimination for spending public money that legislators knew was necessary just to keep the economy creaking along.

In effect, Reagan helped make the Democrats a kind of schizophrenic political party: on the one hand, Democrats knew they had to spend, and spend they did; on the other hand, feeling the full weight of Reagan's anti-government, anti-spending tirades, Democrats engaged in endless self-criticism for doing just that. As early as 1982, none other than the old FDR Democrat Tip O'Neill, speaker of the House of Representatives, cried *mea culpa*. There would be no additional pump-priming to end the 1982 recession, he lamented. Democrats must confess to their sins, and "one of the sins of our party has been to over-legislate and over-regulate."[19] O'Neill's theological metaphor fore-told much about the resurrection of old-time fiscal religion in U.S. politics.

The new, more conservative Democratic party line was reasserted in the 1984 election. Then, leading Democratic presidential candidate Walter Mondale proclaimed that spiraling deficits formed issue Number One of that year's campaign, and he called for politically self-destructive tax increases to pay it down. Others, such as "New Democrat" Gary Hart, fought to lower the river, scorning liberal "special interests" for constantly demanding more public spending. In 1988, renouncing any ideological commitment whatsoever, candidate Michael Dukakis refused to debate George Bush's dismissal of the "L-word," that is, liberalism, promising instead that he would engineer the economy toward fiscal rectitude. Dukakis promised to import the miserly virtues of the suburban city manager right into the Oval Office. More and more in the 1980s, Democrats sounded like Republicans, even though in Congress they continued to behave in crucial ways as big-deficit liberals. In 1992, running against the jobless economy of Bush, Clinton was notably more compassionate about labor needs than recent Democratic candidates had been. But, as we have seen, Clinton's priorities still echo conservative preferences. On the one hand, to the extent he fully accepts the corporate capitalist framework, Clinton is unlikely to spotlight corporate irrationality as the source of the nation's economic troubles. In particular, as Clinton tries to rationalize the health-care finance system, the last thing he wants is an ideological war with business in general. On the other hand, Clinton inherited the Reagan-Bush era's deficits. The basic problem for him is that Washington is now bedeviled by the fact that most federal spending is itself running on something like automatic pilot. Approximately 50% of federal spending is legally obligated to entitlements, such as Social Security, Medicare, farm-support payments, and military pensions. Another 14% is bound to interest payments on the debt. And approximately 17% goes to defense. Most of the discussions about "hard choices" in the budget debate have centered on all the remaining programs and agencies within the remaining 19% of federal spending, everything from the FBI to the Labor Department.

Obviously, military spending can, should, and probably will experience more cuts. But the fact remains that domestic entitlement spending is now the main upward force in the budget, and, given the way the economy is currently jettisoning jobs, expenditures on income entitlements are bound to rise even higher. In this sense, we can see how the federal budget already expresses one kind of administrative response to the post-labor economy: Washington now pays millions of non-working people to consume economic goods and services, to keep purchasing the goods of a hyper-productive, slow-growth economy. Under these circumstances, even if Congress had accepted Clinton's 1993 deficit-reduction package in total and all his assumptions had proved accurate down to the last dime, the federal government would still have to borrow nearly $1 trillion between 1994 and 1997 just to keep itself afloat and the economy bumping along at its current snail's pace. For this reason, deficit-mania, what we call balanced-budget conservatism, figures to be around a long time as the prevailing orthodoxy. All of which means that other crucial matters, such as joblessness, urban decay, and impoverishment, will continue to receive secondary attention at best.

But more than general deficit and ideological forces are moving Clinton to the Right. He is, after all, a product of the Democratic Leadership Council (DLC), a group of conservative young Democrats, many from the South, whose goal was to recapture the White House at any cost, including acceptance of Republican definitions of the economic situation. Most fundamentally, DLC Democrats agreed with Republicans that the main problems of the U.S. political economy must be located and resolved in the state, not the private corporate sector. The DLC was quite happy to move the Democratic Party to the economic Right. As described by political scientist William Crotty,

> The major concerns of the DLC at the end of the 1980s were a strong defense (modified somewhat by the end of the Cold War) and an emphasis on fiscal responsibility, economic growth, and opportunity—stands it hoped would appeal to the middle class. In a real sense, the DLC had been seduced by the Republicans and, more pointedly, by Reagan's definition of the major concerns facing the nation.[20]

And it is clear what Reagan viewed as the Number One question facing the nation. As he never tired of repeating, government is the problem. Reagan's unceasing invocations of the magic of the marketplace surely helped to justify elite inaction on any of the major social issues fueling domestic discontent. But Reagan's greatest contribution to the fractured political economy was not his ideological celebration of markets; it was the $1.3 trillion deficit that he left the regime to deal with. The deficit became the central ideological prop in the long-term conservative attack on the public sector. Like his young judicial appointments to the Supreme Court, Reagan's deficit will be around for decades, keeping the Rightwing in charge of political priorities.

The deficit, more than any other ideological factor in the current situation, conveniently legitimates elite indifference to economic stagnation and social need. The deficit has become the great elite excuse for avoiding economic activism. In a real and vivid sense, deficits haunt contemporary public policy. They are a fiscal specter that frightens people into submission, distracting public attention from the "real" economy, thereby smothering opportunities for alternative discussions concerning a rapidly automating economy or indeed how to reap more fairly the benefits of change. Political scientist Donald Kettl describes the ideological framework quite well when he writes that "the federal deficit has become the most prominent issue of domestic politics—indeed, perhaps of all American politics. It is the backdrop of every policy issue and debate, of every new idea and proposal."[21] Not the agonizingly long "jobless recession," not the end of the Cold War, not the 1992 presidential campaign—not even the Los Angeles riot, the single worst urban riot in national history—nothing seems able to dislodge deficits as the framing limit of politics and policy.

Cut-Throat Federalism

The invisible federal response to the troubles in Los Angeles highlights the third major fracture in the nation's political economy: the increasing fiscal isolation, or autonomization, of state and local governments. The prevailing theme of inter-governmental relations is now "go-it-alone-federalism." In the face of slow growth, hyper-mobile corporate capital, and diminishing financial support from Washington, every unit in the sub-national government system must preserve, protect, and expand its own tax base, if necessary, at the expense of every other unit. The law of fiscal federalism is "every jurisdiction for itself." "The Cold War is over," advises the chief economist of the Los Angeles County Economic Development Corporation, but "now you have a new war between the states. It's an economic development war, and the stakes keep getting bigger."[22] In fact, this war has been going on for a long time. As early as the 1950s, after all, West Coast cities such as Los Angeles and San Francisco "stole" sports franchises, such as the Dodgers and Giants, from New York. Still, as late as 1978, *The Wall Street Journal* could still report that "scores of companies have been turned away from Southern towns because of wage rates or their union policies."[23] Not any more. Two decades of stagnation, coupled with sizeable federal aid cutbacks, have left virtually every city and state in an ever-quickening race for capital. Even once anti-industrial Southern bastions such as Kentucky and Georgia now aggressively advertise all the tax abatements, construction subsidies, and regulatory clearances any site-hungry business could want. Meanwhile, the states up North, just as needy of new capital, gamely struggle to outdo each other as well as their Southern rivals, to lure new business. Consider, for example, the mid-Atlantic commercial war between New York, New Jersey, and Connecticut. In 1992 and 1993,

> New York City handed out $362 million in tax breaks, offered cut-rate energy, and other concessions to four companies and five commodities exchanges to keep them from calling the movers and heading west to the Garden State (New Jersey) or north to Connecticut. New Jersey fattened its business incentives with a new $234 million economic development fund. Connecticut passed a package of tax breaks and loans for businesses that it's advertising nationally.[24]

Give-aways to business, such as those noted above, are not purely matters of public charity. Though they function well enough as a kind of corporate welfare, their purpose is to generate tax-paying jobs, jobs for workers whose collective tax payments will be hefty enough to head off local tax-rate increases, spending and program cutbacks, and layoffs of public employees. In other words, the underlying premise of business-attraction policy is really shifting taxes onto labor. But even Republican governors, who, after all, have to deal with the same economic realities as Democrats, wonder whether this kind of competitive fishing for investment is a good idea. "Once you get something," says Illinois Governor James Edgar, "you might have given up so much it wasn't worth getting [the business], and everyone else that [sic] pays taxes is frustrated." The irony is that officials court and lure business in order to head off tax revolts by their constituents; but since the most typical price of corporate location is tax abatement, local taxpayers end up paying more no matter what, especially since the most productive new enterprises will probably use more capital relative to labor anyway. Thus for all the local effort and cash spent on attracting new business in the last decade or so, "the corporate share of local property tax revenues dropped from 45% in 1957 to around 16% in 1987."[25] When push comes to shove in the politics of taxation, it is the traditional residents, not the new commercial ones, who foot the bill.

In part, the problem is that even as Washington gets locked onto an upward deficit trajectory and into a vicious circle of fruitless anti-spending debates, state and local governments have to balance their budgets year after year. Forced by local constitutional edict as well as by the watchful eyes of Wall Street credit raters, governors and mayors must struggle to avoid deficits at all costs. In Chapter Three, we shall have more to say about the past impact of balanced-budget conservatism on states and cities, particularly in relation to possibilities for progressive versions of grassroots democracy. Here, the key point is that while deficit preoccupations radically unsettled Washington's responsibilities for macro-economic management, the slowing post-labor economy greatly heightened urban and state dependencies on local business. Current economic conditions make states and cites across the nation hungrier than ever before to add more private investment to their economies. Yet, as we have just seen, because businesses produce fewer jobs, such investment produces profits that state and local governments do not heavily tax, without generating enough working-class jobs whose wages they do tax.

For these reasons, in the 1980s and 1990s, most governors and mayors were unable to avoid the politics of retrenchment. They succeeded in achieving legally mandated balanced budgets only by gutting needed public services, raising taxes, or by putting the heat on their workforces to increase productivity. To avoid handing out massive numbers of pink slips, cities and states nearly everywhere forced civil servants to accept speed-ups, wage cuts, attrition, and reduced benefits. As we shall see in later chapters, often it mattered little how many cuts government workers absorbed. Despite pressures and promises to work harder for smaller rewards, tens of thousands of public employees simply lost their jobs anyway. Political leaders, constantly reminded by local businesses that other places were beckoning, studiously avoided raising taxes on capital. Limited in their ability to tax local businesses for fear of losing them, public officials either fired workers, slashed programs, forced productivity increases, or raised taxes. It is a sign of the times that while overall state employment did increase in the 1980s by about 13%, mostly during the fatter years between 1983 and 1987, the majority of new state jobs came in prisons, where the number of employees almost doubled. In a society battered by inequality and economic turmoil, the administration of discipline, incarceration, and security had become a new growth industry.[26]

Confirming the new fracture between Washington and the states, as times got harder for state and local governments, the national government made things tougher yet. As one component of the 19% of discretionary spending left in Congress' immediate control, federal grants-in-aid to states and cities became obvious targets for cutbacks. In the 1980s, the federal Revenue Sharing program was eliminated entirely, and federal grants-in-aid to states and cities fell from about 21% of domestic spending in 1980 to 17% in 1988. States felt such reductions in virtually all areas of policy. "In the 1980s, federal dollars for clean water, sewage treatment, and garbage disposal shrank by more than $50 billion per year. The federal share of spending on local transit shrank by more than 50%." Federal spending on new public housing collapsed entirely. And as Washington crunched the states, the states just turned around and crunched the cities. State aid to cities plummeted from 62.5% of locally generated revenues to 54.3%.[27] The cities, like the states, have to make up the revenue somehow or go without. In either case, they too are on their own.

The Fractured Political Economy

These developing trends—corporate displacement of labor, the national deficit-mania, and "go-it-alone-federalism"—illuminate how the once loosely integrated U.S. national economy is now fracturing along at least three major fault lines. The incorporated private economy, no longer buttressed by massive military spending or unchecked hegemony in world markets, fetches as much growth as it can from replacement of labor by automatic capital as well as from public subsidies, tax write-offs, abatements that lower the costs of capital, and, as we shall see in Chapter Two, by exporting U.S. jobs abroad. This economy currently provides the society with little more than slow, weak growth. Enfeebled by a slack corporate economy, the federal government is constrained by debt politics and forbidden to gun the corporate engines. All of which leaves states and cities facing a tough new world of economic insecurity and cutthroat competition. In this environment, local officials spare no effort to limit spending, seduce capital and discipline labor. In sum, the newly fracturing political economy means that corporations are too lame to help the national State, Washington claims to be too poor to help the governments down below, and most grassroots governments are too eager for investments to assure any social climate but one that is good for business. And business is not very good anyway.

The idea of a fractured political economy is only a slight exaggeration. The U.S. society, state, and economy have always been divided by class, property, gender, and race. As economist John Kenneth Galbraith noted back in the 1950s, private opulence, an expression of class power, has long co-existed with impoverished public services.[28] Within the public sector itself, state and national governments locked horns over any number of issues, especially race; and at least since the beginning of the twentieth century, the large industrial cities have been segregated by class and race from the fortified suburbs in their hinterland. But perhaps the most pernicious divisions of all are the fractures within the ranks of the economic majority of ordinary working people. As we stress in Chapter Three, economic and political elites have manipulated and reinforced at every turn these separations and stigmas of race, gender, ethnic origin, religion, job, skill, and property. The historical manipulation of such differences by elites has done much to weaken and disorganize the working class, rendering it much less capable of forming itself into a politically effective economic majority. In all these respects, tensions, conflicts, and inequalities have long characterized the U.S. political economy.

But we think that these long-existent fractures, lessened at least somewhat since the Great Depression, have deepened and become more prevalent in the last two decades. Between the 1930s and the late 1960s, state-managed corporate capitalism furnished enough growth and sufficient wealth to keep a loose lid on the conflicts between governments, labor, and business; to permit a rising standard of living for millions of workers, especially white males; and to allow Washington to spread some of the fiscal gravy to states and cities, in the form of federal grants-in-aid. In those more abundant days, labor unions could demand more pay and benefits; civil rights and women's movements could arise and actually expect to gain their social rights. States and cities could even raise business taxes on occasion, without shuddering in fear that companies would shut down plants or leave town. The fractures were there, but new unities across class, race, and gender seemed possible. Public and labor-based interests made claims on private power for social expenditure and community-oriented regulation. Democratization built up a head of steam; at least democracy seemed to be moving forward rather than in reverse.

Because the fate of the private economy was then more closely linked to federal policy and Washington was more supportive of state economies, the various segments of labor could face capital in each of these domains with greater hopes of winning a key battle here and there. Expansive, labor-intensive capital furnished more room for maneuvering in the class struggle over who controls the wealth of society. For as capital relied heavily on labor, labor's discontent was more urgent to address. Indeed, compared to today's prevalent logic of universal cutthroat competition, the more unified political economy of yesteryear afforded workers a more democratic backdrop in their battles for larger shares of the pie. Now, each segment and group of the fractured economy is preoccupied with its own internal dilemmas, and because of weak growth, business at every level demands and usually gets priority attention. But times are much tougher for labor, and time is running short. Only 11.5% of U.S. workers still belong to unions, and while public-sector unions are still growing, the state fiscal squeeze is putting dents into public-employee unions, too. And, as we have seen, even an administration such as Clinton's, with heavy political debts to what remains of the Left—"organized" labor, people of color, women, lesbians and gay men, neighborhood advocacy groups, environmentalists—cannot or will not muster the political, economic, or ideological firepower to dislodge deficits from their top spot on the national agenda.

Power Elites:
Trading Public Well-being for Corporate Survival

The strangeness of the current ideological situation is that so much about the real economic ills facing the country is well known. Clinton's first economic speech to Congress stated many of them. Indeed, Clinton led off his list of economic troubles not with references to deficits but to "two decades of low-productivity growth and stagnant wages; persistent unemployment and underemployment." Only after citing these labor troubles did the president mention needs to overcome "huge government deficits."[29] Similarly, mainstream news reports abound with stories on jobless recovery, the steady takeover of jobs by machines, stalling wage increases, expanding inequality, and so on. The problem is that mainstream discussions invariably accept such trends as inevitable. One finds in these sources little or no talk about doing anything to alter or modify the basic configuration of capital, technology, and labor, much less of reorganizing the whole economy along lines that might redistribute more fairly opportunities for work and income.

As C. Wright Mills argued years ago, the power of an elite is measurable as much by its patterns of inaction, irresponsibility, and evasion as by its actions and decisions. In this sense, too, the power of an elite must be judged by how it frames issues for public deliberation as well as by the looming issues it refuses to acknowledge or to confront.[30] In an epoch of crisis and basic transformation such as ours, well-worn ruts lead to dead ends. In the context of U.S. economic decline since 1973, it is evident that, by their inaction as well as by explicit decision, the U.S. power elite has in fact followed a policy of letting the political economy fracture. The fractured economy weakens labor, reduces the social costs of economic change for business, and, all things being unequal, such reduction helps capital compete in the world market. At the same time, millions of people now live more insecure and impoverished lives. Local officials do not know how they will find the money to pay for programs their citizens demand and need. Outside the suburbs, cities unravel, with hold-ups and hijackings aimed at suburban drivers, symbolizing the difficulties of escape.

But what can be done, the lament goes, government is already spending well beyond its means. Public penury, it is now widely argued, preempts public policy. Yet why is the public sector poor? In part, slow growth reduces tax payments. But just as important, the corporate rich have used slow-growth, pro-investment rationales to gain huge tax concessions from the state, to help impoverish the public sector, thereby justifying continued inaction. Consequently, as one study recently noted, while virtually the entire increase in the national deficit can be accounted for by the multiplier effects of the $80 billion in tax cuts that the richest 1% of the population have enjoyed since 1977, the federal government will not tap this source of wealth for fear of offending business.[31] Clinton's 1993 tax increase proposal would hike the top rate on personal and corporate income to 36% from 31%; this is a step in the right direction, but it is a small one compared to the conditions of public need and private opulence accumulated over the last two decades. All told, the U.S. power elite has chosen to trade public revenue and public regulatory authority, the necessary power resources behind the public interest, for the vain hope of reviving a corporate economy that has never needed labor less than it does right now.

Taxpayers, not Citizens, as the Basis for Government

Strikingly, the power elite organized and administered this trade-off pretty much in full public view. There was nothing especially secretive or conspiratorial about it. Indeed, in crucial ways, this bad deal was arranged with the active complicity of voters. Conservatives in particular have successfully promoted their political ideas and interests in ways that have invited voters to rubber stamp the bad deal. That is, the conservative deficit-mania does more than simply put the onus on government for economic failure. In more subtle ideological ways, it dislocates the very relationship between constituents and government. The following summary, a list of political impulses behind the popularity of balanced-budget conservatism, suggests how:

1. the sheer magnitude of deficits, their astronomical size, easily bewilders and frightens people.

2. endless mammoth deficits focus public attention on the continuing inability of government to get spending under control, thus making government seem perpetually deranged, crippled, and gridlocked.

3. huge deficits keep the threat of higher taxes looming on the horizon, especially as politicians cannot cut spending very much because voters demand entitlement programs, especially Social Security, that government provides. This contradiction only exacerbates popular irritation with taxes.

4. rising deficits and the fear of higher taxes to pay for them make people more than ever willing to believe that much government spend-

ing, the kind that does not help them, is ludicrously inefficient, wasteful, and excessive. Newspaper stories documenting wastes such as $600 military toilet seats regularly reinforce such impressions.

5. big deficits, anti-taxism, and anti-statism go together. Cumulatively they legitimate a political preoccupation with putting chains on government. Thus, balanced-budget conservatives press a litany of rules and procedural changes in government operations designed to make spending and taxing as difficult as possible.

Such chains include proposals for a balanced-budget amendment to the U.S. Constitution, a line-item veto for the president, term limitations for members of Congress, tax and spending caps on state and local governments, and requirements for direct voter approval of tax increases.

As the above summary suggests, balanced-budget conservatives make taxpayers rather than citizens the true constituency of government. The distinction may seem intangible and immaterial, but it is very important. Historically, going all the way back to the Golden Age of Athenian democracy, citizenship has been understood by theorists as a public, political status. Formally speaking, citizenship is indifferent to economic standing, indeed, it implies that politics has little directly to do with economics at all. Thus, in democracies, citizens can come from any social class, rich or poor, and from any place or background. Citizens are equal members of a city or political community. They are associates in communal publics, groupings larger than themselves, in associations that give people a common public identity with other citizens. Common membership in a community reflects their mutual interdependence and shared concern for betterment of the whole. Citizenship is, in short, an inclusive, publicly oriented concept. It implies a view of government as an instrument of communal life for serving a variety of public goals, as these are debated and selected by democratic majorities; citizenship, equality, and democracy go together.

On the other hand, in capitalist societies, citizenship and class are not easily separable. The State in capitalist society exists in large part to justify and protect capitalists' economic power. Through laws protecting private property, through rules that impede the ability of non-propertied citizens to vote or speak with a unified voice, through institutions that afford organized pressure groups from the business sector privileged access to the State, through the sheer weight of financial markets on government policy, capitalist governments have universally operated with more sensitivity to private economic demand than broad public purpose. In the real world of capitalist democracy, only private wealth confers first-class civic standing and civic access. Most important, though, government rules that protect private property also exclude the economic majority of citizens who don't own capital, or the means to produce capital, from a direct voice in deciding the use of the nation's wealth.

With control of the means of producing wealth "legitimately" concentrated in the hands of a few, the majority of citizens have little or no direct say in how, whether, and in whose interest the economy will work. In the United States, for example, the top 10% of all U.S. families own 78% of the nation's private real estate, 89% of the corporate stock, 90% of the bonds, and hold 94% of the business assets.[32] In this richest tenth and, more directly, in the institutions of corporation and government that represent their ownership interests, lies the predominant economic power to set directions and limits for public policy, to shape what economics and politics will and will not be about. In all these respects, capitalism inextricably links wealth and power, class and citizenship.

On the other hand, political democracy, meaning governance by the economic majority, represents a real threat to the rich. A strong, pro-democratic government, one that governs in the interest of the economic majority, is empowered to tax and regulate business; to redistribute and reallocate power and wealth; to use deficit spending as a tool of economic management and social justice; to bring pressure on business elites to use their wealth in the interest of the vast majority. Indeed, the closest that working people can come to power over the economy is in their powers to tax and to set the priorities of public spending. If it means anything, after all, democracy means the power of the people themselves to direct how taxes will be raised and spent, *without* being lead around by elites who regularly urge people to think and care about what elites think they ought to care about. Because democracy threatens concentrated economic power, balanced-budget conservatives, who are stalwart defenders of private economic power, try hard to steer politics away from a focus on equal citizenship or broad common interests, especially the common interests of the national economic majority and their common powers to tax and spend. Conservatives prefer a focus on the private interests of "taxpayers." They know how a politics organized around taxpayer interests is a politics that can immunize private economic power from challenges by publicly oriented economic majorities. A politics preoccupied with taxation is a politics that is bound to fracture the link between public spending and the public interest.

The concept of "taxpayers" carries very different symbolic meanings from that of "equal citizens." For one thing, the category of taxpayers heightens the economic relationship between property owners and government. Taxpayers fund governments. However, tax payment defines the political relationships between individual and government in private, economic terms. In this sense, a political focus on taxpayers rather than citizens re-admits the intimate relationships of economics and politics on the safe, conservative grounds of private economic self-defense. Tax payment, after all, is the basis for economic and political citizenship.

But isn't everyone indeed a taxpayer? Of course, but though everyone pays taxes, individuals do not pay taxes in the same ways. Tax structures are very much class structures. Like class structures, the tax system apportions public obligation and benefit in subservience to economic power. Private power inverts public responsibility: Those with the most to give find ways of shifting responsibilities to those with the least ability to pay. People in different classes pay taxes in very different ways and carry very different levels of relative burden.

For example, everyone is required to pay income taxes each April 15. With all its complicated forms and tables, its myriad deductions, exemptions, and changes, its hovering threat of an Internal Revenue Service audit, the income tax gets on everyone's nerves. The percentage of Gross Domestic Product absorbed by the personal income tax has remained virtually unchanged, sticking at about 8%. Are taxpayers out of their minds about rising taxes? Not at all. Payroll taxes, the taxes that employees pay for entitlement programs, such as Social Security and Medicare, have gone way up. In 1962, for example, when measured in relation to Gross Domestic Output, payroll taxes equalled less than half the take of the income tax. By 1992, however, payroll taxes more than doubled, to 7% of GDP.[33] Just as important, payroll taxes, a portion of which are automatically withheld from weekly paychecks, fall heaviest on lower-income workers. Because only about the first $53,000 of income is subject to the payroll tax, those who earn more than this amount escape higher taxes.

Corporations are supposed to pay income and other taxes too, just as individuals do. Between 1962 and 1992, however, corporate income taxes *dropped* from 3.7% to 1.7% of U.S. Gross Domestic Product; estate and gift taxes, owed mainly by the wealthy, also dropped by half in this period. "Tax finance," as James O'Connor has written, "is and always has been a form of economic exploitation." Power elites in all societies have carefully designed tax structures to enrich themselves at the expense of underlying populations.[34] Claims about the unanimous interests of the "taxpayers" disguise real economic differences and injustices. But for defenders of the status quo, that is precisely the point: enmity between "the taxpayers" and wasteful government exists. The category of "taxpayers" falsely unifies all people, regardless of their varying economic status as owners and non-owners. All are welcome in the tax-rebel army.

Indeed, in U.S. lingo, the political category of "taxpayer" does more than unify; it also confers a kind of high civic status to people who think of themselves as paying the freight for the State. The invocation of hard-working taxpayers conveys images of independent, self-reliant property ownership, especially middle-class home ownership. The taxpayers are different folks from the "tax eaters," as one nineteenth-century reformer once labeled the poor. Say the word "taxpayer," and images spring to mind of diligent homeowners tending their lawns, going to meetings of the local school board, the suburban equivalent of Jefferson's yeoman farmers trundling off to public meetings on the village green. The term resonates with classical Aristotelian and Lockean liberal ideals that see middle-class land owners as the moral, civic bedrock of society, a class whose primary political virtue is that they know how not to rely on the State for much more than the preservation of "law and order."[35]

For Locke, as for today's balanced-budget conservatives, the most important thing people share in society is not association in a common endeavor, but an agreement to stay out of each other's way. Government is a necessary evil for insecure property owners. Its role is to keep everyone in their rightfully earned economic place. Some modern Lockeans, such as University of Chicago professor Richard Epstein, are perfectly prepared take this logic to its ultimate conclusion. Government may legitimately force people to pay taxes, Epstein claims, only when taxpayers get "some equivalent or greater benefit as part of the same transaction."[36] For every forced tax payment, individual taxpayers must receive an immediate dollar-for-dollar payback in services or benefits from coercive government. Otherwise, says Epstein, government is guilty of violating the constitutional prohibition against takings of private property without "just compensation."[37] As Epstein well knows, applying the "just compensation" theory to taxation means that government may never shift or reallocate wealth between persons or classes, or even demand taxes from anyone, unless the State "leaves individuals with rights more valuable [and Epstein clearly means commercially valuable] than those they have been deprived of."[38] For Epstein, the whole welfare state, encompassing everything from Social Security and unemployment compensation, to labor union protection rights and zoning, is downright unconstitutional.

Conservatives know that the welfare state is not going to disappear overnight because of such legal arguments. Even the most conservative judges are not about to dismantle Social Security. But the ideology of balanced-budget conservatism, with its harsh politicized attack on public spending and taxes, is an ideology that echoes the spirit, if not the letter, of Epstein's ideas. It tells taxpayers and hard-pressed wage earners what they want to hear: that the tax collector is akin to a thief, that welfare is unfair to the taxpayers, that its recipients are morally suspect. Such arguments help to erode public claims on private fortunes. And a government that loses its capacity to raise new funds, that is confined to a state of permanent relative poverty, is a government that cannot tread where conservatives believe it does not belong. Balanced budgets limit government to basic municipal housekeeping services, such as police, fire-fighting, and sanitation. Balanced budgets are thus conservative in the fullest sense of the term: their effect is to keep the social order the way it is by denying government the fiscal or political power to change it. By the same token, as balanced-budget conservatism elevates protecting taxpayer interests to the highest priority of government, it necessarily stigmatizes poorer, property-less people as somehow less than fully citizens. They are lazy, indolent, wastrels, quarrelsome and contentious, as Locke described them, always hankering after politicians to use power to change the results of fair market competition. Anything constitution-makers do to limit the power of such tax eaters is all to the good, therefore. Thus, as we shall see in Chapter Three, from the very beginning of the Republic, the economic minority has gone out of its way to limit and divide the political power of the economic majority, or, in Epstein's words, to control the risks of popular sovereignty by making sure that the electorate cannot speak at once with one voice.[39]

Obviously, balanced-budget conservatism is, like any effective political ideology, a strategic theory of political unity and division. It seeks to ally enough angry members of the working class with the upper class of the corporate rich to win control of government and then use that very government power to weaken government and cut public spending. The point was never more directly stated than by Republican strategist, Lee Atwater:

> In the 1980 campaign, we were able to make the establishment, insofar as it is bad, the government. In other words, big government was the enemy, not big business. If the people think the problem is that taxes are too high, and government interferes too much, then we are doing our job. But if they get to the point where they say the real problem is that rich people aren't paying taxes—then the Democrats are going to be in good shape.[40]

Atwater erred only in underestimating the power of balanced-budget conservatism to insinuate itself across the political spectrum, to dominate Democratic priorities, too. As we shall see later, in Chapters Four and Five, the real social target of balanced-budget conservatism has never been simply "the poor," but the power of the much larger economic majority of working people, for whom democratic government has been the primary means of controlling elites from taking over. Balanced-budget conservatives know that if they can arouse enmity and suspicion within and among segments of the working population, they will have gone a long way toward creating the kind of fractured working-class politics that will keep the economic minority safe and secure for a long time to come.

Chapter Two

WHOSE DEBT TO WHOM?

The inherent contradiction between a political democracy and a capitalist economy has yet to be resolved.

Business Week, December 1, 1975

In order to meet with unqualified approval, any economic fact must approve itself under the test of impersonal usefulness—usefulness as seen from the standpoint of the generically human.

Thorstein Veblen[1]

When U.S corporate power rode high in the early 1960s, brilliant radicals such as Herbert Marcuse and C. Wright Mills argued that U.S. society had evolved into a kind of Orwellian State, a "brave new world" whose main form of class domination consisted of mass manipulation of consumer appetites. With its technological prowess and advanced forms of salesmanship, corporate capitalism had, for Marcuse, become a system that effectively transformed independent-minded citizens into "one-dimensional" consumers. As U.S. corporate capitalism mass-produced consumer goods as well as the means of war, its power elite—a triumvirate of the corporate rich, military chieftains, and top-rank political executives—all but decimated the chance for popular resistance from below. In Mills' words, most citizens were on the verge of becoming little more than "cheerful robots."[2]

The social movements of the 1960s showed that Mills and Marcuse overestimated the ability of the power elite to engineer consent. People of color, students, women, lesbians and gay men, environmentalists, consumers, and young workers all showed they could still demand that the social system reform its ways. Ordinary people demanded liberation from historic forms of racial and gender oppression; resisted a war they thought unjust; fought for reform of business practices to protect the environment, consumer rights, and worker health and safety. In another, more important, sense, however, the Mills-Marcuse analysis proved accurate, for none of the major movements of the 1960s effectively challenged the right of corporations to run the U.S. economy. For all the turbulence of the 1960s, the issue of corporate capitalism as a system of private power never really got onto the nation's political agenda. In this respect Marcuse's words remain a relevant signpost of the shrinking scope of political debate in advanced industrial society:

> Independence of thought, autonomy, and the right to political opposition are being deprived of their basic critical function in a society which seems increasingly capable of satisfying the needs of the individuals through the way in which it is organized. Such a society may justly demand acceptance of its principles and institutions, and reduce the opposition to the discussion and promotion of alternative polities *within* the status quo.[3]

That advanced industrial society could deliver the goods to most people gave the U.S. power elite reasonable claims on popular support of the corporate State. After all, why should people reject a political-economic system that furnished an ever rising standard of living to the majority? Power could "justly" demand popular consent in exchange for rising consumption levels.[4] But what happens when the organization of society seems increasingly incapable of delivering the goods, especially the jobs? Nowadays, most people continue to abide by the rules of the game, even though the system's ability to satisfy popular needs has deteriorated. Economic data from the latest stage in the history of U.S. capitalism are a record of growing stagnation, inequality, and debt, but most U.S. citizens do not need to see the data: they know from the experience of their daily lives that the economy isn't working as it once did. As the now famous banner hanging in Bill Clinton's Little Rock campaign headquarters proclaimed, the issue of 1992 was "the economy, stupid." But in what sense is "the economy" the issue? The mainstream view, as we saw in Chapter One, holds that government policy is the primary culprit behind the poor performance of an otherwise sound economic system. Conservatives blame interest groups for driving up the debt and liberals blame Reaganomics. Both sides agree, however, that fixing the government deficit is the pre-condition for economic progress. In other words, come what may, it is the State's fault that the private economy is not working as before.

In an attempt to pacify and gain control of a restless electorate, the U.S. power elite has revived the old public philosophy of balanced-budget conservatism to deflect attention from the true source of today's economic ills, the very structure of the economy itself. This has been no easy ideological task. Modern political strategists now find themselves in the unenviable situation of having to explain away trends of economic weakness, insecurity, and growing inequality not seen by most North Americans since the first third of the century.

Most important, any ideology successful in obtaining mass acceptance must have some connection to reality. It must specify conditions and results that make sense in explaining and justifying why events happen. Balanced-budget conservatism fails this test because it won't make the economy work better. Mere changes in State budgeting will not cure what is rotten in the economy; indeed, a drastically curtailed deficit could make the core economic problems much worse than they already are.

The main socio-economic problems of U.S. society—deepening stagnation, growing inequality, and exploding debt—each grow out of a terrible paradox inherent in the design of the current economic structure: the inability of the corporate capitalist system to use profitably all the resources and labor power at its disposal. For the big corporations that dominate the advanced industrial system, what cannot be used or made profitably will not be used or made at all. The end result of this logic is that society as a whole is systematically shortchanged. Instead of rising affluence, adequate provision of public services, and socially liberating free time, we experience chronic stagnation, or the long-term tendency of the U.S. economy to use much less than its full productive capacity of capital and labor. The results include the all-too-familiar problems of people who can't find a way to make a decent living: unemployment, impoverishment, wasted school systems, homelessness, crime, narcotics, illness, and early death. The cost implications of this fundamental economic deficit—the difference between what can be and what is produced—reverberate outward into society, creating a huge social deficit of unmet human needs. At the same time, just to hold the social system together and keep the laggard economy afloat on an ocean of credit, the State spends itself wildly into debt. As real economic growth slows to almost microscopic rates, State spending rises to make up for the shortage of economic opportunity. Yet the more debt the State accumulates, the more business complains that the State is ruining the economy. So leaders, Democrat and Republican alike, demand "sacrifice" from "the people," as if a people made poorer in public goods and services will make for a stronger economy, as if somehow it is popular self-indulgence, not corporate irrationality, behind the current State of affairs.

The point of this chapter is that the growing economic deficit of underproduction is not an isolated problem of the business system. Just as the United States is run by what Mills described as an interlocking directorate of private powers and public government, an interlocking relationship of economic malfunction, social debt, and fiscal crisis is the major consequence of integrated corporate and political power. These are not simply parallel developments. The socio-economic crisis and the system of power go together. The problems result from the way power works in this society, from the way power elites have behaved in response to systemic crisis, from the rules and institutions they control. As a result, fracturing the political economy will not relieve the interlocking debts of the economy, society, and State, nor will dealing with such problems bit by bit. The tendency to view stagnation, social crisis, and fiscal crisis as separate matters, a tendency the mass media, politicians, and business elites encourage, is itself an enormous ideological obstacle to developing a popular movement that demands substantive change in the relationship between power and political economy.

Corporate Capitalism and Stagnation

The economics North Americans learn from their high school and college textbooks insist that corporations cannot behave in ways that systematically produce social harm. There may be bad side-effects, or "externalities," that arise from otherwise sound business practice, but the textbooks promise that government regulation can take care of these. Externalities aside, businesses profit from selling more goods to people who want such goods, which requires that firms increase production, hire more workers, and enhance the efficiency and productivity of their resources. As businesses strive to outdo their rivals, technology advances, production and employment go up, and consumer prices are driven down. In this best of all possible capitalist worlds, the invisible hand of competition ensures that private interests produce social benefits. Everyone wins.

But this idealized image of competitive capitalism fails to seriously consider that if the primary motive of business is monetary gain, gain can sometimes best be increased not by expanding, but by restricting output, in other words, by "cornering the market." In a classically "free" market, of course, no single producer or group of producers controls enough of the output of a product to appreciably affect supply or prices. But the growth of giant corporations in the late nineteenth century put an end to this fairy-tale image of free competition. That is, most large corporations have something that Adam Smith ruled out of his economic utopia of free competition: enough influence over the total volume of goods produced in their industry so that whatever they decide about output, price, and quality will have an instantaneous effect on the decisions of their handful of rivals, who respond in kind. Until the 1970s, at any rate, the handful of firms that dominated the key sectors of the U.S. economy enjoyed such power. With little foreign competition to worry about, they could limit production, raise prices, and control the rate of their industry's technical progress.

Beginning in the 1960s, the great post-World War II boom began to peter out. Even worse, U.S. companies started to confront a nasty grab for markets and power by rival corporations based in Asia and Europe, companies that enjoyed the strong backing of their own governments. Slow to react, U.S. corporations lost much of their ability to regulate global developments in economics and politics. Facing a competitive squeeze from abroad and stagnation at home, the big companies were nonetheless reluctant to re-examine market strategies or lower prices. They were much quicker in taking dead aim at the economic security of U.S. workers. U.S. business internalized the pressures of world competition by moving aggressively to enlarge its share of U.S. wealth at the expense of domestic labor. To achieve this objective, U.S. companies battled to heighten their domination of domestic class relations and public policy at every level. Big Business slammed wages down, broke unions, exported jobs, forced the introduction of labor-saving technology, and invented mindboggling new ways to profit from financial manipulation. At the same time, corporate capital forced governments at every level to lower taxes on business, thus transferring to the public sector the Hobson's choice of raising taxes on labor or slashing public services. In either case, working people ended up taking additional hits from tax hikes and losing public goods.

Later, we will describe how this program worked in New York State, and in Chapter Three we examine how balanced-budget conservatism has become the preferred ideology of business rule today. In this chapter, however, we examine what all the ideological double-speak is meant to conceal: the inner workings of an irrational political economy that, even at its best, creates large social and budgetary deficits. To explain our real economic fix today, we turn now to the series of interconnected forces that stand behind the dilemmas of U.S. society: the nature of modern corporate economic power at its highwater mark in the 1960s, how corporate power reacted to the global competitive threat, and how such reactions contributed to the simultaneous expansion of social inequality and public debt.

Corporate Power and Global Threat

Until the gale of global competition hit the U.S. economy in the 1970s, a handful of corporations, usually ranging between four and eight firms (see Table One), controlled key U.S. industries. Working through a variety of interlocking directorates, joint venture agreements, trade association memberships, as well as advisory boards in government, the corporate giants were closely linked with one another as well as with corporations in other sectors.[5] Together, the business giants controlled

Table One
Selected Industries in Which Four Firms
Controlled 60% or More Shipments, 1966[6]

Industry	Percent
motor vehicles	79%
computing	63%
aircraft	67%
tires	71%
photographic equip.	67%
steel ingot	70%
soap, detergents	72%
household refrigerators	72%
organic fibers	85%
biscuit crackers	59%
cereal preparations	87%
cigarettes	81%

well over one-half of all U.S. manufacturing wealth. As Douglas Dowd notes, "The 500 largest industrial [manufacturing and mining] companies in 1972 controlled 65% of the *sales* of all industrial companies, 75% of their total *profits,* and 75% of total industrial *employment.*" The top 100 companies alone held 47.6% of all U.S. manufacturing assets; the top 200 held 58.7% of manufacturing capital.[7]

Centralization of capital of this magnitude gave big firms the power to effectively manipulate supply and therefore prices, enabling them to fetch a pre-designated or target profit rate, usually between 10% and 20%.[8] In the case of the automobile industry, prices were typically set four or five years before the cars reached market.[9] Thus, even in recessions, when sales dropped, the auto makers could lower their output, mothball some capacity, and hike prices. *Business Week,* a journal that ought to know, noticed the phenomenon in the late 1970s, a time when the already stagnant economy should have dampened inflation and lowered prices:

> By all the textbook rules, inflation and excess capacity should not coexist...But these textbook rules are not working in the industrial economies of the West in the mid-1970s. In the past six months, prices have surged throughout the world even though redundant plant is highly visible everywhere.[10]

Business Week explained this crazy pattern by noting how corporations engaged in "anticipatory, or hedge pricing," that is, raising prices in anticipation of even more inflation; but companies could get away with this *only* if they first enjoyed the power to raise prices "in spite of spare capacity."[11]

Target pricing was decisively important to the big firms. It meant that they could now regularly expect to achieve returns more than adequate to their profit requirements. No longer dependent on banks, brokerage firms, or Wall Street to accumulate borrowed capital, giant corporations achieved financial independence.[12] Corporations gained financial freedom and relieved themselves of the pressures of competition by imposing their prices on everyone else. Corporations applied economic coercion on suppliers, in addition to consumers and workers, but through their sheer power over assets, equipment, advertising, and sales, they avoided other firms applying those same forces against their own markets.[13] In essence, financial independence released the giant corporations from control by outside forces. Big Business wielded power without financial, much less social, responsibility.

The large firms' key to target pricing and the power to regulate output was their ability to lower the break-even point, the point at which revenues precisely cover costs. By increasing efficiency (or lowering costs) for each additional unit of output, corporations reduced the volume of production and the rate at which they could earn profits. By making steady technical improvements in efficiency, corporations reached their target profit rates more or less independently of market conditions. Such corporate power was never perfect or complete, of course, though it helped when one firm overwhelmingly controlled an industry and its "rivals" could play follow-the-leader, as in the case of General Motors and the auto industry. Even with such power,

> Price setting has always been dicey. But when domestic auto makers competed primarily among themselves, each producer could assume that its rivals were paying about the same rates for labor, tooling, facilities, and so forth. Traditionally, the domestic auto makers keyed their prices to General Motors Corp., because that company controls more than 60% of the market for U.S. built cars.[14]

The new structure of modern corporate power changed the rules of capitalism. Running a company's factories at full throttle no longer made sound business sense. As big corporations systematically put a portion of their resources on hold, there would be a gap between what the economy could produce and what it really did produce. And the more efficient the economy became, the greater became the gap of unused surplus capacity, a phenomenon Paul Baran and Paul Sweezy call the tendency of surplus to rise.[15] The crucial meaning of this tendency was that not even competition held the corporations in check. To the contrary, the very privacy of corporate power ensured that the tiny economic minority in charge of the large corporations could simply shift the costs of unused surplus capacity, wasted people and resources, and rising prices to the economic majority. After all, the State was not about to order business to produce when business preferred not to; the United States does not have a "command economy" after all.[16] As long as large corporations had the field to themselves and were free to run huge sectors of the U.S. economy according to their own needs and interests, society witnessed a process of rising private profitability that had no necessary connection to government's capacity to meet social needs. Since large companies did not have to maximize output or lower prices, the promised link between private corporate interest and general social progress was broken.

Thus emerged two mammoth social problems. The tendency of surplus to rise created the potential for a legitimacy crisis for corporate capital. If corporate performance did not automatically contribute to a better society, why should the economic majority continue to support "free enterprise"? On the more mundane level of economic reality lurked another problem. If the expanding workforce could not gain access to well-paying jobs, wouldn't the corporations have a harder time selling their goods? The potential for a shortfall in aggregate demand coupled with rising popular discontent created more than a little support among the corporate elite for a government big enough to absorb the slack. Thus, in 1964, a writer in the *Harvard Business Review* observed that

> the American business community has finally and with un-expected suddenness actively embraced the idea of the interventionist State...Important elements of American business have now come to the clear understanding that the federal government can and probably should be an active agent of social and economic betterment.[17]

In light of the broken connection between private economic performance and social progress, the corporate elite clearly understood and endorsed the State's role as the "active agent of social...betterment," or, in our terms, as the active agent of surplus absorption. To overcome, or at least to limit, the underlying production deficit, and to assure adequate outlets for their increasingly unused capacity, corporate capital was delighted to have government stimulate business activity through such devices as deficit spending to increase consumer demand, and the

Cold War military system, which delivered billions in guaranteed profits to defense contractors. The resulting warfare-welfare State was not only a treasure trove of benefits for the organized interest groups of U.S. politics. It kept business going domestically while protecting U.S. business expansion globally. State expenditures on everything from military hardware and highways to unemployment compensation, Social Security, and welfare gave corporate capitalism an enormous boost. State-sector contracts provided business with incentives to use more of their excess capacity while State social payments and credit programs gave millions of people more money to meet their everyday needs by purchasing more commodities, everything from food and clothing to college loans and mortgage payments.

But the more the State supported business expansion, the more business kept building its production capacity. In turn, the more government had to spend to help absorb this capacity and keep the whole process from grinding to a halt. Between the 1960s and late 1970s, for example, the federal deficit jumped from about 2.3% of fixed private investment to 24.2%.[18] In effect, it was taking more and more public bucks to get a bang out of the private economy.

Amidst this endless cycle of waste, stimulus, expenditure, and subsidy, even massive State spending could not eliminate the tendency of surplus to rise. Indeed, as State spending reinforced the expansion of corporate capital, the economy's capacity, or its potential surplus, increased, although real economic growth lagged.[19] This paradox was rooted in the rise of global competition and overproduction, but also in U.S. capital's tendency to waste its wealth on unproductive uses, especially financial manipulation and, to a lesser extent, luxurious consumption.

Does the evidence of economic performance really support this thesis? We think it does.

Michael Dawson and John Bellamy Foster have attempted to use Baran and Sweezy's theory as a framework for calculating contemporary trends in the size of the surplus going to corporations. According to their estimate, "the gross surplus...has slowly but steadily risen from about $300 billion in current dollars (50% of GNP) in 1963 to about $2.3 trillion (55% of GNP) in 1988."[20] At the same time, despite, or rather because of, the increase in corporate-controlled surplus, the overall economy grows weary, unable to absorb fully the benefits of its own productive capacity. The corporate surplus rises while the data of unemployment, GNP growth, and even profitability all attest to the U.S. economy's inability to expand at rates achieved in earlier decades, leaving ever more people poor and unemployed, more factories shut down, and more economic potential rotted away. For example, Table Two documents the rising

Table Two
Average U.S. Unemployment Rates,
1950s-1980s[21]

1950-1959	4.5%
1960-1969	4.8%
1970-1979	6.2%
1980-1988	8.4%

surplus of labor over the past four decades. Most important is the shocking 35% uptick in average unemployment during the 1980s, a clear signal of the economy's inability to absorb the available labor power. The same dismal pattern shows up in the sagging growth rate of GNP over the post-World War II era (see Table Three). Once again, a nearly 50% slide in economic performance occurs following the 1973 recession, as the post-World War II boom petered out and business failed to hold its own as the driving force of economic expansion. Thus, even though the rich got richer in the 1980s, corporate profits stagnated, and elites shifted their use of wealth from investment to hoarding, speculation, and consumption.

Table Three
Annual Percentage Change, Gross National
Product, Averaged by Decade [22]

1950-1959	4.03%
1960-1969	4.02%
1970-1979	2.83%
1980-1988	2.31%

All told, since the 1970s, corporate profits have moved up and down with the business cycle, but the major trend line points toward a downward rate of profit growth. Adjusted corporate profits, which grew by 79% between 1963 and 1973 and 115% between 1974 and 1979, slowed to a 45% increase in the 1980s.[23] In particular, the twelve-year period from 1977 to 1989 was very poor for corporate profits. Total profits of U.S. non-financial corporations (taxed and untaxed) remained essentially flat, rising slightly from 5.3% of GNP in 1977 to 5.9% in 1985, only to slide back to 5.3% in 1989.[24]

Naturally, business did not take falling profit rates lying down. For one thing, companies used their political power in the 1970s and 1980s to lower the tax rate on corporate profits, so the giants kept more of what they accumulated, even though at the same time, most U.S. taxpayers ended up paying more of their income to government. Thus, untaxed corporate profits rose from 0.3% of GNP in 1977 to 2.9% in 1989.[25] Moreover, in the late 1970s, just before the most intense wave of global competition hit the U.S. economy, corporations piled up huge hoards of cash, as the top 400 firms accumulated more than $60 billion—an amount almost triple the corporate cash stock on hand at the beginning of the 1970s. Recovery from the steep economic decline of 1973-1975 also helped to revive profits, but just as important, many big corporations chose not to reinvest their profits in production, selecting more intangible and lucrative investments, such as foreign bank certificates of deposit and Japanese utility bonds, a key trend we will comment on later.[26]

But there was even more bad news for business. Even as stagnation inhibited domestic expansion of the big companies, leaving more of their surplus either unused or invested in paper assets, by the late 1970s U.S. capital faced unprecedented commercial attack from European and Asian corporations. Massive investments in new plant and equipment by these upstarts dramatically accelerated the global tendency to increase surplus. The effect on U.S. corporate power was stunning. In one industry after another, U.S. corporations lost whole chunks of the world export market. In fields as diverse as textile machinery, electronics, and pharmaceuticals, the share of U.S. corporate exports plunged as a percentage of global trade. (See Table Four.) Imports, which in 1960 had been virtually irrelevant to industries such as automobiles and steel, now equalled 25% or more of U.S. markets. Whole industries, such as consumer electronics, were essentially wiped out by international capital. By 1982, as U.S. companies fought to get back into the world market, "more than 20% of all domestic industrial production was exported, along with 40% of the agricultural production, and trade accounted for one-third of all corporate profits."[27] By 1983, foreign trade accounted for up to one quarter of the U.S. economy, up from just 10% in 1960. In the words of a worried congressional report, "Fully 75% of all goods produced in this country are now subject to international competition, up from 25% two decades ago."[28]

The threat from world competition to U.S. corporate dominance proved enormous. In the first fifteen years of the post-World War II period, the basic logic of corporate power worked pretty much as Baran

Table Four
Decline of U.S. Exports as Share of World Trade,
Selected Industries[29]

Industry	1960	1980
electronics	25%	9.6%
plastics	27%	13%
drugs	27%	15%
agricultural machinery	40%	25%
textile machinery	15%	7%

and Sweezy theorized. In those days, as Left economist Samuel Bowles and his colleagues have written, the "great majority of large U.S. corporations did not have to worry much about price competition…and they could generally maintain a substantial margin of price over production cost." But the onset of global competition threw U.S. monopoly capital for a loop. Clearly, it was not only domestic corporate power that served the corporations well, but "the containment of intercapitalist competition" on a world level that reinforced their healthy balance sheets.[30]

In hindsight, economic "containment" was clearly as important to large U.S. corporations' success as the warfare State's military containment of communism. Indeed, though the two forms of containment were always linked, in light of the disappearance of the U.S.S.R., the containment of world economic competition looms even more important as a contributor to the post-World War II success of U.S. capitalism. For once the European and Asian capitalist States successfully rebuilt their own economic foundations with much U.S. financial support and military protection, U.S. capitalists lost much of their power to regulate competition, control output, administer prices, and dictate consumer choice. They were shaken right down to their moorings.

There was no more potent sign of the crisis than the fact that U.S. firms were fast losing their financial independence to Wall Street banks and global finance. In the key turnaround year of 1973, U.S. companies raised more capital from domestic and foreign lenders than internally from their own profits for the first time since 1950.[31]

This was an absolutely crucial development. The whole point of corporate target pricing, after all, was to generate enough revenue internally to meet all company needs, thus relieving management of "subjection to financial control" by outside banks. Suddenly, as companies had to go hat-in-hand to outside lenders, the decisions of external economic power, bankers, and the stock market became factors of major importance in the plans of a corporate elite that could not set its own course. Heightened reliance on external capital exposed even the once invulnerable corporate titans to wild financial depredations by Wall Street raiders such as T. Boone Pickens, junk-bond manipulators such as Michael Milkin, and their cohorts in the prestigious investment banking and corporate law firms. Mergers and acquisitions, most driven by the logic of stockholder gain, exploded in the mid-1980s, leaving many giant firms just a memory. "Of the 500 companies that *Fortune* included on its first list of the nation's largest industrial companies in 1955, only 35% remain on the list" in 1993.[32] To cite one striking example: "In 1985, with the largest non-oil merger in history, GE purchased RCA for $6.3 billion, making it the seventh largest corporation. GE had amassed its funds by way of tax shelters; this allowed it to pay no income tax on income of $5.5 billion." All told, between 1983 and 1987, as many as 12,200 companies, valued at $490 billion, changed ownership, merged, disappeared or were restructured.[33] And not only did many major firms such as RCA, Pan Am, and Gulf Oil disappear or get gobbled up in mergers, but top corporate managements, including chieftains of some the most famous blue-chip companies—GE, Zerox, GM, and IBM—were actually given the pink slip by their boards of directors. Global competition made the once almighty U.S. corporations reel and quake.

Pronouncing "the end of the cowboy economy," far-sighted business voices that in the mid-1960s declared their acceptance of the welfare State now decried "egalitarianism" as a "threat to the free market." Warning against a continued drift toward equality (as we note below, income distribution actually has changed little since 1900), *Business Week,* perhaps the most liberal of the corporate journals, worried over the spendthrift, pro-egalitarian ways of democratic government. Reminding its readers that "differences in pay and profit are essential" to the market system, it concluded in ominous tones that "the inherent contradiction between a political democracy and a capitalist economy has yet to be resolved" in the United States.[34]

Inequality

The corporate elite was not about to accept anything as serious as responsibility for the sagging economy. The very notion is absurd in a society that claims that major economic decisions result from anonymous market forces, not the specific actions of a class of owners and managers. The economic minority thus looked to re-establish their power by shifting the responsibility for corporate failure onto others, especially workers and the government. By scapegoating labor and the public sector, business could lower costs, raise profits, and elevate stock prices. In what amounted to a dramatic revision of the New Deal social contract, business would rule the economy not through concessions to the lower orders, not through promises of a rising standard of living and ever more goods and services, but through a policy of economic coercion that would strike directly at the gains ordinary people had won with the aid of unions and the welfare State. The corporate few would now prevail by de-legitimizing government as a means of progressive social change. In the new era, the de-legitimation role would be played by balanced-budget conservatism. With government out of the way, the elite would have freer reign to increase the wealth and income gap. As the economy sagged, capitalists extracted more of their income directly out of the hide of the working majority.

Companies hit unions with demands that workers take wage and benefit cuts or face unemployment. The corporations pressed with all their might to lower break-even points by slashing labor costs and shutting surplus capacity. In a process that it is now called, much too politely, "deindustrialization" or "restructuring," U.S. business destroyed no less than 2.3 million factory jobs between 1980 and 1985, many permanently. GE, among the most ruthless and successful corporate warriors, eliminated about 124,000 jobs all by itself in the 1980s.[35] But GE was hardly unique. By 1986, factory employment had dropped 17% in textiles, 30% in primary metals, and 40% in steel.[36] And the process of cutting jobs just goes on and on. In 1992, General Motors announced that it would cut 70,000 jobs and close as many as twelve assembly plants. This news was soon followed by IBM's 1993 proclamation that it would abandon its once vaunted "no layoff" policy and eliminate 40,000 jobs.

As millions of workers lost their jobs, the point was not lost on those lucky enough to keep theirs: In the new economy, "job security" had become an oxymoron. When your next paycheck may be your last, you do what the boss says, or else. Thus, as corporations fought to lower their production costs and break-even points, the 1960s gains were taken out of working-class paychecks. In the deep recession year of 1982, for example, 38% of the unionized workers absorbed wage cuts, and 15% enjoyed no wage hike at all. Three years later, at the height of the Reagan "recovery," but still very much fearing the pink slip, one-third of all workers covered by new collective bargaining agreements accepted total pay freezes or wage reductions, and 40% of covered workers lost cost-of-living adjustments clauses in their contracts.[37]

Enlarging their anti-labor strategy, U.S. corporations took aim at the once formidable industrial unions. First, the Business Roundtable, the most prestigious of the corporate political organizations, surprised the AFL-CIO by pulling out all stops to defeat organized labor's bid for a national Labor Law Reform Act that would help unionizing Southern workers. Business continued its anti-union strategy by widely violating worker rights in such unionizing drives. According to the National Labor Relations Board, the number of workers illegally fired for union activity increased 216%, from 2,723 in 1970 to 8,592 in 1980. Not surprisingly, union victories in representation elections reflected the higher cost of organizing activity, dropping from about a 50% rate in the early 1970s to 45% by 1981. Corporations also sabotaged unions by pressing for de-certification elections, in which management often succeeds in getting workers to sack their union. Such elections, which averaged about 240 per year in the 1960s, quadrupled to nearly 900 a year in the 1980s.[38]

In the wake of the anti-union campaign and continuing layoffs, the big industrial unions suffered huge membership losses: the Teamsters lost 400,000; United Automobile Workers nearly 100,000; the United Steel Workers, almost 300,000. And while local and State public employee unions held their ground and even grew in the 1980s, President Reagan symbolized the ultimate managerial prerogative by firing nearly 14,000 federal air traffic controllers at a single stroke, when their union, the Professional Air Traffic Controllers, went on an illegal strike in 1981.[39]

Unions weakened by corporate assault were in a poor position to resist further demands for retrenchments, such as two-tier wage structures in which new workers are paid less than established workers for doing the same job, or the spread of part-time jobs, which pay less than full-time work and provide little or no benefits. Estimates vary on the size of the part-time labor force, but it adds up to a figure ranging between 17% and 25%, approximately one-fifth of U.S. workers.[40]

In the effort to force all working-class incomes down, the power elite took the fight to even the lowest ranks of the working class. What Francis Fox Piven and Richard A. Cloward call "the new class war" targeted the poorest of the poor, "the unemployed, the unemployable, and the working poor." By the summer of 1981, with Reagan now in power, the Democratic Congress followed his lead by approving $140 billion in cuts from social programs over the years 1982-1984, more than half of it from income-maintenance programs that provide low-income people with cash, food, health care, and low-cost housing.[41] The point was not merely to press wages down, but to lower the so-called "social safety net" so that all workers would have to compete for jobs at lower wages. The new business discipline would spare no segment of the working class.

Finally, in what was perhaps the most punishing and intimidating attack on U.S. labor because it was the least resistible, corporate capital simply exported production. This not only denied U.S. workers access to employment; the export of jobs by U.S. business effectively pronounced Third World wage levels the acceptable standard for U.S. workers to meet. Expanding aggressively in Europe, Canada, Asia, and especially the Third World, corporations made it clear that unless U.S. workers were prepared to accept pay at the lowered global wage rate, they could forget about their jobs. Liberal economist Bennett Harrison and Barry Bluestone well describe the new intimidationist logic:

> Following the maxim, "if you can't beat 'em, join 'em," thousands of U.S. firms set up operations abroad, substituted foreign-made components for ones that they had originally made for themselves at home, cultivated agreements whereby they would share trade secrets and new technology with foreign firms in order to gain access to foreign markets, or simply turned themselves from producers into importers of foreign companies' products.[42]

To add insult to injury, Washington's tariff laws permitted U.S. corporations to re-import duty-free goods whose parts originated in the United States but which were assembled abroad. Between 1969 and 1983, the total value of such re-imports jumped from $1.8 billion to almost $22 billion, about half from Japan, West Germany, and Canada, the rest from such Third World capitalist states as Mexico, Malaysia, Singapore, the Philippines, and Taiwan, to name just the top five. By 1987, General Motors alone maintained twenty-three auto assembly plants along the Mexican border, the now infamous *maquiladoras,* which perform the wondrous feat of exploiting cheap Mexican labor, U.S. taxpayers, and U.S. workers all at once. Indeed, by the mid-1980s, a large group of American multinationals, including Dow Chemical, American Brands, Colgate-Palmolive, and American Home Products (not to mention the major U.S. energy companies and international airlines), extracted the bulk of their profits from sales of foreign-manufactured goods and services.[43] But the trend did not stop at the export of manufacturing jobs. U.S. firms also exported even the lowest-wage service jobs, such as keypunch operators, to nations such as the Philippines, Barbados, the Dominican Republic, Ireland, and India. Chicago publisher R.R. Donelly, to take one example, began "sending entire manuscripts to Barbados for entry into computers," while New York Life Insurance Company forwarded its insurance claims to Ireland, where workers punched up the numbers at a fraction of U.S. wages.[44] Overall, the corporate attack on wages brought big economic rewards to some

companies, which saw their break-even points drop. U.S. auto corporations, for example, can now profit on a volume of 24% fewer sales than
before 1980, while the chemical industry can break even at about 65%
of capacity, with Du Pont able to profit by using less than 60% of its plant
and equipment. After its massive layoffs of the 1980s, G.E. reached the
point where it could increase earnings by 50% on a sales increase of just
12%, although in fact the company did much better than that in the last
decade, raising sales nearly 250%, from $27 billion in 1981 to $65 billion
in 1992.[45]

For labor, the cumulative effect of these trends is crystal clear:
Real wages have sunk, not merely since the onset of recession in 1990.
They have been sinking for most of the twenty-year period during which
stagnation and intensified competition have dominated world business.
The contrast between the early and late post-World War II era could
hardly be more striking in regard to wages. Between 1946 and 1973, real
wages of U.S. workers, especially the white workers who found their
foothold in Fortress Suburbia, grew impressively. Backed by strong
unions, an expanding manufacturing base, the rising demand for goods,
a host of government supports for economic growth, such as highway,
housing, and defense programs, as well as a broader social safety net,
wages averaged a 1.84% annual increase. This growth formed the economic base for what activist Michael Harrington calls "the honorary
middle class." This class included all those folks who earned enough to
live a tenuous middle-class lifestyle—they could buy a house and a car
or two, and put the kids through a good, four-year public university,
though they probably lacked the resources to survive long layoffs or
illness without losing almost everything. Since 1973, these honorary
blue-collar members of the middle class have learned just how fragile
their situation really is, and as we shall see later in our studies of tax
revolts, they are not pleased at the discovery.

Between 1973 and 1990, wages grew at an annual rate of *negative*
1.22%. The real weekly income dropped from $327.45 in 1973 to $276.95
in the recession year of 1982, plunging yet further to $264.76 in 1990, a
19% drop all altogether. As the 1990 recession dragged into 1992, wages
continued to fall at a 0.4% annual clip.[46] Inflation also contributed in a big
way to the drop in real wages. For not only did global competition drive
U.S. wages down, but wild inflation, ratcheting upward especially after
the two oil price shocks of 1973 and 1979, ate up workers' purchasing
power. The Consumer Price Index measures changes in price levels due
to inflation, and Table Five summarizes the big price swings since the
1950s. Later, in Chapter Five, we will look at how the inflation of the
1970s contributed to Ronald Reagan's political success. For now,
though, the key point is that by the early 1990s, slackening of wages

Table Five
Average Change in Consumer Prices[47]

Decade	Percent Change
1950-1959	20.7%
1960-1969	23.9%
1970-1979	87.1%
1980-1988	33.3%

became a generalized tendency in the whole economy, hitting just about every income category, including white-collar and even college-educated workers. By 1992, average pay increased faster than inflation for only two groups of workers, black female college graduates and workers with at least two years of post-graduate education. Everyone else fell behind.[48]

Even when we look at the wage picture from the standpoint of median household income, thus taking into account two- and three-earner families whose incomes did grow, the situation still got bleaker in the 1990s. Between 1989 and 1991, median household income slid 5.1%, down by $1,077 per household.[49]

Perhaps most dismal is the fact that in today's labor market, jobs, including full-time jobs, no longer furnish the route to a decent living. Fourteen million full-time workers—nearly one-fifth of the full-time workforce—now fail to earn even enough to carry themselves over the poverty line.[50] Thus, while the deficit-driven expansion of the Reagan era did generate more than twelve million new jobs, because the majority of such jobs fell into the non-unionized, lower-wage service sector, they did not lead to economic betterment. And why should they? As one business observer noted, in the 1980s U.S. employers "had plentiful supplies of female labor at bargain prices," women to do the often dirty, demeaning, and servile tasks of attending to their economic betters at 65% to 70% of men's wages. As we stressed in Chapter One, estimates on likely job growth in the 1990s hold little cause for optimism about the future. According to the Bureau of Labor Statistics, between 1984 and 1995 the fastest growing employment categories will be, in order: cashier, registered nurse, janitor, truck driver, waiter and waitress, wholesale and retail salesperson, nurse's aide and orderly, accountant and auditor, and kindergarten and elementary school teacher. Among these occupations, only nurses, retail salespeople, and accountants earned above the average wage in 1984.[51]

In other words, due to the heavy downward pressure on wages, inflation, the shift from manufacturing to low-pay service jobs, and the accumulated bias of gender and race discrimination within the economic majority, the brutal truth is that even if poor people work harder in the next few years they will probably not do much better. Indeed, one recent study found that poor people did work 4.6% more hours in 1989 than a decade earlier, but their incomes still *dropped* 4.1%. By contrast, the richest fifth of the population worked 2% more, for a 19% *increase* in income.[52] No wonder the poverty rate jumped to a ten-year high of 14.2% in 1992, or that one person in ten now uses food stamps. Nor is it any less surprising that in a stagnant, wage-depressed economy, one aggravated by a history of racist employment practices, median family income among people of color is $14,000 less than that of whites. The bottom line of all these developments is that "hourly labor costs in the U.S. are [now] among the lowest in the industrialized world."[53]

The U.S. has become a cheap-labor country relative to other advanced industrialized nations, and business is reaping the benefits. Even as the national unemployment rate edged up to 7.8% in the summer of 1992, before-tax operating profits of U.S. corporations rose 1.7% between April and June, following a 10.6% jump in the previous quarter and a 12.5% increase over the previous year. There is little doubt that business is taking these profits directly out of labor's hide, a reality that *Business Week* bluntly described:

> One of the reasons that personal income isn't growing is the dichotomy between sagging household earnings and rising profits. Despite weak demand, companies are lifting profits by cutting costs—a euphemism for cutting jobs…Companies are lifting their profit margins, because unit labor costs have slowed even more than prices.[54]

The link between declining wages and rising profits suggests two critical and interlocked tendencies of the new economic order. One is the weakening connection between jobs and access to a decent standard of living. The other is the growing disconnection between business success and the fate of labor. Weakened by chronic stagnation, the trickle-down effects of the warfare-welfare State have run dry. Today, business thrives only by making things worse for labor. And, at least from an income standpoint, the corporate rich have never done better.

Before we look at precisely how much better the corporate rich have done since the attack on labor began, it is important to reiterate that U.S. society has always been economically unbalanced, indeed very much so. The story of recent income and wealth trends is not a tale about this society's abruptly abandoning a principled commitment to equality.

It is a story of how the economic minority has increased what was an already huge lead in wealth and income, without apology or concession to the underlying population.

Even if we look at the first six decades of the twentieth century, by far the most fabulously productive period in the history of U.S. capitalism, the fact is that the basic structure of class inequality hardly changed. Indeed, class inequality slightly increased over this period. Between 1910 and 1959 the poorer 50% of the population went from a 27% share of national income to a 23% share.[55] By the early 1960s, the high point of U.S. corporate power, the richest 10% of families controlled almost twice as much wealth as the bottom 90%. Of course, as we have seen, average real wages rose considerably in the twentieth century, especially after World War II, and the standard of living enjoyed by millions of workers improved dramatically. But because no discernible equalization of economic power matched rising income, more money for workers did not mean lessening vulnerability to economic insecurity. This was the terrible secret of the great post-World War II boom, an invisible truth that confused even sophisticated radicals such as Mills and Marcuse, who frequently tended to overstate the government's ability to manage economic tensions and avoid crisis.[56] For all the abundance packed into Fortress Suburbia, most people remained dependent on and vulnerable to the decisions of the private, unelected elite that runs the economy. And it is this vulnerability to the decisions of others that makes class the central structural factor of power and weakness in this society. What happened in the 1980s is that the highest class *increased* its economic advantage over everybody else, which meant that more of the economic surplus was under private control and that less of the surplus was available to meet the needs of the majority.

By the early 1980s, the corporate rich just began to pile even more money onto their already enormous holdings (see Table Six). Needless

Table Six
Change in Distribution of Wealth Between 1963 and 1983[57]

Families	1963	1983	Percent Change
top 0.5%	25.4%	35.1%	+6.6%
top 10%	65.1%	71.7%	+9.7%
bottom 90%	34.9%	28.2%	-6.7%

to say, given what happened to wages, the same process was visible in the distribution of wealth, e.g., stocks, bonds, real estate. By 1991, the richest 10% controlled 71.7% of all wealth.

Nowhere was the unequal trend of the 1980s more striking, or more curious, than in the explosion of inequality in pay between the top and bottom of the corporate pecking order. Despite the enormous disinvestment in U.S. business, the loss of global market share in industry after industry, and the fact that most people's pay stubs just inched ahead at best, top executive pay went through the roof. In 1981, corporate chieftains took home average paychecks of $624,996, forty-two times the pay of an average factory worker. By 1990, after Washington reduced the top federal income tax rate from 70% to 31%, *the average CEO made eighty-five times what ordinary workers took home.* In the 1980s, "CEO compensation jumped 212%, while the factory worker saw his [sic] pay increase by just 53%, the engineer by 73%, the teacher by 95%." Yet in the same period, "the average earnings per share of the Standard and Poor 500 companies grew by only 78%." Even conservative voices argued that this "huge runup in pay...seems unjustified by either corporate performance or the historic relationship between executive pay and what other people make."[58]

Debt, Credit, and Finance Capital

Clearly, the tendency of capitalism to increase inequality between classes harms the public. Worse, as private-sector managers huddled to protect their own interests, the domestic debt deepened, the result of planning by the elites and systemic irrationality. Let us examine *how* the rich did so well in the 1980s. One clue consists of the relative growth rates of the various types of income (see Tables Seven and Eight). In the 1980s, the value of capitalist wealth—stocks, bonds, money-market, and other financial instruments—grew three times as fast as income from wages and salaries. If anything, this data *understates* the difference between wealth and salary income because the total for wages and salaries also includes payments to managers and professionals, the very groups that receive the most capital income. Indeed capital as a percentage of total national income has nearly doubled since the end of World War II, although half of that increase (from 10.7% to 19.3%) occurred between 1979 and 1989. The main reason for this was the high interest rates launched by the Federal Reserve Board in 1979 in order to crush inflation. As interest income increased by 73% over the decade, the rich derived an increasing share of their already large income not by investing in plant, equipment, and technology, but by lending money to all the debtors of the U.S. and world economy: corporations, foreign govern-

Table Seven
Real Income Growth by Type of Income, 1979-1989[59]

Income Type	Total Growth, 1979-89
1) Total Capital Income	66.2%
a) Rent	-12.5%
b) Dividends	42.1%
c) Interest	73.4%
2) Total Labor Income*	
a) Wages and Salaries	22.3%
b) Other Labor Income	22.8%
(e.g. bonuses, etc.)	
3) Proprietors' Income**	18.1%
Total Market-based Income***	28.4%

*   Includes pay of executives, professionals, and hourly workers
**   Individual business and farm owners income
*** Personal income less government transfers, e.g., Social Security and other entitlements

Table Eight
Distribution of Ownership of Selected Assets, 1983[60]

Families	Real Estate*	Corporate Business	Stock Bonds	Assets**
Top 0.5%	35%	46.5%	43.6%	58.2%
Top 10%	77.8%	89.3%	90.4%	93.6%
Bottom 22.2%	10.7%	9.7%	6.3%	

*   Private homes excluded
**   Includes ownership interests in incorporated businesses, farms, and professional practices

ments, consumers, and of course, best of all, Washington, whose bonds and notes were sold on "full faith and credit," which means that only the collapse of the political system itself would stop payment of principle and interest. More, attracted by the lure of high interest rates, corporations joined the ranks of the big investors in paper assets. As we noted earlier, by the late 1970s, the 400 biggest U.S. firms enjoyed a $60 billion cash hoard, much of which corporations used to speculate on the international money markets.

Mainstream economic critics see the growing gap between investment in finance versus investment in production as the sign of a dangerous new stage in the U.S. economy's development. *Business Week,* for example, worries over the advent of a "Casino Economy" that sacrifices productive investment for speculation, while Secretary of Labor Robert Reich laments the rise of "paper entrepreneuralism."[61] Such critiques pretend an innocence about the real purpose of capitalist production, which has always been to make money, not goods. In the history of capitalism, manipulation of paper assets is hardly novel or unforseen; if opportunities for profit were greater from investing in paper than goods, smart capitalists have always been quick to shift their money into these more lucrative outlets.

In fact, as Thorstein Veblen argued nearly a century ago, the distinction between "business"—the making of profits—and "industry"—the making of goods—is crucial to understanding how modern corporate enterprise actually works. All corporations are essentially institutions of "business," not only because they are oriented toward profits, but because in a more subtle sense, they are legal empires whose very existence is based on stocks and bonds, paper assets whose value the market determines. To survive in a capitalist economy, corporate managers must focus on bolstering the value of their paper base. Whether firms enhance the value of their assets by increasing industrial production, by sabotaging production and raising prices, or by manipulating the relative values of their paper assets is purely a strategic question: Enhancing the market or exchange values of their stock is, along with the making of profit itself, one of the main goals that drives corporate business. But as Veblen noted, in times of economic instability and disturbance, when paper values abruptly rise and fall, long-term industrial investments become particularly risky. Such periods offer bountiful opportunities for "gain or loss through business relations simply," that is, exclusively, by manipulating stocks, bonds, and other forms of credit and paper.[62]

Developments since the 1960s offer vivid proof of Veblen's century-old analysis. Indeed, according to Michael Dawson and John Bellamy Foster, in this recent period of extreme economic turbulence for the large corporations, and despite the brutal reduction of wages, we can account for virtually all of the rise in surplus as a percentage of GNP by growth in categories of business activity that are occupied mainly, if not exclusively, with financial manipulation: net interest, surplus employee compensation (in fields such as finance, legal services, and real estate), advertising costs, and the profit element in corporate officer compensation, e.g., benefits such as stock options, bonuses, special incentive plans, "golden parachutes," and "greenmail." In their words, between 1963 and 1988

> the rise in gross surplus...can be accounted for entirely by factors reflecting the general shift away from production toward finance and marketing in the economy as a whole.[63]

As we have seen, the twin evils of chronic stagnation and anarchic global competition have rocked the foundations of the U.S. corporate structure. The most ominous sign of this erosion was the declining value of the dollar in world trade. The U.S. war in Vietnam, rising military spending, and worsening U.S. trade deficits all combined to inflate the world economy, push the dollar's value down, and accentuate the forces of stagnation.[64] As Europeans refused to accept ever cheaper dollars in exchange for goods, the sinking dollar led in 1971 to the break-up of the fixed-rate monetary system that had governed world trade since 1944. Europeans were not the only ones sick and tired of accepting cheap U.S. dollars. Inflation caused Third World producers to rachet up their prices. The most important example, of course, was the four-fold hike in energy prices by the Organization of Oil Exporting Countries in 1973. This development itself greatly accelerated inflation, vastly increased the circulation of dollars through the world banking and trading systems, and seriously compromised the economic sovereignty of many nation-states, which now depended heavily on global banks to finance their debts. As petro-dollars, Euro-dollars, and global interest payments poured in, banks in the United States, Europe, and Asia created and sold all sorts of new financial instruments to attract even more capital. As Joyce Kolko summarizes these developments,

> The new information and communications technology, the floating currency exchange, and the floating interest rates had an enormous effect. Banks moved from expanding assets (loans) to "managing" liabilities (deposits) and continuously developing new "products."[65]

And the more instability there was in the value of money, the better it was for the banks' many new "products," as momentary movements of paper assets proved the best way for capitalists of all stripes to make money quickly. While lenders continued to have a strong interest in stability, Kolko notes, echoing Veblen, "The new money traders had a vested interest in instability" and manipulating disturbances.[66]

The profitability of disturbance became even more influential for world capital after Congress deregulated the domestic banking industry between 1980 and 1982 and the Federal Reserve Board pushed interest rates up.[67] And, despite lower inflation after 1984, interest rates stayed high. The combination of declining inflation and high interest, coupled with the release of U.S. finance capital from restrictions on lending, motivated corporations to take advantage of the new "financial products." They could now move money around the world in seconds to benefit from fast-changing exchange rates, to trade in money-market accounts, to bet on stock index futures and junk bonds, or on virtually any piece of commercial paper that promised quick returns on capital. And each trade and sale brought lucrative commissions to brokers on Wall Street, to merchant and investment banks around the world, and to the law firms that wrote and defended the legal rules underpinning the mysterious new forms of paper wealth. Between 1980 and 1985 the volume of daily trades on the New York Stock Exchange more than doubled; the marketing of tax-shelters, such as real-estate investment trusts, increased nearly six-fold between 1981 and 1985. Markets in futures, where money merchants bet on the future prices of everything from pigs to Treasury notes, also took off. In 1983 alone, the value of U.S. futures trading equalled $7 trillion, or $28 billion daily. The trading of paper assets became so vast that in 1984, just one investment banking house, First Boston Corp., handled $4.1 trillion in trades, more than the total value of the entire U.S. GNP that year.[68]

Caught up in the frenzy of deregulation and fast profits, owners of the nation's Savings and Loan (S&L) banks tore into virtually any financial outlet they could find. Knowing full well that despite deregulation, Washington guaranteed all S&L accounts up to $99,999.99, S&L owners pulled in vast sums of no-risk money for speculation in livestock, condominiums, junk bonds, anything that promised a return on a no-risk investment. In one instance, for example, the Sunrise S&L of Boynton Beach, Florida, went from $5 million to $1.5 billion in assets between 1980 and 1985 by luring outside capital into "no money down" real-estate deals.[69] When such ventures failed, as thousands did, especially after the stock-market and real-estate crash of 1987-1988, the U.S. government and taxpayers were left holding the bag, to the tune of more than $100 billion.

Of course, fast and loose financial ethics were not confined to S&Ls. As ever higher paper values shook traditional financial expectations, stockholders in the once mighty U.S. corporations grumbled that their dividends failed to keep up. In other words, the real productive assets of many corporations were not generating returns at the level of rival investments. Enter a whole new business substratum of "corporate raiders," such as T. Boone Pickens and Henry Kravis. Funded by "junk bond" traders and financiers, such as Michael Milkin, Dennis Levine, and Ivan Boesky, figures who were among the most well-regarded names on Wall Street and who each ended up in jail for illegal insider-trading, the raiders made a mockery of the once vaunted power of the U.S. corporate elite. By purchasing large blocks of corporate stock with funds borrowed on Wall Street, raiders threatened to take command of targeted firms. They put blue-chip managements on notice that established managements must either yield corporate control or buy out the raiders at the now elevated stock prices. If managements choked and the raiders took control, the new "owners" could repay their own lenders by selling off pieces of the company one at a time and still make gigantic profits, as much as "$10 for every $1 of equity invested."[70] On the other hand, if managements kept control by bidding up stock prices, the raiders grabbed the difference between what they paid and the new selling price. Either way, the raiders won millions without lifting a finger, save to make the appropriate phone calls.[71]

Companies "put into play" by the raiders comprise a virtual hall of fame of U.S. business: Gulf Oil, Pillsbury, Kraft, Union Carbide, TWA, among many others. In 1984 alone, $140 billion was spent on takeovers, mergers, and buy-outs. All this financial activity absorbed much potential surplus, and the strategists of finance capital (brokers, bankers, lawyers) got richer beyond measure, but they added little or nothing to the country's industrial base. The damage was not limited to growth in inequality, increased instability of managerial rule, and a vast waste of capital. As if all that were not bad enough, the effect of shifting corporate liabilities from stock to bonds tremendously increased the financial vulnerability of the big companies to the same kind of bond-holder power that lurks over the State. Stockholders, after all, hold a risk investment; the value of their shares fluctuates with the market value of the company. But bond purchasers expect to be paid a fixed rate of interest, and their principle represents a first lien on the bond issuer. Hence, although it was initially cheaper for management and raiders to fight their financial wars through bond sales because interest payments are tax deductible and stock dividends are not, the longer-run effect of such maneuvering was to undermine the economic base for hundreds of U.S. companies. In effect, thousands of corporations went massively into debt in order to finance their own self-protection. Between 1982 and 1988, the corporate debt load nearly doubled, reaching $1.8 trillion, nearly 25% of total corporate cash flow.[72]

Of course, amidst the instability and confusion of stagflation, big corporations were hardly the only segment of the U.S. economy to borrow as a means of economic survival. Through their credit-card operations, corporate capital urged all consumers to buy now and pay later. And the resulting change in household debt patterns over the last decade is, to say the least, unsettling. As a share of personal incomes, household debt grew slightly between 1967 and 1979, rising from 63% to 67%. However, between 1979 and 1989, household debt leapt to 80% of personal income.[73] Indeed, compared to the debt loads that private households, non-corporate businesses, and farmers accumulated, the corporate sector's share of total private debt actually declined in the 1980s. And for all the scary talk about the federal debt, when it came to living on borrowed money in the 1980s, Washington actually trailed all segments of the private sector: in that decade, federal debt actually grew more slowly than the whole of private domestic debt. The fact is that in the credit-happy capitalism of the 1970s and 1980s, every sector of the economy became addicted to borrowing as a way to keep the economy going. By 1985, the total debt of households, corporations, and governments was slightly more than $7 trillion, nearly twice the nation's GNP, one-third higher than a decade earlier.[74]

Behind this trend toward a universalization of debt was a severe weakening of U.S. corporate enterprise, rooted in deep-seated patterns of chronic stagnation, inflation, accelerating world competition, and overall financial insecurity. In the face of this increasingly vulnerable financial condition, all segments of the economy became more dependent than ever on government spending to avoid financial collapse.[75] In the words of economist Albert Wojnilower, of the First Boston Corporation, the federal budget deficit is "a large part of what has stood and will be standing between us and a Depression with a capital 'D.'"[76]

As Wojnilower's comment makes clear, the fact of big federal spending does not mean that government has lost financial self-control. Instead, it suggests a dangerously weakened corporate economy, a private economy that cannot keep going, much less growing, without massive injections of federal spending to absorb its very capacity to generate surplus.

Stagnation, Inequality, and the Deficit

As everyone knows, U.S. government deficit spending has grown substantially since the 1980s. The numbers are mindboggling in absolute size, but it is their magnitude relative to historic trends in national output that is actually more important. For example, during the glory years of the U.S. post-World War II boom, from 1962 through 1973, the federal deficit averaged about 1.1% of Gross Domestic Product (GDP) annually. During the next seven more stagnant years, deficits rose slightly as a percentage of GDP, averaging about 1.5% annually. As Table

Table Nine
Federal Deficits and National Growth[77]

	Federal Deficits	Deficits as Percent of GDP
1981	79.0%	2.7%
1982	128.0%	4.1%
1983	207.8%	6.3%
1984	185.4%	5.0%
1985	212.3%	5.3%
1986	221.2%	5.2%
1987	149.8%	3.4%
1988	155.2%	3.2%
1989	152.5%	3.0%
1990	221.4%	4.0%
1991	269.5%	4.8%
1992	290.2%	4.9%

Nine indicates, however, the consistently big uptick in deficits began in the Reagan years, when deficits nearly doubled as a proportion of GDP between 1981 and 1986, falling off a bit as the expansion of the mid-1980s reached its peak, only to start rising once more as the most recent recession rolled in. The up-and-down relation of government deficits to the overall economy is just what mainstream economists expect. As the economy contracts, tax revenues fall while the so-called automatic stabilizers of unemployment compensation, Social Security, and welfare payments rise, pushing the deficit up; as the economy expands once again, tax payments go back up and unemployment compensation and food stamp costs should fall, lowering the deficit. If we take a broader view and look at how recent deficits have accumulated on top of the historic debt of the federal government (the total accumulated borrowings of the federal government throughout the years), it is obvious that today's debt is actually much smaller than it was in the years immediately following World War II and the Korean War, when the federal government's borrowing requirements mounted, as they do whenever governments make war.[78]

Spurred by the fast growth of the early post-World War II decades, Washington sliced the debt-GNP ratio nearly in half by 1970. Consistent with our analysis above, stagflation, coming to a head in the mid-1970s, drove the debt-GNP relation sharply upward, especially in 1982, the worst year for the U.S. economy in the whole post-1945 era, when the

Table Ten
U.S. Federal Debt as Percentage of GNP,
Averaged by Decade[79]

Decade	Average Debt as Percent of GNP
1950-1959	59.3%
1960-1969	39.3%
1970-1979	30.0%

relation of debt to GNP increased by almost 5%, from 29.3% to 34%. Since 1983, the debt-GNP relation has never fallen below that level.

Yet for all the problems posed by the debt-GNP relationship, the truly worrisome aspect of the deficit is not so much its size as its irrational and wasteful composition. And the bogeymen here are not the usual suspects, such as Aid to Families with Dependent Children (also known as welfare). AFDC takes up less than 2% of federal funding, and for years spending on welfare has failed to keep up with inflation anyway. The huge trouble spots are in three areas: health expenditures, principally Medicare and Medicaid; the still disproportionately high levels of military spending; and, worst of all, the rising percentage of the deficit that goes just to pay interest on the debt.

Though the United States ranks below the top of the list of the world's healthiest nations, we spend more on health care than anyone else. Medicare and Medicaid costs leapt from 8% of the federal budget in 1980 to 14% by 1993. According to Congressional Budget Office projections, if the nation does not adopt basic reforms, these two programs alone will absorb almost one-fourth of all federal spending by 1998. As *The New York Times* recently commented, unless health finance is reformed

> even if the Government *abolishes* food stamps, welfare, farm supports, child nutrition programs and veterans pensions— an extreme step that no one is advocating—entitlement spending on these two programs alone would still be a higher percentage of the federal budget in 1998 than it is now.[80]

The tragedy is that much of the money spent on U.S. health care does not go directly to human care at all, but to the corporate treasuries of insurance, pharmaceutical, medical technology, and private-sector hospital firms, which profit from health care's ever more byzantine administration and commodification. Similarly, despite the end of the Cold War, federal defense expenditures in 1992 remained almost one-third greater than spending on non-entitlement, civilian programs.[81] The health and military complexes are obviously enormously powerful institutions. But they are not immutable. Mass pressure can change their habits of feeding off the federal budget.

Moreover, if the economy were to find a way to grow at its earlier rate, even these irrational expenditure patterns would not come close to bankrupting the country. Budget expert Allen Schick argues that "If the economy had been as expansive in the 1970s and 1980s as it was in the two preceding decades, the deficit would have been moderate" and the cost of financing it would not have been a problem.[82] But even a stagnant U.S. economy is rich enough to support *at least* the current level, if not the direction, of government spending. In 1989, for example, the United States spent *less* of its domestic output on public activities (36%) than almost any other advanced industrial society; only Japan and Switzerland spent less. At the same time, the United States extracted fewer taxes (29% of GDP) than any other capitalist government, except for Japan (which taxed 27% of its GDP). In addition, as we noted in Chapter One, between 1960 and 1990, the share of corporate taxes as a percentage of federal revenues shrunk by more than half (from 23% to 9%), while payroll taxes, which ordinary workers cannot avoid, more than doubled (from 16% to 37%).[83] In short, capital's method of dealing with global crisis, which has been to grab more of the surplus for itself, has trounced labor in the private sector and left labor holding the bag in the public sector. Today, working people must not only finance needed programs, such as Social Security and health care, with much less help from the corporate rich, but also the profit-driven waste inherent in the corporate-State complexes of defense and health.

The fact is that if federal spending were channeled into socially useful expenditures that enhanced the productivity of labor and improved the real quality of life, if the State channeled public money into a growing economic capacity to provide for social needs, deficit spending would harmonize with the public interest. "A deficit," as economists Robert Heilbroner and Peter Bernstein note, "is not necessarily a drain on our well-being."[84] The deficit only becomes a drain when government spends the borrowed money on futile and wasteful purposes, when elites use such irrationalities to justify repression and distortion of more urgent domestic priorities, and when the overall economy grows less capable of financing its obligations. This is precisely the situation we face today.

The combined effects of slow growth, irrational modes of expenditure, and tax exploitation have led to a situation in which deficits and debt now grow faster than the economy. This means that just as Washington must spend more and more to keep the economy afloat by absorbing a larger potential surplus, the cost of financing this added government expenditure keeps rising too, both because interest rates rise as government borrows more of the available capital and because the principle the government must service (that is, the total debt) also keeps growing. In turn, as the debt gets bigger, interest payments expand as a percentage of total federal spending. In 1992, interest payments on the national debt equalled 14% of all federal spending, more than the total amount of federal aid that goes to the State and city governments of the United States.[85] If the deficit continues to grow at its post-1981 rate, the General Accounting Office estimates that interest payments would, by 2020, eat up almost a third of all federal spending, essentially the amount now spent by Washington on Social Security and health care alone. By this point, the U.S. government would have lost virtually all its power to control events.[86] In other words, if the above trend continues and interest keeps eating greater chunks of the national budget, the federal government would be unable to absorb surplus, fund social programs, and advance the interest of U.S. capital worldwide. The days of the U.S. empire would truly be over. As the editors of *Monthly Review* summarize the basic problem,

> the stimulation generated by unending and ever more red ink is self-limiting. Deficits piled on top of deficits provide fuel for new inflationary spirals and help sustain high interest rates; and at the same time they set in motion forces that eventually arrest growth and lead to a new business decline. In short, today's capitalism finds itself on the horns of a dilemma: It can't live without deficits and it can't live with them.[87]

That the expanding debt holds the potential to further rattle the foundations of U.S. power is the main reason even liberal segments of the nation's power elite have concurred: fiscal conservatism must be the new ruling ethos of U.S. politics. But as we have seen throughout this chapter, the budget deficit is not the cause of U.S. economic woes. The real culprit is the irrationality of a capitalist economy. The social relations of corporate power constrain the enormously powerful forces of technical progress that this nation could turn to satisfying human needs. Government deficits mount in order to counteract the underlying structure of constraint, along with the social deficit to which this constraint corresponds: growing inequality, impoverishment, stagnant wages, declining living standards, the whole degradation of the nation's urban civilization. Meanwhile the rich, foreign and domestic, who hold more than 50% of the federal debt, grow richer still on the interest payments, an upward redistribution of wealth that further spreads the wealth gap between the economic minority and the economic majority.[88] Thus, by focusing on the federal deficit "as the root of all evil," the leading politicians serve the interests of capital in two ways: first, by cloaking the real economic source of the problem, and second, by shifting the burden onto the shoulders of working people. They tell us we must slash government programs; we must raise taxes. Everyone must sacrifice, proclaim both Democrats and Republicans. But the question needs to be asked: For what and for whom? Why should working people end up taking a double hit, first from the business attack on their jobs, wages, and living standards and then from government's attack on their services, programs, and taxes? The apparent answer is that this is the only way to try to heal an economic system that—whether it works well or badly—empowers and enriches elites at the expense of everybody else. Whether the economic majority will continue to accept this answer is, of course, the key political question of the 1990s.

Chapter Three

BALANCED-BUDGET CONSERVATISM AND THE SQUEEZE ON THE STATES

> The debt is like a crazy aunt we keep down in the basement. All the neighbors know she's there, but nobody wants to talk about her.
>
> Ross Perot

> ...by no stretch of the imagination can "reducing the deficit" be considered as America's number-one problem, as it *is* considered by 44 percent of the population and probably by a larger percent of economists. If it were America's number-one problem, we would be very well-off indeed.
>
> Robert Heilbroner and Peter Bernstein [1]

Twenty years of stagnation, not the federal deficit, left much of the economic majority either laboring for lower wages, working part-time, jobless, or downright poor. In an economy as complicated as ours, it would be absurd to think that everyone experienced stagnation the same way. Inevitably, that experience depends on a worker's industry, skill level, union membership, education, gender, race, and geographic location. Still, in one sense at least, stagnation does treat all workers more or less alike. It has certainly left the economic majority as a whole far more economically insecure in the 1990s than at any time since the 1930s. The vulnerability of all workers to dislocation—whether in the form of joblessness, lost benefits, lower wages, weakened unions, or the fear of shutdowns—is now better understood by most people than at any time since the 1930s. One huge difference between then and now, however, is that in the 1930s working people, especially less skilled white men, responded by forging unions to enhance their economic and political power. In the process, they won more economic security for themselves and their families. This time around, growing economic insecurity has been accompanied not by a strengthening and unifying of the working class, but by a fracturing of organized labor and a severe weakening of the political power of the majority.

As we shall see in Chapter Four, such fracturing is nothing new in the history of the relationship between working people and the U.S. political system. Particularly striking today is the way leading politicians of both major parties have refracted the economic crisis. Democrats and Republicans share the view that federal deficit reduction must be Washington's leading economic priority. Even Bill Clinton, who tried lamely to stress that he thinks a $19 billion government "investment" is necessary to kick-start the slow economy, promised to cut federal spending by $500 billion and the federal workforce by 100,000 workers over the next four years.

When leading Democrats, such as Clinton, and Republicans agree that federal deficits are a root cause of the nation's economic ills, they effectively take the heat off the managers of the corporate economy. They act as if the profit and investment priorities of corporate capitalism are inherently legitimate—as if they deserve to be encouraged and stimulated—while government spending choices are tainted by "politics," thus requiring special examination, discipline, and restriction.

In effect, Democrats together with Republicans have revised an archaic ideology, which we call balanced-budget conservatism. Balanced-budget conservatism divides the economic majority and shields corporate power from responsibility and mass political challenge. Balanced-budget conservatives wed a tough-sounding rhetoric of fiscal common sense to a more soothing appeal to grassroots democracy. Thus they justify shifting as much economic responsibility as possible onto the shoulders of state and local government.

The problem for adherents of grassroots democracy is that, when it comes to economic power, state and local governments are the weakest links in the political system. These governments face much tougher budgetary constraints than Washington; the cookie line of public spending ends in the lower ranks of federalism. As national economic burdens are transmitted from the corporate sector to the national government and then from Washington on down the line to the state and local governments, the inherent vulnerabilities and divisiveness of the federal system are sorely aggravated. Instead of people at the grassroots pressing leaders on Capitol Hill for a more responsible, productive national economy, the economic majority, scattered throughout more than 80,000 local jurisdictions, attempts to make its own way as best it can, fighting for lower taxes here, for more social programs there, to attract a business here, to hold onto a plant there. If there is anything that brings out the inherent weakness of a disunited majority, it is fiscal federalism.

By contrast, balanced-budget conservativism candy-coats economic reality with a tantalizing vision of grassroots democracy, states' rights, community empowerment, and local control, a vision that in certain crucial ways resounds with the communitarian spirit of radical democrats on the Left. But we believe that the grassroots democracy envisioned by balanced-budget conservatives, a democracy without economic power, is doomed to fail. That is why the populist veil of balanced-budget conservatism is so dangerous to the interests of working people.

In this chapter we will illustrate that point in two ways. First, we will look at how stagnation has played havoc with state and local budgeting. Then, we will examine how balanced-budget conservatism both seals and celebrates the economic weakness of local governments and sets the stage for a politics of divide and rule.

State and Local Retrenchment

Grassroots federalism is, to say the least, poorly equipped to compensate for a financially strapped national government. State and local governments have to live under the constraint of big federal aid cutbacks, a hard squeeze on their own budgets, and fierce global competition for new investment. During the Reagan years, while the president sang the praises of the states, he presided over retrenchment in aid to those very governments. Between 1981 and 1988 national grants-in-aid to state and local government dropped from almost 26% of state and local expenditures to barely 18%. To cite just one instance, during the 1980s, Washington sliced the federal share of New York City's spending by 50%, from 20% to 10% of the city's budget; the city lost almost $30 billion. And as we saw in the last chapter, federal interest payments on the debt now exceed total federal aid to all states and cities.

Still, state and local governments tried to fill the economic breech. During the recession of 1982-83, even though it threatened their ability to recover, many states attempted to pick up the slack of lost federal aid by raising taxes. This was especially true in the older industrial states, where tax increases were the steepest in the nation. Between 1981 and 1983, for example, taxpayers in at least thirty-eight states began paying more out of their income in state and local taxes even as their federal taxes were cut. The recovery boosted state and local surpluses, from a $2 billion deficit in the third quarter of 1982 to a $19 billion surplus one year later. Between 1983 and 1984, state revenues overall rose by 14.8%. All told, by the mid-1980s, by combining service cutbacks, public employee layoffs and give-backs, tax increases, and higher service fees, hundreds of cities and the majority of states appeared to have weathered the big changes in federal spending.[2] Indeed, by 1987, as the Reagan-era expansion neared its climax with the October stock-market crash, state taxes amounted to 26.1% of the total tax revenues raised by U.S. governments (excluding trust-fund revenues, such as Social Security and unemployment compensation), up from 20.6% in 1970 and 23.9% in 1980.

Clearly, by 1987, the states were carrying a much larger share of the nation's fiscal burden. It is also worth noting that in this period, some states tried to spread that burden in a relatively fair and equitable fashion. More states attempted to move away from over-reliance on regressive forms of taxation. Several introduced income taxes as well as taxes on the interest and dividends received by the upper class.[3] Overall, state income taxes increased from sixteen cents of every tax dollar raised in 1980 to nineteen cents in 1990, though the tax contribution of business dropped slightly, from five to four cents of each state dollar.[4] Meanwhile, although many cities in the Southwest and Northwest came through the stagnant 1970s and early 1980s in comparatively good economic shape, about a quarter of U.S. cities, mainly the bigger, older, industrial cities, began the new decade facing rapid population losses and rising levels of social impoverishment.[5] In Detroit, Cleveland, East St. Louis, and Newark, the stagnation and inequality described earlier were most painfully concentrated. New York and Boston, on the other hand, temporarily benefitted from the financial and defense booms of the mid-1980s and actually improved their local balance sheets. But these were the exceptions. Many other cities did what usually happens when the economy goes into a downslide. They cut services, fired public workers, sought give-backs from public-sector unions, and found ways to speed up the labor process, causing worker burn-out and higher levels of client hostility. In the short run, this tactic improved these governments' financial situation, but, as we shall see in Chapter Six, fiscal belt-tightening usually comes at a "real cost in the quality and supply of urban public services."[6]

Beginning with the onset of the second recession of the decade, however, these cities, along with most other local and state governments, now confronted the makings of a truly severe fiscal crisis. Its manifestations varied from state to state, but we would not be exaggerating much in saying that, collectively, they produced a fiscal nightmare. Indeed, despite an estimated $10 billion overall increase in state taxes during fiscal 1990, the combined effects of declining revenue and rising costs generated 1991 budget gaps between $40 and $50 billion in almost forty states.[7] And, as we know all too well, state and local fiscal crises translate into a reduction of public services to all citizens, but especially the neediest, and an economic crisis for public-sector workers.

In Florida, for instance, a state that epitomizes the Sunbelt boom, Governor Lawton Childs was forced to call a special session of the state legislature to cut $622 million from the budget and to introduce a state income tax. As the speaker of the Florida House of Representatives explained, Floridians could no longer expect good services and low taxes. "Something has to give," he said. "You can't have a tax haven and at the same time tell people you're going to provide them with a utopia down here." The choice was as stark as it was simple: enact new taxes or face cuts in basic human services, health, and education. [8]

Variations of Florida's experience were repeated throughout the nation. In 1991, Maine's governor was forced to invoke emergency powers and cut state spending by $22 million, primarily in local school aid, only to have to shut the state's government down for one week after funds ran short that following summer. Nearby in Rhode Island, the newly inaugurated governor declared a bank holiday in January 1991, when the state's banking system was endangered by fallout from the Savings and Loan scandal. These experiences were bad. But no state faced a bigger mess than California.

In 1992, California, the biggest and richest state of them all—the state that kicked off the property tax revolt of the 1980s (see Chapter Five) and gave the nation its tax-cutter-in-chief, Ronald Reagan—went without any budget at all for sixty-four days! Unable to agree on how to close a $10.7 billion deficit in a nearly $60 billion budget, California's political leaders ended up paying their bills with "warrants," a euphemism for I.O.U.'s, or "funny money." But there was no other choice, lamented Governor Pete Wilson, "California is running on empty." [9] By September, when the state's political elites finally cut a budget deal, it was a deal all about cuts. More than half the deficit, $6 billion, was made up by slashing expenditures for education, welfare, and health services. As a result, "the gates to the state colleges will narrow, the poor, blind and disabled will find their meager allotments cut even more, and local governments will be forced to shut libraries, fire and sanitation services." [10] Up to 50,000 state and local workers were likely to lose their jobs. And with all this, the state still faced a return to fiscal crisis in the spring of 1993. When combined with the depression in the state's defense and real estate industries, all the cuts in government spending simply accelerated the state's downward economic spiral. No wonder President George Bush hardly campaigned in California prior to the November 1992 election.

California was only the most glaring and desperate example of the continuing disintegration of the fiscal fortunes of the states. According to its 1992 fiscal survey, the National Association of State Budget Officers found that despite a fifteen-year record in the total amount of tax increases and expenditure cuts made by the states, thirty-five were still unable to balance their budgets in fiscal 1992, forcing additional cuts of more than $5 billion. To achieve balance in fiscal 1993, thirty-one governors proposed tax increases, eleven sought more cuts in local aid, five asked for cuts in welfare, eight tried to postpone wage increases for state workers, twenty-three demanded give-backs of benefits from state employees, and fifteen attempted to cut health-care costs. The Association's experts predicted that by the end of fiscal 1993, more than 180,000 full-time state jobs would be eliminated, either by firing or attrition. In New York State alone, as we shall see later, New York's liberal Governor Mario Cuomo has laid off no less than 25,000 of the state's 230,600 workers since 1990. [11]

The latest spate of public-employee firings came on the heels of years of layoffs. In 1990 alone some 6,000 state workers lost their jobs in Illinois, Massachusetts, and New Hampshire. New York and Pennsylvania fired another 2,500 that year. And the research department of the American Federation of State, County and Municipal Employees estimated the overall loss at 50,000 state jobs in 1991.

Against this tide of layoff and constriction, public workers have limited options. In moments of economic crisis, unions' vaunted lobbying power, a tool highly touted by their critics during good times, is of marginal usefulness. As we shall see in Chapters Six and Seven below, the unions can, and do, wield power. But unions cannot create revenues where they do not exist. Meanwhile, along with state employees, the poor bore much of the burden of fiscal crisis in the states. New Jersey and California refused to provide additional aid to women on welfare who had more than two children, and a number of other states, including Massachusetts, Michigan, Arkansas, Louisiana, West Virginia, Wyoming, Nevada, and Kansas, either eliminated or greatly reduced their "general relief" programs, which go to single men and women who are poor. It is worth noting in this vein, by the way, that in Michigan the majority of those on general relief are white men, and the fastest growth in applications for relief was in the suburbs.[12]

By the end of 1990, when President Bush finally admitted that a national recession was underway, expenditures were rising faster than revenues in more than half of U.S. cities. In the words of Henry Aaron, an economist of the Brookings Institute, a center-liberal Washington think tank,

> I think you would have to go back to the Great Depression to find similar anguish, in terms of the number of states that are facing an unprecedented cutback in service or significant increases in taxes.

The situation in New York City got so bad at one point that its leading fiscal watchdog, investment banker Felix Rohatyn, pronounced the unthinkable: that the state confronted financial conditions so awful that government leaders actually had to consider suspending the law of the balanced budget. "At some point," declared Rohatyn, "the tradeoff between balancing the budget and the long-term social and economic harm may not make sense," particularly when the size of needed cuts threatens to do "extreme brutality" to the lives of New Yorkers. [13]

In effect, while Washington found itself increasingly immobilized by budget battles, states and cites had to do the real dirty work of stagnation politics. It was up to the governors, mayors, state legislators, and city counselors to cut, slash, and burn the voters' expectation that government should meet public wants and needs. For these officials, the political life of incumbent legislators was rapidly becoming, in Thomas Hobbes' famous phrase, "poor, nasty, brutish, and short." As the politics of retrenchment worsened, fist fights broke out on legislative floors, governors and legislators were spat upon by constituents and even received death threats (someone actually fired shots at a pro-income tax legislator in Connecticut!), and angry rallies gathered in capitols and town squares across the nation. Perhaps most telling of all, just as nearly one-quarter of the members of Congress decided not to run for re-election in 1992, up to one-third of the nation's state legislators also refused, the largest departure in thirty years. And this estimate does not count the number of legislators who were defeated in their re-election bids in November. "I've begun to feel like the singer of 'Bye, Bye, Miss American Pie,' " said the president of the National Conference of State Legislatures. "Bad news on every doorstep; I couldn't take one more step" was a refrain that spoke plainly to the miseries of the politics of retrenchment. [14]

By 1993, the accumulation of tax increases, combined with the effects of what passed for an economic recovery amidst the longer pattern of stagnation, pushed state revenue collections up about 6%. For many states, the worst was over, at least for a while. Moreover, President Clinton's call for a small tax increase on the wealthy as part of his national deficit-reduction package helped to build the courage of officials in some states to consider raising taxes on the rich. Indeed, even before Clinton, when Congress hiked the top income tax rate from 28% to 33% as part of its 1990 budget deal with President Bush, a dozen states lifted their own upper-bracket rates. But state legislatures hesitate to raise taxes on business and the affluent; these groups have the political power to resist proposed tax increases through lobbying and threatening to withdraw campaign contributions. Even more important, state officials continue to worry that, in the words of one state tax official, "When you get too far out of line" with the tax rates of other jurisdictions, "you have to be concerned about the impact of taxes on [corporate] decisions about where to locate." [15]

Empowerment and the New Federalism

Given the fear of corporate flight and local tax-base erosion, balanced-budget conservatism is no mere ideology for most state and city officials; it is the main *fact* of their everyday political life. And while "it is clear that there is no overall plan to guide the various actors and units in the system" as they try to meet the fiscal imperatives of balanced budgets, it is just as clear that federal policy toward intergovernmental relationships in the 1980s was deliberately molded by conservatives to make economic insecurity the main consideration, both ideological and practical, in the calculations of state and local officials. [16]

Certainly, President Reagan wanted Washington to get out of the domestic public policy business. As far as he was concerned, most domestic policy matters belonged in the realm of local governments, where taxpayers had the greatest say over taxes and spending. Indeed, the trouble with the nation's economy, as Reagan viewed it, was not a malfunctioning of corporate capitalism at all, but an overly centralized and intrusive administration in Washington that both hampered business freedom and impaired the ability of regional and local majorities to work out their own solutions to problems. A central goal of Reagan's presidency, then, was "restructuring the power system which led to the economic stagnation and urban deterioration." The power system he had in mind was an overweight federal government, and restructuring meant "returning power to states and communities" as "a first step toward reordering the relationship between citizen and government." [17]

As we have just seen, however, to empower states and cities in a time of private stagnation and federal aid reductions was to force sub-national officials into terrible decisions that national political elites refused to make for themselves. As far as the states and cities of the nation were concerned, this was the age of "Fend-For-Yourself-Federalism." [18] In fact, this new regime really meant a return to the nineteenth-century U.S. political system, one in which "the states did almost all the governing." [19] In this old federal regime, each state was equal to every other, and each was the full repository of "the police powers," which covered everything from property regulations to marriage laws, from health to safety, even the regulation of community morals.

Legally speaking, the states were then and are now very powerful governments. But along with their autonomous legal power, the states had to own up to a heavy economic responsibility. The more disguised economic meaning of the old federalism was that states and cities, regardless of their resources, size, wealth, or poverty, were responsible for maintaining and guarding their own economies. But unlike the feudal townships of old, states and cities enjoyed no power to erect tariff walls, to coin money, to issue passports, or to make any rules keeping local business in place—or the competition out. And because state or municipal socialism was clearly never an option, the practical effect of economic independence was to make states (and cities) hypersensitive about creating business climates that would attract and hold capital, which only accentuated state economic competition. For state officials, keeping taxes low, unions out, and social expenditures down were all but inevitable.[20] From this perspective, one that places political auton-omy in the context of economic vulnerability, the case for returning power to the states and cities looks more like a case for empowering business and increasing its control of the surplus. The inner meaning of Reagan's "New Federalism" was empowering not grassroots govern-ments, but Wall Street fiscal monitors, for-profit corporations, and the world market for low-tax, low-wage, big-subsidy business sites in this country and abroad.

Wanting It Both Ways

From a purely strategic point of view, Reagan's most remarkable achievement was his ability to persuade the public that he was a staunch fiscal conservative at the same time that his administration went on one of the biggest domestic-spending sprees in U.S. history. This was no small triumph of political sales strategy, and credit should go where it is due. But the bill of goods Reagan sold the country was more than flim-flam. Reagan's balanced-budget political philosophy embodied a set of ideals, principles, and rules with real political and economic conse-quences. Indeed, rarely has ideological double-speak played a more important material role in the economy than in the 1980s. The fact that Reagan failed to live up to his own rhetoric, or even that he failed to focus adequately on the real economic roots of the fiscal crisis, is not the crucial point here. For if the Rightwing did nothing else, they did establish an ideological rationale for going back to a retrogressive set of rules that do two painful things. First of all, balanced-budget conser-vatism pits Americans against one another and against their national government. Thus, it persuades citizens to forgo united efforts to control national political power as a means of controlling corporate power. Then, in the name of local control and states' rights, the ideology encourages citizens to rely almost exclusively on their state and local governments to meet needs that such governments often lack the economic ability to satisfy. In short, the political strategists of the 1980s vastly increased the problems of government without doing anything to enhance the capac-ity of government to meet those very problems. By wasting vast deficit expenditures on a fruitless economic strategy, and then turning around to lambast that very expenditure, Reagan did the impossible: he set the financial gears of government and politics into forward and reverse at the same time. Balanced-budget conservatism formed the ideological cover for what was a most remarkable act of governmental derangement.

Balanced Budgets and Political Morality

The heroics and rewards of entrepreneurs and financial wizards, of the Steve Jobs, Donald Trumps, and Michael Milkins, as most everyone knows, dominated the 1980s. Reagan cheerfully proclaimed that it was all right to be rich, good to get fat off the land. Markets were magical, and in the words of the fictional tycoon of the movie *Wall Street,* which mimicked the real words of financial speculator Ivan Boesky, "Greed is good." But, as we saw in the last chapter, it is dangerously one-sided to see the 1980s solely as a time of economic excess and fabulous rewards.

Another side existed to the Reagan heyday. Not only were the 1980s a very bad time for large segments of the economic majority; Reaganism also meant strict government regulation of significant spheres of personal life. On questions such as abortion, prayer in school, and the freedom of cultural expression, the Reagan Administration stood with fundamentalist religious groups that favored strong, locally imposed limitations on private freedom. In the realm of culture, local majorities could have things their way; constitutional rights of privacy belonged to property, not individuals. Robert Bork, Reagan's nominee for Supreme Court justice, defended "the community's right to make moral judgements" in strongly toned constitutional terms. Similarly, conservative economist E. S. Savas pronounced that "The concept of national community...has failed to gain acceptance" because "with respect to social issues, America is not so much a single national community as it is a nation of small, diverse communities, each of which can be empowered to define and solve for itself the problems it considers most important." [21] Conservatives now imagined themselves to stand for power to the people via local democratic self-government. But communal democratic morality in the Reagan years had a fiscal aspect, too. The belief that government must live within its means was a cardinal principle. In this civic economic morality, deficit spending is wrong, evil, even a sin. To prohibit fiscal sin, fiscal morality requires government rules that forbid unbalanced budgets. Local governments understand this better than national government.

However, before examining this balanced-budget morality, we should note that not all conservative Reagan followers accepted the doctrine of fiscal sin, just as Reagan himself did not follow the principle in practice. Supply-side conservatives, such as Jude Wannisky, Jack

Kemp, Paul Craig Roberts, and others, preached the gospel that much lower taxes would produce much higher government revenues. They knew the economy was in the doldrums and that continued stagnation would bar both a rise in corporate profits and Reagan's re-election.

Hence, they were fully prepared to accept unbalanced budgets as the price of faster growth and the president's popularity. To the supply-siders, the traditional Republican defenders of balanced-budget conservatism were anachronistic, ideological enemies; they were almost as intensely disliked as liberal Democrats. One of the most excited ideologues of supply-side economics, George Gilder, warned old-fashioned fiscal conservatives that their balanced-budget conservatism "will inevitably require rises in tax rates and the closing of the horizons of growth." As Gilder pleaded, *"There are free lunches under capitalism,"* but not "within [their] calculus of pay-as-you-go lunches." The supply-siders insisted that tax cuts would produce growth (Gilder's "free lunches under capitalism") while Reagan's fiscal experiment required fiscal conservatives to change their stripes and accept big deficits. To call balanced budgets the be-all and end-all of political economy was, in Jude Wannisky's words, to succumb to "Fat Cat America's budget-balancing mania." [22]

It is obvious in retrospect, even if it was unclear to voters in 1981, that Ronald Reagan wanted both kinds of Republicans gathered under his tent, just as he wanted a fiscal policy that went in two directions at once. He wanted to cheerlead an economic experiment in fiscal adventurism by sharply reducing taxes on the richest citizens. At the same time, he sternly preached the morality of balanced budgets, which would ultimately require tax increases and major cuts in government programs.

The Reagan Administration never really thought seriously about this contradiction, much less resolved it. Consequently, as we saw in Chapter One, since 1985, when the supply-side deficits finally compelled Congress to pass the first Gramm-Rudman budget-cutting law, Reagan's "have your cake and eat it too" philosophy had policy debates at the national level boxed into a corner. Today, politicians of all stripes make fierce critiques of government spending only to turn around and become gridlocked when it comes to the task of significantly reducing spending or raising taxes in order to pay down the deficit. As mainstream budget analyst Allan Schick explains, the U.S. government currently faces not only a huge and growing deficit, but a "crisis in budgeting" which calls into question the very ability of the political system to resolve it. [23] In effect, through their spending and tax policies, the Reaganites transformed the real systemic problem of slow growth and stagnation, which had been building up since the late 1960s, into the mainly ideological, though potentially systemic, problem of deficit spending and unbalanced budgets. [24] Transforming the central issue of U.S. political economy from one of corporate-led stagnation into one of public economic deficits is no small feat. But it is an ideological sleight-of-hand that works because it resonates with the traditional Protestant work ethic.[25] Balanced-budget conservatism draws much of its moral fervor from long-held spiritual beliefs and appeals to common sense about personal economic rectitude. The ideology awakens dormant commitments to the eighteenth-century "pay-as-you-go" ideal, and it seeks to apply this ideal to government, despite the fact that "pay-as-you-go" long ago fell out of use as a guiding principle of corporate management, a point we shall return to shortly. Nonetheless, the underlying theology looks something like this:

Individuals who run up big debts live beyond their means and their labor; they consume instead of produce; they spend instead of working and saving. But the only kind of debt worthy of hard-working, hard-saving people is a deficit in their own self-gratification. According to the work-ethic myth, the rich get wealthy not by appropriating the labor power of others, but by working, saving, and keeping their own desires and appetites under control, in effect, by treating themselves poorly. [26] The institution of credit, however, is evil because it urges us spend income we do not have in order to live at levels we cannot afford so as to satisfy appetites that we should not be appeasing. Credit is the devil's lure, urging us to live for today rather than tomorrow and charging us interest in the bargain. [27]

Borrowers have nothing in reserve for a rainy day, they have no stored-up capital to invest in order to gain more wealth, and, worst of all, they stand a very good chance of going bankrupt and losing everything to their creditors. Undisciplined borrowers risk the worst of all things, becoming poor in goods because they are poor in spirit. For all these reasons, borrowing carries the heavy taint of sinfulness, sloth, and undiscipline; it has, to say the least, a bad name in U.S. culture.

Balanced-budget conservatives infuse the moral fervor of this private work-ethic theology into a critique of public spending. Applying moral rules of capitalist behavior to the state, rules that capitalists themselves no longer abide by, balanced-budget conservatives not only misdirect a simplistic moral psychology onto a design for fiscal management, they also mystify and confuse the way the political economy really works, the real relations between government, capital, credit, and power. Precisely because their underlying moral analysis is so appealing to traditional U.S. outlooks, it is essential to treat balanced-budget conservatism not as a serviceable theory of economic morals, but for what it really is: an ideology of private power.

One cautionary point: balanced-budget conservatism is not, in any case, a formal economic theory. For all its appeal to Protestant doctrine, balanced-budget conservatism is not rooted in a single theoretical work or a school of economics; no mature economic theory abjures the credit system. Nor can it be found delineated in a set of principled speeches by Ronald Reagan or anyone else. Balanced-budget conservatism is our term for a related but disparate set of conservative ideas and principles, for pieces of a conservative folk-wisdom, which, when held loosely together, help to explain and justify balanced budgets as a first principle of government. We constructed the concept theoretically by reaching for the kind of assumptions that would be necessary to firm up its claim that balanced budgets are inherently good. We constructed the idea empirically, drawing upon a variety of works, speeches, books, and so forth, which together make arguments for it. Balanced-budget conservatism is, in this sense, less a systematic theory than a cluster of ideas and habits of mind, which more or less run together, and which have a solid place in the economic folklore of U.S. political culture, especially within that segment of it known as the Republican Party, but also increasingly within the Democratic Party. In what follows, we first present the idea critically as a mythology, then connect it to sources deep in the anti-tax bias of conservative politics. Finally, we move on to describe what we see as three main principles of balanced-budget conservatism.

No Taxes!

In the 1980s, balanced-budget conservatism became the stern ideological counter-melody to the free-swinging spending of credit-card capitalism. Under this theory, abundance is terrific, everywhere, that is, but in government. When it comes to government, poverty is best. As liberal economist John Kenneth Galbraith once observed, "The line which divides our area of wealth from our area of poverty is roughly that which divides privately produced [goods]...from publicly rendered services." Fiscal conservatives believe this is good; this is how things should be. Public penury is, for the balanced-budget conservative, the very condition of private affluence. The best way to maintain public penury and private affluence is simply to keep taxes low. "Taxes," as Emma Rothchild once observed, "are the heart of darkness of the Reagan philosophy." [28]

Former Vice-President Dan Quayle offers a clear, straight-forward statement of the anti-taxism that sits at the crux of balanced-budget conservatism. "If you tax wealth," said Quayle, "you diminish wealth. If you diminish wealth, you diminish investment. The fewer the investments, the fewer [the] jobs." Low taxes equal more jobs; low taxes are as good for the working class as the business class. Thus do the interests of the economic minority and the economic majority harmonize. Indeed, taken to its logical conclusion, Quayle's dictum means that the best tax policy is a no-tax policy. Give government taxes and you not only sap the strength of the economy, but you give government the economic power to club the economy over the head with regulations. If the state is necessary, suggests Quayle, keep it small. As Quayle put it, "In man's economic life, the state may be an uneasy ally, but I don't think it is ever a friend." [29] Sound conservative policy would keep the "uneasy ally" just strong enough to protect the taxpayers, but never rich enough to stand as an equal to them. And the most effective weapon against overbearing and intrusive government is simple, raw fiscal discipline: low taxes coupled with a balanced budget.

Fortunately, the enforcer is always at hand; it consists of nothing more complicated than the plain reluctance of tax payers to part with their money. As we saw in Chapter One, conservatives prefer not to make distinctions between different classes of taxpayers. To the contrary, they like to jump from the premise that no one likes to pay taxes to the conclusion that all classes of taxpayers have the same interest in avoiding taxes. Conservatives wash out of their arguments any consideration of the class conflicts inherent in tax politics; the idea, for example, that working people have an interest in ample public services, funded by fair systems of taxation, while corporations have an interest in avoiding their fiscal obligation to society. As long as conservatives persuade working taxpayers to overlook such differences and to believe that somehow all taxpayers have an equal ability to control their own money in the form of power over government spending, the rest is easy: government will inevitably find itself able to raise only the minimum necessary funds, and not a dime more. Obviously, public services will shrink. But by then, the damage will have been done; the taxpayers will have shot themselves in the foot, which is what happened in California, as we shall see in Chapter Five.

Balanced-budget conservatives know that working people will tend to press for more public services: libraries, schools, roads, police, fire and environmental protection, health care, and so on. They see great dangers looming in such pressure. The very rules that give taxpayers the political clout to make demands for public services also create pressures to raise taxes. When mass demands are coupled with progressive outlooks, working people can see to it that corporations and the rich pay according to their ability. Moreover, when such taxes are drawn from the economic base of the nation as a whole, a base that only the national government can tap, corporations lose the opportunity to play local jurisdictions off against one another. For conservatives, then, the nationalization of fiscal power creates fears that national politicians will tantalize the masses, using progressive taxes and deficit spending to lure voters with promises of government booty. Thus, the further taxpayers are removed from the centers of political power, and the broader the tax base, the easier it is for politicians to create mass constituencies for public spending at the cost of private power. Milton and Rose Friedman typify the conservative warning against national power: "The centralization and the enlargement of the functions of government," they argue, "inevitably require a change in the way government operates." [30] Centralization means that government must become more bureaucratic. Once statist politicians are able to place administrative barriers between taxpayers and spending policy, the natural opposition of taxpayers and government may get obscured, obstructed, and coopted by the benefits, programs, and pork that politicians use to dull people's anti-tax sensibilities. Only far-away central governments can print money, after all, or tax corporations with minimal fear that business will flee the country. For the Friedmans and other balanced-budget conservatives, then, full-scale democracy, or rule by the national economic majority in the national government, is the most dangerous kind of government, and even contains the seeds of its own fiscal destruction:

> Throughout recorded history whenever leaders have been chosen by some method of voting, the aspirants for leadership have bought votes. Traditionally they have bought votes either with their own money or with a patron's money. To some extent, they still do so. But something new has been added! Since the 1930s, the technique of buying votes with the voters' own money has been expanded to an extent undreamed of by earlier politicians. [31]

According to this view, all things being equal, in a government simply, directly, and locally responsible to the people, taxpayers would surely deny government the power either to build up surplus revenues, or to print and waste money by going into debt and delivering services inefficiently. [32] Balanced-budget conservatives love to illuminate this point by referring to California in 1978, when the highly unusual combination of a huge state revenue surplus and exploding property tax bills spawned the tax revolt of Proposition 13. [33] As we shall see in Chapter Five, the taxpayers of California felt exploited by what they perceived to be a public policy of raising taxes at a time of enormous government surplus. But polls taken during the battle over Prop 13 showed that voters did not want to cut services—they wanted to cut the state's property tax rates and its surplus. Lurking within this most famous of recent tax revolts was a strong desire for more public services, which politicians will trade upon for votes, that balanced-budget conservatives both fear and hope to contain.

Balanced-budget conservatives believe that voters cannot be trusted to withhold their support from politicians bearing promises. The Friedmans' criticism of politicians' "buying votes with the voters' own money" suggests that voters are gullible creatures. They are easily deceived by politicians into thinking that tax payments are a reasonable price to pay for desired public services. For balanced-budget conservatives, people in their right mind would never actually choose rationally to have a government that furnishes a broad array of services for a reasonable price in taxes. Such a thing could only happen through manipulation, through the promulgation by politicians of a "false consciousness" that disconnects taxes and benefits.

People who can regularly afford to buy any private services they want might well see the world this way. In contrast, ordinary working people living on strapped budgets might just as reasonably have a more positive attitude toward inexpensive, widely available public services, such as education, health care, transportation, and recreation. However, by shifting the focus of public attention onto the problems posed by rising government spending, rather than the need for expanding government services, conservatives hope to build support for institutional rules, procedures, and mechanisms that will limit the possibilities for economic democracy, including the capacity of politicians to answer the demand for change among voters. Hot debates over rules, such as caps on tax-rate increases, or requiring super-majorities to pass new taxes or an explicit balanced-budget amendment, focus political discussion not so much on what government does to address social problems and needs, but on the costs of government to taxpayers and business. By splitting the question of how much money to give politicians from the question of what such money will be used for, conservatives play to the most narrow concerns of taxpayers. In this sense, balanced-budget rules not only limit the potential of democratic politics, they put anti-tax consciousness at the heart of conservative democracy. To help propel this anti-tax consciousness, balanced-budget conservatives rely on three interlocking principles: fiscal balance, shifting governmental power from Washington to the states, and cutthroat competition.

The Imperative of Balanced Budgets

The first principle of balanced-budget conservatism simply states that governments must live within their fiscal means. According to this simplistic, unvarying dictum, no government is genuinely legitimate unless it succeeds in living with the resources taxpayers are willing to supply. Since most taxpayers will not readily part with their money, good government usually means small, cheap government."

"That government governs best which governs least," said the nation's third president, Thomas Jefferson.[34] Politicians who cannot serve efficiently within these monetary confines should leave office, or the voters will certainly kick them out. Government compliance with the taxpayers is the central test of public legitimacy for balanced-budget conservatism.

But why should government budgeting be different from every other institution and household? In the real financial world U.S. citizens inhabit, gaining access to credit and living on borrowed money is the name of the game. The old work ethic may frown on debt, but present-day institutions demand it. As we saw in Chapter Two, the whole economy now floats on a vast ocean of credit. Corporations large and small, homeowners, credit- and charge-card users, just about every participant in the real economy borrows money. Most U.S. families would not be able to purchase a home or finance college for their kids without borrowing money. Corporations would not be able to finance big capital investments without turning to banks and the bond market. The fact is that "to fuel nearly three decades of post-war economic boom at home and export it abroad, this nation...borrowed an average net $200 billion a day, each and every day, since the close of World War II."[35] Modern capitalism is virtually inconceivable without its vast credit system. If credit is an inherent part of contemporary capitalism, "the pivotal factor in business enterprise," as Veblen called it, why should government act differently?[36] Why should the public sector have to meet a higher fiscal standard than anyone else in the economy?

To pose the question this way unveils the inseparable connection between the public ethic of balanced budgets and an archaic vision of capitalism, a capitalism made up not so much of big corporations, but of individuals, independent producers, owners of private property who work mainly for themselves in the manufacture of useful goods. In this inaccurate view, neither government nor the credit system plays a significant role. Most important, government produces no wealth of its own, does not produce useful economic services or possess any substantial economic power. This model of government, which exists only in the mind of the most utopian laissez-faire theorist, does not own land, build schools or highways, manufacture a defense establishment, or educate children. This imaginary state is radically separated from the real economy of work and production and does little more than provide for former Vice-President Dan Quayle's "uneasy ally," that is, a constabulary to defend the property owners, along with courts and prisons to discipline the thieves. This stark separation of state and economy explains why, despite the obvious existence of big corporations, only private individuals can engage in rational economic pursuits. But this individualistic outlook still sits uneasily with the reality of the large company.

Conservatives know, of course, that modern corporations pose a problem for their utopian image of an individualistic economy. Corporations are a form of collective, institutionalized "private" ownership. But the important thing for conservative purposes is that even in the corporate form, the private financial interests of individual stockholders control and govern the behavior of management. Indeed, balanced-budget conservatives want to model public government precisely on the stockholders' relation to their company. Government's owners, the taxpayers, must regularly and closely monitor their organization's economic behavior. As Ross Perot tirelessly told voters in the 1992 presidential campaign: "You are the *owners* of this country. Nobody else can do the job. Our system has been corrupted because we weren't exercising *the responsibilities as owners.*"[37] The true relation between government and individual, in Perot's formulation, is not that of citizen and public, but of shareholder and corporation. Government is, in this sense, not a matter primarily of public interests, but private ones. It is just an economic convenience, business by other means. Unfortunately, for balanced-budget conservatives, government is usually business run badly.

Because the state does not produce wealth on its own, its ability to make rational economic policy is strictly limited. First of all, because government officials do not own the property they use, or confront competition in the market, they will necessarily lack first-hand understanding of the hardships of production, the work, time, and sacrifice it takes, the risk and anxiety, the constant pressure to increase efficiency or risk losing all. Government bureaucrats, the Friedmans' complain, "spend other people's money," and "they have a bottom line...that is very distant and hard to define."[38] Even if public managers tried honestly to guard the public purse as if it were their own, though, the complexities of bureaucracy and absence of profit motive would inhibit efficiency anyway.[39] Government activity is wasteful because public administrators must, by definition, lack the business owner's hard-won experience of dealing with tangible economic problems and pressures, the hard-edge commercial forces that make corporate managers efficient and disciplined users of the stockholders' money. Government is inefficient because its managers are uniquely estranged from the discipline of real economic life.

Such arguments highlight the economic costs of distancing power over property from knowledge of industry and workmanship. What balanced-budget conservatives tend to overlook, however, is that the distancing of economic power from technical competence is, as we saw in the last chapter, a characteristic phenomenon of corporate capitalist organization and behavior. Balanced-budget conservatives can isolate government for special attack on this score only because they like to pretend that the modern corporation hasn't changed the way capitalism works. [40] Fiscal conservatives like to presuppose a vigorous but mythic capitalism in which entrepreneurs possess immediate technical knowledge of production. But in the 1990s, capitalism is no longer organized this way.

Capitalism has evolved into a corporate system that concentrates economic power and then directs such power toward manipulation and exchange of intangible assets. From a localized, small-scale system based on production of tangible goods in the early nineteenth century, capitalism changed into a global credit system driven to capture increasingly abstract and intangible forms of value. This development shattered whatever intimate connections may have existed in the nineteenth century between ownership, workmanship, and efficiency. As the development toward increasingly abstract economic institutions proceeded, the common-sense, materialistic checks and balances supplied by work in a "real" economy evaporated just as much for managers in the private sector as they did for chief bureaucrats in the public sector. Indeed, the distancing of business understanding from technical know-how, once the object of radical critics such as Veblen, has now become a familiar mantra within the business class itself. [41]

Nowadays, the ability to use other people's money for organizational purposes, the power to act independently of market forces, the capacity to manipulate the measurements and meanings of profit and even of money itself are defining features of corporate capitalism. Indeed, if anything, the state itself became more bureaucratic and abstract in its relation to the government work process only after conservative reformers in the early twentieth century demanded that government become more "bureaucratic" and "businesslike."[42] It is always worth remembering that the founders of the best U.S. graduate schools of public administration modeled them on the abstract financial and managerial methods first developed in graduate schools of business administration.[43] If a problem exists in the alienation of bureaucratic administration from real economic life, then, it is a problem rooted not simply in the state, but in the overall organization of modern corporate capital.

But, for balanced-budget conservatives, government's economic irrationality is not just a matter of the absence of business experience. As we saw above, conservatives also see government policy driven by politicians' desires for re-election. They love to point to outrageous public expenditures, $50 million subsidies for bee keepers, for example, or $600 price tags for military toilet seats, what Reagan's budget chief David Stockman breathlessly calls "the booty and spoils of the organized thievery conducted within the desecrated halls of government." [44] The incumbents' desire for re-election is also supposed to explain why public managers go easy on public employees, an indulgence of public labor that conservatives insist reduces efficiency and raises costs to taxpayers. The resulting inefficiencies are only worsened by civil service tenure rules that unnecessarily insulate government employees from economic insecurity, as well as by the political power that public-employee unions muster in elections. Public workers, after all, are the only part of the economic majority that can actually elect its bosses. [45] In the conservative view, when public employees are organized into unions, government does more than merely incline toward socialism; it is socialism incarnate, a full-blown democracy in which a segment of the economic majority actually controls the minority.

For all the reasons that flow from the simple fact that government does not produce wealth, balanced-budget conservatives insist that it is morally irresponsible for public officials to spend beyond what they can persuade the truly productive classes to pay in taxes. Each government expenditure must have a ready and equivalent source of revenue to pay for it. Otherwise the government should refrain from spending. Except for the basic police and security functions, no need justifies government spending at levels beyond what the taxpayers are willing to provide. In the final analysis, the ethic of balanced-budget government means that dollars rather than votes must frame the bounds of public policy. In other words, the most important expression of majority rule is the will of the taxpayers to pay (or not to pay) taxes. This constrained vision of majority rule takes us both logically and historically to the second principle of balanced-budget conservatism: returning political power to the states and cities.

Federalism: Divided We Rule

Balanced-budget conservatives know that the most vigilant taxpaying majorities are located at the grassroots of the political system, in local political systems, especially those that govern Fortress Suburbia. This understanding underpins the second principle of balanced-budget conservatism: in the U.S. political system, state and local governments should have the main responsibility for spending and taxing. Conservatives expect greater fiscal virtue from state and local majorities because, as we have seen, nearly all state constitutions mandate governments to balance revenues and expenditures. There is no choice in this matter; balanced budgets are the law.

In the real world, however, things are more complex. Balanced-budget rules do not stop state and local governments from living on credit. Just the way everyone else does, state and local governments borrow money on the bond market. State and local borrowing represents a huge segment of the U.S. bond market, amounting to nearly $750 billion in 1988.[46] Most of this borrowing goes for long-term capital improvements, such as road and school construction and is, quite reasonably, subject to a different set of bookkeeping accounts than regular, or annual, program expenditures. At the same time, state and local borrowing is closely scrutinized by financial rating firms, such as Moody's Investor Services and Standard and Poor's, as well as by the government bond departments of the large Wall Street brokerage houses that underwrite and market the bonds. When Standard and Poor's or Moody's smells a financial rat, they can lower a local or state government's credit rating, or in the worst case, even shut a city off from credit altogether, thus effectively forcing a local government into a "fiscal crisis," perhaps even bankruptcy.[47]

On the other hand, cities and states have little recourse when it comes to a bad financial grade; there are no external checks and balances on the rating firms. What they say goes. As Detroit's financial director recently lamented after Moody's lowered his city's credit rating, "Who is going to brawl with the ratings agencies?" It did not matter that Detroit had cut its municipal budget, reduced wages and benefits of public employees, and increased its debt reserve funds, or that it even ultimately achieved a balanced budget. In the case of a run-down, ex-industrial city like Detroit, not even balanced budgets are enough. To win Moody's heart, Detroit had to prove that the city will not stay poor; that what the firm called "the pressures exerted by extraordinarily weak credit fundamentals [that is, white-worker flight and auto plant shutdowns] will not lead to recurring fiscal distress."[48] To impress Moody's, one of the ultimate enforcers of balanced-budget conservatism on Wall Street, Detroit not only had to toe the budgetary line; it had to show prospects of becoming rich despite its poverty, either by attracting capital, or presumably, by finding a way to expel its poor. The lesson is clear that only affluent jurisdictions with hefty tax bases will gain honorable credit ratings.

Consistent with this principle, Moody's recently put the fiscal health of twenty-one exclusive New Jersey counties at the peak of its

Municipal Prestige list. These counties deserve such honors not only because they follow a "tradition of conservative fiscal practice," which results in bigger-than-average budget surpluses. These jurisdictions rank well above the national average also in per capita wealth. [49] These financially credible counties, which do not include New Jersey's poorest cities such as Camden and Newark, have broad tax bases, which generate more revenues than the wealthy citizens who live there either need or want to spend on public services, and which more needy cities outside their boundaries cannot tap.[50]

The circular logic of the fiscal-rating game is as obvious as it is vicious. Wealthy cities with limited borrowing needs can get all the credit they need. Poor cities, which need to borrow more to build up their infrastructure, cannot get affordable credit because they are likely to stay poor. Thus does the fiscal noose tighten around those towns already choked by corporate flight and Fortress Suburbia.

As the New Jersey case suggests, and fiscal conservatives expect, bond-rating institutions do not act alone in setting the parameters of fiscal responsibility for states and localities. They have the ready support, both direct and indirect, of taxpayers. Because bond issues are frequently subject to the decision of voters in special bond-issue elections, and many places now have rules requiring voter consent to tax increases, taxpayer majorities assist Wall Street in keeping local and state spenders on a tight leash.

External and internal constraints on capital borrowing leave most balanced-budget conservatives reasonably well-assured that governors and mayors are more responsible agents of fiscal trust than national politicians. Thus, during the 1992 presidential campaign, President Bush was quick to make just this point against Governor Bill Clinton's boasts of having administered twelve consecutive balanced budgets during his years as chief executive of Arkansas. As Bush noted during their final television debate, the Arkansas governor did not act responsibly because he *chose* to do so; he behaved correctly because he was *forced* to do so by law. "Governor Clinton has to operate under a balanced-budget amendment," said Bush. "He has to do it. That is the law." And, as Bush immediately added, "I'd like to see a balanced-budget amendment for America." [51]

The pressures buttressing fiscal constraint in state and local governments do not end with fiscal oversight and rules requiring balance. Not only do local and regional governments lack Washington's power to print money, they also tend to rely for their revenues on the most regressive and unfair forms of taxation, sales and property taxes, which end up forcing lower- and middle-income people to pay more taxes. According to the liberal Washington-based tax watchdog group, Citizens for Tax Justice, "Only two states—Vermont and Delaware—have devised systems of taxation that are even slightly progressive over-all...[I]n the vast majority, of states, both poor and middle-income families are taxed at rates well in excess of the rate at which the very rich are taxed." [52] As we shall see in the case study of New York (Part Two), regressive tax systems are perfectly structured to antagonize taxpayers and to keep the political light focused on questions of the cost rather than usefulness of government programs.

For balanced-budget conservatives, keeping the financial heat on state and local governments has another competitive benefit, too. As sub-national governments can expect less economic help from Washington, they must fend for themselves in a struggle for the only alternative source of revenue: private capital. States and cities have little choice but to compete with one another as well as with other nations to get business investment, even if this means simply bribing another community's plant or business to make its next investment away from home. Unless their own *local* economy expands, elected officials will have no choice but to press for more tax increases and service cutbacks.

Inter-jurisdictional competition for business takes many forms: the offering of tax abatements and enterprise zones, energy and utility subsidies, highway improvements, subsidized training programs for workers, the building of hi-tech industrial parks, schemes for university-business tie-ins, right-to-work laws, and, where unions exist, generous legal support for contracting out to non-union shops. Forced into competition with one another, neighboring states like New York, New Jersey, and Connecticut, or Kentucky, Ohio, and Tennessee, regularly dangle all kinds of rebates, incentives, and subsidies before each other's businesses, each hopeful of enticing capital, as Kentucky did when it recently beat Tennessee's offer to win a new International Paper plant. Kentucky's governor made the fever pitch clear in a stream of ads telecast over Cable News Network. "Locate your manufacturing plant in Kentucky," pleaded Kentucky's chief executive, Brereton C. Jones, "and the state will reimburse your entire investment. In Kentucky, we're serious about jobs." [53]

The mix of federalism, capitalism, and stagnation puts business in the catbird seat, giving capital more power to impose its own terms of investment on local communities and states. Unless the economic majority pushes Washington to change the rules and flatten the commercial playing field, states and localities, representing different segments of the economic majority, will remain locked in a vicious struggle to win business by absorbing more of the costs of doing business as well as government onto themselves. For now, though, as in the instance of municipal credit ratings, only the wealthiest jurisdictions have the freedom to choose, or closely control, the kind of capital they want. [54]

Celebrating Cutthroat Competition

Stagnation not only brings out the worst in local governments, it brings out the worst in taxpayers. In a political economy that makes public government rather than private power the most legitimate object of citizen anger, it is easy to see how stagnation and scarcity can set group against group *within* the various local and state governments. For balanced-budget conservatives, intensifying group conflict within local jurisdictions, fracturing the local economic majority, is the hard fist inside the velvet glove of "grassroots" democracy. Indeed, the celebration of cutthroat competition is the third basic principle of balanced-budget conservatism.

Conservatives want more group conflict, because in the face of a bitterly divided economic majority, local politicians will have to choose more carefully between competing claims of taxation and spending. And conservatives are prepared to bet that, especially in state and local governments, for reasons we have already considered, the pressures favoring lower taxes will prevail over those seeking higher spending.

As incomes fall and jobs grow insecure, as taxes and prices rise, as it gets harder and harder just to make ends meet, taxpayers will naturally strike out at the price of government. They will rail about their wages and complain about prices in the supermarket. But in a bad economic situation, taxes are the one price that the corporate economy permits the economic majority to complain about; taxes are the one aspect of stagnation, people can use their political power to fight. There is a very important point buried deep in this seemingly simple fact of everyday life, and it is crucial to the link between balanced-budget conservatism and cutthroat competition.

We should not automatically equate the voters' preoccupation with taxes with the conservatives' ideological hostility toward government. Many voters, especially those in Fortress Suburbia, may well be conservative. Many certainly do not want urban economic majorities reaching in to extract surplus revenues from "their" tax base. But the roots of anti-taxism are at least as much structural as they are ideological. As we shall stress in Chapter Four, the very distinction between suburb and city is anything but natural. Anti-taxism reflects the way the organization of society and state restricts the themes for public anger and debate. Other topics, alternatives, or approaches that might directly threaten the economic minority—such as demanding that corporations account for their use of capital, or that suburbs share their tax base with cities—are effectively screened out by the prevailing myths and rules. Peter Bachrach and Morton Baratz call this silent form of ideological power, through which potential demands for change are quieted by the very organization of institutions, "non-decision-making" power. [55] That the social system does not ordinarily allow the economic majority to hold private-investment and pricing decisions accountable to the public is a crucial non-decision, one that effectively redirects mass anger about economic inequity toward questions of taxes and government spending. Once again, the failure of corporate activity in the private sector to benefit the larger society is magically transformed into public governmental failure, while the corporate sector is provided a built-in social exemption from public responsibility. In our society, as Left economist Arthur MacEwen notes,

> there is no mechanism by which people can vote for higher wages or less inflation, the elimination of the business cycle or lasting security. They can, however, vote against taxes. Voting for lower taxes and thus higher incomes is the one response that the political system allows to a deteriorating economic situation. [56]

When, as they experience economic stress and strain, taxpayers push to limit taxes, they inevitably circumscribe the purposes and uses of government, the things government can do or pay for. Obviously, conservatives like that. When resources grow scarce, the politics of who gets what from government will get more bitter. A government facing annual gaps between resources and demands has to carefully ration and discriminate between the various claims for tax exemptions, tax payments, and social services; it has to choose among conflicting pressures and demands, giving in to some interests, denying support to others. Ideologically, conservatives praise this sort of competition among interest groups. Such competition is good because it appears to lay the basis for a more high-minded, moralistic, and responsible politics. Offering up a false image of grassroots democracy as a debating society where corporations and individuals debate from equal planks, instead of the raw power struggle that takes place in a class society, conservatives claim that political competition will compel the various interest groups to make the most reasonable, intelligent claims they can. Not only that, but countervailing group pressures will force the hand of politicians toward self-discipline. They will no longer be able, as the Friedmans' feared, to buy votes. Beset by conflicts and the omnipresent need to balance budgets, politicians will no longer have the luxury of promising benefits to pro-spending constituencies, as they did in the days of the New Deal. As our later case studies of California, New Jersey, and New

York will illustrate, public officials now have to make hard, even harsh judgements about which groups will get less and which must pay more. What conservatives see as the permissiveness of liberal "give-away" programs—welfare, farm subsidies, pork-barrel projects—all of what David Stockman heatedly indicted as "the flotsam and jetsam of a flagrantly promiscuous politics," will disappear because scarcity and outraged taxpayers will withdraw the means of logrolling. When the rule of thumb is pay-as-you-go, all give-aways must go.

Such thinking finds its moral high ground in the political writings of contemporary political scientists such as Theodore J. Lowi, who was a big influence on the thinking of Stockman. Lowi believes that responsible and legitimate government cannot be all things to all people. It must stand for something, for one set of priorities, values, and interests at the cost of others. A legitimate democratic government deliberately and painfully chooses between conflicting claims. The end result is a particular definition of the public interest that voters can understand, measure, and judge. When the next election rolls around, voters can support continuing this definitive policy, or choose another. But at least their decisions rest on evaluating clear commitments, not vague promises. In Lowi's words, "A good clear statute puts the government on one side as opposed to the other sides, it redistributes advantages and disadvantages, it slants and redefines the terms of bargaining. It can even eliminate bargaining...Laws set priorities. Laws deliberately set some goals and values above others." [57]

As a theory of pure politics, Lowi's model sets a high and even worthy standard for rational democracy. On the other hand, political decisions are never made in an economic or social vacuum. [58] In a class society, if government is going to stand for one set of interests at the expense of others, it is probably the ruling economic class whose claims will prevail. Whatever the reasonableness or truthfulness of claims made by the various contending interests in the democratic debating society, public officials must first heed the higher claims of financial markets and business investors. Especially in an era marked by economic stagnation and "go-it-alone federalism," the society's "non-decision-making" process all but guarantees not the monopoly but the primacy of capitalist interests. Under such circumstances, it will be the capitalist market, not the moral choices of legislators, that "slants and redefines the terms of bargaining" *before* the politicians ever make their deliberate choices. Under these circumstances, when the non-choices and non-decisions of corporate capital frame the difficult choices of democracy, the effective structure of reasonableness is no more general or public in scope than the private pecuniary rationality of commerce. If brass-knuckles economic pluralism determines the way the political game is played, the economic majority is bound to lose.

Yet, knowing this, even supposedly liberal Democratic politicians who claim to speak for the broad interests of working people, such as Gary Hart in the 1980s and President Bill Clinton today, join balanced-budget conservatives, such as Ross Perot, in the critique of "the special interests," as if all "particular" interests were somehow equal in the weight, power, or justice of their demands. Unless Democrats such as Hart and Clinton make absolutely explicit the profound differences between the claims of the economic majority and the economic minority—and we do not think this is very likely—their anti-group rhetoric will simply fuel the fire of popular hostility against progressive politics.

Ideology and Reality

Even as it seems to triumph at dissimulation, balanced-budget conservativism is at best an imperfect weapon. This ideology can only disguise and deflect criticism from the corporate economy; it cannot change unsatisfactory conditions. The underlying socio-economic order stays in place, with all its weaknesses, warts, and strains. Not least among the strains is the difficulty elites face in their effort to secure a system of decaying social relations. As the power elite's preferred apology for inaction, balanced-budget conservatism offers a framework of diminished expectations for everyone else. But even as the apologetics of disappointment, balanced-budget conservatism is radically divorced from economic reality.

Unlike the welfare-state liberalism that it supplanted, the new conservativism denies the power of the existing means of production to overcome economic constraints; it cites government as the primary limit to progress. But what are the implications of an ideology of sacrifice for a society conditioned to a belief in progress?

From at least the middle of the nineteenth century on, capitalism gradually abandoned the Calvinist belief in the value of work for its own sake. Indeed, in the twentieth century, corporate capital justified the pain of labor with the promise of ever more leisure-time fun. A shorter working day, higher wages, and more consumption would leave workers and their families happier and freer. Economic progress came to be identified with a society capable of supplying ever more Disneylands. Immodestly, the system committed itself to a constant escalation of its own success; but now the solution looms as a problem. [59]

When capital plunged into the twentieth century's first great crisis of stagnation, the welfare state emerged to absorb surplus, stimulate demand, and subsidize consumption. The welfare state demonstrated that capitalism could no longer find its excuse in the self-redeeming quality of work, for business was incapable of securing full employment on its own. It was no longer possible for capital to justify itself by appeals to necessity or nature, for the "natural" workings of the system brought disaster. State intervention to guarantee consistently high levels of employment and consumption shifted the system's apologetics onto the ground of real performance. From the 1930s on, government's provision of "entitlements" turned consumption into a right independent of work, both because social movements pressed hard for such a right, and because ever more consumption had become vital to production.

Through deficit spending, easy credit, and mass advertising, the welfare-warfare state more than answered business' need for consumers. At the same time, such changes forged the public understanding that economic processes were too important to be left solely for market forces to direct. The end justified the means: stimulating the economy supplanted traditional market ideology, and elites adjusted the ideology to reflect and justify new policies and political relations. Welfare liberalism, what Theodore Lowi calls "interest group liberalism," justified a broad democratization of political demand. [60] Celebrating interest group power as a necessary ingredient of democratic policy making, within an interventionist state committed to managed growth, welfare liberals urged all interests to organize and advance their demands for spending. As long as such groups made their demands "within" and not "against" the political system, the working principle of politics became accommodating to group power: "To each according to their organization."

The pluralist image of group power crudely approximated what the political-economic system really aimed to achieve—a generalized incorporating and pacifying of all social classes and interests. Material expansion would bring about the ever widening satisfaction and cooptation of interests, and economic growth would be both the end and means for government spending. Deficits fueled aggregate demand, television provided the required stimulus to buy, capitalist production furnished the goods, and U.S. political science even offered the appropriate theoretical cover of a "pluralist theory" of the state. Pubic policy, economic reality, and public ideology were at least roughly coordinated and synchronized. Even if working-class interests could never realistically aspire to more than influencing the middle levels of power, public spending and public policy brought more than merely symbolic rewards. The standard of private and public living actually rose, albeit, as Galbraith said, very unevenly.

In most of these respects, however, welfare-state liberalism is different from balanced-budget conservatism, and such differences are more than cosmetic; they involve basic shifts in how the prevailing ideology relates to material reality.

Compared to welfare liberalism, balanced-budget conservatism rests on a far more distorted relation to economic reality. Not even the state and local governments that are legally required to balance their budgets actually do so, and elites know that a federal balanced budget would produce an economic disaster. The obsession with deficits does not describe how the real political economy works; nor does it offer a realizable goal for government, or promise real relief from economic stagnation. To the contrary, its goal of fiscal rectitude is a hopeless dream that glorifies the impoverishment of government with a false promise of grassroots democracy and the supposed virtues of self-defeating group combat. As compared with the open secret of cooptation in welfare liberalism, the goal of balanced budgets has nothing to do with the real purposes of elites. The goal of a balanced budget is purely abstract, symbolic, and mythical.

The repeated attacks on government spending deny public responsibility for social costs, and they make increased taxation seem irrational. The anti-tax focus in politics subordinates the question of corporate financial obligation to the public interest; this ideology takes the large corporations off the hook. The deficit obsession serves mainly to undermine social democracy and to consolidate a corporate takeover of national wealth and power.

Balanced-budget conservatism is thus a much "purer" form of ideology than interest-group liberalism. Whereas the strategic purposes of pluralism were always close to the surface—could any thinking person not understand what the term "New Deal" really meant?—the repressive character of balanced-budget conservatism is more veiled. Its claim to economic common sense hides the attempt to coerce. This increased displacement of ideology from material reality is, we have argued, connected to the objective under-performance of the regime. Balanced-budget conservatism is an excuse to economically repress popular expectations masquerading as an attack on the spendthrift state. The irony, of course, is that even as it downgrades the state and lowers wages, business must still constantly raise private expectations through consumption and sales systems. Fredric Jameson puts the point well when he observes that "obviously you can't have it both ways; there is no such thing as a booming, functioning market whose customer personnel is staffed by Calvinists and hard-working traditionalists knowing the value of the dollar," and who, we might add, are desperate to find work at any wage.[61] Inasmuch as balanced budgets offer no prospect of reversing economic decline, inasmuch as it is doublespeak for a corporate takeover that is against the interests of the economic majority, balanced-budget conservatism runs a heightened risk of stretching ideology to the breaking point. The inherent falsehood of balanced-budget conservatism makes it a point of strategic vulnerability in the system.

At the same time, we cannot fail to be impressed by the power of elites to shape the national agenda and public consciousness. After all, balanced-budget conservatism did not result automatically from the mechanics of a faulty economy. Not only were the hyper-deficits of the 1980s aggravated by deliberate changes in federal budgetary policy, but elites of both parties have systematically urged deficit-mania on the public. No less important, we have to acknowledge that the ideological ploy of balanced-budget conservatism fits, hand in glove, into the broader framework of U.S. society. As the next chapter explains, the political and economic systems were made to order for the purposes of an elite politics of divide and rule.

Chapter Four

THE FRACTURED MAJORITY

What happens in politics depends on the way in which people
are divided into factions, parties, groups, classes, etc.

E.E. Schattschneider, 1960

At all levels of politics, balanced-budget conservatism pits group
against group, heightening tensions. Battles rage over taxes, spending,
and budgets. Interest groups desperately try to maintain their shrinking
piece of the pie while fending off tax increases by government or budget
raids by rival groups. Stagnation erodes the tax bases of towns, cities,
and states, fueling inter-jurisdictional competition to attract scarce capital investment. Because businesses expect tax abatements and other
economic inducements as their price of entry, localities and states can
win the struggle for more investment only by shifting the pressure on
taxes and spending over to non-business interests.

Why do people accept such a formula for disaster? Why, in the face
of all the evidence of corporate failure, are people willing to accept a
political arrangement that puts the onus for setting things right on the
backs of taxpayers, and local and state governments? Why are many
working Americans so willing to fight one another, especially when, as
we saw in Chapter Two, a tiny minority of the society controls the vast
preponderance of wealth and uses it to the disadvantage of the majority?

A big part of the answer, we think, is that division is anything but
a new experience to the U.S. working class; the government has always
treated different segments of the working class differently. By giving
assorted groups of workers unequal status, power, and position in
politics, elites have kept segments of the workforce at each other's
throat, sometimes quite literally so, while creating allies for corporate
power among millions of people who work for a living. This inescapable
history of division, we shall argue, prepared today's workers for the
newest ideological incarnation of divide and rule—balanced-budget
conservatism. It is hard to imagine, after all, that a united, class-conscious workforce would tolerate a national social policy that pushed the
working class to compete with itself.

Before turning to the details of the argument, we should be clear
about why we believe so much of U.S. politics depends on the politics
of dividing the masses. The reason is basic. Divide-and-rule governing

is connected to the volatile mixture of mass democracy in a capitalist society.

The oxymoron called "democratic capitalism" rests on a potentially explosive political base: the willingness of the majority of workers to relinquish using their political power against the tiny economic minority of owners and managers that controls most of the nation's wealth.[1] To put it bluntly, democracy gives the majority of working people the power to demand that those who control the economy use that power for the good of society as a whole, or risk losing the privilege. Nominally, even within the normally accepted rules of this society, the economic majority can regulate, tax, and in some cases even plan the uses of private capital to better serve the public purpose and need. Historically, governments at all levels have used such powers to tax, regulate, and channel the uses of private property. From Washington's command of the means of production in wartime to the mundane world of town zoning to protect local property values, government has used its power to control and channel the uses of private property. In the United States, no government has ever systematically drawn together this power to foster the interests of working people as a whole, but all elements of the economy have used scattered fragments—business, labor, agriculture, and consumers—when it served their narrow and divided purposes. More fully extended, a majority-run democracy would demand that business be fully accountable to society. It might even demand that business no longer run some key areas of the economy, such as health care and housing. Democracy, in sum, has the power to put capitalism at risk.

Needless to say, no self-respecting power elite wishes to have the majority breathing down its neck. No self-respecting power elite would even tolerate this. The U.S. economic elite is no exception. Simply put, business in the United States has never viewed the majority as a reliable ally of economic minority rule. Repeatedly, ruling economic and political elites have preempted, inhibited, and thwarted the potential for economic majority rule. Among other devices, such as using state violence against protesters and ideological purging against radicals, elites have regularly used the procedures, methods, and boundaries of government to fracture the economic majority. Elites have regularly manipulated democratic institutions to forge a host of political majorities that are much smaller than the economic majority—smaller, divided political majorities that do not threaten the elite's economic power.

In this chapter, we examine a series of examples of divide-and-rule government and how workers responded. Beginning with James Madison's 1787 incorporation of the divide-and-rule strategy in the Constitution, gradual bifurcation of working-class power into the increasingly disparate channels of trade-union and ethnic machine politics. Our main focus here will be on the rise of labor's voting power and its pacification by machine politics. Most important, we examine how the financial practices of urban party machines inspired a double-edged counterattack by urban power elites against the working class. First, local capital struck at labor's urban political party base, using a host of institutional reforms to weaken party rule and shrink the urban majority down to size. Then, having done much to sabotage machine politics inside the cities, reformers consolidated their gains by building up the institution of Fortress Suburbia outside central cities, thus barring the urban majority's power to tap the expanding revenue base of metropolitan areas. Eventually, of course, suburbia, which once functioned as a means to control labor, became the dream destination for many workers themselves, although throughout most of the post-war era, only whites has a real chance to get there. Indeed, the national Democratic Party did much to encourage and subsidize white labor's flight from the cities. In the process, by enlarging the potential constituency for modern conservatism, the New Deal Democratic Party dug its own grave. As we shall see in Chapter Five, the Democrats' uncritical support for white hegemony in Fortress Suburbia would turn out to be a chief factor in the failure of liberalism to meet the challenge of suburban tax revolt.

The Constitutional Roots of Divide-and-Rule Government

In order to stay in the saddle, U.S. elites have always set elements of the workforce against each other, the best way to keep the majority from challenging minority control of the economy. The strategy goes back to the founding of the nation, and was never more clearly stated than by James Madison in his famous Federalist Paper #10.

Analysis of the work of this "dead, white male" is indispensable for progressives today. For any study that pretends to be concerned with the Left's political options, Madison's ideas about political structure and organization are critical. Madison was a strategic political thinker of the highest caliber; he thought clearly and honestly about how his preferred version of society was inextricably connected to a particular organization of the struggle for power. Moreover, Madison's ideas as expressed in Federalist Paper #10 and other writings are not idle speculation; they were used to structure our political system as a means of protecting the economic minority. Finally, and perhaps most important, Madison's principles are not archaic. They continue to shape politics, influence conservative strategy, and inhibit mass political organizing. In one form or another, such recent developments as twentieth-century "good government" reform, the emergence of Fortress Suburbia, and, perhaps most surprisingly, even the growth of new urban movements on the Left (a subject to which we shall turn in Chapter Eight) reflect Madison's ideas. Clearly, we must contend with his writings.

Strategically, in Federalist Paper #10, Madison attempts to explain why a large republic should limit the power of the economic majority over the economic minority. Madison envisioned politics as, at bottom, a struggle of conflicting economic interests, a long-enduring fight between "those who hold and those who are without property." [2] Madison, of course, sided with those "who hold property," and believed, as modern balanced-budget conservatives do, that because taxpayers pay the freight of government, they deserve special protection from the spending-and-tax proclivities of "those without property." [3] Still, Madison did not believe it a wise political strategy, or even politically just, for propertied interests to monopolize political power. "Give all power to property and the indigent will be oppressed. Give it to the latter and the effect may be transposed. Give a defensive share to each and each will be secure." [4]

On its face, Madison's view seemed balanced; as each side of the class struggle was liable to oppress the other, the government should entrust neither alone with a monopoly of political power. From this standpoint, Madison's ideas about the double-sided nature of class conflict seem to reflect a sense of liberal fair-mindedness. A good government would thus assume the role of independent referee in the on-going economic battles of society. Accordingly, the system of government should manage such conflict "by the exercise of reason and good will," for "politics is not a civil war conducted by other means but a constant process of bargaining and accommodation, on the basis of accepted procedures." [5]

Yet when one examines the Constitution's "accepted procedures," as we will in a moment, it becomes instantly clear that its rules of political organization are not neutral. Their weight falls heavily and deliberately on the side of economic minorities and against the mass power of "those without property." Madison defends such an uneven solution by claiming that the economic majority can always use the principle of majority rule to defend itself against the economic minority. In contrast, because the economic minority can never outvote the majority, it is necessary to give the latter extra protection against the majority's political power. In that way, the system of government prevents poorer classes from carrying out such "improper or wicked project(s)" as issuing paper money, raising burdensome taxes on the rich, abolishing debts, or, worst of all, enforcing "an equal division of property." [6] But this extra protection given by the Constitution to the economic minority consists precisely of a structural attack on the majority's very power to form itself. In depriving the majority of the power to wreak havoc on the rich, the Constitution also cripples the majority's power to use the very principle of majority rule that Madison reassures us will be its self-protection.

The key to Madison's subversion of majority power comes in his proclamation that for minority economic rights to be secured, "those without property...must be rendered, by their number and local situation, unable to concert and carry into effect their schemes of oppression." [7] In effect, Madison devises a plan that will crumple the big economic majority, leaving it unevenly twisted and turned into numerous divisions. The plan rests on a handful of simple but crucial principles. First, Madison called for a system of government that was capable of absorbing very large populations and adding great swaths of territory. Madison knew that with the country's economic development the population would inevitably grow. He also suspected that this new population would hardly come from the ruling classes of Europe. Aristocrats, nobles, and kings would be the last people to pick up and leave the social systems in which they held the cards to make a new life in a poor country that did not even respect feudal titles. Rather, Madison insisted, in the United States the "increase of population will of necessity increase the proportion of those who will labor under all the hardships of life, and secretly sigh for a more equal distribution of its blessings."[8]

But while rapid growth of the poor majority might seem to increase the danger to "those who hold property," Madison theorized that the nation's large size and population would have two negative effects on the economic majority. First, the sheer breadth of the country would make mass communication and organization difficult for poor people. More important, especially as modern technology makes size irrelevant to communication, Madison also theorized that the majority of poor Europeans who came here would reflect so many different regions, cultures, languages, and ethnicities that they would tend to subdivide the economic majority into "many lesser interests," a congeries of mutually exclusive identities and groupings more likely to "vex and oppress each other than to cooperate for their common good." Amidst this hodgepodge of clashing identities, this "multiplicity of interests," a cohesive mass organization of "those without property" would be virtually impossible.[9]

Madison was nothing if not a brilliant student of political organization and group dynamics. His "cure for the mischiefs of faction" rested on the key insight that the most suitable contexts for rapid and effective political organization are small, relatively homogenous communities— systems resembling what he called "pure democracies." Madison understood that people who know one another, speak the same language, share customs and habits, live in similar ways, and believe in similar goals and ideals, are much more likely candidates for unified action than people who are strange or mysterious to one another. The point may seem obvious, but it is not. Revolutionaries like Karl Marx, who wrote after Madison's death, believed that workers throughout the world would come finally to appreciate their joint interests as a members of a global economic majority. Yet contemporary students of social movements have frequently confirmed Madison's insight. Writing of the conditions most favorable to the formation of today's social movements, for example, Richard Flacks stresses that mobilizing poor communities for political action needs more than sharing a common problem.

> Threats must be perceived, and action against them must be felt to be possible if collective action is to occur. Such shared perception depends on communication with others sharing the life situation and the threat. The more accessible such others, and the more interaction about the situation takes place, then the more a sense of common definition and of possibilities for collective action can be achieved...Because such communication is a crucial condition for collective action, we suppose that the ideal locale for its emergence is a relatively self-contained and homogeneous community that is experiencing threat.[10]

Indeed, precisely because the existence of small, homogeneous communities increases the probability of action by the economic majority, Madison strongly opposed direct or "pure democracy":

> a pure democracy, by which I mean a society consisting of a small number of citizens, who assemble and administer the government in person, can admit of no cure for the mischiefs of faction. A common passion or interest will in almost every case, be felt by a majority of the whole, a communication and concert results from the form of government itself; and there is nothing to check the inducements to sacrifice the weaker party or an obnoxious individual.[11]

We are thus left with a seeming paradox. Madison opposed local democratic self-rule, or direct democracy, because it increased the ease and probability of political organization by the property-less. Yet he understood that the more such local communities existed, the more likely these communities would frustrate and compete with one another, thereby weakening the majority's opportunity to organize. Federalism—the division of power between the national and state governments—proved the perfect one-sided resolution of Madison's paradox.

As under the reigning legal theory of Madison's day, whose essence still holds true today, communities and cities have no independent constitutional status. As one legal scholar writes, in the U.S. political system cities "have no 'inherent' or 'natural' power to do anything." They enjoy only powers the states grant them. [12] Because they are legally subordinate to state governments, Madison could reasonably expect the states to discipline any excesses of local economic majorities. In this respect Madison offers the propertied elite the best of both worlds: a large republic with a huge workforce politically divided against itself.

Madison's goal in the Constitution was not only to allow for a vast and differentiated population, but also to maximize the opportunities for local and state governments to reflect and represent such differences. This would ensure that as the various segments of the underlying population congregated in particular regions, areas, or neighborhoods, their local representatives in state and national legislatures would surely reflect and accentuate their parochial outlooks far more than unified class perspectives. And, again, the more local governments (and there are approximately 80,000 local units of government today), the more such disparate voices, perspectives, and interests will proliferate, the more secure the economic minority is from the potential political power of the economic majority. In Madison's oft-quoted words,

> Whilst all authority in [the government] will be derived from and dependent on the society, the society itself will be broken up into so many parts, interests and classes of citizens, that the rights of individuals, or of the minority, will be in little danger from interested combinations of the majority.[13]

Adding to the localization of political power in the United States, the Constitution mandates that either local or state majorities elect all offices of the national government. The House of Representatives is elected by 435 local congressional districts; the Senate by fifty state districts; even the president of the United States must collect a majority of votes in the electoral college, which are apportioned state by state. This means that even if, against the odds, the economic majority did form a unified political force, the fact remains that the U.S. political system has no at-large election district for a national majority to control. The end result of this very complicated set of rules and boundaries is a weird sort of *absentee* democracy. It is an absentee democracy in two interconnected senses. First, the people are rendered only indirectly present in government through the device of representation. Second, due to the localization of the representative system, the national economic majority simply vanishes as a political force. The established institutions make it politically invisible. Absentee democracy preempts national majority rule, encourages localism, and prohibits even local majorities from making anti-capitalist rules. In short, Madison's argument promises majority rule as the safety valve against the domination of the few, but then withdraws that very opportunity through its intricate system of fractured political constituencies. It is no wonder that balanced-budget conservatives want to push politics down to the state and local levels; that is just where the inner divisions of the majority are most faithfully represented and most likely to erupt.

Nor is it any wonder that Karl Marx, whose whole political program aimed at uniting the economic majority throughout Europe, argued that for the purposes of majority rule, "The machinery of government cannot be too simple. It is always the work of knaves to make it complicated and mysterious." [14]

But there was more to the early strategy of divide and rule than we find in the byzantine structure of the Constitution. Serving further to divide labor against itself, the founding elite simply denied certain broad segments of labor—women, slaves, Native Americans—the right to participate in politics at any level or in any forum. Of course, the main reason for the economic elite to exclude such groups was not to divide the working class, but to exploit their labor and land to the hilt, with no political questions asked. We must not believe that racism and sexism are merely cultural or psychological phenomena; they are expressions and justifications of power inextricably intertwined with economic exploitation. Despite Madison's moralistic claim that as a means of controlling the causes of class conflict it would be "folly to abolish liberty," the elite did precisely "abolish [the] liberty" of many so that the latter could not use political power to redress their grievances.

The uneven exploitation of labor had the additional political benefit of segmenting the economic majority. Defining certain sub-groups of the working class as "slaves" or " second-class citizens" (women) was undoubtedly psychologically empowering for white male laborers. The poor farmers and workers who kept their civil rights understood the message of unequal citizenship: no matter how bad their economic situation might become, white male workers were at least fully free public citizens, equal in civic rank to the wealthiest man in society, and much higher in dignity than those women, slaves, and Native Americans who were not. By elevating some workers, many among the oppressed could themselves feel the dangerous psychic high that comes from the ability to lord it over others. In effect, through its provision of unequal standing within the working class, the political system turned the feeling of power back onto the consciousness of white male laborers, lending such men an enhanced sense of status, a surplus of psychic income, and a bigger stake in the ongoing system of unevenly arranged power. So while the presence of a large population of unpaid labor held down white male wages, those wages were still above the pay of women and slaves. Plus, white men could enjoy the invidious social pleasure of what W.E.B. DuBois once called the "wages of whiteness." We might just as well add, of course, that such workers also enjoyed the "wages of maleness." To extend a powerful argument made by historian David R. Roediger, the nineteenth-century U.S. elite partially compensated white male workers for suffering alienating and exploitative class relationships by conferring intangible status privileges over "the truly disadvantaged" races and gender.[15]

The relatively early granting of suffrage to white male workers also inhibited working-class consciousness. By 1840, virtually all white male workers had won for themselves the right to vote in the various states, which meant that they never had to organize as a national class in order to win political power.[16] Because it conferred the vote on white males regardless of class, Madison's fractured, anti-majoritarian political system seemed democratic, at least in the absentee sense. In the United States, people came to consider democracy a set of fair procedures through which individuals vote for and try to influence government officials. This image of democracy was a far cry from Madison's "pure democracy," a political system whose very make-up specifically empowered the working class. This modern absentee democracy, made up of seemingly neutral procedures that actually distanced the masses from the inside levers of government power, did not appear to have any particular social or class content at all. Rather, because all citizens could vote for their leaders, absentee democracy ostensibly embraced the good of all classes; this despite the fact that large parts of one class had no representation at all, and the remainder of that class was largely reduced to seeking local influence.

By contrast, until well into the nineteenth century and beyond, European workers not only suffered economic exploitation; they were also excluded from governance. As their economic and political domination by the minority went hand in hand, they developed a sense of their own class identity. Indeed, nineteenth-century Europeans of all ideologies, whether they stood for or against democracy, generally understood that the essence of democracy lay not, as Madison said, in its small size or the absence of representative institutions. The real essence of democracy was in the power it conferred on the economic majority, and this form of socio-economic democracy was not at all inconsistent with representative government. The issue was not "representation or no representation," the issue was whether the economic majority had a real chance to "conquer political power" as a *class*.[17]

In the United States, the experience of nineteenth-century labor failed to bring working people to a common sense of their class status mostly because the political system actively intervened by conferring unequal statuses on working individuals and by manipulating geography.[18] Government divided labor against itself in two ways: first, by forming labor into separate geographic, political communities and second, by dividing it again into vastly different political statuses, some much more free and equal than others. Indeed, in this second division, something radical happened. As David Roediger argues, recalling similar arguments by W.E.B. DuBois and Thorstein Veblen, by imposing the most difficult, unpaid drudge work on women and slaves, more privileged workers developed "a disdain for hard work itself, a seeking of satisfaction off the job, and a desire to evade rather than confront exploitation."[19] In the nineteenth century, many white workers already saw consumption and leisure at home—and in the neighborhood—as the legitimate price for their consent to capitalist rule in the workplace.

This emerging division between workplace and community consciousness is crucial, for it not only confirmed workers' accommodation with capitalism, it also laid the groundwork for their later incorporation into Fortress Suburbia. But as far as labor is concerned, the path to Fortress Suburbia was both tortured and conflicted. White labor first passed through the crucible of urban machine politics, an institution whose offenses against property were sufficiently great to bring about the first, upper-class demands for reform of urban government.

The developments here are connected to the tendency, hinted at by Roediger, for U.S. workers in the nineteenth century to view the spheres of work and community as more or less distinct. As Ira Katznelson has argued, the segmentation of class into distinct industrial and communal arenas was a major factor in shaping the political consciousness of U.S. workers. Most important, viewing issues at work and in the neighborhoods as different, largely separate matters gave rise to distinct institutions for the expression of working-class grievances, unions and party machines. These were institutions that did not always work in harmony, to say the least.[20]

Unions and Divided Labor

Katznelson argues that U.S. workers gradually came to rely on individual unions to propel their bread-and-butter demands within the workplace. Nineteenth-century workers widely understood unions to be the most direct vehicle for taking on "the bosses" over issues of wages, benefits, and working conditions. In an economy based on contracts, workers enjoyed a clear right to a say in the conditions established in labor contracts. They were, after all, the party of the second part. This was hardly a foolish choice: unions collectivized the power of workers to make immediate demands in a way that roughly matched the economic power of factory owners over labor's access to work. Collective bargaining over contracts was simply the legal expression of this political fact. But there were also dangerous drawbacks to labor's preoccupation with unionism.

The victory of one set of workers over an employer is not the same as the victory of all workers in their relation to capital. The danger always existed that a labor strategy exclusively focused on union action would divide the working class, as distinct groups of workers fought for their own benefits while remaining indifferent to the fate of their peers. In particular, forming narrow, exclusive, and segregated unions offered the better-established craft and skilled workers the chance to distance themselves from unorganized, unskilled immigrants, women, and ex-slaves, who brought up the rear of the U.S. workforce. Under these conditions, unionism played directly into the elite's divide-and-rule strategy.

Moreover, the ability of workers to depend on unions as the machinery for raising class-related economic issues helped submerge the battle to get democratic government to join labor's side of the class struggle. Indeed, for men such as Samuel Gompers, a founder of the American Federation of Labor (AFL) and Selig Perlman, a key theorist of bread-and-butter unionism, the most effective way to organize labor was to define goals in narrow, economic terms and fight for them only within the private sector. In Perlman's words, because U.S. workers were preoccupied by jobs, pay, and working conditions—what he called "job consciousness"—the "economic front was the only front on which the labor army could stay united." [21]

Perlman's theory of narrow economic action had, in turn, several crucial implications. First, because "the economic front" was divided into as many battles as there were companies and industries, the AFL strategy was a recipe for dividing the working class. Second, if labor could unite only around bread-and-butter issues, there was no point in trying to build a national labor party to politicize the class struggle. Indeed, because the AFL leadership did not trust the state to intervene in class conflicts on behalf of labor, Gompers stuck firmly to the principle that unions should fight for economic improvement only *within* the private sector, where, he felt, at least labor could bargain with management on equal footing.[22] In all these ways, mainstream union politics became an apologia for the unequal distribution of union benefits to organized workers while allowing business to intensify exploitation of the unorganized.

Of course, more radical, class-conscious labor organizations, such as the National Labor Union (NLU) formed after the Civil War, and the International Workers of the World (the Wobblies), fought against Gompers' defense of parochialism and the "labor aristocracy." These and other labor organizations understood that, as one labor newspaper stated in 1869, labor's power as a class would come "only by nationalizing the struggle, and by establishing unity among the working classes throughout the states."[23] Groups such as the NLU were important to labor's fight for the eight-hour day, and the Wobblies led some very courageous and bloody class battles, especially among Western miners. Even so, the radical labor organizations failed to persuade a majority of workers to see beyond their differences. The elite strategy of treating different parts of labor differently was still paying dividends at the end of the nineteenth century.

Madisonian Politics, Machine-Style

While labor battled within its own ranks over how best to organize and focus its economic power, workers wielded political power in their communities, and the dominant political parties courted their votes, especially the Democrats. Connections between working-class communities and local Democratic Party organizations were already a fixture of the political landscape by the time of mass immigration from Southern and Eastern Europe.[24] Bonds between neighborhood associations and local political organizations had been growing in working-class areas since the early nineteenth century. What became the Tammany Hall democratic machine in New York City grew out of a local fraternal organization, for example, and its spreading of political power was helped by ties to such local groups as neighborhood volunteer fire-fighting companies organized on ethnic lines. [25] Similarly, in Kansas City, home of the famous Pendergast machine, Jim Pendergast parlayed his neighborhood connections—legal and otherwise—as a local saloon owner to build a loyal Irish following that would carry him to leadership of the city's Democratic Party.[26]

In exchange for their votes, of course, workers expected politicians like Pendergast to deliver benefits, but nothing so dramatic as change in the structure of economic power. They hoped for smaller, discrete benefits that could tangibly improve the quality of everyday life—a job in local government, for example, or a place to live after a fire, or help getting a drunken husband out of jail. And if it was politically helpful to do so, and it frequently was, machine politicians were not averse to appealing to working-class neighborhoods on explicit class grounds, as defenders of the poor against the rich. Pendergast, for instance, positioned "himself as a champion of the working class, successfully fighting against salary reductions for firemen, promoting a city park in the West Bottoms [the city's tough factory section], and successfully opposing an attempt to move a fire station out of his ward." [27] Machine politicians such as Pendergast offered their ethnic constituents a kind of unstated social contract. As the infamous Tammany Hall leader George Washington Plunkitt explained:

> When the voters elect a man leader, they make sort of a contract with him. They say, although it ain't written out: "We've put you here to look out for our interests. You want to see that this district gets all the jobs that's comin' to it. Be faithful to us, and we'll be faithful to you."[28]

Although machine politicians like Pendergast and Plunkitt would stalwartly claim to stand for "the little man," and in some instances did actually challenge Big Business interests—in Jersey City, for example, machine Mayor Frank Hauge raised taxes on the large railroad companies and even the giant Standard Oil Company of New Jersey to pay for the city's large public payroll [29]—machine politicians were not interested in fueling class warfare. While ever prepared to use the rhetoric of class to win votes, machine politicians were more likely to appeal to labor on the basis of district-bound, ethnic ties. They appealed to a consciousness of kind more than to a class consciousness and, in doing so, reflected the matter-of-fact, pragmatic, and crucial insight that the easiest way to overcome Madison's fracturing of the majority was to reassemble it one deal, one ward, one group at a time. Minority ambition piled on top of minority ambition. Machine politicians pulled the newly arrived immigrant laborers into the political system by promising disparate rewards, a stream of benefits, patronage, services, jobs, all in exchange for nothing more than a vote. These slick urbane pols and ultimately self-serving leaders took the system as it was—and for all it was worth.

By responding to many of the most immediate social needs of workers in their communities, machine politicians undoubtedly helped many individual families get through hard times. More broadly, machine politics offered ethnic neighborhoods a degree of political incorporation within the Madisonian system. But, like the higher economic elite, machine politicians often reinforced the segmentation of labor. The reason had more to do with raw economics than political strategy. Plunkitt may have likened the big industrial cities to a cornucopia of booty, "a sort of Garden of Eden...full of beautiful apple trees," but as Steven P. Erie carefully demonstrated in his study of Irish machines, late nineteenth-century local governments were, just like today's cities, economically pinched. Irish politicians were faced with needs to ration benefits, and they usually made sure to apportion the lion's share of the spoils first to their compatriots.[30] Other white ethnic groups had to struggle hard for a small piece of a not-very-large pie, either by pushing their way into the machine, or by joining the machine's rivals among the out-party, usually the Republicans, or by allying with Reformers, who as often as not were Republicans by another name. New Haven's Italians, for example, opted for the Republican Party when the Irish dominated the city's Democratic Party, while many Jews in New York City were split between the radical labor movement and more conservative affiliations with Republicans or Reformers.[31]

The partisan reinforcement of ethnic differences by machine politicians served the interests of the urban economic minority in a number of crucial ways. For one thing, it helped to keep labor pinned down in what Katznelson calls the "the trenches" of ethnic and neighborhood competition.[32] It also helped take some of the heat off economic class conflicts by providing immigrants an alternative channel to economic rewards. As politics provided a salve for some of the worst hurts of economic life, there was less reason to challenge the economy.[33] The economic minority benefitted from machine politics in another way, too. Urban machines were generally hostile to radical labor and political organizations. Like most successful business organizations, party machines were not interested in competition. When socialist or radical elements threatened the allegiance of workers to the machine, such as when radical mayoral candidate Henry George took on Tammany Hall in New York City in 1886, established politicians were as ruthless as needed in using bribery, red-baiting, and fraud to deny political power to insurgents.[34] As Erie observed of the old Irish machines, "Both repression and corruption were used to defeat the machine's labor and Socialist Party rivals. The machine's henchmen intimidated labor party speakers and voters. The machine-controlled police force broke up Socialist meetings, revoked the business licenses of insurgent immigrant entrepreneurs, and enforced Sunday-closing laws to stifle Jewish dissidents."[35]

Political entrepreneurs on the make, machine politicians were as hostile to radicalism as any of their private-sector brethren. In this spirit, machine Mayor James Michael Curley of Boston is reputed to have offered some pointed, if sarcastic, advice to radically minded workers: redistribution of the wealth might not be such a bad thing, Curley opined, indeed it might even be right; but in the United States socialism was not in the cards, so it was best for workers to back the machine and be happy with some "redistribution of the graft."[36]

The Business of Machine Politics

Clearly, machine politicians were anything but idealists; theirs was a tough, cynical, business-like brand of politics in which success was measured in votes and cash. For the upwardly mobile machine politicians, politics was a way to make money; it was a business, plain and simple. As Plunkitt put it, "Politics is as much a regular business as the grocery or the dry-goods or the drug business." [37] Like any "regular business," machine politics worked through the exchange of deliverable commodities: votes and bribes for patronage and "the right decisions." Party leaders simply took the normal brokers' fee. After all, "Men ain't in politics for nothin'," Plunkitt declared. "They want to get somethin' out of it." [38]

But most machine politicians understood that business was much more than a matter of equal exchange; the big profits do not come from fair trades; they come from exploiting unfair exchanges between people of unequal economic power. Like John D. Rockefeller, Jay Gould, or any of the corporate "robber barons," Plunkitt said, "I seen my opportunities and I took 'em." [39]

And in this context, "opportunity" meant the chance to exploit government for profit. Just as huge corporations, such as Standard Oil, exploited labor in the production process or secured monopoly control of a key raw material, ethnic political entrepreneurs, whose backgrounds excluded them from the higher precincts of corporate power, exploited political power to turn a fast profit. As far as the machine politicians were concerned, the use of political power for private gain was simply good old-fashioned U.S. business. [40]

Machine politicians understood the simple fact that in capitalist economies, governments do not just protect private economic power; they can create it. Through the shrewd distribution of utility franchises, tax abatements, contracts, jobs, inside information, regulatory exemptions, the machine politicians capitalized on any government decision that might fetch a price from business owners dependent on it. Plunkitt called such maneuvering "honest graft," and as a manipulation of power for profit the machine simply mimicked what big corporate powers were doing, exploiting power advantages for profit. As Plunkitt understood the normal rules of private enterprise, exploitation, manipulation, and corruption were not extraneous to the pursuit of profit. They were its essence. The system was one of mutual exploitation: politicians accepted bribes; businessmen offered them.

Bribery, corruption, and graft were the *primary* means of doing business between government and business elites in the old industrial city. But private enterprise had its limits in subsidizing machine rule.

Especially when it came to matters of budgets, bonds, and taxes—always the core financial issues for balanced-budget conservatives—machine politicians would frequently go too far, spending well beyond available revenues in order to pay for the big public payrolls that were the meat and potatoes of patronage politics. Indeed, a big factor limiting the largesse of machine government was the potential for electoral and, even worse, fiscal retribution from middle- and upper-class taxpayers. Many of the early exponents of balanced-budget conservatism did not want to see their money siphoned off on public works controlled by Irish politicians, especially when the resulting municipal services, such as street and bridge construction, were less than second rate. Inefficiencies in public provision could be bad for business, especially when it came to the facilities necessary for the movement of goods. But just as important, the economic minority did not enjoy paying taxes that were likely to end up in poor people's pockets. Upper-class tax resistance was a main factor behind the relative poverty of cities at a time when their private economies were exploding. In the latter third of the nineteenth century, when large numbers of tax-sensitive middle- and upper-class voters still lived in cities, machine politicians would generally avoid taxing big property and risking a tax revolt that might drive them from power. Staying away from taxes on the rich did not come easy to machine politicians. It took much self-discipline. After all, as the renowned crook Willie Sutton once explained why he robbed banks, "That's where the money was." Moreover, a policy of keeping taxes down did little to improve the quality or quantity of public services, which made local business owners all the more angry.

Machine politicians were nothing if not political realists, and their great fear was an upper-class-led tax revolt or capital strike that would drive the machine's finances into ruin and its power into the dust. That is why they would typically turn to other revenue sources, especially the graft extracted from illegal activities. In New York City, for example, Tammany Hall leader Richard Croker "developed a police graft system in the late 1880s, substantially filling Tammany's coffers with the payoffs from gambling, drinking, and prostitution."[41] Croker's reliance on graft for revenue did not grow out of his fondness for the underworld. It stemmed directly from lessons learned by the Tammany Hall machine after it was driven from power following the New York City fiscal crisis of 1871, an event that not only reflected the power of capital to limit taxation, but which precipitated the modern reform movement to destroy machine government.

Fiscal Reform and the New Taxpayer Majority

In the 1860s, Tammany sidestepped taxation of real property by selling bonds at a rate far exceeding the city's tax base, at least insofar as that base was limited by the wealthy's willingness to pay. Between 1867 and 1871, while the city's tax rate dropped and Boss Tweed even sponsored a bill that restricted the property tax rate to no more than 2% of assessed value, the city's bonded debt ballooned from $30 million to $90 million, much of it placed with banks on whose boards the loyal men of Tammany served. When the machine's own city auditor died suddenly in a sleigh accident in 1871, its vast overselling of bonds became public knowledge.[42] Capital reacted swiftly and with punishment. The European financial exchanges suspended trading in the city's securities, and New York faced imminent bankruptcy, much as it would again in the 1930s and 1970s. And just as in those more recent cases, a committee of the city's economic minority formed to directly challenge the machine by leading the business and professional classes in a tax and investment strike. All at once, "one thousand of New York's largest taxpayers announced that they would not pay their taxes until the municipal government's books were audited, and the city's major bankers indicated that they would not extend any loans to the municipal government until a man of their own choosing, Andrew Haskell Green, was granted full authority over the city's finances."[43] When the city's capitalists said, "No more money," the Tweed ring collapsed.

Recurring crises brought on by the fiscal expansionism of Tammany Hall and other urban machines generated bitter reactions from urban financial capital. The anger ran very, very deep, to the point where many among the financial elite began to question the legitimacy of political democracy. The most ideologically minded of such men, along with followers from other factions and sectors of the business and professional strata, became known as "good government" Reformers. For these forces of "good government," the logic of a municipal government elected by working-class renters rather than by land owners and property taxpayers represented a profound internal contradiction. Logically, it meant that those who paid for government were regularly outvoted by those "without property," just as Madison feared would happen in "pure democracies." Local political democracy, especially when machine politicians organized and ran it, put control of municipal expenditures in the hands of a spendthrift class that had no interest in or respect for fiscal discipline. If "the people" ruled, they would never balance the public budget.

Urban working-class democracy was, for these interests, anathema; it led inexorably to fiscal madness. The only thing that might bring the fiscal democrats to their senses was a nasty bout of fiscal crisis, but relying upon fiscal crisis to check democracy was a bad way to protect a city's reputation as a good place to do business. Fiscal crises and capital strikes might prove to be salutary breaks on governance by the economic majority, but, as Madison might have said, they were cures worse than the disease. There were no alternatives to sound financial judgement: the methods and procedures of urban democracy would simply have to change. In essence, capital would have to gain increased representation at the expense of people.

The Tweed ring crisis led reform-minded men to just this conclusion. New York City attorney Simon Sterne, an early and influential government reformer, was among the first to insist that the financial integrity of municipal government must rest on a political structure that unequivocally reflected the higher interests of capital, the interests of the class that paid the bills, or rather, received the interest payments from municipal bonds. At least Sterne agreed with Plunkitt about one thing: each thought of city government as a business enterprise. Unlike Plunkitt, however, who saw the business of government as exploiting government's economic power through deals with outsiders, Sterne drew his business analogy from inside the company: from the sober, fiscal logic of balanced accounts and tight-fisted economic management. For Stern, the city was not Plunkitt's "opportunity" but an administrative arm of the state whose general purpose was to facilitate the growth and protection of private enterprise. Sterne's was a government of, by, and for the property owners. In his words, local government was "a decentralized portion of the general government of the state and a cooperative organization of property owners for the administration of property owners."[44] City government existed to serve the collective interests of property owners, mainly land owners, who invested in city bonds and paid taxes for municipal services that complemented their commercial establishments and real estate. Sterne did not shrink from the plainly anti-democratic logic here:

> In applying the doctrine of universal suffrage indiscriminately to the management of mere property interests as well as to governmental functions, a state of affairs has been created by which the mass of nontaxpayers and unthrifty inhabitants obtain the control of all these expenditures relating to property, in which they have, it is true, a remote interest, and which puts the taxpayers at the mercy of the tax eaters.[45]

Sterne's position was far more extreme than Madison's on the question of the working class' admission into political power. Madison at least conceded the right of "those without property" to vote, form factions, and influence the state. His solution was to weaken such factions through the political structures of divide and rule. Now, Reformers such as Sterne, the predecessors of today's balanced-budget conservatives, were willing to concede to workers only a "remote interest" in government. This was an interest insufficiently direct to merit the working class' full democratic right to set its own priorities in government. The state must check the populace's power to write government checks. Sterne's solution is as familiar as today's headlines: give taxpayers a veto over municipal expenditures. This way, poor people—in Sterne's day, "the little people did not pay taxes"—could make any political promises to themselves that they dared, but the fiscal rod of the taxpayers would apply the necessary monetary discipline. The taxpayer veto would make normal democratic governance by majority rule subject to the higher pecuniary will and smaller numbers of "those who hold property." In effect, Sterne wanted to roll back part of the victory of working-class political rights by retreating to a venerable Lockean principle: no representation without taxation.

Municipal reformer Albert Shaw, an ally of Sterne, went a step further. He recommended changing the very basis of the city's electoral system, arguing that only by destroying the ward basis of machine politics could the city's property owners expect men of their own kind to run the city. Candidates should therefore run at-large and city-wide, not in the small districts that reflected the patronage demands of the poor ethnic neighborhoods.[46] But some fiscal Reformers wondered why it was even necessary to bother with the votes of non-owners at all. The Tilden Commission of 1877, which was formed to recommend changes in New York City government following the 1871 fiscal crisis, took the last step toward urging outright oligarchy when it recommended that "the choice of the local guardians and trustees of the financial concerns of cities should be lodged with the taxpayers."[47] Stern approved of the Tilden proposal. While the plan did not have any chance of passage, Stern's analysis of its underlying principle spoke volumes about the civic spirit behind the urban reform movement that was soon to sweep through hundreds of U.S. cities. "We must stop organizing [local government] on the basis of arbitrary population and organize on the basis of interests," Stern declared, "and let the few or the chosen few, who are at the top of these interests *ipso facto* into government."[48]

Stern and Shaw recognized that U.S. city government had reached a true watershed. Madison's divide-and-rule system was no longer effective in restraining the economic majority. The party-led democracy of machine government showed how it was possible to get the divided ethnic factions of the majority to cooperate on the basis of mutual benefit and self-interest. The Plunkitts of this world successfully used a politics of deals and grafts to link the diverse white ethnic minorities of the working class into political majorities. Reformers understood that party machines posed no threat of radical income redistribution, but the machines did something almost as bad: they were effective in forming a loose majority of working-class voters who might then tax and spend according to their own predilections. Through machine rule, such voters could then expect to receive benefits in jobs and services at the cost of upper-income taxpayers. Madison's feared majorities were apparently smart enough to learn how, within Madison's own rules, to use their political power to exploit the wealth of the economic minority.

Just as in 1787, taxes were driving class conflict. Once again, the fight was ultimately waged not on the basis of competing theories of taxation or social justice, but over the proper scope, procedures, and methods of democratic government. The Reformers grasped that the key to reasserting upper-class control of government budgets, taxes, and spending was to cripple the mechanics of majority democracy. The rules of government, said Reformers Stern and Shaw, would have to change to "render" majority parties "unable to concert and execute their plans" of taxing, borrowing, and spending on behalf of themselves and their immigrant constituents.

Madison had earlier claimed to stand for regulating factions; now, good government Reformers proclaimed to stand for purifying party-led government. But there was that critical difference between Madison's approach and that of the new Reformers. Madison endorsed the right of working people to form political organizations to pressure government. Madison's hope was that the nation's immense size would encourage the organization of so many groups that the national majority would fall apart through the weight of its own internal divisions. His plan at least conceded the usefulness and the desirability of politics, if only in fomenting what he called a "multiplicity of interests." The problem for the next generation of anti-majoritarian Reformers was that Madison's strategy underestimated the ability of people "to cooperate for their common good."[49] His strategy of setting ambition against ambition was at least partially overcome by the ability of ethnic interests to coalesce behind a series of deals. Party-machine politicians such as Plunkitt used the glue of patronage to connect the various ethnic ambitions into a political majority. In this sense, through the ways and means of distributive politics, or "logrolling," parties brought a kind of half-baked working-class democracy to local politics. Given the structural and ideological limitations of U.S. politics—the fracturing and localizing of government power and the strong ideological aversion to anti-market, anti-property economic policies—machine politics represented the easiest route to political power for political organizations that pretended to represent mass interests.[50] Therefore, concluded the Reformers, they must eliminate from government any traces of politics, political parties, and the freedom of politicians to divvy up the spoils of patronage.

To replace politics, Reformer's sought to put government on a new footing, that of apolitical, efficient, scientific administration.[51] They wanted to replicate in government the professional bureaucratic management model then sweeping the boardrooms of giant corporations and new university graduate schools of "business administration." Instead of deals, logrolling, and patronage, there would be hierarchical organization by trained administrators. Experts and technicians would run the state, not politicians. Selected on the basis of merit, the technocrats would work according to scientific principles within a framework of sound fiscal judgement. Scientific analysis of civic problems, subject to tight fiscal accounting principles, could produce the best and the cheapest government possible. With professional administrators rather than politicians at the helm, society's need for government administration and the taxpayers' desire to keep their payments as low as possible could harmonize into a single "public interest."

To put their thinking in the best possible light, Reformers insisted that their recommendations would benefit the poor, whom machine leaders widely manipulated, as well as the more affluent. Furthermore, anticipating the arguments of modern-day fiscal conservatives such as David Stockman, the early Reformers insisted that wealthy and knowledgeable elites had a moral responsibility to protect the poor and ignorant from the corruption and organized thievery of machine politics. "It is a duty of perpetual obligation on the part of the strong," as judicial reformer John Dillon insisted, "to take care of the weak, of the rich to take care of the poor."[52] Those whom Madison called "enlightened statesmen" must govern; they must not delegate such responsibility to self-interested party hacks.

Buried deep within the Reformers' strangely moralistic logic of scientific accounting, however, lay questionable assumptions. Reformers took it for granted that technical considerations of efficiency and cost, the only matters about which experts might even come close to agreement, would somehow objectively reveal who should get what from government. But science, which rests upon a belief in a fundamental split between "facts" and "values," cannot offer "scientific" answers to the hard questions: how should public priorities be ranked? Which people should get what share of the benefits of government? Indeed, what action should government take on which social problems? Science has neither the intellectual right nor the capacity to tell government what to do. That is what democracy is supposed to do.

To get around this problem, Reformers hoped to match their economically rational administration with an economically rational citizenry. Reformers attempted to perfect democracy by removing its corrupting elements: political parties, patronage, the parochial interests of neighborhoods, and uninformed, easily manipulated voters. In cities across the country beginning about 1900, Reformers advanced a series of political rule changes designed to break the grip of machines on their ethnic, working-class constituencies. These changes included such seemingly pro-democratic modifications as the secret ballot, direct primaries, voter registration requirements, city-wide or at-large election districts, the powers of initiative, referenda, and recall, and civil-service merit examinations. By weakening the ability of parties to pull voters inside the political tent, such reforms emphasized the responsibility of the individual voter to be a *self-mobilizing citizen:* to follow closely the issues of politics, to read up on the candidates and their positions, to be familiar with government policies and proposals. Smart citizens did not need to be informed, galvanized, or mobilized by mass organizations; only the uneducated and apathetic needed parties to stimulate their civic interest. Besides, in a true democracy, politics should represent the views of individual citizens, not special interests; at its best, grassroots democracy was a matter of "do-it-yourself" politics, not collective action.[53]

When Reformers spoke of democracy in these individualistic terms, they effectively stripped it of its social class content. They neutralized Democrats' ability to mobilize political power collectively on behalf of the working class. The fact was that most working-class immigrants from Southern and Eastern Europe were illiterate. Even to many literate English speakers today, the U.S. political system, with its endless list of elections, offices, and levels of government, is a mystery. How much more alien it must have seemed to people who had never voted in any kind of political system before. For such reasons, the newcomers desperately required mass political organizations to assist their integration into the political system. But even more important, the immigrant laborers constituted an economic class with different interests than those of the taxpaying and business classes. For workers, class-based political organization, even if it assumed the bastard form of machine politics, was indispensable to getting at least some of what they needed from government. The attack on party government was at its core an attack on the political power of the working class.

Some critics of reform argue that to view reform as a form of class conflict overstates the case. Gerald Frug, for example, a writer who clearly sees the pro-capitalist implications of reform government, nonetheless insists that it is an exaggeration to argue that Reformers represented "a crude effort to advance the interests of the rich or of private corporations at the expense of the poor inhabitants of cities."[54]

At least on the matter of crudeness, we think Frug is right; reform was anything but crude. Its devices were smothered in a mystifying, moralistic, and confused quasi-scientific language that did not belie anything so crass as class interest. But the key issue behind reform is not its style. The key issues concern whether Reformers consciously identified the good of the public with the good of business owners and upper-income taxpayers, and whether they tried to reshape the electorate to conform with that class bias. And on that issue little doubt can exist as to cause and effect. The business-like government Reformers sought a government committed to the virtues of balanced-budget conservatism, and they believed that such a government was incompatible with a straightforward democracy based on economic majority rule. Their preferred government had little room in it for interests that could not be stated in business-like terms. They were intolerant of ideological outlooks that clashed with possessive individualism. Their version of reform was anti-political only when it came to what they saw as the spendthrift politics of the working class. Reform was the anti-political politics of the business class. [55]

And, for the most part, conservative reform worked. In the Age of Reform, between 1896 and 1920, overall voter turnout in the most popular and attractive of all U.S. elections, elections for the presidency, dropped from 79% to 49% , with most of the fall-off coming from the lowest income ranks. Still, the drop in labor's participation does not mean that machines, immigrants, or agitators simply disappeared from politics. In some cities such as Chicago, New York City, and Albany, machine politics continued to hold sway, either by driving Reformers from power, as in New York, or in making peace with the business class, as in Chicago. [56] Indeed, some Reformers, especially those in charge of urban land development, made their own peace with the logic of machine politics. Developing quasi-machine-like bureaucratic empires, such as Robert Moses' Triboro Bridge and Tunnel Authority in New York or Justin Herman's San Francisco Redevelopment Agency, these once-upon-a-time Reformers created powerful urban growth machines outside the regular local governmental structures, development machines that became a prime nexus of power for local builders, bankers, real-estate interests, newspapers, and construction unions in the post-World War II era.[57] Meanwhile, insurgent and radical political groupings continued to hammer away at the power of capital. Early in this century, the Wobblies (International Workers of the World) led dozens of strikes in the Western mining fields; the Socialist Party, led by Eugene Debs, won 6% of the presidential vote in 1912; agrarian radicalism spread through the northern Midwest, inspired by the North Dakota Nonpartisan League and the Minnesota Farmer-Labor Party. [58] But with that duly noted, the main trend of civic reform did cut hard against the political power of immigrants and the working class. During the first two decades of the twentieth century, the years in which the giant corporations consolidated their hold on the U.S. economy, civic reform significantly weakened the ability of ordinary workers to engage even in the democracy of machine politics.

Fortress Suburbia and the Private Majority

The Reformers' struggle against machine government was a crucial expression of the continuing struggle by the economic minority to twist democracy into a shape that would not threaten its class rule. But, as many Reformers themselves understood, urban reform was an imperfect weapon. Short of adopting the Tilden Commission's recommendation to abolish universal suffrage, middle- and upper-class Reformers knew that ultimately the exploding population of workers in the big cities was too overwhelming to control. In addition, the machine politicians were nothing if not wily political entrepreneurs. They were professionals who knew how to manipulate or get around and through the rules for their own advantage. Consequently, in cities like Chicago and Jersey City, which forbade party names to appear on election ballots, machine politicians used their web of precinct and ward connections to spread the word about who the party was for and against, and local Democrats stayed in power for years.

Finally, for many upper-class critics of machine rule, the problem of living with the working class was more than a question of numbers, power, and taxes. Immigrant workers were widely seen by established citizens as dirty, uneducated, corrupt, and illbred, as inferior beings who were not fit to live with respectable people. A report in the magazine *Massachusetts Teacher,* published as early as 1851, captures this elitist and xenophobic spirit:

> The constantly increasing influx of foreigners…continues to be a cause of serious alarm to the most intelligent of our people. What will be the ultimate effect of this vast and unexampled immigration…Will it, like the muddy Missouri, as it pours its waters into the clear Mississippi and contaminates the whole united mass, spread ignorance and vice, crime and disease, through our native population?[59]

Half a century later the same xenophobic attitude found its voice at a meeting of the National Society of the Daughters of the American

Revolution, whose president warned: "We must not so eagerly invite all the sons of Shem, Ham, and Japhet...to trample the mud of millions of alien feet into our spring."[60] These views were hardly the isolated rantings of extremists. They were heard among the most distinguished representatives of the nation's political elite. In 1894, for instance, a group of well-known and honored New Englanders, lead by Massachusetts Senator Henry Cabot Lodge, formed an Immigration Restriction League to keep poor foreigners out altogether. Its preferred method was a literacy test to exclude non-English readers. And, once more reflecting divisions within the working class, the nativist elite won support for this idea from the better-situated craft unions, which opposed competition from cheap imported labor. As the political pressure of U. S. residents mounted against the tide of immigration in the early twentieth century, Congress passed a series of bills requiring literacy tests, though each died at the hands of a presidential veto. Finally, after World War I and amidst the anti-communist hysteria of 1919, Congress passed laws carefully restricting the number of new immigrants in 1921 and 1924.[61]

Anti-immigration laws were another example of how conservative elites tried to control the problem of economic majority rule by squeezing and compressing the majority. But these laws did little to help elites overcome the problem of the immigrant population already in the cities. Many began to solve the problem for themselves by moving away from the central city. Suburbia loomed as the elitist political alternative to urban democracy. Developments in transportation, such as the streetcar and automobile, supported by an enterprising real-estate and construction industry, beckoned middle-income workers to purchase housing on the city's outskirts. Such developments allowed the affluent to think increasingly of the city only as a place to work, or perhaps as the destination for an occasional shopping or entertainment trip. Also pushing the suburbanization trend was the outward move by capital. Between 1899 and 1909, for example, suburban manufacturing employment grew nearly twice as fast as inner-city factory jobs. New corporate manufacturing centers sprang up "in open space like movie sets," writes New School economist David Gordon, as companies set up shop in satellite towns such as Gary, Indiana, near Chicago; Lackawanna, New York, outside Buffalo; and Chester and Norristown, Pennsylvania, near Philadelphia.[62]

Apart from the space it provided for larger homes, the proximity to green grass and quiet, tree-lined streets, suburbanization had decisive social and political advantages for the economic minority. First, it distanced affluent people from the poorest of the new arrivals. Moreover, because companies could build integrated factory and working-class housing complexes outside the city, suburbanization afforded corporations more control of their workforce.

But the suburban solution had its limits. First, as transportation and housing got cheaper, poorer workers could move further out themselves, especially if businesses continued to shift semi-skilled and unskilled jobs outside the city. More important in the short run, even great geographic distances could be easily traversed by the long arm of the central city's political power. By annexing far-flung hinterland developments to the city's political jurisdiction, machine government could still tax and borrow on the basis of its now enlarged geographic property base, simply shifting the cost to more affluent outlying property owners and companies. Nineteenth-century U.S. cities did that all the time; that is precisely how the big cities grew. Cities annexed, or simply added, surrounding territories and populations and enclosed them within the city's municipal limits. Between 1870 and 1900, the towns that would comprise the nation's twenty largest cities in 1940 all expanded their territories by about 18% each decade, and during the 1890s, these cities increased their geographic boundaries by as much as a third.[63] In fact, until and even beyond the late nineteenth century, central-city business interests themselves pressed for annexation of surrounding developments in order to increase the efficiency of urban services, spread the reach of regional markets, and gain police control over scattered settlements of the poor which, as in European cities today, were occasionally to be found on the urban fringe. The largest urban annexation in U.S. history, the merger of the five separate counties of New York into the singular and monumental City of New York in 1898, followed heavy pressure from New York's business elite.[64]

New York's decision was the high point of a process that characterized late nineteenth-century urban expansion across the industrialized northern tier of the country. The mature industrial cities followed a simple rule: to never let their economic populations or geographic market areas escape their legal control. This constant game of geographic catch-up allowed urban business to benefit from economies of scale when it came to the planning of regional infrastructure, such as highways and energy facilities. It also, at least in theory, allowed a single, large administrative jurisdiction to ensure the existence of a single set of legal rules, regulations, and taxes to govern the local economy. No firm or group of firms would thereby be in a position to exploit competitive advantages from the arbitrary gerrymandering of economic jurisdictions. In effect, urban annexation assured capital a level playing field for business interests to compete upon.

If prevailing patterns of annexation had continued into the twentieth century, cities like Boston and New York would now embrace the majority of their exclusive suburbs. Chicago, for example, might today cover half the distance to Milwaukee.[65] But the annexations did not continue; Fortress Suburbia very much slowed down annexation with a powerful countertrend, a countertrend that showed why a level playing field was just what many in the upper classes did not want.

The power of cities to annex their suburbs meant that distance in and of itself was not enough to protect upper-class property and status from the presence of labor. Suburbanites needed the power to keep their distance from labor, the power to stop the out-migration of labor, the legal authority to deny the central city jurisdiction over "their" land, taxes, and budgets. To work as a class political strategy, suburbanization had to become much more than a mere physical process of geographic and residential dispersion. To gain fortress-like protection for taxpaying interests, as well as for companies desirous of benefitting competitively from lower taxes and fewer regulations, suburbs had to wrap themselves in the protective armor of a government that could tax, zone, and legislate for itself. Only establishment of carefully tailored governmental jurisdictions would give suburbanites precisely this public power to make their own laws, raise and spend their own taxes, and regulate use of their own land.

To give themselves such truly fortress-like power against the urban majority, the economic minority of the new suburbia began a struggle to create new "democratic" governments in which they constituted the majority. In effect, through governments of their own, the private interests of relatively small groups of property owners could become "public interests," backed by all the coercive strength that the public law affords. In this way, the taxpayers would no longer have to worry about the preferences of "tax eaters" in the cities.

As in the case of the anti-immigrant fervor more generally, suburban opposition to annexation represented a mixture of social and economic motivations. As the editor of one suburban Chicago newspaper explained his town's demand for independence:

> The real issue is not taxes, nor water, nor street cars—it is a much greater question than either. It is the moral control of our village...Under local government we can absolutely control every objectionable thing that may try to enter our limits—but once annexed we are at the mercy of city hall.[66]

Snobbery and elitism, hate and fear, have always provided powerful motivations for political action.[67] But suburbanization had an economic logic too. Suburbanites understood that by separating themselves into distinct political jurisdictions they could monopolize the benefits of urban capitalism, benefits produced by the city's giant working populations, while excluding the social costs of reproducing labor, costs of public education, sanitation, transportation, housing, fire, and police. Theodore J. Lowi, a political scientist who knows power when he sees it, put the point squarely when he observed that "A suburb is ultimately an instrument by which the periphery can exploit the center, by which a single unit of the whole can exploit the rest." The onset of Fortress Suburbia was a matter of urban "parasitism." [68]

Beginning in the 1870s with suburban Brookline's defeat of Boston's attempt at annexation, middle- and upper-class suburbanites began triumphantly to carve out social, economic, and political spaces for themselves that were separate and more than equal to the big city next door. Using their economic and political influence with conservative, often Republican-dominated state legislatures, suburbanites took advantage of the vast open field for manipulating government rules, boundaries, and procedures that exists under the umbrella of state government. From rurally dominated state legislatures anxious to limit the power of cities, early twentieth-century suburbanites obtained legislation easing the creation of new governments and making urban annexation more difficult, typically by requiring dual-voter approval for annexation. The successful class opposition to annexation, coupled with the liberalization of suburban incorporation laws, ensured that, in most cities of the North and Midwest, suburban wealth was now off-limits to urban economic majorities and tax rates. Long before Ronald Reagan demanded "privatization" of government, the public sphere was already privatized into fortress-like compounds of public power.

Conclusion

The exclusionary logic of Fortress Suburbia was the most powerful force in twentieth-century local government. Today, most large cities are surrounded by dozens and dozens, sometimes by hundreds, of suburban governments, each of which maintains autonomous control of their taxing, spending, and service policies. [69] Chicago has more than 1,200 governments around it; New York City more than 500 surrounding governments just within the boundaries of New York State alone; Philadelphia, more than 800; Pittsburgh, almost 700. The list of urban fracture and fragmentation could go on and on; suffice it to say that the average U.S. metropolitan area has no fewer than eighty-four separate governmental jurisdictions that function to carve and divide its potential area-wide majority. [70] All of this means, simply, that the clashing class and group interests of the nation's huge metropolitan populations do not have to make political peace with one another. In the fractured metropolis, where classes and races may legally live apart, no public framework exists requiring majority rule to resolve clashing interests. In this neat world of separate and unequal interests, conflicting political ambitions need never collide, much less counteract one another. Avoidance, not conflict, now checks Madison's fearsome urban majority.[71] Ironically, for all their talk about the "public interest," when suburban Reformers recarved the governmental boundaries of the metropolis to ensure the tightest possible control of their taxes, they demonstrated the utterly arbitrary and ideological character of appeals to the "public interest." With the carefully planned fracturing and limitation of big-city power by fleeing property interests, the idea of an urban "public interest" lost whatever claim it had as a general ideal. The battles over annexation and suburban formation illustrate how, in the class- and race-divided metropolis, there is not even a generally agreed upon political unit within which public or communal interests are shared at all.[72] The very existence of suburbs as escape hatches from the poorest strata of the working class showed that specific groups and classes formed particular public governments to serve their particular private interests. Judged in this light, the great issue of balanced-budget conservatism is not so much the conflict between private interests and public spending. The real question is whether a genuine "public" can be said to exist at all within a society whose class and race divisions go hand-in-hand with its structure of local government.

Chapter Five

DEMOCRATIC FAILURE AND MIDDLE-CLASS REACTION

There are really so many things that make me mad.

John Budzash, leader of the New Jersey tax protest

Suburbanization shattered the principle of a broad public interest in the fast-growing metropolitan areas of the post-World War II United States. The rapid growth of Fortress Suburbia both reflected and deepened splits between competing "public" interests in taxing and spending, dividing segments of the working class, as well as the different classes that lived in separated communities. Today, through their celebrations of federalism and grassroots democracy, balanced-budget conservatives can manipulate these divisions to keep working people fighting amongst themselves over taxes, spending, and business locations. Nonetheless, the development of Fortress Suburbia was not a purely conservative Republican phenomenon. With a host of attractive and popular public policies, Democrats in the 1950s and 1960s helped millions of white, and even some non-white, workers to escape the urban majority. Indeed, by encouraging suburbanization, Democrats helped make the urban majority a political minority. By 1992, the majority of all votes cast in the presidential election came from the suburbs, which is why candidate Bill Clinton courted "the Reagan Democrats" who lived there. Clinton, however, is not the first Democrat to appeal to conservative-minded working-class suburbanites. Enduring historic connections exist between Democratic policies and working-class suburbanization. These ties have much to do with the Party's current failure to challenge and overcome many of the rules and assumptions of balanced-budget conservatism. Beginning with a brief review of the Democrats' role in creating working-class suburbanization, this chapter offers two case studies of Democratic failure to challenge Fortress Suburbia: the explosive tax revolts that dominated California in 1978 and New Jersey in 1991.

We focus on these cases for several reasons. First, they conveniently bracket the most recent political epoch of balanced-budget conservatism. Although California's revolt grew out of the real-estate boom that marked the high point of its post-World War II rise to power, the

state's experience helped pave the way for conservative political dominance in the era of stagnation. By contrast, New Jersey's tax revolt
emerged from the bitterness of recession and stagnation, from the
failure of supply-side policies to set the nation on a long-term growth
track. Yet New Jersey's experience also dramatizes the inability of
Democratic liberalism to counter the Right's diagnosis of government
as the main cause of economic disarray.

In addition, these cases symbolize the great political power of
middle-class tax resistance as a force working against a unified public
sector that stands for equal benefits for all workers.[1] But these examples
share more than symbolic significance. Each case spawned major conservative policy victories that helped institutionalize balanced-budget
conservatism. California's Proposition 13 not only drastically reduced
state revenues, it permanently changed the rules of taxation to benefit
the economic minority. In New Jersey, an upsurge of lower-middle-class
opposition to Governor James Florio's tax-reform proposal led to a
conservative Republican landslide in the state legislature, which, in turn,
produced a sharp right turn in both social and economic policy.

Finally, these illustrations have one more thing in common, perhaps the most important. Thoughtless Democratic politics and strategy
contributed directly to the conservative triumph in both California and
New Jersey. In quite different ways, Democratic Governors Jerry Brown
and James Florio played vital roles in the onset, development, and
ultimate success of conservative reaction in their states. Perhaps if they
had acted differently, conservatives would not have gained the political
power to make public policy. Of course, to intervene effectively against
the tide of fiscal conservatism, Democrats would have to assume a role
as leaders and organizers of the joint interests of working people. Yet
"by the late 1980s," as William Crotty notes, "the Democratic Party had
lost faith in its traditional issues and appeared almost embarrassed by
the coalition of the less well-off that normally supported it."[2]

Crotty may be too kind to the Democrats. Since 1932, Democrats
have regularly favored programs that divide the working class. In great
measure, their legacy of integrating white labor into Fortress Suburbia
lies at the heart of the Party's inability to move in progressive directions,
of standing frozen in fear of tax revolt and an angry middle class.

Democrats and the Suburbs

More than any other political organization, the Democratic Party
deserves credit for helping white workers gain the privilege of joining
the more affluent ranks inside Fortress Suburbia. Only about 15% to 20%
of suburbs are precincts of great wealth. Fifty percent of the members

of the AFL-CIO now live in suburbs, and so do nearly one-quarter of African Americans. [3] Of course, for many of the middle- and lower-income strata who live outside the political reach of cities, the suburb is no pleasure dome. Today, suburbs such as Yonkers, New York, or Somerville, Massachusetts, know many if not all the problems of their larger urban neighbors, New York City and Boston. Indeed, in many cases, but for the formal boundaries that exist between jurisdictions, pedestrians who crossed the street between big city and suburban satellite would hardly notice a change in social character. Many cities and their nearest suburbs have blended imperceptibly into a single dreary urban mass. Still, it is just as true, especially for the more distant and exclusive suburbs, that their status as separate governments continues to fortify their neighborhoods, schools, land, and taxes against the claims of urban pro-spending interests. The Democrats, we must emphasize, helped workers reach suburbia, but they did not then work to change suburbia's political economy.

Class integration of the suburbs commenced with the large-scale build-up of low-cost tract housing in the two decades immediately following World War II, years in which the economic force of Cold War spending and state-subsidized suburbanization were crucial absorbers and stimulators of corporate surplus. These were the years in which white workers began moving out of the city in droves. The Democratic Party stood ready to help pay for this white flight with massive doses of public capital. There was $50 billion for the national defense highways and urban loops to make moving to and living in the suburbs easier and cheaper; billions more in public-mortgage subsidies for returning veterans to purchase new "private" homes in the suburbs; billions more yet in public planning, sewer, and water grants to construct the vast networks of public utilities to supply the suburbs and their resident corporations and homeowners with energy and water. And, of course, much of this post-World War II suburban development was in fact Cold War related. In states as different as California, Massachusetts, and Georgia, suburban expansion was linked directly to government military investment that reached $8.2 trillion between 1949 and 1990.[4]

At the very same time, the Democrats were complicit in the federal government's use of racist criteria to allocate Federal Housing Administration (FHA) mortgage aid. "Blacks purchased less than 2% of all the housing financed with the assistance of federal mortgage insurance between 1946 and 1959." A look at the FHA's 1938 Underwriting Manual suggests some of the difficulty faced by non-white buyers. As if they needed any reminders, the FHA instructed bank loan officers to keep in mind that:

If a neighborhood is to retain stability, it is necessary that properties shall continue to be occupied by the same social and racial classes. A change in social or racial occupancy contributes to instability and a decline in values.[5]

Democratic administrations from Truman through Johnson were reluctant to pay much more than lip-service to changing such explicitly racist policies or to overcoming the racist underpinnings of Fortress Suburbia. But Democrats not only left suburban racism alone; they also shied away from challenging the underlying political economy of exclusion integral to suburbia, the framework of property-based government power that the economic minority invented to insulate itself from the economic majority.

Though millions of workers now live in suburbs, the class dynamics of local fiscal conservatism has never changed. Inside the politically barricaded domains of the more affluent suburbs, much of the private wealth lies beyond the control of the economic majority. Most of this wealth is concentrated inside the richest 15% of the suburbs, of course. But even in the poorer suburbs of the middle and working classes, the same dynamics of property, race, and exclusion tend to dominate local politics. For example, when the federal government finally did insist on locating integrated public housing in such working-class suburbs as Warren, Michigan, or Yonkers, New York, many of the residents protested vigorously to keep such development out. The reason goes back to basic institutional ties between suburbanization and the attempt by economic minorities to monopolize control of their property taxes, ties that Democrats rarely, if ever, challenged as they helped to build Fortress Suburbia.

For all the twentieth-century expansion of national government power and spending, for all the economy's reliance on technological capital as its engine of wealth, most U.S. cities and towns still use the real-estate property tax as their main, locally generated source of revenue. And even though many localities now supplement their property taxes with sales taxes, user fees, state and federal grants, and in some cities, even income taxes, the property tax is still the most critical and conservative component of home-grown revenues. For example, in 1985 property taxes generated about 75% of the total tax revenue of local governments, including 93% of the locally generated revenue of townships and 97% school districts. All told, local governments raised nearly $100 billion in property taxes in 1985, $40 billion more than Washington raised from the corporate income tax that year, and a little less than a third of what the federal government generated in individual income taxes.[6]

As far as local politicians are concerned, no one can overstate the importance of municipal reliance on property taxes. Real estate has always driven much of U.S. community development, and raising property values has long been what local boosters mean by "civic health and well-being."[7] Building community government on the real-estate tax ensures that those who control the most important local resource will have the main say about how much of it comes under public control—and for what purposes.

But an even more significant point lurks here. Because taxes on land and property pinch the value of people's homes and backyards, taxpayers who own property feel real pain, especially when cheaper private homes are assessed at disproportionately higher values than wealthier ones. In 1977, for example, just before the anti-tax fever of Proposition 13 swept the nation, one-third of U.S. property owners named the property tax as "the worst tax, that is, the least fair."[8] In part because of the pain and injustice involved in the raising of property taxes, suburban taxpayers widely feel that property taxes should be kept to a minimum and *only* used collectively for local services, such as schools, police, local roads, and parks. Property taxes should not go into a general, statewide pool; they should keep up the town, that is, sustain the value of real estate and/or pay for the local schools. In this sense, property taxes have gained a semi-private status that makes any talk of redistributing them sound particularly dangerous, subversive, and radical.

This sense of communal possessiveness of property taxes explains much of the seeming contradiction between tax rebels' demands for lower taxes coupled with their continuing penchant for public services. Through local confines of the property tax, suburbanites can finance the services they want without fear of wider redistribution. They can actually be fiscal liberals at home while favoring fiscal conservatism nationally.[9] Balanced-budget conservatives understand this logic well and play into it all the time when they demand power for local taxpayers. As conservative economist William Craig Stubblebine put it, the shift toward more localized fiscal responsibility minimizes the redistributive effects of taxation and "will tend to increase the volume of public services in upper-income communities and to reduce the volume in lower-income communities, while increasing fiscal effort in both."[10] For precisely these reasons, heavy reliance on property taxes by municipalities is much more than a purely fiscal matter. The local structure of taxation also plays a critical role in forming social consciousness and public policy, and fortifying exclusionary, separatist, and parochial habits among suburbanites. "Community" ends up as little more than an "unsentimental economic brotherhood" of local homeowners, of people who feel their enclave exists truly apart from society as a whole. [11] Local property-tax dependence both reflects and reinforces this strong sense of communal possessiveness as well as the anti-redistributive bias that accompanies it. It insures that public wealth is available only for the enclave's purposes, not for the needs of alien publics. Seen in this light, the contradictions within the U.S. idea of a "public" are obvious.

From the 1950s onward, Democrats tried to overcome these fiscal and political limitations by using federal grants-in-aid to reallocate tax monies to poorer jurisdictions. But grants-in-aid did not alter the basically conservative fiscal structures of local governance, nor the exclusionary, possessive consciousness enmeshed with it. Thus, when in the 1970s and 1980s the federal government cut back or abolished the Revenue Sharing program and later, other grant programs, only the conservative political economy of local and state government remained.[12] About this, Democrats had little to say. They gave the working class access to the suburbs, but they never changed the fiscal ground rules of suburban politics to accord with the needs of broad metropolitan majorities. When push came to shove in the tax revolts of the last decade, Democratic governors could do little more than stand by and let the old conservative institutional and ideological forces play themselves out, much to the disadvantage of the Party's old working-class, urban constituency. Such are the roots of responsibility for the lamentable case studies to which we now turn.

California's Proposition 13: Prelude to a Protest

Proposition 13 was the opening shot of the era of new balanced-budget conservatism. It gave conservative ideologues focus, momentum, and most important, a constituency of angry taxpayers who they could appeal to on issues of fiscal integrity, toughened management, and a return of political power to the states. Passed by an overwhelming two-to-one majority in June 1978, Proposition 13 took dead aim at the capacity of California's state government to raise revenue. It shrunk the size of the economic base subject to taxation and then increased the size of the electoral majority needed to pass tax legislation at the state and local level. Specifically, Proposition 13 lowered tax rates on property to 1% of its market value, based on the 1975-76 assessment. Next, the new law limited the increase in assessed valuation to no more than 2% a year; property could be reassessed at its full market value only when it was sold. Finally, Proposition 13 amended California's constitution to require a two-thirds majority of the state legislature to increase taxes. And local governments could raise taxes within their own borders only if two-thirds of the jurisdiction's voters approved. In these ways, Proposition 13 accomplished two things that are near and dear to the hearts of balanced-budget conservatives. The law not only trimmed the percentage of private wealth subject to public taxation; just as important in the long run, it gave the economic minority much more direct power to stop tax increases. Now one-third plus one vote of the state legislature, or a local community, could prevent upwards of 65% of the voters from raising taxes to meet needs they thought important. In effect, Proposition 13 gave life to the balanced-budget conservative principle that issues of tax rates and public-spending levels were matters too important to be left to government officials or the economic majority; in effect, a minority of the angriest taxpayers should decide for everyone else.[13]

Frustration with taxes is, of course, as "American" as apple pie. It is always lurking beneath or near the surface of U.S. politics. What helped conservatives make anti-taxism *the* big political issue in California, however, was a confluence of factors unique to the state in the late 1970s, a time when inflation rampaged across the whole U.S. political economy.

To understand Prop 13, we must look back at earlier tax politics in California. Throughout the 1950s and 1960s plenty of tax resentment swelled in California's Fortress Suburbia; there was even some scattered but very active local tax resistance. In the mid-1960s, for example, suburbanites in San Gabriel Valley organized tax strikes against local government and, in one explosive moment, actually stormed a meeting of their board of supervisors.[14] Yet for all the anger, California's property evaluation practices were actually more than fair to the middle class. In California, as in other states, the state's elected tax assessors typically undervalued more affluent middle-income homes. Also, their assessments varied greatly among jurisdictions, and in some cases business properties were actually appraised above the state norm of 25% of market value, thus, in effect, providing a subsidy to politically vocal suburbanites.[15] In a state that insisted upon taxing residential and commercial property at the same rate, loose assessment practices became a way of informally shifting fiscal burdens off the shoulders of homeowners.

In 1965, around the time San Gabriel homeowners vented their spleen, the *San Francisco Chronicle* published a series of articles that documented how local businesses attempted to even the score by bribing assessors with campaign contributions. *The Chronicle* stories created such a fuss that state lawmakers pushed through a tough tax-assessment reform measure. The legislature tried to remove the politics from property evaluation by establishing assessment as "a non-discretionary administrative function." It also required reassessing all property in the state within three years and regular reassessments thereafter to keep evaluations up to date with fluctuations in the market. From now on, said the legislature, everyone would pay their fair share.[16]

The reform gave California one of the most modern, competent, and rigorous tax assessment systems in the nation.[17] But because assessors were no longer so lenient, many homeowners saw their property tax bills shoot up even as some business rates went down. For example, "Between 1975 and 1978, assessed evaluation of all owner-occupied homes in California went up by 110.9%, compared to 34.2% for apartment buildings, and 26.4% for businesses."[18] Assessment reform brought formal equity to California tax practices, but it also created a simmering sense of popular injustice.

In 1968, amidst the flurry of tax resentment aroused by the assessment scandals and the following rise in property tax bills, Howard Jarvis, a conservative political activist and lobbyist for California landlords, launched his first petition effort to limit property taxes by amending the state constitution. But, along with a related tax-limitation plan that Los Angeles' tax assessor pushed, Jarvis failed. In an important pattern that would repeat itself over the next few years, California's political leaders countered a series of proposed tax limitation initiatives coming from Jarvis with moderate forms of tax relief—in this instance, an exemption on the first $750 of assessed value of owner-occupied homes. This step, like others that followed over the next few years, illustrated how timely, well-modulated responses by elected leaders could coopt suburban anti-taxism and nip an incipient tax rebellion in the bud.[19] This point is so important, it warrants a slight pause in our narrative.

As political elites smothered suburban discontent with the blanket of limited concessions, their measures narrowed the scope of anti-tax politics. In other words, elite concessions on taxes helped to keep white taxpayers bitterness over assessments from linking up with other, even more socially divisive suburban discontents, such as growth restrictions and racist opposition to busing and housing integration. This was no mean or trivial feat. Since the end of World War II, the most powerful social movements in Southern California were resistance movements not of the poor, but of well-to-do suburban homeowners, for whom, as Los Angeles social commentator Mike Davis writes in *City of Quartz,* the term community meant "homogeneity of race, class, and especially, home values."[20] That is, like most U.S. suburbanites, Californians wanted higher land values and fewer people in their communities, especially poorer non-whites and immigrants. So they used a host of exclusionary devices, especially zoning and planning ordinances, to remove land from development. Democrats at all levels of the political system aided in constructing Fortress Suburbia, but having helped better-situated workers to create it, Democrats now became hostage to its privatism and, as often as not, its racism. By the stagnant 1970s, Democrats had to step ever-so-delicately around the tax issue in order to avoid inciting mighty conservative opposition to other forms of egalitarian social change. The sad truth is that liberals found it very important to isolate the tax question, because once middle class money worries got tied up with other social anxieties, especially questions of growth control and integration, the middle-class would be likely to unleash its defensiveness in favor of balanced-budget conservatism.

On the one hand, Democratic tax concessions to the middle class would necessarily reduce the revenues available for needed social programs. But on the other hand, tax concessions would also stem the tide of even more radical anti-tax measures that would stop social spending in its tracks and even reverse its upward direction. As we have emphasized throughout this book, public policy is not simply a matter of doing what is best or most rational for the society as a whole. It is first and foremost a reflection of private power, especially the power to make non-decisions and choices that considerations of private interest and private property dominate.

Thus, in the early 1970s, as California Democrats in the state legislature offered deals that successfully lowered the political boiling point on taxes, Jarvis and Los Angeles Tax Assessor Philip Watson consistently failed to pass their tax limitations amendments. Californians were still unhappy with their property tax bills, of course, but they were not nearly angry enough to back major changes in the state tax system, especially cuts that might endanger cherished public services, such as local education, which the property tax almost exclusively finances. [21]

Political strategy was by no means the only reason for the relative quiescence of taxpayers, however. California's economy was booming, helping Democrats to lower the anti-tax fever. The paper value of California real estate drove upward even faster, pushed along by a big dose of good old-fashioned land speculation. The big payoff in California real estate commenced in 1974, just as the rest of the nation struggled to get out of the worst recession of the post-World War II era and to overcome the political crisis of Watergate. At that moment Californians began to enjoy in superabundance what U.S. citizens always dream of, a seemingly everlasting expansion of fabulous real-estate values. Without doing a thing, Californians saw the value of their homes double, even triple, in value. In the span of only a few years, the value of California properties leapt by as much as 200% and 300%. "In Beverly Hills, median home values increased $200,000 in a single year. Averaged over all of Southern California, homeowners were reported to be earning 30-40% on their equity per annum...and home values increased almost three times faster than income."[22] Californians lucky enough to be in on the ground floor of the boom found themselves suddenly sitting on a mountain of inflated wealth. It was as if they were getting something for nothing, with compound interest to boot.

But the joys of expansion had a dark side. With California's modernized assessment system in place, property taxes, which had to be paid in real money, shadowed the rise in market values. But the explosion of real-estate prices was fictional; it was an explosion of paper values; homeowners could not "realize" their profits unless or until people sold their homes. In effect, Californians were being taxed real money on the basis of anticipated paper profits, profits that might never actually materialize if the land boom collapsed. For example, "the property tax bill on a home purchased in Los Angeles for $45,000 in 1973, when the average selling price was $39,600, would have risen from $1,160 in 1973-74 to $2,070 in 1976-77, an increase of 80% over three years."[23] By 1977, a year before Proposition 13 hit the political scene, California property taxes were about 52% above the state average for the country, while the total per capita tax burden in the Golden State was exceeded only by New York and Alaska. Under the conservative administration of Governor Ronald Reagan and his liberal successor, Jerry Brown, state tax collections increased by nearly 90%.

When More Became Less

By 1978, California was rolling in cash. Inflation was pouring dollars into the state coffers, and politicians did not even have to raise tax rates. Estimates of the state surplus ranged anywhere from $1.6 billion to upwards of $5 billion. [24] In this climate, the prospect of a state fiscal crisis seemed ludicrous; it was the farthest thing from anyone's mind. If anything, California seemed to have found the goose that lays the golden egg. The state was living proof of U.S. Senator Patrick Moynihan's dictum that with rapid growth, the biggest problem facing politicians is how to find new ways to expend public funds in the public interest.[25] Was Moynihan kidding? How could a government budget surplus be a problem?

As we saw in Chapter Two, balanced-budget conservatives see government surpluses as a potentially great problem indeed. Surpluses indicate that government is taking in more money than it really needs, which means that taxes are unnecessarily high. Not only can such over-absorption of private surplus act as a drag on the economy, but conservatives insist that surpluses create incentives among politicians to hunt for useless projects that serve their power interests over those of society as a whole. For balanced-budget conservatives, surpluses exploit the taxpayer and corrupt the state. That is why fiscal conservatives will quickly grab on to surpluses as an issue with which to mobilize the electorate against government.

For these reasons, Moynihan's comment was on target. As state officials in California recognized the impact of inflation on tax revenue, it became politically crucial for them to come up with some combination of tax reform and necessary social spending to relieve the hostility of taxpayers and take the potentially explosive issue of surpluses out of conservative hands. For without seeing a rational plan to redistribute the state surplus back to society, taxpayers could well conclude that they were indeed paying something for nothing.

The state's ability to defuse the surplus issue became the key to avoiding a tax revolt. And this, we must stress, was fundamentally a *political* problem. A solution was well within the capacity of state government leaders to find. Indeed, California's Governor Jerry Brown may well have been among the last state officials of his growth-era generation to have the chance to reduce taxes, increase needed social spending, and not increase his government's debt. Brown, in other words, had it within his economic and political power to solidify a political alliance of taxpayers and the working poor behind a combination of tax reductions, rebates, and improved services. Of course, there was a powerful economic limit in this situation, and it was the taxpayers' determination to see more of their money back in their own pockets. But a package of rebates and spending might well have a gone a long way toward limiting the wrath of suburban taxpayers.

As things turned out, however, Brown did not meet the political challenge. Part of the problem was the predictable wrangling over which political party would get credit for tax relief. This familiar but debilitating habit was the source of much battling over the surplus. Republicans were naturally loathe to help Democrats build a coalition around a sugary sweet program of tax cuts and more spending. Democrats turned around and blamed the Republicans for stalling; indeed, the Democrats needed just two more votes to get their tax reform package out of the state Senate. But, to be fair, as we have seen throughout the decade of balanced-budget conservatism, partisanship was also entwined with more genuine party and class differences over the structure of tax relief and spending, especially over how much relief the state should target to working-class families. [26] Furthermore, Brown faced another difficulty. Even before passage of Proposition 13, California law required a two-thirds majority in the state legislature to pass a budget. In this sense, the state's constitution already favored conservative, anti-spending minorities. [27]

Nonetheless, Governor Brown, well-known for his aloofness and weak ties even to Democrats in the legislature, proved unable to pull enough Republicans over to pass a comprehensive surplus-reduction package. And there is little evidence that he tried actively to mobilize urban constituencies in his favor. To the contrary, in 1977 Brown consistently favored legislation giving most of his proposed tax relief to business, not homeowners, despite the fact that California corporations earned record profits that year. Moreover, when Republicans blocked the legislature's proposed tax reform, which, among other things, promised $550 million in tax relief for homeowners and another $285 million for renters, "Brown refused to attack the Republicans for putting partisan politics ahead of property tax relief." As Dean Tipps explains, Brown could have been much more aggressive in challenging conservative minority rule. "By denouncing the partisan Senate vote, calling an immediate special session of the Legislature, and urging the people of California to help him get the two additional needed votes to make property tax relief a reality in 1977-78, the Governor could have forced a legislative solution to the property tax crisis."[28] But without his leadership, and driven by serious social differences, the parties kept snapping at each other and the taxpayers just grew angrier.[29] And as taxpayers became more irate, estimates of the surplus kept rising, ranging from $1 billion in January 1977 to almost $6.8 billion just after the voters passed Prop 13.

Californians smelled a rat. As Rabushka and Ryan comment in *Tax Revolt*, "Perhaps no issue more strained government's credibility with the public than the state's volatile surplus."[30] With a fat state surplus, skyrocketing tax bills, and endless partisan bickering, Californians had good reason to complain about the mess in Sacramento. However, in California, when politicians fail to act on important problems, or when they act against the wishes of key sectors of the population, the state's constitution gives citizens the power to use the institutions of direct democracy, such as a voters' initiative, to change public policy. In four earlier stabs at tax-reform initiatives, Howard Jarvis did not even gather enough signatures to make it on the state ballot, though he did obtain more signatures each time. Five was the charm. After Jarvis and his ally Paul Gann introduced their newest version of tax reform—what became known as Proposition 13—people joined the tax-limitation bandwagon in droves. By July 1977, Jarvis had signed up 1.2 million voters to put Proposition 13 on the June ballot. This number was approximately 15% of *all* registered voters in the state, and as many as 20% to 25% of the likely turnout in the election itself.[31]

What drew the voters? The most immediate attraction was a $7 billion cut in state taxes. But there was also the promise of structural reform.With the passage of Prop 13, not only state budgets but any new increase in taxes or tax rates would need the backing of a two-thirds super-majority in the state legislature, or the approval of two-thirds of the voters in local taxing units, such as municipalities or school districts. This rule-driven reform, which would quickly spread to other states, was a vital principle of the new balanced-budget conservatism, one whose real target, as Jarvis boasted, was the financial strength of the public sector itself. The politicians, he insisted, had to be put in legal chains by the taxpayers. As Jarvis well knew, this was "a strategy far more menacing to liberal objectives than past haggling over tax rates and program budgets."[32]

For Jarvis, the big state was indeed a "liberal" state motivated by "liberal objectives. Very much attuned to the balanced-budget mythology of the individualistic economy, it did not occur to him that the increase in the scope, size, and cost of California government was in any way related to the fantastic expansion of the state's private economy itself and the gigantic costs this imposed on all sectors of the state and its resources. The state's corporate elite thought otherwise. Not only the Democratic political establishment and public employee unions fought Prop 13, but many of the state's largest corporations, including Standard Oil of California, Atlantic Richfield, and Bank of America, also balked. Even California's leading Republicans opposed Prop 13, including two future governors, Dukmejian and Wilson. Big business was worried that the nation's largest state economy could not be effectively managed by a revenue-poor, administratively weakened state. Corporate elites understood that the bureaucratic bottom line of post-World War II U.S. development had always been the existence of a strong state to subsidize and absorb the social costs of growth.[33] By contrast, middle-class Californians were now willing to risk much on the bet that parochial local government was all they needed to get and keep the kind of limited growth they wanted. It was one thing to reduce the state's surplus and lower taxes all around on a one-shot basis. It was quite another to chain the state's ability to act in the interests of large-scale capitalist enterprise over the long haul. "Californians," warned one business publication, "have threatened the strength and stability of the boom and have raised serious doubts about the state's ability to accommodate future growth." A vast, sprawling political economy such as California's had to overcome immense problems of traffic, pollution, waste, land management, education, and energy, problems that even a well-financed state would have a hard time gearing up to manage. Put the state on a fiscal diet and California might begin to strangle on the cords of its own expansion.[34]

In effect, the debate between big and small property interests over Proposition 13 exposed the ultimate irrationality of balanced-budget conservatism as an adequate approach to managing the capitalist state. It also showed that there were limits beyond which big business was not willing to go in supporting balanced-budget conservatism. As pure ideology, fiscal conservatism was useful to the corporations in keeping the state off their backs; as an institutionalized policy, however, it threatened to weaken the social framework of capitalist development itself.

In this context of heated division even within the propertied classes, political battle lines formed quickly. Jarvis took advantage of free time on the media, especially on the radio talk shows, to spread his anti-tax gospel. With the state's institutional elites arrayed against him, Howard Jarvis' excited brand of talk-show populism was extremely important to Prop 13's success. It became the route through which he could reach the vast population of Fortress Suburbia and turn their incipient anger into militant anti-taxism. But to advance his push for Prop 13, Jarvis could also count on the landlord interest groups for which he regularly lobbied: his own California Taxpayer League, an organization dominated by senior citizens, for whom school taxes were a pain in the neck; and a handful of real-estate development companies that gave him several thousand dollars in campaign contributions.[35]

But the key to Jarvis' victory lay in the tract homes of the working- and lower-middle-class white suburbs. Jarvis proved that in an intensely emotional election, grassroots activism can overcome elite organizational backing, especially when the grassroots groups include well-entrenched, effectively organized suburban civic associations. Indeed, the solid, organizationally effective core of political support for Proposition 13 was in the many middle- and upper-class civic and homeowner associations of suburban Southern California. As L.A. commentator Davis has noted, Jarvis "drew heavily" for his votes upon the sub-culture of homeowner activism, especially in its heartland of Southern California.[36] By failing to act effectively on the surplus, Governor Brown only encouraged activist suburban civic groups to link their tax anxieties, and the possibility of a direct $2,000 cash benefit, to the larger cluster of dangerously divisive suburban worries. For homeowners in average middle-class areas like the San Fernando Valley, the tax revolt overlapped with a series of other issues that all, in one form or another, involved challenges to suburban self-rule. Brown's and the legislature's inaction allowed conservative suburban leaders to fire up neighborhood concerns over issues such as growth regulation and integration with the heat of anti-taxism. In this way, the civic associations energized the "unified protest culture" in the California suburbs, a culture that was bent not only on lowering taxes, but on defending, perhaps even raising still higher, the already big walls around suburbia. [37]

Such people were not, as some observers suggest, "on the fringe of the dominant institutions in U.S. society."[38] These were folks who occupied the middle niches of power in U.S. institutions, the people who directly administered the controls of such institutions, supervised the line workers, manipulated ideas, delivered services, and managed the core economy. The loyal servants of institutions run by power elites, middle-level power holders who were among the greatest beneficiaries of Democratic Party growth policies, were the fervent ideologues of conservative grassroots democracy, of direct self-rule within their guarded enclaves.

To recapture the fiscal loyalty of this angry middle class, California Democrats finally offered up another moderate tax reform package that, they hoped, would once again cool off the discontent. Their alternative, Proposition 8, promised a $1.6 billion property tax cut, but it also added an important and progressive new twist. Prop 8 finally broke with the state's conservative tradition of taxing all landed property at the same rate. By creating a new legal basis of separate rates for commercial and residential property, Proposition 8 created the chance for liberals to create a dual tax structure, one for homeowners, the other for business.

Organized labor, especially the public-employee unions, spent heavily on behalf of Prop 8 and against Prop 13. The California Teachers Association pumped $225,000 into the fight, the California State Employees Association invested $100,000, and the state's firefighters another $52,000. Major unions such as the American Federation of State, County and Municipal Employees, American Federation of Teachers, and the state AFL-CIO also supplied campaign and organizational aid to the anti-Prop 13 cause.

But strikingly, the unions, including the public-employee unions, did not generate anything like a strong pro-government ideological argument on the key questions of taxes and spending. As post-election opinion studies revealed, while public employees and their families were among the strongest opponents of Proposition 13, their motivations reflected much more the self-interest of what Selig Perlman called "job consciousness" than a political awareness of why a strong public sector is important as a bulwark of social justice. "Public employees' unique role in the governmental system apparently did not spur them to any exceptional defense of the public sector," write Sears and Citrin, in *Tax Revolt.* "They were outspoken defenders of their own jobs and wage levels, but aside from that, their attitudes were very similar to those outside the public sector."[39] Of course, if public employees failed to mount a persuasive ideological defense of government, neither did any other group. If anything, corporations made as much of a case against radical tax cuts as the unions did.

Moreover, as befits the historic pattern of class and race bias in U.S. elections, recipients of welfare and public housing—the people and policies most endangered by conservative opinion—played little role in the politics of Proposition 13. On the other hand, it is just as important to note that African Americans, many of whom are poor, are not necessarily averse to anti-tax themes themselves. In fact, ample data suggest that of all groups in the population none is angrier about taxes than urban blacks. Given the regressiveness of state and local property and sales taxes, such resentment should come as no surprise. [40] It is really only through the magic of television punditry that many people have come to believe that anti-taxism is somehow an exclusively white obsession. But to the extent that people of color joined with whites in feeling that Sacramento's politicians did need their comeuppance, the fact remains that at the level of mass politics, Jarvis and the tax rebels had the field pretty much to themselves.

· Still, the California political establishment urged support for Proposition 8 as responsible tax reform, the kind that would give taxpayers a needed break without causing structural damage to state government. But instead of trying to rally the poor and labor in a coalition with the lower middle class, California political leaders clearly pitched their arguments to the not-at-all-forgotten middle class. Anti-Prop 13 forces tried to strike fear into the hearts of the middle class by warning of economic disaster if the tax cuts went into effect: massive reductions in services, deterioration of the state's highly regarded education system, layoffs, even a severe recession that might cost the state as many 250,000 jobs, many in the private sector. Raising such fears was a natural strategy, but under the circumstances of elite disarray and the fast-changing estimates of the state surplus, the scare-tactics approach reflected the faulty assumption that middle-class voters would believe elite claims.

Many voters, witnesses to the partisan game-playing over the state surplus and egged on by Jarvis' reminders that lying politicians needed to be hog-tied by anti-tax rules, rejected the prophecies of doom. Indeed, surveys done shortly after the election found that most people were prepared to dismiss elite warnings and believed that there was plenty of room for more efficiency in state government. Prophesies of doom fell on deaf ears. [41] A majority of Californians believed that they could have tax cuts and their desired government services, too. In short, the state would achieve the simple virtues of good government with an instant dose of populist tax cutting.

There was one big exception to this middle-level optimism. A majority of voters did believe that if anything had to go it should be welfare and public housing. As far as these urban, minority-identified problems were concerned, Proposition 13 became a way for suburbanites to pull the financial rug out from under the most objectionable features of the welfare state. For them, "Proposition 13's explicit promise to roll back assessments and let homeowners pocket their capital gains was accompanied, as well, by an implicit promise to halt the threatening encroachment of inner-city populations on suburbia," writes Davis.[42]

When the votes were finally tallied, Proposition 13 won by a landslide: 65% to 35%, a margin so big that even if every eligible voter in the state had turned out, including all of the state's poor, the outcome would probably have stayed the same. As Californians went to the polls, it is obvious that not only were they extremely angry with the state's political leadership, they also believed that they were voting for nothing more radical than much lower property taxes, hefty cash returns, and the maintenance of *their* government services. If this was, as economist writer Robert Kuttner has said, a "revolt of the haves," it was a most peculiar kind of revolt, one that was aimed at more of the same of everything people already enjoyed from government, everything, that is, except taxes.[43]

The Big Sweep of Proposition 13

Proposition 13's influence on both political consciousness and public policy was enormous. This was not simply because of the vast media coverage that any California event attracts. Across the nation, inflation was driving up taxes and state revenues, and stagnation was already driving down real wages and incomes. California's tax revolt symbolized a direct way for U.S. citizens to resist what many already sensed was a long-term threat to their standard of living. Moreover, anti-tax, balanced-budget conservative interest groups, such as the National Taxpayers Union, the American Conservative Union, and the National Committee on Tax Limitation, aggressively capitalized on growing popular discontent with the economy. Such groups, abetted by Ronald Reagan's 1980 presidential campaign, effectively defined high taxes as the source of the nation's economic problems. They actively propagandized around the country to promote procedural changes, such as a federal balanced-budget amendment and state spending caps, that would, as one conservative activist put it, "impose limits on the total capacity of government to tax and spend." In this way, conservatives believed they could alter "the relationship between government and society." Many voters accepted their message. In the year following passage of Proposition 13, twenty-two states lowered their property taxes, eighteen reduced income taxes, fifteen limited sales taxes, eight voted to limit spending, and a dozen more repealed or reduced an assortment of other state taxes. And the majority of the benefits of these changes went to upper-income homeowners and businesses. In California itself, owners of commercial property enjoyed 60% of the tax relief offered by Proposition 13. California oil corporations did especially well: Standard Oil saw a tax windfall of $47 million, Shell got $16 million, Getty Oil received $12.3 million, and ARCO saw a $10 million tax break. Overall, business owners in the state received $1.80 in property-tax relief for every dollar that went to homeowners. But the same pattern reappeared in Delaware, where most of the loot from its $21.5 million income-tax cut was slated for the highest tax brackets; in Utah, which voted for a property-tax rebate, but against repealing the sales tax on food; and in Texas, where tax relief was designed to help homeowners, but not renters. [44]

The anti-tax mania of the early 1980s put many states deeper in the financial hole when, between 1981 and 1983, the nation experienced its worst post-World War II recession. It also wiped away years of Democratic Party efforts to convince people of the positive link between rapid economic growth and big government. Indeed, it seemed to wreck whatever confidence Democrats themselves may have felt about their ability to manage the economy with a tilt in favor of the poor. That the 1980s would end with a Democratic governor of a major state prepared to tilt in favor of more equality was, therefore, a surprising development, not least among Democrats themselves.

New Jersey's Winter of Discontent

Twelve years after Proposition 13 hit California, New Jersey experienced its own winter of discontent. The circumstances were different, although the outcome was much the same: a strong message of suburban antipathy for high taxes and policies that smack of a threat to suburban self-control. But the differences between California and New Jersey are important, particularly for what they reveal about the kind of politics that may be necessary to overcome balanced-budget conservatism. In California, Governor Brown's sins of political omission spurred on Jarvis' campaign to turn the table on liberalism. Say what one will about New Jersey Governor James Florio, but one could not accuse him of wimping out on what balanced-budget conservatives like to call "the tough decisions." Breaking decisively with orthodox anti-tax politics, Florio was outspoken in his desire to up-end the socially regressive consequences of balanced-budget conservatism. He moved aggressively to restructure his state's tax system, equalize funding for education across the state, and make the rich pay more in order for the middle and bottom to pay less.

On its face, Florio's version of class politics promised to challenge balanced-budget conservatism on its own terms. That is, Florio was going to balance his state's budget, but on the backs of the state's richer rather than poorer citizens. Here, at last, it appeared, was a Democrat with the nerve to raise a direct, frontal counterattack on the upper-class bias of Reaganomics. No wonder Democrats across the country closely followed events in New Jersey. As Florio sought to make his state a laboratory of tax fairness, Democrats sensed that, as one party leader explained, either Florio would lead us to our "last defeat of a terrible decade or our first success story" in a new political era. Or, as Rutgers University Professor George Sternlieb put it, by wagering that "class warfare is back," Florio took "one of the great political gambles of the century."[45]

When Florio was elected governor of New Jersey in 1989 with 61% of the vote, the third largest margin of victory in the state's history, there was little hint in his campaign that he would soon be betting the ranch on "class warfare." Though Republicans would later pin the tag of "the Lenin of Trenton" on him, Florio campaigned as a tough-minded, sober leader, a man solidly in the Woodrow Wilson "good government" tradition of politics. Appealing directly to the state's suburban middle class, he made familiar managerial vows to bring "old-fashioned efficiency" to New Jersey government. Florio declared himself to be a "lean and mean Liberal." He also promised not to raise taxes. But why should he? New Jersey's abundant economy was producing plenty of revenues.

The New Jersey Miracle

The mid-1980s were economic glory years for New Jersey. The state's economy added more than 650,000 jobs and enjoyed the lowest unemployment of any big industrial state; the jobless rate dipped as low as 3.7% in 1987. Expansion generated tremendous regional land booms in places like the Princeton corridor, where many hi-tech firms located their plants, and in northern New Jersey, across the Hudson from New York City, where spanking new office parks and housing enclaves abounded. Atlantic City became the East Coast's gambling capital in the 1980s, and the Meadowlands development project, just a few miles from Manhattan, became the new home of the football Giants, super-bowl champs of 1987 and 1990. Republican Governor Tom Keane went on television and became a popular pitchman for New Jersey's virtues as vacation playland and business site. The state was doing so well that one year Keane was able to turn a $1 billion revenue surplus into tax rebates for nearly every taxpayer in the state. In the 1980s, everything went New Jersey's way.

Unfortunately, when Florio took power, New Jersey, like most other states, went into an economic nosedive. The deepening national recession had swallowed up the forces behind the 1980s boom. In 1990, faced with plunging revenues and rising deficits, states across the nation raised taxes by $16 billion—the greatest single-year tax increase in the history of U.S. federalism. And this happened even as the states cut spending by a collective $7.5 billion. [46] Like other Northeastern states, the recession hit New Jersey hard, particularly when compared with the 1980s glory years. But aside from economic decline, New Jerseyans had other reasons to be worried, if not downright angry.

Suburban Discontents

As in California, the recent boom in New Jersey's real-estate values helped push property taxes up an average 10% a year in the 1980s, this in a state that gets nearly 50% of its revenues from property taxes (the average for U.S. states is only about 30%). [47] Rapid growth brought other familiar problems too, problems of density, traffic, and waste. Like their California counterparts, New Jersey suburbanites wanted growth on their own terms, and so they developed their share of land-use controls against "excessive" development. One poll, for example, found that fully one-third of New Jerseyans wanted "very strict" growth controls, while over half favored development controls that were "somewhat strict." [48]

Also fueling the uptick in suburban defensiveness was a series of strikingly progressive legal decisions by the New Jersey Supreme Court. One required all suburban communities in the state to provide land for low-income housing in proportion to the state's population of poor people; another that the state's system of school finance be made equal. These strongly egalitarian legal mandates directly threatened the small government strategy of Fortress Suburbia. And redistributive politics were no more popular among suburbanites in New Jersey than they were in California, especially when unelected liberal judges sitting in Trenton were ordering equality. Keane, Florio's predecessor, tried to relieve white distress over housing integration by creating a state Council on Affordable Housing, which encouraged suburbs to buy their way of out of "forced integration." The Council tried to meet the problem by proposing that suburbs give nearby cities the money to build new low-income housing units within urban borders. As far as Fortress

Suburbia was concerned, redistribution of a little income was easier to take than outright class and racial integration.

Undoubtedly, the bad recession of the early 1990s soured many middle-class New Jerseyans on such buy-out strategies. At the same time as communities faced court-ordered pressure to restructure their systems of housing access and educational opportunity, New Jersey began hemorrhaging jobs: it lost 104,000 jobs in 1991 alone. The state also faced a $3 billion budget deficit. Furthermore, Wall Street bond-rating firms were breathing down the state's neck, threatening to lower the state's credit rating if it did not get its fiscal house in order. Finally, Florio also faced a series of more localized problems, including fast-rising automobile insurance rates and severe pollution problems caused by the state's huge petro-chemical complex.

Most of these problems were of long standing, but Keane had so masterfully played the game of consensus politics that he studiously avoided taking steps that risked antagonizing powerful constituencies. Like Ronald Reagan nationally, Keane's administration tended to "roll over" the state's problems to his successor. And, like Reagan's successor, Keane's successor did not have the luxury of a short-lived boom to help people forget their troubles. Florio did not anticipate the politics of decline when he ran for governor. As the keynotes of his very mainstream 1989 campaign, Florio wed the "competence" pledge of Michael Dukakis to the anti-taxism of George Bush. He thought the state's abundance would help him avoid the "hard decisions."

The First One Hundred Days

Florio got off the mark quickly, striking hard to change the state's automobile insurance system, ban assault rifles, and strengthen pollution controls. On the social issues front, Florio proved indeed to be very much the activist reformer. Within weeks he began work on an economic package to deal with the state's now fast-mounting fiscal problems. Here, too, he showed some of the fire of the activist reformer. Rejecting finger-in-the-dike incrementalism, Florio thought comprehensively. Indeed, he began to work toward an economic program that specifically linked questions of political economy to issues of social equity. Noting the "harsh realities" facing the state, he felt that people were tired of anti-government tirades, that they were "hungry for leadership" from a government that worked to promote needed change.[49] "Determined to pronounce the age of Ronald Reagan dead in New Jersey," Florio advised his fellow Democrats that leaders have to risk political confrontations in order to achieve progress. "The easiest way not to have anybody against you," he proclaimed, "is to go into hibernation for a two-year period in Congress or a four-year period in a State House."[50] But now was the time for Democratic leaders to wake up and lead.

In late March 1990, just two months after becoming governor, Florio "stunned" the Democratic-controlled state legislature with a comprehensive, sweeping, and redistributive tax proposal. [51] The pivot of the plan was a doubling of the income-tax rate on the state's wealthiest citizens. For the top 17% of the state's taxpayers, those earning $55,000 and above, Florio proposed to increase the income-tax rate from 3.5% to 7%. The increase would raise $1.2 billion, and much of it would go toward equalizing spending by New Jersey's public school districts. Under the plan, 220 wealthier suburban school districts would lose money to over 600 other districts, especially the state's poorest, such as Newark. In addition, Florio proposed to raise the state sales tax from 6% to 7%. Finally, to appease fiscal conservatives and Wall Street, Florio promised to launch a drive to cut $1.1 billion in state spending, reductions affecting programs in transportation, the arts, drug treatment, and the elderly. For lucky New Jersey, these would be the first real cuts in state spending in fourteen years. At the same time, for all the audacity of Florio's program, corporate and business taxes were left conspicuously untouched.

Florio expected to sell this package on the simple populist premise that it would help many more people economically than it would hurt. He believed that traditional Democratic constituencies—poor, working and lower-middle-class people—would get behind tax reform because they and their children stood to gain most of the benefits. The governor calculated that as long as Democrats maintained reasonably tough, socially conservative positions on themes such as law and order (for example, favoring capital punishment and gun control), they could present an economically progressive program that would be very popular with the working class. Moreover, by letting business off the hook, the governor figured that he could both retain business confidence and still add populist force to his plan by taxing the rich as consumers, not investors. This would help to gain corporate support for rationalizing the state's tax system and doing something once and for all about education. In sum, the politics of the plan were to pit the bottom half of the income distribution against the suburban upper-middle class, all with at least the tacit support of New Jersey's business establishment.

Naturally, Florio realized that many working-class people would be angry about the sales tax increase and many of the spending cuts. But if the proposal was made early, the bad news would wear itself out as the economy began to grow again and the real benefits started rolling into working-class neighborhoods and school districts. In any case, as governor, he had to do something about school equalization because he knew that the liberal New Jersey Supreme Court would soon force his hand.

Florio's thinking *was* bold; the political theory behind it was daring, though much depended, as it usually does in politics, on timing. If the inevitable conservative taxpayer opposition was slow in building, if the recession ended early, if the plan's benefits flowed sooner rather than later, if, in short, time was on his side, Florio might well transform expectations of the politically possible. At least he could count on the fact that New Jersey, unlike California, does not provide mechanisms of direct democracy, such as initiative, which give anti-tax conservatives the power to resist change from below. If some New Jerseyans were angry about the tax plan, they would have to wait until 1993 for the next gubernatorial election, while the earliest state legislative election was a year away. Meanwhile, as governor, Florio expected that he could use the powers of his office and healthy Democratic majorities in both houses of the state legislature to ward off potential opponents long enough for the plan to work.

Radio Populism

Even his fellow Democrats were surprised by the breadth and daring of the program. Unfortunately, like the citizenry at large, the state's leading Democratic professionals were neither consulted nor coached by the governor about the changes to come. Yet Florio had broken virtually every rule in the playbook of balanced-budget conservatism: raising taxes, redistributing income, imposing sacrifice on the most affluent constituencies. Conspicuously designed to deal in one fell swoop with the inter-connected realities of school finance equalization, fiscal imbalance, and the need for more equity in state taxation, Florio's program showed the potential for tax reform to become social reform. But the program needed a majoritarian politics to back it and make it work.

As Florio's tax plan became public in March 1990, political reactions ranged across the dismal band that separates anxiety from outright condemnation. Republicans scorned a liberal governor who would cynically raise taxes on the wealthy to build a surplus that he would use later to buy the votes of taxpayers. For Republicans, the "Lenin of Trenton" was the arch-evil expropriator of their well-earned wealth.[52] Shrewder Republican heads sensed, however, that Florio's model was not to be found in the Communist East, but the American West; that he might better be cast as an East Coast resurrection of Jerry Brown, with Republicans in the role of the "mad-as-hell" Howard Jarvis.

Meanwhile, Democrats in the state legislature gave little more than polite support to their party leader. Ringing speeches in defense of class justice did not abound. Aware that Republicans were gearing up to cheerlead a tax revolt, and that tax protest was already driving Connecticut's Democratic Governor William O'Neill from another run for his job, Trenton Democrats agonized that Florio's scheme threatened to put their political heads on the block, too. [53] Just weeks after the proposal went public, New Jersey's suburban voters confirmed such anxieties when they rejected nearly half the state's local school budgets, a state record. By contrast, there were no spontaneous urban demonstrations in favor of egalitarian school tax reform or "soak the rich" schemes. Most important, like Jerry Brown, Florio made little or no effort to mobilize urban, African-American, or Latino interests in favor of his program, or to link urban and suburban constituencies, or even to portray his program as having excited the interest of the economic majority it would most benefit. In essence, Florio offered a program, but not a countervailing ideological alternative to balanced-budget conservatism as the framework of political debate. And that was really what the voting public needed.

Under no mass pressure for egalitarian tax reform, Democrats in the legislature joined with Republicans in sensing that the politics of Florio's economic plan had best be cast in terms of suburban anxieties about tax-and-spending levels. Almost immediately, jittery Democrats in the legislature responded to taxpayer criticism. First, they raised the income level to which the top rates of Florio's tax increase would apply from $70,000 to $150,000. Then, in order to get more money to preserve New Jersey's homestead tax rebate, the legislators put their hands deeper into the pockets of ordinary people by expanding the reach of Florio's proposed 1% sales tax increase to cover a batch of everyday products, among other things, soap and paper products, including toilet paper, as well as cigarettes and alcohol. In effect, Democrats tried to assuage the growing tax discontent by narrowing the class that would actually have to pay higher income taxes while raising taxes on items ordinary people use every day. From such concessions most voters would rather be spared. [54]

Tax-sensitive legislators were not the only political forces Florio had to contend with. Interest groups also mobilized against his plan, including groups long tied to the Democratic Party. By early June, for example, the New Jersey Federation of Teachers, a liberal group upon whose support Florio had counted, complained that his plan to shift $800 million in pension costs from the state to local school districts threatened the security of teacher pension funds. Although not opposed in principle to equalizing school finance, the Federation did not want education reform to come out of its members' hides. Similarly, Democratic officials from affluent Bergen County, a largely suburban jurisdiction slated to lose approximately $100 million in school aid under equalization, complained that such cuts were going to hurt moderate-income families, too. Amidst all such complaints, Florio's failure to mobilize mass support was clearly beginning to hurt. After interviews with scores of New Jersey voters, *The New York Times* reported that many "were confused by Mr. Florio's complex agenda and clearly understood only that taxes were going up." Consequently, Florio's popularity rating crashed; by June he could count on the support of only one-third of New Jersey's Democrats; his overall approval level sank to 23%. [55]

Not all the news was bad. Florio was able to count on backing from the state AFL-CIO and from big-city mayors, such as Sharpe James of Newark, and the New Jersey Council of Churches, who urged the faithful to repel the racist claims of those who opposed school finance reform. [56] But, with little or no guidance from Trenton, these backers did not galvanize mass demonstrations or rally community and neighborhood organizations behind the governor. Nor did such groups fight to make the central issue of his economic plan the need for government to combat unequal policies and satisfy broad public needs. The real anger across the state was being expressed in suburban districts and in the anti-tax rhetoric of balanced-budget conservatism.

As with Jarvis in California, local radio talk shows became popular vents for taxpayer outrage. One radio personality, a disc jockey on WKXW in Trenton, challenged his angry listeners to stop complaining and do something about Florio's insult to the taxpayers. Put up or shut up, he dared. Several took up the challenge.

With radio as their link, callers John Budzash, a 39-year old mailcarrier, and Pat Ralston, a grandmother and real-estate title searcher, banded together to form a new protest group called Hands Across New Jersey (HANJ). For lower-middle-class people like Budzash and Ralston, taxes had sparked their discontent, but their anxieties went deeper, much deeper. HANJ touched a whole assortment of concerns that grew out of the long era of stagnation, problems of falling real wages and living standards, rising auto insurance rates, traffic snarl-ups and urban growth issues, and legislative pay increases. And while these citizens also feared educational finance reform and the portent of new pressures for racial integration, the unifying theme of lower-middle-class anxiety seemed more economic than racial insecurity. As Budzash explained, "There are really so many things that made me mad...I was really incensed that my mother all of a sudden had to take a $3 salary cut, from $9 to $6, and she's sixty-five years old and ready to retire on her last salary scale." And, as he added, "I know other people who have to take salary cuts, and with the economy in the state as bad as it is and our so-called deficit and fiscal problems, the Assembly gets a raise."[57]

Out of their anger with falling wages, HANJ moved against taxes and the state. That was the only money, after all, that working people could get their angry hands on. Thus, HANJ quickly spawned a program of its own to reverse directions, one that bore the clear stamp of balanced-budget conservatism. Its mass petition campaign aimed at three simple demands: rollback of the entire Florio tax package; a constitutional amendment granting direct democracy powers to the citizens of New Jersey (initiative, referendum, and recall); and a complete and independent audit of the state's finances. The group's strategy was to confront their governor with the signatures of a million angry New Jerseyans. The force of popular protest would command conservative change from below. Mass petitions would substitute, as well as be the pre-condition for, the winning of even more direct democracy.

Florio answered HANJ with a patronizing civics lesson: in our system, he proclaimed, the people elect representatives to make the big decisions; direct democracy, he lectured, runs "counter to our American system of representative democracy," and he would oppose it. As for the substance of taxpayer discontent, while understandable, it came to more bark than bite; the protest would surely fade as the benefits of reform spilled across New Jersey. Resistance would be spotty and there was nothing to worry about. "There was no backlash," he said.[58]

Meanwhile, throughout the summer and fall of 1990, HANJ pushed its petition drive forward, organizing noisy demonstrations in Trenton. To protest the expanded sales tax, the tax rebels even sent toilet paper (some of it used!) to state legislators. By September, though, signs of fragmentation, division, and faction marked the movement, and from the other side of the Hudson River, *The New York Times* suggested that Florio's original political calculation might prove accurate. As "tax protestors have no immediate recourse at the ballot box" to register their feelings, they would have to stay angry for a whole year before gaining the right to hold state officials accountable.

As political scientist V.O. Key once observed, however, voters are not fools.[59] Nor is their memory all that short. Voters are, among other things, wise enough in the ways of federalism and representative government to register state-focused protests even in "national" elections, elections to the U.S. Senate, for example. Thus, only weeks after reports of disaffection and weakening among the protestors, and months after pundits ranked Senator Bill Bradley among the politically invincible, New Jersey voters sent political shock waves across the nation as they came within a hair's breadth of defeating their highly popular senator.[60] Popular irritation was showing signs of longevity.

HANJ leaders eagerly claimed credit for the rebuke against Bradley. "We were able to channel a political storm this year," said one. "And all legislators who fail to heed the message...will be blown out next year by a hurricane."[61]

Right Moves by the Democrats

Democrats, including Florio, got the message. Finally conceding his failure to explain the tax program to voters, Florio now promised greater sensitivity to middle-class concerns. The middle class wanted lower taxes, tougher management of state government, and more understanding from liberal politicians about the virtues of its unequal school system. While refusing to roll back the 1991 tax increases, and unable to go against a state court mandate for equalizing school funding, Florio now vowed to do what he could to bring the most vocal New Jerseyans a smaller, cheaper state government. Gradually, but unmistakably, Florio now turned right. And he made his main scapegoat state workers.

In January, the governor presented his new budget, replete with attacks on government employees. Demanding that public-sector unions produce half the $800 million in spending cuts required to balance the state's budget, Florio announced the elimination of 8,000 state jobs, including 4,000 from layoffs, a 9% reduction in the state workforce, and a trimming of the state's departments from nineteen to sixteen. He also exacted from public labor a wage freeze and cuts in state contributions to health and pension plans. [62]

Confirming the reactionary trend in Florio's administration, the governor did not stand in the way as frightened Democrats in the state legislature disemboweled the equalization commitments of his own 1991 school finance program. Attempting to recapture suburban support, Democratic legislators in March moved $360 million of $1.1 billion in new tax money from aid to poor districts into a replenished fund for homeowner tax relief. Then, in order to give homeowners another $229 million, the legislature also set strict spending caps on both rich and poor school districts. Next, to redeem the faith of taxpayers, the legislature began explorations into a new welfare reform program, one that would, among other things, deny added benefits to women having children after they have gone on welfare. Finally, to seal his new balanced-budget conservative covenant with the middle class, Florio switched his position on direct democracy and backed including initiative and referendum powers in the state constitution. In every respect, including his refusal to lower taxes, which were needed to balance the state's budget, the governor had submitted to the social forces of balanced-budget conservatism. [63]

As if to proclaim their conversion, Florio and the Democrats now bombarded the state with radio and newspaper advertising, promising money for the voters, money from lower automobile insurance rates, and more money from property tax rebates up to $500. [64] The monetary lure, Democrats hoped, would re-certify their pro-middle class credentials. But, in fact, the Democrats now seemed desperate. It appeared they would do anything short of cutting taxes and expanding the deficit to win middle-class votes, including reversing the basic principles for which they had fought just a year before. As journalist Peter Kerr observed after Florio's new budget went into effect in July,

> This year, with the Democratic majorities in both houses facing re-election, Mr. Florio and the legislators produced a budget that a Republican would be proud of: it raises no taxes, increases aid to suburban homeowners and slims down government by several thousand workers...So marked is the turnabout that the Republicans can be expected to ask in the coming months what exactly Mr. Florio and the Democrats stand for, or if they stand for anything at all.[65]

The Democrats, of course, stood for one thing: their own re-election, but the voters remained unimpressed. Florio's poll numbers stayed in the tank, and soon some key Democratic legislators announced that they would forego bids for re-election. Even the party's links to the organized working class broke down. A coalition of seven public- and private-sector unions, fed up with Florio's scapegoating of workers and demands for give-backs, announced a campaign to support independent candidates, and the unions matched Republican anti-Florio ads with their own. [66] As one official of the Communications Workers of America proclaimed, with anger as well as with hyperbole, "This is the end of the relationship between the Democrats and the labor movement." As he bitterly added, "if we are going to get hurt, we'll take a lot of [Democratic politicians] with us."[67] Indeed, by November, a key labor group, the New Jersey Education Association, actually threw its support to Republican candidates.

Labor's anger, counterproductive in the short run, was understandable. Where else could unions go politically after the Democrats turned their back on the working class and poor people? At least, the unions' contribution to defeat of irresponsible Democrats might remind party officials of their class base. In either case, the old Democratic constituencies were caught between a rock and a hard place. If they abandoned Democrats, they got Republican policies; if they supported Democrats, they still got Republican policies. Thus did New Jersey public employees learn the lessons of balanced-budget conservatism the hard way, although along with the middle and upper classes, they extracted their pound of flesh from the Democrats in November.

In what can only be termed a landslide, Republicans swept into power in both the New Jersey Assembly and Senate, taking complete, veto-proof control of the legislative branches for the first time in twenty years. The Democrats' right turn helped themselves not a whit. All they could do now was bluster and feint about overturning their own tax package and thus force the Republicans to raise taxes themselves. A truly tawdry political show unfolded in the closing days of Democratic legislative rule as vengeful Democrats threatened to bring on a fiscal crisis. Meanwhile, Republicans and their business allies in the Chamber of Commerce and Business and Industry Association now attacked a tax rollback as the height of fiscal irresponsibility, warning of economic "chaos" if the state ran out of money. But bluster was all there was to the sorry condition of the New Jersey Democratic Party, and the legislators left office with their heads hanging between their donkey tails, the tax increase still very much in place.

When Republicans took power they completed the policy U-turn that the retreating Democrats had already begun. Overriding Florio's veto of their budget, Republicans made good on their promise to cut the sales tax back to 6%, giving New Jerseyans a $608 million tax cut that was the largest in the state's history. In addition, Republicans boasted of finding another $400 million in excess spending, so that together with the $600 million sales-tax reduction, they passed a budget $1 billion smaller than Florio's. The balanced-budget conservatives found their savings in predictable places: layoffs of public employees (estimates varied between 1,400 and 7,500 workers); a $190 million cut in the budget of the Department of Human Services; elimination of the state's Office of the Public Advocate (a recent sin was the advocate's backing of a lawsuit permitting busing across school-district lines).

For New Jersey and Florio, this was a truly astonishing turnabout. Committed originally to an experiment in activist, redistributive public policy, Florio's program was worse than a failure in its own terms. For its very failure helped to legitimate a reaction of balanced-budget conservatism in what had been for decades a state marked by moderate to liberal social policies. The governor's inability to take political charge of his own program, to rally the urban economic majority on its behalf, to build class and interracial links between constituencies with real economic interests in common, helped to certify balanced-budget conservatism as the only reasonable way to approach the state's economic difficulties.

But in important ways Republicans were only slightly less faithful to their constituents than Democrats were to the poor. Indebted to a host of corporate interests such as the utility and real-estate industries, which feared citizen lawmaking like the plague, Republicans were not about to give New Jersey's middle-class voters the direct political power they wanted. The new majority simply let the initiative and referendum die on the vine. [68] John Budzash, feeling double-crossed once again by the politicians, condemned "Rat-publicans," and set about to start a new protest group to fight for direct democracy.

But the real tragedy of Florio's impoverished and cowardly reformism was best captured by another citizen who felt double-crossed, a long-time activist for school finance reform, Marilyn J. Morheuser. By timidly fostering balanced-budget conservatism, by exacerbating divisions between the middle class and the poor, the suburbs and cities, Florio had rubbed raw all the anxious nerves of ordinary people in the state. Now the "two New Jerseys—[the] rich one and...[the] poor one...—are further apart than when the governor first talked about ending the two New Jerseys in the early 1990s."[69] Florio actually ended up leaving social relations in his state in a worse, more divided condition than when he first became governor.

Conclusion

As key cases of failed liberal leadership, the tax revolts of California and New Jersey bracket the era of balanced-budget conservatism. Contrary to conventional wisdom, in neither instance can we find the fundamental cause of rebellion in a middle class seething with anger and anxious to throw off the shackles of the welfare state. In California, Jerry Brown and his cohorts in the state legislature mangled the opportunity presented by a $6 billion surplus, clearing the way for conservative activist Howard Jarvis to build a following. New Jersey's Florio, on the other hand, did have an activist program; his goal of reuniting the working poor and middle class in a coalition for tax reform and social justice was worthy of the best in the U.S. liberal tradition. But instead of taking the time to prepare and galvanize the various segments of his proposed coalition, Florio aggressively pushed his program through from the top down; a compliant Democratic legislative majority gave its consent, only to turn around and withdraw it once the political waters roiled. What might have been a test case for liberal activism in the 1990s became a political disaster as the shock of big tax increases and reduced school funding produced fiery suburban reactions. The end result was a political right turn by Democrats who then did nothing to stem a Republican takeover of the legislature.

We do not mean that the middle class in these states was a constituency ready and waiting for the cause of social justice. Any such interpretation would be naive to a fault. But we believe that between spirited commitment to social justice and incipient middle-class reaction, political space exists. This space existed both in California and New Jersey. More creative strategies for social change could have filled it. These strategies must show a sensitivity to the subtle balance of political necessity and possibility more acute than that shown by Brown and Florio. Brown could have knocked partisan heads together to produce a policy for dealing with taxes and surplus; Florio could have been a more democratic leader, perhaps moving more slowly, though with no less determination, to bring about fairer systems of taxation and school expenditure.

The tragedy of the tax revolts of California and New Jersey is that in each case an impoverished liberal leadership created richer opportunities for conservative forces to gain political power and thereby shift the dynamic of change toward more suffering and hardship than even capitalism requires. But the fact that each of these Democratic governors failed to ward off an incipient tax revolt is only partly to be blamed on their personal and strategic inadequacies. Much of their weakness under fire stems, we think, from the Democratic Party's historic ambivalence toward social differences within its working-class base, differences that the Party has done much both to reinforce and at times even to criticize. Florio's oscillation on equalizing school finance is as good an example as there is of the Democrats' hesitancy to challenge the prerogatives of Fortress Suburbia. In the age of balanced-budget conservatism, when push comes to shove, Democrats usually end up pushing in the same direction as conservatives, away from, rather than toward, the interests of the economic majority. Having subsidized white workers in their move from the cities, most Democrats leaders are disinclined to remind workers of their roots, especially those lucky enough to hold onto decent jobs.

Chapter Six

NEW YORK STATE TURNS TO THE RIGHT

The first section of this book laid bare the concept of balanced-budget conservatism. We traced the roots of balanced-budget conservatism to the dual forces of a declining economy and the pressures facing today's government, a government caught in the ongoing political struggle between the property-owning classes and the non-propertied for protection and amenity of their wealth on the one side, and for social assistance on the other. High levels of public expenditures on social welfare programs mean higher taxes to the former group; cutbacks in social spending reduce services for the latter. This, as we showed, sets up a zero-sum dynamic that ensures that the victory of one side will come only at the expense of the other. In short, the politics of balanced-budget conservatism clearly define who wins and who loses, and, most importantly, the stakes of this political game become higher as the national treadmill economy continues its slide toward the abyss.

Balanced-budget conservatism, we have attempted to show, is more than a new kind of politics. It also has important ideological implications. In fact, we argue that balanced-budget conservatism has replaced what political scientist Theodore Lowi calls "interest-group liberalism" as the nation's dominant public ideology. This is the heart of our work. For if balanced-budget conservatism has indeed become the new public philosophy, the implications for developing new political strategies and tactics for change are far-reaching. New political strategies will have to address a changing reality, one in which elected officials of both political parties, driven by the restrictive principles of balanced-budget conservatism, become increasingly alike. Progressives, then, face major obstacles in implementing their policies. Balanced-budget conservatism views the goals of progressives as unattainable, since their strategies—enlarging the welfare state—are inherently bad. This ideology teaches that reducing the size of government is a good in and of itself, and thereby restricts the nature and variety of policies pursued by liberal political leaders in the first place. Obviously, these beliefs place progressive leaders in a political straightjacket, severely limiting their range of "viable" actions. And should a progressive be foolish enough to challenge the pragmatism of balanced-budget conservatism, the ill-fated experience of New Jersey's James Florio serves as a reminder of the likelihood of failure. In other words, balanced-budget conservatives place harsh restraints on the most progressive politicians.

The second section of our work looks more closely at the tenets stated above. We do this by examining New York's experience with balanced-budget conservatism during the past decade. We decided to study New York for a number of reasons. First, the state has a long tradition of progressive politics. The New Deal itself, the institutional setting underlying interest-group liberalism, has its roots in the progressive democracy of Governor Al Smith and the state's own experiment in fighting the Depression under Franklin D. Roosevelt, architect of the New Deal. But New York's progressive tradition stretches well beyond the confines of the Democratic Party. Teddy Roosevelt, for instance, played a leading role in the progressive movement in the two decades following the turn of the century, and Nelson Rockefeller gave new life to the Republican version of "pragmatic liberalism." Rockefeller's variety of liberalism defined and shaped the progressive wing of the Republican Party for more than a generation. Indeed, New York's progressive tradition is so deeply rooted in the state's political culture that conservative Republicans such as George Bush and Dan Quayle seized every opportunity to make political points with the conservative electorate by lambasting New York's liberalism.

There is at least one other important reason for looking closely at New York. Mario Cuomo was elected governor in 1982 as a liberal Democrat during the heart of the so-called "Reagan Revolution." Cuomo built a winning electoral coalition modeled on the one that most political observers and pundits thought Reagan had put to rest: the old New Deal-type coalition of organized labor, ethnics, poor people, peoples of color, and women. The governor's already impeccable liberal credentials received national acclaim when he gave his brilliant keynote address at the 1984 Democratic convention. Cuomo's reliance on New Deal values and his attack on Reagan's social Darwinism catapulted him into the national spotlight and strengthened his position as the symbol of liberalism. Expectations among liberal Democrats ran high. Cuomo, more than anyone else, would develop a liberal response to the forces of balanced-budget conservatism, and many expected New York to emerge as a showcase of progressive success in an era of Rightwing reaction.

Cuomo's position was complicated by Republican control of the New York Senate. But this was nothing new; the Senate had always been the bastion of upstate conservativism. Other liberal governors had managed to tame the Senate, and so would Cuomo. There were other problems, of course. New York's fiscal crisis of the mid- and late-1970s almost threw the state into bankruptcy. The bitter struggle for political control over New York City, the desperate appeal for federal assistance, massive retrenchments in the public sector, the precipitous drop in the quality of life, and the imposition of new taxes and fees reminded people of the dire consequences of "overspending." This, too, would make the liberal Cuomo's task more difficult. But the circumstances of the early 1980s gave liberals an opportunity to show how progressivism works. With Cuomo at the helm, progressives had another occasion to create a model illuminating the success of liberalism and the failure of conservatism; in essence, Cuomo, more than anyone else, was going to lead liberalism back into the promised land. He was the person to turn things around, to reset the political agenda. Roosevelt had done it, and now it was Cuomo's turn. Unfortunately, things did not work out as planned.

The following three chapters analyze the rise of balanced-budget conservatism in New York, its emergence as a fundamental tenet of public policy, the kinds of problems these policies create for those who support a progressive agenda, and strategies for an effective Leftist response. In short, we look at the ability of conservatives to set the political agenda, the failure of liberalism to alter it, and the prospects for the Left. The first of the three chapters traces business' attempts to overcome intra-class conflicts and present a united front against the re-emerging New Deal coalition. New York's businesspeople, we argue, led by the state's largest corporations, learned a lesson from their national counterparts: they formed a statewide organization, the Business Council of New York, to spearhead their collective political efforts. Their political agenda both created and expressed the principles of balanced-budget conservatism. Backing the ideology of balanced-budget conservatism with the promise of jobs, wealth, status, and influence, the Business Council tied Mario Cuomo's hands, splintering the coalition that elected him and driving him down the fiscally restrained path of balanced-budget conservatism. But, we argue, Cuomo could have done worse. His political skills and reluctance to put up a fight that he could not win kept a bad situation from getting worse. This, of course, raises the issue of what strategies would work against balanced-budget conservatism.

The second chapter of this section analyzes labor's response to balanced-budget conservatism. We do this to gain insights into what worked, what reasonable alternatives failed and why. In short, public labor tried to meet the centralized power of business by concentrating its own power. Solidarity became the buzzword of labor's offensive. But for the reasons discussed below, public-sector unions' solidarity efforts fell short. Solidarity within the public sector was only one issue. There were others. And public labor fell short in these arenas, too. The unions failed to build a winning political coalition with private-sector unions, and they did not join forces with that growing segment of the population outside the organized labor movement. The fourth and concluding chapter of Part II looks at the New York experience from the Left. Bush and Quayle might attack New York at every opportunity because of its Leftist ways, but progressive-minded people, as we have argued, are aware of the limitations of the welfare state, particularly an under-financed one that processes people through large, insensitive bureaucracies. This chapter looks at the limitations of liberalism and draws upon labor's failure in New York to suggest strategies to build an alternative political movement, one that goes beyond the pain of conservatism and the bankruptcy of liberalism.

Chapter Seven

BUSINESS REORGANIZES

For virtually every law taxing big money, there is a way those with big money can avoid or minimize it.

C. Wright Mills.[1]

Congratulating the "Italian kid from Queens," the Civil Service Employees Association (CSEA), the largest public-sector union in New York State, celebrated Mario Cuomo's 1982 election victory with a media blitz forecasting great things ahead. And why not? The union representing close to 250,000 public employees had broken tradition by endorsing Cuomo six months before the Democratic primary, even though he was an underdog in the polls. CSEA's media campaign illuminated the iconoclastic aspect of its early endorsement. Since Mario Cuomo broke tradition during his campaign by publicly backing labor, CSEA also departed from tradition by throwing early support to the pro-labor candidate. Now the union would reap the rewards from its astute political maneuver, for they predicted that with Mario Cuomo in Albany "the 80s would be remembered…as the decade of job security."[2]

Time and events proved CSEA wrong. As happened to liberal governors in California and New Jersey, something went awry. Nine years after his first gubernatorial election, when Cuomo was the front runner for the 1992 Democratic presidential nomination, CSEA president Joe McDermott declared that his union would not back its old friend. Instead, CSEA supported Bill Clinton, governor of a right-to-work state that prohibited public-sector collective bargaining. Within days, Cuomo's dreams of the presidency died. Citing the state's fiscal crisis and the inability of the legislature to develop a budget program, New York's governor announced that he would not run for the presidency. Leaders of the Republican Senate watched the CSEA-Cuomo sideshow with glee, while a sigh of relief emanated from the White House.

People outside New York State may find CSEA's reversal baffling, to say the least. Why would the state's largest public-sector union torpedo the presidential aspirations of the home-state, pro-labor governor it helped elect in the first place? But McDermott was not alone in attacking Cuomo. Leaders of the state's other public-sector unions all joined the anti-Cuomo chorus at one time or another, and they eventually united with McDermott in singing the praises of Arkansas' Clinton.

As strange as this scenario may seem, CSEA's (and labor's) about-face toward Cuomo mirrors the changing realities of political power that began nationally and eventually took hold in New York State: the re-emergence of business interests as aggressive political players willing to put intra-class differences aside.[3]

Responding to victories by public-interest groups on the federal level, in the early 1970s business groups launched a new and aggressive political offensive in Washington. They increased the number of corporate PACs, introduced new grass-roots lobbying efforts, expanding existing ones, and found innovative ways to coordinate their political efforts, including the formation of the Business Roundtable, a lobbying organization consisting of CEOs of the nation's largest firms. In short, they stopped assuming that their economic power alone ensured victory over less powerful players and dedicated more resources to the governmental process. A decade later, New York's business community followed suit. [4]

Since the early 1980s, New York's corporations have assumed the leading role in reorganizing business's political power on the state and local levels. Forming political organizations to represent their class interests and actively pursuing pro-business political and public-relations campaigns, the state's unified business community led the charge for balanced-budget conservatism in New York. And the times were ripe for the reemergence of this pro-business ideology. Balanced-budget conservatism fed on the nation's worst recession since the end of World War II. Nationally, unemployment had climbed to a post-World War II high of almost 11%, productivity was declining, and exports dropped, as the overvaluation of the U.S. dollar further aggravated the nation's trade deficit. [5]

Business's rejuvenated political power presented New York's Cuomo with obstacles different in degree from those confronting his liberal counterparts in California and New Jersey. Not only did Cuomo feel the economic and ideological pressures of balanced-budget conservatism, he also had to respond to the revitalized political clout of the state's business interests. And respond he did. Learning from the California and New Jersey debacles, Cuomo attempted to fight balanced-budget conservatism by yielding to its precepts. Indeed, the power of business interests helped transform the liberal Cuomo into a fiscal conservative, despised by large segments of the New Deal-type coalition that elected him in the first place. In this chapter, we examine the reorganization of business interests in New York, how it was fueled by the fiscal crisis, the role business plays in setting the state's political agenda, and the paucity of options available to even the most progressive elected officials. Chapter Eight examines the impact of the corporate political agenda on the fiscal crisis, the depth of the crisis, and how public labor has responded to the changing political economic environment. Chapter Nine explores the failure of liberal strategies and offers some new strategies for progressive change.

Cuomo Woos Labor

New York City's Ed Koch had a lock on the 1982 Democratic gubernatorial nomination, at least according to the polls and political pundits. Every poll picked Koch as the sure winner of the primaries. Koch, after all, was a well-liked mayor of the nation's most populated city, and his primary opponent Cuomo was then the little-known lieutenant governor and former secretary of state.

Cuomo did not stand a chance. He had already lost to Koch in the New York City mayoral race of 1977. And this time around, his chances looked even worse. With the backing of the state's business interests, New York City's mayor had millions to spend on the primary election. After receiving the Democratic Party's endorsement at its June convention, Koch's campaign coffers were bursting as he prepared for the September primary election. Cuomo, on the other hand, did not have Koch's money or any immediate prospects to match the mayor's spending. Worse yet, prior to the Democratic convention, rumors had surfaced suggesting that Cuomo might play the spoiler in the general election in November by refusing to endorse Koch, who at the time seemed a certain winner. In fact, unless Cuomo agreed to support Koch, it appeared that he might not even get the 25% backing necessary to appear on the primary ballot. Yet all this was almost beside the point, for with the polls showing Koch way ahead, the primary election would be a mere formality. When Hugh Carey, the outgoing governor, passed up his lieutenant governor to endorse Koch, it was all over but for the voting. It looked like Koch had it won.

But Koch's strength was overstated. Over the years, he had alienated many downstate voters with his anti-union policies, particularly his attacks on public-sector unions, even though they employed over 200,000 workers, and his abrasive personality angered many upstaters. Koch, after all, had committed a serious blunder by ridiculing suburban and rural life in a *Playboy* interview. Public workers mistrusted Koch, viewing his treatment of New York City's public unions as miserly and confrontational. Koch was elected mayor as New York City was still teetering on the brink of bankruptcy. During the peak of the crisis in 1975-1976, the city's employees suffered massive layoffs and large wage cuts. Even though Koch did not take office until 1978, fiscal austerity was the watchword of his administration, and the recession of 1982 illuminated his predicament. [6]

Looking for ways to alleviate the fiscal crisis, New York's mayor did what others had tried in the past and what has become the popular solution today: Koch attempted to balance the city's budget on the backs of public workers by threatening to lay off 10,000 public employees. His words were not idle threats. A series of layoffs, speed-ups, and attacks on public-employee pensions had created contentious labor-management relations between the mayor and municipal unions. Indeed, no matter what happened, public employees thought that Koch always wanted more in the way of give-backs and concessions. Although recognized by some in the business community as the savior of New York's fiscal integrity, Koch had made many enemies among public-sector workers. So many that he was, as it turned out, politically vulnerable.

Cuomo was astute enough to recognize his opponent's weakness. He openly courted New York's state and municipal unions, getting their enthusiastic backing. CSEA, for instance, which had openly fought Koch's efforts to weaken municipal unions through changes in the civil-service law, provided the candidate with a ready-made state-wide organization. The quarter-of-a-million teachers represented by the New York State United Teachers (NYSUT) and led by its 125,000-member New York City local, the United Federation of Teachers (UFT), funnelled money and, most importantly, hordes of volunteers into the Cuomo campaign. Cuomo's primary campaign enlisted 10,000 volunteers who spent primary day bringing voters to the polls. Campaign volunteers, according to most analysts, made the difference for Cuomo, and the volunteers overwhelmingly came from the ranks of labor, particularly government employees.

The Civil Service Employees and the United Teachers were joined by public-sector unions across the state. The Public Employees Federation (PEF) and the huge District Council 37 of the American Federation of State, County, and Municipal Employees (AFSCME), to name the larger and more active organizations, played important roles in Cuomo's primary campaign. District Council 37 made a number of especially important contributions to Cuomo's primary campaign. Its president, Victor Gotbaum, who viewed Koch as a vehemently anti-labor candidate and adversary, committed the resources of Council 37 to Cuomo, including volunteers and campaign funds. But Council 37 also gave the Cuomo camp something else of importance, a deputy campaign manager, Norman Adler, a District Council 37 staffer who took on the responsibility for the "get out the vote effort."

When the primary ballots were counted, the voters proved the pollsters wrong.[7] Although outspent by Koch by about three to one,

Cuomo pulled a major upset. He won the primary handily, getting 53% of the vote and beating the mayor by more than 80,000 votes. The surprising primary victory gave Cuomo a new image. Almost overnight, the reformer from Queens shed his loser's reputation and became the darling of the labor movement, and public employees loved him most of all. After all, their money, phone banks, votes, brains, and energy had paved the way for his September primary victory. The apparent marriage between public-sector workers and Mario Cuomo created an entirely new political scenario. As the general election approached, the Democratic nominee emerged as the leader of a labor-driven political movement that galvanized large numbers of rank-and-file unionists to action. In the wake of Reagan's anti-unionism, this signaled, to many, the rebirth of organized labor—with public-sector unions at the forefront.

The budding new labor-driven political coalition still had at least one more obstacle facing it. The general election in November pitted the Cuomo coalition of labor, women, and people of color against the wealthy, far-Right candidacy of Republican Lew Lehrman. Observers hailed the Cuomo-Lehrman contest as a test of traditional liberalism versus the free-market, anti-labor, balanced-budget conservatism of Reagan Republicanism. Perhaps this overstated the ideological and organizational cohesiveness of Cuomo's coalition, for Mayor Koch's anti-unionism and the extreme Right wing candidacy of Lehrman may have made Cuomo's coalition seem more liberal and stronger than it really was. Cuomo recognized this when he decided to run as a "moderate," but in the euphoria of the primary upset and Lehrman's unacceptability to labor, the implications of this ideological decision were overlooked. After all, as one public-sector union newspaper noted during the campaign, there would be no unions if Lehrman had his way. [8] Besides, this time labor had bet on a winning horse. Cuomo was the favorite.

But Koch had also been the favorite, and there were no guarantees that Cuomo would avoid the same fate as his former primary opponent. Lehrman, of course, did his best to prove the pollsters and pundits wrong. The Republican candidate spent over $11 million, including more than $8 million of his own money. The $11 million was as much as both gubernatorial candidates combined spent in the 1978 gubernatorial election and almost three times more than the $4.1 million raised and spent by Cuomo, whose campaign was again buttressed by labor's money and volunteers. In fact, in early October when Lehrman was outspending Cuomo by more than four to one and it appeared that the tide was shifting to the Republican, labor leaders came to the financial rescue, pledging $400,000 to the Cuomo campaign.

Unions remained committed to the pro-labor candidate, and their efforts made the difference. As election-day approached and Lehrman's well-financed campaign gained momentum, Cuomo's lead began to slip. For a while it appeared that Lehrman might even win. But once again organized labor came to the rescue. Cuomo's aides recognized that a big pro-Cuomo turnout on election day was essential to victory. AFSCME's Norm Adler, Cuomo's deputy campaign manager and field coordinator, observed that election day phone calls could account for between 4% to 6% of the vote. Conceding nothing, Adler led the drive to recruit 20,000 volunteers to staff telephones on election day. The volunteers called more than 200,000 voters identified as Cuomo supporters and urged them to go to the polls. As noted above, the New York State United Teachers had volunteers phone each of its almost 250,000 members, and CSEA set up state-wide phone banks. In fact, these scenarios were repeated in virtually every large public-sector union in the state.

Complementing the "get-out-the-vote" efforts, some of the unions preyed on their members' fears. The Public Employees Federation, for instance, ran a two-page story in its newspaper, *The Public Employee Press,* which had a circulation of over 100,000. Under the heading of "If Lehrman Had His Way There Would Be No Unions," the story chronicled the "slave-like" conditions workers at Lehrman's non-union Rite Aid drugstore chain experienced. [9] The underside of the message was that a Lehrman victory would cost public workers their jobs.

We all know the results of the November election. Cuomo won a squeaker with a winning margin of only 3.6%, or about 110,000 votes of the more than 5,500,000 cast. Unions had helped elect a progressive governor in a state noted for its progressive tradition, a tradition going back to Alfred E. Smith and Franklin Roosevelt on the Democratic side and Nelson Rockefeller liberalism on the Republican. Cuomo would now build upon and expand this tradition, so organized labor thought. But public-sector unions barely had a chance to celebrate Cuomo's electoral victory before a different reality set in.

Balanced-Budget Conservatism Gains Momentum

Even though Lehrman's spending failed to bring victory at the polls, the Republican candidate's campaign opened up new vistas for balanced-budget conservatism. Parroting Reaganomics, the owner of the Rite Aid drugstore chain successfully promoted balanced-budget conservatism by promising to restore the state's economic health through huge tax cuts, to reduce state taxes by some 40%, and to cut the size of government by reducing waste and privatizing many public functions. Feeling the effects of a severe recession, the public found the ideology of balanced-budget conservatism so attractive that they almost elected Lehrman as governor, even though Democrats out-registered Republicans by about a two-to-one margin in the state. Despite the results of the election, Lehrman waged an ideological assault on what conservatives label the "tax-and-spend" policies of New Deal liberalism, and his ideas gained a strong grip on the state's population.

The ideology of balanced-budget conservatism received a boost days before Cuomo's inaugural when Bethlehem Steel announced the closing of its mammoth Lackawanna plant on December 27, throwing thousands of workers into the streets. The death of Bethlehem's Lackawanna plant, once the world's largest steel mill, symbolized the depth of the recession and the declining role New York State and the nation would play in the changing world economy.[10] The United States was no longer the world's dominant economic power and this impacted heavily on New York's manufacturing base. Indeed, the state's industrial foundation was disappearing. By January 1983, plant shutdowns and corporate flight had taken their toll in New York. The Cuomo Administration took office with only 1,100 firms employing 500 or more workers left in the state.[11] Lehrman's campaign had played on the issues of economic recession and corporate flight, blaming government regulations, meddling bureaucrats, and high taxes for the state's fiscal woes. Balanced-budget conservatism may have oversimplified New York's economic woes, but there was no getting away from it: New York was in the midst of an economic downspin that the new governor would have to reverse.

The possibility that Cuomo could successfully rely on traditional New Deal economic solutions to reverse New York's economic plight became less likely when the state's business community reorganized as a major political player espousing many of the ideas of balanced-budget conservatism. Emulating the political efforts of corporations on the federal level, in 1981 New York's business interests, seeking new ways to increase their political clout in state politics, put aside their past political differences and formed a new political lobbying group: the Business Council—New York's version of the Business Roundtable. Upon its creation, the Business Council immediately became "the state's largest business lobbying organization and the biggest organization of its kind in the nation."[11] With an annual budget in the millions, and with more than 3,000 members employing over three million workers, the Business Council became the political arm for a pro-business balanced-budget agenda. The Council had the political means to gain politicians' attention, and it did, as it effectively espoused many of the balanced-budget ideas of the Lehrman campaign, including reductions in corporate and personal income taxes.

The ability of the Lehrman campaign to frame the issue in balanced-budget conservative terms, the emergence of business as a major lobbying group, a serious economic recession, and the long-term effect of corporate flight upon the state's economy increased the pressure on Cuomo to play by the rules of balanced-budget conservatism. During the gubernatorial campaign, Cuomo responded to the increasingly conservative environment by rejecting the "tax-and-spend" rhetoric that conservatives love to hate. Candidate Cuomo had even vowed to "use all the powers of my office" to convince the legislature to place a cap on the state budget—a kind of Gramm-Rudman policy for New York—and to lower the maximum personal income tax rate to under 10% during his first term. At the time, Cuomo's conservative statements did not daunt leaders of the liberal coalition, including public-sector unionists, who continued to back him; their candidate's fiscally conservative public statements were seen as necessary but tasteless campaign rhetoric that accomplished the necessary evil of bowing to balanced-budget conservatism. After the election, however, Cuomo had to replace campaign rhetoric with concrete political policies and programs. At this juncture, the political and economic power of balanced-budget conservatism surfaced.

Cuomo's Economic Program

When Cuomo took office in January 1983, the recession was not New York's only problem. Balanced-budget conservatism had another institutional ally in the federal system of government. Competition among the states for business reached new heights, as states offered tax breaks and incentives to lure investors who increasingly found New York's skilled and productive labor force less attractive than non-union labor in the Sunbelt states. The national recession intensified economic competition among the states and gave credibility to the Business Council's program for lower taxes and more state assistance to business.[13] Failure to recognize the growth requirements of the private economy would exacerbate the state's economic plight, so the argument and the conventional wisdom went, and if anyone doubted this, they had only to look at New York's economic condition during the Hugh Carey years.

Carey's eight years in the Statehouse saw New York lose approximately 400,000 residents, and the state's relative income dropped from 13% to 9% above the national average, even though the Carey Administration, with the urging of business, had made significant cuts in the personal income tax. Indeed, despite reducing the state's highest tax bracket from 15.5% of personal income in 1974 to 14.2% in 1981, Carey left office with New York's tax position unchanged relative to other states. Competitive pressures to attract new business forced other states to meet and even exceed New York's tax cuts.

The Carey tax reductions failed to give New York a competitive advantage over the other states, but they did trigger a spate of attacks on a weakened public sector. Tax cuts mean reduced revenues, and this in turn usually forces cuts in government spending. And this is exactly what happened in New York during Carey's tenure as governor. Indeed, during the Carey Administration per capita real expenditures declined by about $100. But the issue is not simply tax or spend. Public spending is crucial to the health of the private economy. The spending reductions of the Carey Administration may have temporarily met a political goal, but they deferred a number of maintenance and investment projects essential to the economic infrastructure.[14] Revenue losses associated with tax cuts were making it increasingly difficult for the state to provide the usual functions of law enforcement, education, sanitation, economic development, or environmental regulation. Other crucial policy programs, such as those addressing health care and poverty, were increasingly underfunded.[15] Additional cuts, on top of the deferment of numerous capital projects, threatened to permanently cripple New York's economy; and the cuts were inevitable, for President Reagan's "New Federalism" crippled states with a developed public sector. Between 1977 and 1982, federal aid to the states dropped from $72.4 to $54.6 billion in 1977 constant dollars, and New York's share of federal grants fell from 10.6% to 10.2% of the total during the Carey years.[16]

The combination of a new business political offensive, economic stagnation, competition among the states for new investments, a changing global economy, and declining federal assistance presented New York's newly elected governor with a sizable deficit. By the time Carey handed the reins to his successor amidst projections of a budget deficit of about one-half billion dollars, Cuomo could not afford to ignore the political realities and pressures of balanced-budget conservatism. Since the Cuomo Administration had to play by the same economic rules and influences applied to all the states, how could it differ from the rest? Cuomo's position was actually worse than most, as New York's deficit jumped to $1.83 billion and business interests stood by as political watchdogs against public programs. Clearly, New York was in trouble again, and this time the problem appeared insurmountable.

The state's crisis worsened in early 1983 when the Standard and Poor's 500, a leading bond-rating firm functioning as the guardian of balanced-budget conservatism, placed the state on a "budget watch." As noted above, during the campaign Cuomo had countered Lehrman's "trickle down" rhetoric with a pro-business platform of his own, something he was driven to do by the recession and business' political clout. Financial institutions and real-estate developers had made contributions to his campaign, but other factors were at play here. Cuomo knew that he could not afford to incur the Business Council's wrath, and when the Council announced that cuts in the personal income and corporate taxes ranked at the top of its political agenda, the governor listened.

The Business Council was not alone in seeking tax cuts. Cuomo had pledged to lower taxes during his campaign. In fact, tax cuts were a key element of his economic plan to attract and keep existing businesses in the state. But once in office, his "trickle down" campaign promise to reduce the top rate of the personal income tax below 10% during his first term presented an interesting dilemma. If Cuomo kept his campaign promise to lower income taxes, the already large deficit would increase, and the state's credit rating would worsen. Despite this fact, the Business Council pressured him to make good on his campaign promise. Less spending, however, was likely to alienate public-sector workers and their clients, the very groups that had helped elect the governor in the first place. The governor's campaign pledge to lower taxes made the latter scenario inevitable; it also made any upward tinkering with the personal income tax as a way to raise revenue to meet the deficit politically unacceptable.

The governor's predicament was complicated by Standard and Poor's budget watch. Poised to ensure that the new governor took a "fiscally responsible" path, Standard and Poor threatened to lower the state's bond ratings, thereby forcing the state to pay higher interest rates and increasing the cost of borrowing. The squeeze was definitely on. Caught in the tightening vice of business and financial pressures, the governor took what he perceived as the best and perhaps only politically viable way to achieve a balanced budget: he opted for significant reductions in public services and new taxes that disproportionately hurt the poor and lower-middle classes.

As in the cases of California and New Jersey, the dilemma facing the new Cuomo Administration illuminates one of the key characteristics of the politics of scarcity. In short, unlike the politics of New Deal Liberalism—the ideological and organizational principle of Cuomo's electoral strategy—where the expansion of wealth allows all organized interests to get a piece of the pie, balanced-budget conservatism ensures that the victory of one interest comes at the expense of another.[17] Balanced-budget conservatism gives new meaning to the Madisonian dictum of "interest against interest." When the size of the pie remains stable or shrinks, politics openly becomes a sum vector game. The victory of one interest comes at the expense of another, and losers feel the pain. Elected officials face what they and the pundits call "tough decisions." Not surprisingly, they base their decisions on the distribution of power, and the weakest groups take the hardest hits. As one analyst put it in 1983:

> Someone is going to have to pay a stiff political price—The State must, therefore, set aside liberal sentiments about the funding of welfare facilities and egalitarian opportunities. [18]

Why punish the weak? As an aide to Deputy Assembly Speaker Arthur Eve recently put it, politicians "punish those the most who can hurt them the least and reward those who can hurt the most." The weak, in short, are incapable of punishing those in power. They will remain weak until they organize and fight back. On this score, the New Deal governor of New York read the political cards quite well. Upon taking office, Cuomo could not keep his pledge to lower the personal income tax. The deficit and the national recession postponed that for awhile. But, unlike his counterpart in New Jersey who gambled and lost, Cuomo played it differently. His policies soon mirrored the balanced-budget conservatism that ultimately responds to the needs of business at the expense of the politically weak.

Under the watchful eyes of Standard and Poor and responding to the vociferous demands of the Business Council, the governor unleashed an unprecedented attack on public-sector workers. His budget proposal for the 1983-1984 fiscal year, the first of the new Cuomo Administration, was criticized by downstate liberals as "indistinguishable from what a conservative Republican might have submitted."[19] And for good reason. Cuomo's first proposed state budget addressed the deficit through a number of cost-cutting devices and gave credibility to those who were beginning to characterize Cuomo as a "pay as you go" liberal, an economically austere liberalism that remains socially generous, but fiscally conservative.[20] The centerpiece of Cuomo's pay-as-you-go liberalism was what he called the Workforce Reduction Program.

The Workforce Reduction Program recognized the inflexibility of the bulk of state spending. A large proportion of state spending is committed to such things as contractual increases, pension obligations, capital projects, and other relatively fixed obligations. As a result, at the state and local levels, government budgetary axe-wielders often find it expedient to shrink the labor force because salaries make up the bulk of expenditures.[21] And this was the approach of the Workforce Reduction Plan, which sought to eliminate some 1,400 jobs at an annual savings of $219 million. The reduction program included 8,190 layoffs,

2,297 positions lost to attrition, and another 3,400 through early retirements.

Labor's initial response to Cuomo's proposal was predictable—shock and disbelief at this attack on public workers. Lehrman, after all, was the Business Council's candidate, not Cuomo. CSEA President Bill McGowan, who just weeks earlier had worked for Cuomo's electoral victory, vilified the plan. A retirement incentive bill, McGowan claimed, would attract some 10,000 state workers, not the 3,400 Cuomo claimed, so he did not need to lay off any state workers. "I met with Mario," the CSEA leader said, "and I told him his figure of 3,400 is all wet."[22] McGowan's charge that Cuomo was placing the burden of social services on the very "backs of people who depend on the state for services" echoed the public gripes of other labor leaders who had now joined the anti-Cuomo choir.[23] Notable among these was Victor Gotbaum, Cuomo's key labor supporter who helped orchestrate his electoral success.

Labor's offensive against the governor was accompanied by a legislative proposal from members of Cuomo's Democratic party to impose a 2.5% income-tax surcharge as a way to raise revenue and avoid reducing state services. But Cuomo responded to the surcharge proposal by characterizing it as "short-sighted." Publicly proclaiming that there is too much fat in government, he claimed the state would not have to cut services because we would do "more with less."

The promise that New York State would do more with less was not restricted to speed-ups resulting from massive public-employee layoffs. As public criticism of Cuomo's assaults on public workers increased, his ideological assault on the state took another turn. He initiated a new attack on public labor unions by blaming the deficit on contracts negotiated with the state the year before. His aides in charge of contract negotiations with public-sector unions told the press that the state's public unions should renegotiate their agreements because they were too expensive. Meyer Frucher, former head of the Governor's Office of Employee Relations, the agency charged with negotiating contracts with public unions, went so far as to blame the unions for the layoffs. Frucher noted that unions were warned a year earlier during negotiations that there were insufficient funds to pay for their wage increases; layoffs, he observed, provide the only way to pay for the wage hikes. Within the context of a severe fiscal crisis and mounting political pressure from the business community, the pro-labor governor, less than three months after taking office, had singled out labor as a primary cause of the state's fiscal woes and was now placing the blame for layoffs on the very same leaders who had engineered his election.

Cuomo's fiscally conservative policies, his offensive against public employees, and his pledge to eventually lower income taxes and reduce the size of government may have damaged his standing with organized labor, but they increased his popularity in conservative areas of the state. One public opinion poll disclosed that Cuomo ranked almost as high with upstate conservatives after five months in office as with those who had elected him.[24] In short, as support within the Cuomo coalition waned, his appeal to voters outside the coalition increased. He knew that scapegoating public workers would garner sufficient political support to resolve the immediate deficit. But Cuomo and his aides also knew that their old allies had no place else to go and would be won back over time.

As labor became increasingly alienated from Cuomo's policies, the governor attempted to mend his political fences by meeting with key labor leaders, including AFSCME's Gotbaum, who had become one of his most outspoken critics. Angered by Cuomo's attacks on public employees, Gotbaum publicly lamented the governor's failure to communicate with his allies in labor. In the end, however, Cuomo won him over; he promised to stop his verbal attacks. A truce now existed, but labor, particularly public labor, needed more than kind words. Amidst signs that economic recovery was on the way, it appeared that public workers would finally get some positive actions from the governor they had helped elect.

A quicker-than-expected recovery enabled Cuomo to return to the politics of plenty. This postponed the "hard decisions" that necessitate attacks on the weak and allowed him to follow policies pleasing to all organized interests. The fiscal prosperity of fiscal year 1983-1984 enabled Cuomo to respond to the needs of business, labor, and clients of human services. Government grew and spending increased until the next fiscal crisis. It was up to the business community to create the crunch.

The Politics of Plenty Revisited

The 1983 economic recovery proved stronger than expected. Nationally, the growth rate climbed to 6%, and New York was among the top three states in creating new service-industry jobs, although these jobs paid less than the traditional blue-collar work they replaced. As jobs in the service sector proliferated, New York's economic surge mirrored the national trend of a dual economy characterized by growing disparities between professional white-collar workers and service employees.[25] Still, in 1983, the full implications of this trend were not yet clear, and the most visible economic indicators suggested a full and robust economic recovery.

The indicators were right. The recovery was so swift and complete that the budgetary deficit of the previous year was replaced by a large surplus. The exact amount of the surplus was not entirely clear. Cuomo pegged it at $124 billion; others thought it larger. Whatever the actual amount, state finances were so improved that Standard and Poor put their seal of approval on the state's fiscal condition by upgrading New York's short-time notes, which effectively lowered the cost of borrowing by investors. The state was well on the way to financial recovery, and it appeared that the days of budget cutting were over, at least for now.

The revived economy and the budgetary surplus alleviated the pressures of the public labor squeeze. Abundant public coffers allowed all organized groups to share, however unequally, in the prosperity. Cuomo's proposed budget for the 1984-85 fiscal year—which increased spending by more than 10% over the previous year—reflected the state's growing prosperity and the return to the politics of plenty. Some groups did better than others, of course, but the fiscally induced pain of the previous year began to dissipate. Indeed, Cuomo's efforts to shore up support with labor received a boost as the state began to hire and rehire many new workers. New York's Republican comptroller, Ed Regan, even complained that the Cuomo Administration had put more workers on the payroll a year after the layoffs than prior to implementing the Workforce Reduction Program.

Other labor victories followed, including Cuomo's support of a supplemental pension bill over the objections of Mayor Koch. The new law increased pensions by more than 40% for workers who retired before public employees could receive Social Security benefits. Cuomo signed the legislation over the vociferous objections of Koch, who complained that pension reform would cost the city some $434 million over ten years. The governor's support of the bill, in light of Koch's cry that "[t]his bill signals that union raids are being launched against our treasury again,"[26] provided him with the opportunity to contrast his policies toward public unions with that of labor's old nemesis. Politically, Cuomo still was labor's friend.

With the fiscal crisis apparently out of the way, Cuomo responded to the needs of his labor supporters in many other ways. Public-sector unions closed the year with long lists of victories. CSEA's McGowan, who had spent much of the previous year locked in battle with the Cuomo Administration, now declared that his union had achieved seventeen major victories in 1984. McGowan was not alone; his union's experience exemplified the positive relationship public unions had with the Cuomo Administration. The economic prosperity of 1984 fueled a revival of the old New Deal-type coalition that had elected Cuomo. But given the governor's campaign pledge to cut taxes, his aggressive assaults on public workers in 1983, growing public sentiment for a massive tax cut, and the increasingly aggressive posture of the Business Council, public labor should have entered the new year with more distrust than complacency. Large tax cuts, after all, could produce new deficits and divert the funds that held the coalition together.

Business Flexes Its Muscle

The Business Council used its political clout in framing public discourse on the tax issue. By now a well-lubricated lobbying machine, the Council released a study designed to show that between 1975 and 1980 New York's tax structure, that is, its high taxes, had reduced employment opportunities for the state's workers. The report argued that some 300,000 members of New York's labor force, including 100,000 professional and managerial workers, had left New York for opportunities in other states. The Business Council's "trickle down" message was clear: high taxes hurt the state's economy and drive its working people away. A growth economy, the Council argued, required a government with tax and spending policies that did not chase potential employers to other states.

The following year, another budget surplus, this one estimated at between $200 and $700 million, gave further impetus to the drive to cut the personal income tax. Finally, in early April 1984, Cuomo kept his campaign pledge to lower taxes when he signed legislation reducing the top personal income tax rate from 10% to 9% over a three-year period. Cuomo's chief fiscal officer, echoing the celebratory tone of the Business Council, hailed the $3 billion three-year tax cut as beneficial to all New Yorkers.

The combination of tax cuts and a revived economy boosted the Business Council's ideological assault against big government and what they characterized as high taxes. The Council's trickle-down economic theory caught the public's attention as the tax cuts of $3.2 billion were accompanied by an additional $4.4 billion in new revenue before the end of Cuomo's first term. State revenues increased drastically because the economy was growing rapidly, creating some 900,000 new jobs between 1982 and 1986. Under such booming economic conditions, the Business Council was sowing extremely fertile soil. And sow it did. Its public relations and political efforts convinced the ordinary citizens and politicians alike that tax cuts stimulated the economy and were crucial, not only to ongoing growth, but also to future economic expansion. Gloating over the business community's political success in 1985, council president Ray Schuler commented that "[i]t has taken us several years to perfect the mechanism."[27]

The Business Council could point to numerous legislative victories in 1985, running the gamut from the elimination of toxic torts reform to the implementation of tax cuts passed in 1984. But Council representatives still railed against big government and big spending. Recognizing the growing public acceptance of balanced-budget conservatism, business thought the political environment was becoming increasingly hospitable to their developing clout. They wanted more and knew how to get it. With Cuomo's popularity reaching unprecedented heights as the 1986 gubernatorial election approached, Council members covered their bets by making major contributions to the governor's re-election campaign. In fact, according to a *New York Times* report, between the time he beat Koch in the 1982 primary and October 27, 1986, just prior to the 1986 election, Cuomo raised $12 million dollars in campaign funds, with business interests among the largest and staunchest contributors.[28] The turning point came when Cuomo secured the Democratic nomination in 1982. From then on, campaign contributions from big business increased annually.[29] The governor happily described the magical moment when money began pouring into his campaign coffers by stating that his finance chairman for the 1982 race "didn't have enough room in his office to accommodate all the people who came rushing in to make contributions."[30]

Campaign finance laws in New York are similar to federal laws as they were prior to the 1974 reforms. In statewide elections, the maximum contribution is high; single contributors may give a candidate up to $65,000: $15,000 in the primary election and another $50,000 for the general election. Corporations may donate up to $5,000 per calendar year, but there are so many loopholes that they usually give much more. In one day, for instance, Drexel Burnham Lambert contributed $20,000 to Cuomo in four checks from affiliated corporations. This was not atypical.

Labor still remained the largest single contributor in Cuomo's 1986 reelection drive, accounting for twenty-five of the 134 contributions of $10,000 or more. But business groups collectively gave more. Real-estate developers and financial institutions combined accounted for thirty contributions of $10,000 or more. The list of major business contributors, in addition to Drexel Burnham Lambert, included Phillip Morris, NorStar Bank, and Morgan Stanley, to name just three. And while the governor could rightfully boast of the influx of unsolicited donations following his victory over Koch, the Cuomo Administration actively and aggressively pursued contributors, collecting about 50% of total contributions from people doing business with the state. In the words of one anonymous observer, "The Cuomos have raised [fundraising] to an art form."[31]

Cuomo won the 1986 election by a record-setting margin, garnering about two-thirds of the vote. His war chest of more than $13 million made his victory a certainty, as he far out-raised and out-spent his Republican opponent, Andrew O'Rourke. Indeed, just prior to the November election, O'Rourke had raised a total of $1.2 million, about half as much as Cuomo spent on radio and television advertising alone during the last ten weeks of the campaign. Having received about half his contributions from labor, financial institutions, and real-estate developers, including Republican Donald Trump, Cuomo finished his campaign with a campaign surplus of almost $4 million.

With the 1986 election behind and the governor safely re-elected, the Business Council took advantage of its growing political power. It launched a two-pronged offensive against big government and what it characterized as wasteful spending. The first leg of the campaign was to gain major new tax cuts. This, in and of itself, could reduce revenues sufficiently to threaten New York's traditional social services and contribute to the shrinking of the public sector. But that was not enough. Despite its rhetoric against "big government," the Business Council viewed some facets of the public sector as worthwhile. For example, it wanted the state to assume a more active role in economic development by providing direct financial subsidies and incentives to business and by cutting back on regulations. The business community's understanding of its power within the political environment of the late 1980s was on target. Despite Cuomo's early indebtedness to labor, by the time the 1987 legislative session ended, business had achieved the largest personal income tax cut in New York's history, a massive cut in corporate taxes, and major breakthroughs in the arena of economic development.

The 1987 tax battle was at the head of the Business Council's agenda, and the Council was in extraordinarily good shape. Its officials initiated an anti-tax campaign based on the claim that the 1984 tax cut had brought prosperity back to New York. The Council's political efforts were supported by federal tax reform in 1986 that removed a number of tax deductions, thereby thrusting many taxpayers into higher tax brackets. In effect, this made it likely that New York's taxpayers would pay more state taxes, unless, of course, the state restructured its tax laws. The additional state taxes—called "windfall taxes"—were estimated to range between $1 billion and $4 billion annually. Republican leaders in Albany had parroted the Business Council's call for massive tax cuts even before the 1986 elections, but when Cuomo pledged during his re-election campaign that he would not use the windfall for new programs, tax reform appeared certain. The remaining questions centered on the timing and type of reform.

The developing consensus in favor of lowering the state's personal income tax grew primarily out of arguments made by the Business Council as well as the real competition for business among the states. The Council buttressed its anti-tax position by pointing to the federal tax reform mentioned above. Besides, Council officials continued, taxes in New York were too high and negatively affected the state's competitive position. Over a period of twenty-eight years, New York, had lost 659,000 jobs, according to Council president Daniel Walsh, with many going to the low-tax South.[32] Again, the Council pointed to the 1984 tax cuts as the model for economic prosperity. Clearly, their argument concluded, another round of reductions would do the same. When skeptics suggested that the benefits of trickle-down tax cuts exclude large segments of the population, the Council added to its mantra a concern for the working poor. Walsh noted that tax reform was necessary to remove the working poor from the tax rolls.[33]

Although favoring tax reform, Cuomo approached the issue cautiously. Massive tax reductions, he feared, would create revenue shortfalls, throwing the state into a new fiscal crisis and forcing "hard decisions" that could fragment his electoral coalition. Urging caution, Cuomo took a wait-and-see attitude. Arguing that the uncertainty of the size of the federal windfall, which he had put at $1.7 billion but Republicans estimated as high as $2.5 billion, made any changes in the tax structure premature, Cuomo offered to put a giant, colored thermometer on the facade of the capitol building. The thermometer would illustrate the size of the windfall, or what Cuomo called "the sunny day fund," which would be returned to the state's taxpayers. Once a clear determination of the amount of excess taxes collected was made, then, and only then, Cuomo argued, the legislature should reduce state taxes.

The thermometer gimmick did not convince the Business Council or politicians hungry to put money back into the pockets of their voting constituents. A public flap developed when the new speaker of the assembly, Mel Miller, who later resigned in disgrace after being convicted of a felony fraud charge, which was later overturned, led a number of his Democratic colleagues in calling for massive new tax cuts. Recognizing the importance of a growth economy, Miller, upon taking office, noted that "New York has many needs. Three are at the top of my list. Number one is jobs, number two is more jobs, and number three is many more jobs."[34] The way to create jobs, according to Miller, who characterized himself as "one of the most progressive members of the Assembly," was a reliance on the trickle-down theories of Reaganomics. As at least one lobbyist noted, Miller's focus on creating jobs when the already low unemployment rate (4.9%) was dropping suggested that he was out of touch with social issues.[35] Miller's concern with economic growth over social issues illuminated the growing importance of balanced-budget conservatism in New York. It demonstrated that even one of the most progressive members of the legislature would reverse long-standing positions to support business' needs for low taxes over the need to expand social welfare programs.

Miller's challenge, growing public support for a tax break, competition among the states for business investment, and a report by Republican comptroller Ed Regan noting that surplus revenues for 1987 were larger than Cuomo anticipated, led Cuomo to reverse his position on the tax cut. Unwilling to fight a battle that he knew he would not win, Cuomo reluctantly backed tax reform to the tune of $1.7 billion more than the projected windfall. But even this was not enough. The legislature wanted more, and they got it. Within weeks Cuomo signed the largest personal income tax cut in the state's history, a reduction of $4.5 billion. Cuomo claimed to sign the legislation hesitantly. The cut was too large, he said, but legislative support was overwhelming.

Tax Reform Comes to New York

The 1987 tax cut was the culmination of a series of reductions in the personal income tax initiated by Hugh Carey and continued by Cuomo. The cuts reduced the top rate from 15% in 1974 to 7.5% after the five-year phase-in period of the 1987 tax reform. The 1987 reform accelerated a trend toward regressivity in New York's tax structure. At one time, New York's personal income tax structure had twelve brackets, but the 1987 reform reduced it to four. The law set the top income bracket at $26,000, so a family with that modest income would pay the same tax rate as one with an income of $26 million, or $26 billion, for that matter. According to estimates by the Coalition on Economic Priorities (CEP), a labor thinktank established by the New York State AFL-CIO, three-quarters of the tax cut would go to the richest fifth of the state's population. And CEP's projections were not out of line. By the end of 1991, according to one study, the wealthiest 5% of New York's population paid $1 billion less in personal income taxes.[36] Other studies claimed that the wealthiest New Yorkers benefitted to the tune of $16 billion.[37]

The implications of the 1987 tax reform began to surface just days after Cuomo signed the legislation. Five days after signing the new tax bill, Cuomo proposed a series of new regressive taxes to fill a projected revenue gap of $1 billion. He attributed the revenue shortfall to the size of the tax cut and proposed new taxes and fees on a large number of items, running the gamut from beer and cigarettes to new fees on drivers' licenses. Failure to impose these new regressive taxes, Cuomo noted, would lead to cutbacks in public services.

Having secured generous breaks in the personal income tax, the legislature now pointed its tax axe at the corporate sector and passed a corporate tax bill with a Christmas tree of gifts for the state's largest companies. Claiming that high business taxes made New York uncompetitive, corporate officials had sought lower corporate and business taxes for years. Despite endless studies showing that state and local taxes have little impact on investment decisions, that it is like "pushing on a string," business leaders play on the fear of corporate flight to withhold millions from public coffers.[38]

Since 1978, New York's corporate taxes have dropped by almost half. During the 1978-1979 fiscal year, corporations paid 9.1% of all state tax revenues, but a decade later, following the 1987 Business Tax Reform and Rate Reduction Act (BTR & RRA), corporate tax collections plummeted to 5.5%, despite higher levels of corporate profitability.[39] Corporate tax reform reduced corporate income taxes from 10% to 9%, significantly less than California's 12.6% and below neighboring Connecticut's 9.6%; provided for the deduction of long-term debt prior to applying the Business Capital Alternative Tax rate; abolished the Officer's Salary Alternative tax; and eliminated the Interest Add-Back provision. Despite the earlier talk of revenue shortfalls and the call for new regressive taxes, Cuomo responded to the pressures of balanced-budget conservatism and signed the bill into law. Observers estimated that corporate tax cuts would return some $150 million of the windfall back into corporate coffers. In the words of then Business Council president Raymond Schuler, New York's corporate tax reform was "the best set of tax incentives for job retention, expansion, and investment in the country." After all, as Schuler surely knew, it would save the state's corporations several hundred million dollars over the next four years.

Just in case corporate tax cuts were insufficient, the legislature also passed a $160 million economic development package that included a Strategic Resurgence Fund designed to retain and attract new business into the state. A little more than a week later Cuomo, acting under legislation passed the year before, identified the first ten of up to forty communities to receive the designation of Economic Development Zones (EDZ). EDZ incentives included a 25% state tax credit against wages, decreasing to 5% over a five-year period; a 3% savings in utility bills for certified business customers; an investment tax credit up to 10%; and a credit or refund of the 4% state sales tax. Localities provided additional tax incentives, and New York City business received extra utility savings. The New York State Power Authority would compensate utilities with extra hydro-power. The establishment of Economic Development Zones came on the heels of legislation consolidating the state's economic development agencies—the Urban Development Agency, the Commerce Department, and the Job Development Authority—into a new super-agency, the Department of Economic Development. The combination of reduced tax obligations, a large package of direct subsidies, and a more focused and coordinated effort to promote the state's commercial interests convinced the Business Council that the state's Democratic party was friendly to business after all. Business Council president Ray Schuler talked of a new pro-business partnership in New York and expressed his gratitude by sending roses to Mel Miller. Business' old nemesis, the Democratic-controlled assembly, had joined the Business Council's bandwagon.

Shrinking the Public Sector: Taxes and Economic Development

Supporters of tax reform held that tax cuts and more aggressive economic development efforts would attract new business to the state, keep current ventures from moving, and provide a general stimulus to the economy. The pundits were wrong. The tax cuts, the backbone of Cuomo's economic development program, contributed to a series of unending budget deficits that galvanized the dismantling of large segments of the state's public sector. This also tended to aggravate the recession by reducing public spending and throwing thousands of public-sector workers into the streets.

The state's other economic development programs did little to help. In fact, they too may have worsened the fiscal crunch by giving massive tax breaks and other expensive goodies to business without reversing the exodus of jobs out of New York. Additionally, key economic development programs took business ventures off the local tax rolls and increased tax burdens on local governments, contributing further to the growth of anti-statist political sentiment. In short, examination of the tax cuts and the state's economic development efforts suggests that the combination of huge personal and corporate tax cuts and aggressive pro-business economic development programs failed to resolve the state's economic plight while fueling the anti-statist attitude that calls for further attacks on the public sector. In New York, as elsewhere, balanced-budget conservatism was giving ideological cover to a laissez-faire public policy, while simultaneously justifying more direct government support for business.

Before the first phase of the income-tax cut was a year old, Cuomo's warnings about budgetary shortfalls began to look real. The October 1987 stock market plunge of 508 points, the largest drop in history, signaled the end of what *Business Week* called the "Casino Society." The crash cost the state millions in tax revenue, leaving Cuomo to search for new ways to raise revenues and stimulate the economy. In January 1988, he announced a new program that would make available a $100 million fund for loans to small businesses. After all, Cuomo concluded, small businesses were responsible for about one-quarter of the state's 1.2 million new jobs since 1983. The fact that the funding came from public-employee pensions rather than new state revenues was overlooked by many during these precarious times.

The state's situation worsened in April 1988, when tax revenues dropped by $500 million. Within weeks, Cuomo estimated that the shortfall had dropped to about $900 million. But several years of good times provided a cushion for New Yorkers to escape the fiscal bullet, at least temporarily. In July the state's political leaders reached agreement on closing the deficit by further manipulations of existing funds. The fiscal manipulations saved the day, but they proved to be a stay of execution rather than a long-term solution to the state's fiscal problems. Just weeks after resolving the shortfall, a new deficit of $133 million surfaced. Again, the latest shortfall was attributed to declining tax revenues. In fact, by now the problem was becoming so severe that Budget Director Dale Forsythe publicly stated that unless the next phase of the income tax cuts was stopped, New York would face massive fiscal problems in 1989. By fall of 1988 the budget director projected a budget deficit of $2 billion for the following year. The state attempted to recover $100 million by imposing a hiring freeze and cutting 2,500 jobs through attrition. Although layoffs were again avoided, it became clear that further deficits would lead to massive firings. With a mounting deficit and the next phase of the tax cut about to kick in, the fiscal prognosis for 1989 was grim.

Forsythe's dire budgetary predictions galvanized public workers and community organizations into action. Under threats of cutting public jobs and services, closing college campuses, and raiding public workers' pension funds, a collection of labor, educational, community, religious, and government organizations, under the umbrella of the New York State AFL-CIO, formed the New York State Coalition on Economic Priorities (CEP). CEP represented a diverse coalition aimed at maintaining New York's public sector. "We intend to work together as family to insure this state has an adequate, fair and equitable tax base," said Ed Cleary, CEP chair and president of the New York State AFL-CIO.[40] The coalition's immediate goal was to stop the final two phases of the income tax cut, reductions that would reduce revenues by about $1.9 billion, putting most of it into the pockets of the wealthiest New Yorkers.

CEP's appearance on New York's political scene triggered responses from business supporters. Governor Cuomo, concerned with the state's rating in the bond market, spoke of the need to maintain credibility by imposing a "new discipline" on spending cuts. Reneging on promises to the business community, Cuomo said, would undermine government's political credibility with business. James Houghton, chair of the Business Council, picked up on the credibility issue and summarized business' position in a letter to the editor of *The New York Times* in which he argued that abandonment of the next stages of the tax cuts would hurt New York's credibility and its competitiveness. The 1987 tax cut, Houghton concluded, "rightly has been hailed as the cornerstone of New York State's strategy for economic growth."[41] With bond-rating firms breathing down the state's back and business interests impatiently waiting to turn political promises into profits, Cuomo announced his opposition to delaying the next phase of the income tax cut for 1989, even though the state's budget division projected large budgetary deficits through 1992.

Cuomo's refusal to discuss delay of the tax cut for 1989 may have pleased the business community, but it exacerbated the state's fiscal problems. Facing a growing deficit, he scrambled to find ways to balance the budget. He and the state's Republican comptroller once again turned to public-employee pensions as a way out of the budget mess. In an attack on public pensions hailed by experts as a "dangerous precedent," the state saved approximately $325 million by reducing contributions into the pension funds. Public-sector unions groused over the attack, but took no direct actions against the program, for they too had an interest in restoring the state's fiscal rating and preserving public-sector jobs.

In mid-April 1989, Cuomo and legislative leaders and the governor approved a new state budget. The budget resolved a potential deficit of about $2.8 billion by including huge spending cuts and about $1 billion in new taxes and fees. The taxes were mostly regressive, covering, among other items, alcohol and tobacco products and fees on traffic tickets. The new taxes provided the financial foundation to maintain the next phase of the income tax cuts. Additionally, Cuomo attempted to increase the burden for financing social programs on local governments. More and more, New York State tax policy was becoming a mirror of federal policy, prompting one state assembly official to observe that "The Governor wanted to paint himself as a conservative liberal, but instead he was painted as Reagan."

New York's journey into Reaganomics was not the misguided effort of naive liberals or of politically corrupt politicians. It reflected the realities of the late twentieth-century U.S. political economy, characterized by economic competition among the states and by the ability of financial institutions to pressure policy makers to tighten their fiscal belts. The latter became crystal clear less than two weeks after the state adopted its new budget. Standard and Poor, citing the state's resolution to the "enormous short-term fiscal problems it faced in the last two years," gave New York's short-term bonds its highest credit rating. Moody's followed suit. The change in the short-term bond rating was especially welcome, since short-term borrowing had increased annually, were following the 1987 tax cuts, and the new rating would lower interest rates. The savings for 1989 was projected to run into the millions, as New York was scheduled to sell $3.9 billion in one-year notes.

The bond firms' optimism proved premature. Before the 1989-90 fiscal year was up, another deficit emerged, this one approaching a billion dollars. The size of the revenue shortfall prompted Cuomo to change his position on the tax cut. Like it or not, Cuomo had to resist further revenue losses, even if it meant fighting with fiscal conservatives over implementation of the next phase of the tax cut. But the tax cut alone was not responsible for the fiscal crisis. In 1989, New York's Industrial Development Authority (IDA) attempted to promote the state's economy by issuing about $1.5 billion in tax-exempt bonds. This effort to promote business, according to an estimate by the state comptroller, had the unintended effect of reducing revenues by $500 million for the year.[42] IDA expenditures tend to shift local taxes to existing homeowners and businesses and frequently fail to create new jobs. In fact, in some instances in the retail-trade sector IDA spending actually has reduced the number of jobs.[43] The vast amounts spent on IDAs and other economic development programs provide a stark contrast to the fiscal squeeze on the public sector. The contrast between the two illuminates the ascendancy of balanced-budget conservatism as a public philosophy.

Cuomo's budget proposal for the 1990-91 fiscal year recommended more than $800 million in new taxes and fees and proposed saving $400 million by suspending the last phase of the income tax cut. But Standard and Poor found this unacceptable. The bond-rating firm announced that the proposed budget was insufficiently austere to justify New York's current bond rating. And Standard and Poor were on the mark. The state was in such dire fiscal straits that it was unable to meet its payroll obligations without additional borrowing. In early March, it borrowed $665 million just to meet expenses.

The other fiscal shoe fell three weeks later when Standard and Poor dropped New York's credit rating two notches to level A, the lowest in state history. New York now had the third-lowest credit rating in the nation. To make matters worse, both Standard and Poor and Moody's dropped the bond ratings on the short-term notes the state uses to raise cash for current expenses, and this just as New York prepared to sell $775 million in short-term notes. Higher interest rates would cost taxpayers tens of millions on this transaction alone.

Plummeting credit ratings strengthened the political hand of the state's business community. With a projected deficit of $4 billion, the annual partisan quarrel over the proportion of the deficit to be filled by cuts or new taxes and fees took new meaning. After Cuomo and legislative leaders reached agreement on extending the sales tax to services such as management consulting and computer programming, business interests pressured legislative officials, particularly Senate Majority Leader Ralph Marino, to renege on the agreement. The budget finally agreed upon some seven weeks after the April 1 deadline contained another $1.8 billion in new regressive taxes and fees and $1.4 billion in one-shot revenues to meet the estimated deficit of $4 billion.

The numbers never added up. In November, shortly after election day—an election in which Cuomo received a dismal 53% of the vote in a race that could have signaled the death of the statewide Republican Party—Cuomo bowed to anti-tax business interests and opened the way for new attacks on the public sector. These attacks are comprehensible when viewed within their political context. First, his narrow electoral victory against a weak Republican and a strong conservative suggested that people were tired of the endless rounds of regressive new state taxes. Also, by 1990 the Business Council had become one of the most, if not the most, influential players on New York's political scene. Business controlled the financial and structural resources, including jobs; they were united as in the days of the robber barons; the new anti-tax public ideology and a severe recession provided a favorable ideological climate; and within months after the election the political strength of the business community increased with the formation of CHANGE-NY, a pro-business anti-tax think tank.

Founded by two former gubernatorial candidates, Republican Lehrman, the Rite Aid mogul, and Conservative Herb London of New York University, along with a former state Republican head, Evan G. Galbraith, a director at Morgan Stanley, CHANGE-NY sounded very much like New Jersey's HANJ and California's Jarvis-Gann operation. But while HANJ and Jarvis-Gann were basically lower-middle-class or petty bourgeois populist movements, CHANGE-NY had a different class base; its members included New York's highest-paid executives from the state's largest firms.[44] The newly created political arm of the state's corporate sector sought to emulate the tactics of the Business Round-Table on the specific issue of taxation. Following the trajectory of

Jarvis-Gann and HANJ, CHANGE-NY intensified the ideological on-slaught against the public sector and further centralized business' political efforts in the state. Characterizing itself as a grassroots organi-zation that supported more "pro-growth tax cuts," CHANGE-NY sought term limitations on elected officials, the privatization of public services, and tuition vouchers to subsidize families who choose, at taxpayer's expense, to send their children to private rather than public schools.

The new anti-tax organization became a political force in New York almost overnight. CHANGE-NY initiated its program with a direct-mail campaign criticizing state spending and calling for additional cutbacks in the public sector. Two months after its formation, the anti-tax organi-zation took a major step toward increasing its public credibility by hiring a high-powered public personality, Lawrence A. Kudlow, to serve as a co-founder. Kudlow, chief economist and senior managing director at Bear, Stearns & Co., brought with him a reputation as a radio and television commentator on economic issues. He even wrote an occa-sional column for *The Wall Street Journal*.

But Kudlow delivered more than skill and a recognizable name to CHANGE-NY. His association with Bear, Stearns connected him, how-ever loosely, to the Cuomo Administration. For, as we shall see below, officials from Bear, Stearns participated in the Friends of Mario Cuomo fundraising events, and company officials contributed thousands to Cuomo's campaigns. It is also worth observing that Galbraith, one of the co-founders of CHANGE-NY, serves as a director at Morgan Stanley & Company, a firm whose officials played important roles in Cuomo's fundraising events and also gave considerable amounts to his electoral efforts.

Business interests eventually emerged as the largest contributors to Cuomo's campaign. The Friends of Mario Cuomo, the fundraising arm of the Cuomo campaign, included representatives from the largest and most influential corporations and financial institutions in the state and the United States. (See Appendix) By 1989, financial, legal, and real-estate interests had contributed 25% of Cuomo's campaign contri-butions (since 1982). Employee organizations, including labor unions and professional organizations, gave only 8%. Individuals associated with business and individuals on state contracts gave more. Ninety percent of the engineering firms doing business with the New York State Thruway or the Department of Transportation contributed to Cuomo's campaign between 1982 and 1987.[45] The Rich Greene Adver-tising Agency, for example, which has a $30 million contract for the "I Love New York" campaign, gave a total of $42,000. Bear, Stearns & Co. contributed $235,000, and the Republican law firm of Rogers and Wells gave $64,200 over the years.

The money going to Cuomo's coffers is only part of the story of the re-emergence of business's political power in New York. For instance, in 1990 and 1991, commercial bankers spent $1.8 million trying to influence Albany's policy makers, according to a joint report by New York State Common Cause and New York Public Interest Research Group. Tobacco interests invested another $1.7 million, and real-estate interests spent nearly another million. This does *not* mean that business interests crudely purchased influence. Teacher unions and public-employee organizations also spent large amounts.[46] The point, however, is that campaign contributions are usually not made for altruistic reasons. As the New York State Commission on Government Integrity observed, "...the perception persists among lobbyists that by contributing, they may curry favor and good will—or, at the very least, will avoid the perceived risk associated with not giving."[47]

Business's assertion of its political power restricted Cuomo's political options, but he drew on the experience of his New Jersey colleague, Governor Florio. As noted in Chapter Four above, Florio sought to overcome revenue shortfalls by instituting a more progressive income tax system. Unlike Cuomo, he directly challenged the ideology of balanced-budget conservatism. But public reaction to Florio's tax program was sufficiently hostile to secure victories in both houses of the Legislature for tax-cutting Republicans, thus exacerbating the crisis and rendering Florio powerless to stop radical conservative attacks on state government. As the New Jersey fiscal crunch worsened, the anti-tax Right tightened its grip on the political agenda, and the prospects for Florio's re-election appeared grim, to say the least. By side-stepping direct confrontation with the Business Council, Cuomo may have avoided duplicating the Jersey scenario, thereby keeping a bad situation from getting worse. The point, however, is that Cuomo understood the significance of the ideology of balanced-budget conservatism and recognized the ability of business interests to define the political agenda and put progressives on the defensive.

The ideology of balanced-budget conservatism and the growing power of business were not all Cuomo had to confront. Moody's again cautioned against more borrowing and threatened to drive up the cost of borrowing by lowering the state's bond ratings. Within this context it is not surprising that Cuomo, interpreting the election results to mean "no taxes," announced shortly after his successful 1990 re-election campaign that he would fill the growing deficit—now estimated at $1 billion and rising for the current fiscal year which still had almost six months to go—with major new cuts.

Once again Cuomo's liberalism was tempered by the strength of balanced-budget conservatism and the organized power of the corporate and financial communities. He had no place else to go. As Cuomo noted in an interview, he shared the values of labor and did not want to cut human services: "I want what they want," he said. But he cautioned, "I can't do what I want to do."[48] In short, New York's governor knew his options were limited. Indeed, he said it best at a meeting with leaders of the United University Professions. Referring to the gigantic cuts imposed on the State University of New York, Cuomo noted that he did not want to impose cuts because a strong public university is fundamental to economic growth and prosperity. But, he lamented, "I had to."[49]

Even though the deficits were driven by the 1987 tax cuts, cuts that gave disproportionate breaks to the wealthy, the prospects for tax reform during the 1991 legislative session appeared remote. Instead of seeking new revenues, Cuomo continued to buy into the balanced-budget conservative approach of reducing public services. And Cuomo's post-election attack on public-sector workers made his 1982 Workforce Reduction Plan look like child's play. In 1991, for the first time in state history, the state would furlough public employees without pay. The cost-cutting plan would eliminate 18,000 jobs over a seventeen-month period, lay off 17,000 workers during the same period, and fire 2,000 by the end of the ongoing fiscal year. Additionally, Medicaid payments would drop, and state assistance to hospitals would decline by $55 million. Aid to school districts would fall by 2.5%, and revenue sharing to local governments would plummet by 10%. After years of tax breaks for the wealthy, plummeting revenues were used to justify major new attacks on the public sector.

Cuomo's belt-tightening recommendations pleased the Business Council. But, as usual, it was not enough. With contract negotiations about to open for 200,000 state employees, the Council called for a freeze on public workers' wages for a two-year period, something the governor viewed as a sound idea. In addition to saving the state $800 million, the wage freeze would also preserve some 25,000 public jobs, so the Council that argued.[49] The business organization also launched an offensive against the benefits unionized state employees received compared to workers in the private sector. Simply put, the ostensible message was that unionized public workers were too costly during these hard times. More subtly, however, the Council was attacking the right of the public sector to pursue collective bargaining. In fact, the report concluded, the cost of benefits for non-unionized state employees approximated costs in the private sector, at least in some important areas. The implications were becoming crystal clear: the Business Council was launching a new offensive to break public-sector unions in New York State.

The budget battle for the 1991-92 fiscal year was crucial to public-sector unions. Cuomo had been forced to move to the Right, having succumbed to the pressures of public opinion and the business community; the Democratic-controlled Assembly also followed suit, sounding very much like the Republican-dominated Senate. However reluctantly, the Democrats had opted for what they hoped would bring growth over ideology. All sides accepted the business community's political agenda, an agenda becoming increasingly hostile to organized labor in the public sector. With their very survival at stake, public unions had to reassert their political punch in an increasingly hostile political environment. Under ordinary conditions the battle would not be easy: a fragmented public-sector labor movement, characterized by a tradition of internal suspicion and distrust, faced a unified and increasingly powerful business sector in desperate battle. And, as the examples of California and neighboring New Jersey demonstrated, these were not ordinary times. Balanced-budget conservatism had taken hold, delimiting the kinds of options open to even the most liberal government.

The 1991-1992 state budget finally agreed to in July 1991 contained huge cuts and layoffs—in the words of CSEA's McDermott, "The state isn't just looking at a little belt tightening. They're wiping out whole titles."[51] The budget raised personal income taxes for those with gross incomes above $150,000. But this tax hike was not a "tax-the-rich" victory. It was a technical modification rather than a restructuring of the personal income taxes, and was projected to raise about $100 million in revenue. As a source of new revenue, it helped, but was far from sufficient.[52] By the middle of the fiscal year, plummeting revenues produced another deficit, reaching $875 million by Thanksgiving. Worse yet, there was still no light at the end of the tunnel. The budget for the next fiscal year looked just as grim, as experts predicted a shortfall of another $3.6 billion for the 1992-1993 fiscal year.

Cuomo, still considered a potential presidential candidate, worked with the Business Council to seek a long-term solution to the deficits. He wanted a fifteen-month budget that would save money by restructuring state spending and the state's labor force. But Republican leaders, following President Bush's request "not to make Cuomo look good," refused to cooperate and scuttled Cuomo's cost-cutting plans. As the new year approached, the 1991-92 deficit remained in place, massive new deficits loomed for the coming year, and New York still teetered on the edge of financial disaster without a fiscal plan. Labor's cry for tax equity had fallen on deaf ears. By now Cuomo knew that Florio's soak-the-rich approach had failed, and he certainly wished to avoid a similarly divisive struggle. Consequently, there was no dialogue on restructuring the corporate or personal income tax systems. The consensus viewed more cuts and less spending as the solution, but there was no agreement on what and where to cut. Balanced-budget conservatism led to a political stalemate.

The nation's largest financial institutions refused to tolerate continued inaction and uncertainty. So they took action. In early January 1992, Moody's downgraded all state bonds that were backed by annual legislative appropriations, citing the state's failure to assert effective budgetary control. This, the second downgrading in two years, left the targeted bonds just two steps above junk-bond ratings. Despite years of budget cuts, by 1992 the state's fiscal situation was worsening, and now the cost of borrowing had increased.

The worst was yet to come. A week after Moody's fiscal assault, Standard and Poor stepped in. The financial agency took sweeping action against a broad range of New York's bonds, including the state's strongest and most sound. The broad nature of Standard and Poor's downgrading drive interest rates up and undercut the credit worthiness of bonds sold by school districts, driving school and other local taxes further up. Again, representatives of the financial institution blamed New York's political leaders for failing to resolve the crisis and inflaming Wall Street's loss of confidence in the state.[53]

Standard and Poor's verbal assaults on New York's political leaders echoed the sentiments of the Business Council's political campaign against the public sector. In a widely distributed document entitled "Just Do It," the Council chastised politicians "who talk but won't do," and called for an immediate budget freeze of salaries, taxes, hiring, in fact, "of everything that can be frozen." The Council report also proposed a number of long-term structural reforms, such as downsizing state and local governments, merging agencies, and abolishing or reforming civil service to allow for the privatization of as many government services as possible.

The ascendancy of balanced-budget conservatism as the new public philosophy, fueled by the Business Council's political efforts and the fiscal squeeze by Moody's and Standard and Poor, was not lost on New York's politicians. Unlike the experience of previous years, the 1992-1993 budget passed close to the deadline of April 1, 1992, coming in less than a day late. But, as one newspaper headline characterized it, in some quarters the reaction to the budget was one of anguish—anguish because it was a budget of cost containment. It slashed state services, eliminating 5,000 more jobs, thereby cutting the total workforce by almost 14% in a two-year period; on an experimental basis, it required welfare and Medicaid recipients to carry identification cards and subjected them to mandatory fingerprinting. Overworked public servants would now police the poor more directly, as the new rule required them to treat clients bureaucratically and with suspicion, no matter what their specific needs and personalities.[54] The budget also cut assistance to New York City by $3.6 million and raised taxes on hospitals and nursing homes. It again delayed the final phase of the income tax cut, but within the halls of the capitol during this election year, there was no real debate or discussion of the need to restructure the state's tax system. Labor's fair tax agenda dialogue, at least to this point, had failed.

Still, all this was not enough for CHANGE-NY. The anti-tax organization opposed the new budget because it did not go far enough in slashing programs and restructuring state government. CHANGE-NY wanted deeper cuts and the implementation of the next phase of the income tax cuts. Consequently, the political group went after politicians who supported the budget deal, publishing a list of targeted officials, mostly Republican senators who had "betrayed" their ultra-conservative cause by supporting the new budget. Among those targeted was Senate Majority Leader Ralph Marino, a conservative Republican, who now found himself fighting attacks from the Right political flank, as CHANGE-NY promised to unseat him in his re-election bid.

Angered by CHANGE-NY's vicious attacks, Marino chronicled the organization's willingness to further its anti-statist agenda by bringing New York to a grinding halt. The Senate leader mentioned a conversation with, in his words, "one of the millionaires of CHANGE-NY" who, on the eve of reaching a budget agreement, had advised him against reaching an agreement. "You have to bring the state to its knees," the CHANGE-NYer told Marino. The Senator replied that this would close the schools and create chaos, to which the CHANGE-NY leader responded, "So what?"[55]

The strategy to discredit the state as much as possible was designed to make it appear that the public sector and elected officials are inept and incompetent. More public failures and inefficiencies would make people angrier, thereby accelerating the dismantling of the public apparatus and increasing the likelihood of more privatization. The attacks on Marino and others, however, did not immediately realize this goal. Instead, they revealed a schism in business's ranks. The far-Right extremists of CHANGE-NY were not satisfied with the speed and degree of attacks on the public sector. Now, they were turning on elected officials who took pro-Business Council positions. Perhaps this will push the Council further to the Right, or it may lead to the discrediting of CHANGE-NY. Although it is too early to tell, Marino's attacks on CHANGE-NY indicate serious disagreements within the business community.

The appearance of schisms, however nascent, in the business community provides an opportunity for organized labor to wage a successful political offensive against the business juggernaut's political power. The following chapter chronicles public labor's efforts to resist balanced-budget conservatism, its attempts to build a unified front, the problems and obstacles working against this, and labor's prospects for the future.

Appendix

Friends of Mario Cuomo Dinner Committee 1988

Bear, Sterns & Co
Brown and Wood
Citibank
Communications Workers of America
Debevoise and Plimpton
Dillon Reed and Company
Drexel Burnham Lambert
First Boston Corporation
Fleishman Management Company
Goldman Sachs and Company
Hawkins, Delafield & Wood
Lazard, Freres and Company
LeBoeuf, Lamb, Leiby and MacRae
Manuel Elkin Co.
Merrill Lynch and Company
Metropolitan Life Insurance Company
Morgan Stanley and Company
Mudge, Rose, Gurthrie, Alexander and Ferdon
Paine Webber
Paul Weiss Rifkind Wharton and Garrison
Peat Marwick Mitchell and Company
Smith Barney Harris Upham and Co., Inc.
The International Longshoreman's Association
The Mack Company
The Mendik Company
The Savings Banks Association of New York State

Chapter Eight

UNIONS STRIKE BACK

When labor really mobilizes its forces, neither the Business
Council nor anybody else can stand in its way.

Frank Barbaro, NYS Assembly Labor Committee chair

Since the emergence of balanced-budget conservatism as the new
public philosophy more than a decade ago, opportunities to attack labor
unions have increased dramatically. Scholars may debate the exact date
of the turning point in capital's latest offensive against labor, but few
deny the current reality: organized labor took some serious hits in the
1980s.[1] In both the private and public sectors, union membership has
plummeted; labor law makes organizing difficult; the National Labor
Relations Board moves at a snail's pace and is more likely to undercut
than uphold the sanctity of collective bargaining. Many states place
restrictions on the right of public workers to organize, and some even
prohibit it; and corporations, often with a wink and nod from national
and state elected leaders, wage the most virulent anti-labor campaigns
imaginable, sometimes in violation of the law.

Despite the successful attacks on labor over the past decade or
more, some observers still are optimistic about labor's power and future
prospects. Frank Barbaro, for instance, chair of the New York State
Assembly's Labor Committee, applauded labor's experience in 1990,
when public and private unions collectively marshalled their forces to
win several important victories. As discussed in Chapter Seven above,
in 1989 labor lost its battle to delay the final scheduled phase of the
income tax cut. But the following year, unions succeeded in delaying
the cut and also won an increase in both the minimum wage and workers
compensation benefits, two issues on the top of its political agenda.
Labor's success on these issues led others to join Barbaro in hailing
unions' political clout. Dean Ronald Seeber of the New York State School
of Industrial and Labor Relations at Cornell University, for instance,
noted that "New York labor's political machinery seems to be a model
in a lot of ways."[2]

Barbaro's and Seeber's optimistic view of labor's political power is
somewhat exaggerated. Despite the important victories they point to,
public labor in New York, as elsewhere, took a beating during the
budget battles of the late 1980s and early 1990s, and the state's private-

sector unions were teetering from massive plant closings and ongoing corporate flight.[3] Yet Barbaro's and Seeber's observations are not totally ungrounded. In 1990, after all, organized labor could point to these two important victories, victories extracted through collective action that ran against the grain of balanced-budget conservatism.

But, as numerous studies have chronicled, cooperation among organized labor tends to be the exception rather than the rule. All too often, organized labor fails to act as part of a larger collective movement. Instead, unions frequently pursue their immediate narrow competing interests,[4] fall victim to ethnic, gender, racial, and skill differentials,[5] and fail to develop coalitions with community groups and the clients they serve.[6] As we shall see, labor's inability to meet the centralized power of business with unified collective action of its own undercuts its political potential and plays into the hands of capital.

Never was organized labor's need to act collectively more apparent than during the critical budget battle of New York's 1991-92 fiscal year. By January 1991, business had tightened its grip on the state's political agenda. Business, in fact, was in command. The business community—always aware of its class interests but sometimes bogged down in intra-class struggle—was now politically unified, highly financed, and strategically positioned.[7] The merger of competing business groups in 1981 had helped organize the state's business interests under the umbrella of the Business Council, and its think tank, the Public Policy Institute, kept the general public informed of the issues dear to business' heart and pocketbooks. The Council's prize political victories—the corporate and personal income tax reductions of 1987— contributed significantly to growing budget deficits, deficits used to justify shrinking the public sector.

Public-sector unions responded to business' growing political cohesiveness by trying to centralize and coordinate their own efforts. Recognizing the importance of collective efforts and the need to work as part of a larger political movement, public unions intensified their attempts to end internecine quarreling and turf battles. They sought to confront the business juggernaut with a united political front of their own, one capable of projecting labor's interests as the general interest of all New Yorkers. For union leaders know that political debate in a democracy is always ideological, and their problem was to show the "truth" of their position to policy makers and the public. This, they also knew, is best done through collective action. But the basis for labors' solidarity was shallow and sometimes self-serving, and the unions failed to build real solidarity. Thus they never realized their potential to mobilize as part of a larger class movement. Although somewhat more united than previously, organized labor in New York remains relatively fragmented, politically weak, and divorced from many of its potential political and class allies outside organized labor. This chapter analyzes labor's response to business' political efforts, the steps unions took to unify and become a movement, and the obstacles preventing this.

Prelude to Solidarity

By Fall 1990, public labor's political agenda was becoming crystal clear. Public workers wanted job security. After experiencing years of cutbacks in the public sector, rank-and-file workers were looking to their elected leaders to reverse this trend. Public employees also began to grumble loudly over the political endorsements their unions had given Cuomo and were becoming increasingly vociferous in their criticisms. With contracts of state workers scheduled to expire in spring of 1991, both leaders and rank-and-file members were becoming increasingly anxious abut their future prospects. Public-sector leaders knew that they must take drastic steps to reverse the attacks against their members, and they increasingly saw the need for tax reform and the formation of a broad-based political coalition for reform as the solution to the state's fiscal problems. Leaders of public-sector unions knew that without tax reform, the fiscal crunch would worsen and continue to threaten their members' jobs. And that is exactly what happened.

Labor's problems became even more acute following the 1990 election. For shortly after winning his second re-election attempt, Cuomo, with New Jersey's "tax-the-rich" debacle unfolding across the Hudson, made it clear that he could not ignore the Business Council's agenda. With the state facing a $1 billion shortfall for the last third of the 1990-91 fiscal year, Cuomo once again took swift action against public-sector workers. Saying he regretted it but "there's not a whole lot I can do about it,"[8] Cuomo announced 2,000 layoffs and the abolition of an additional 4,000 jobs by attrition during the fiscal year. He also called for the elimination of another 18,000 jobs during the next fiscal year.

Cuomo's proposed budget for 1991 sought to slash spending by $4.5 billion, deeply cutting into such crucial programs as health inspections of eateries, AIDS testing, a wide gamut of senior citizen programs, drug abuse and crime prevention programs, public education, job training, snow plowing of state roads, and a broad range of other human and social services. In fact, the cuts in human and social services were so severe over the years that the Community AIDS Association testified before the state legislature in 1992 that:

> if many of the Governor's budget cuts are enacted in health
> and human services programs, we will be guaranteeing, as
> a matter of state policy, more hunger, homelessness, family

breakups, untreated illnesses, unnecessary deaths, and widespread despair.[9]

Although they struck at the heart of New York's underdeveloped and debilitated welfare state, Cuomo's proposed cuts made barely a dent in the growing deficit. So he asked for more. This time, Cuomo wanted give-backs from public-sector unions. His aides from the Office of Employee Relations—the agency charged with negotiating with the state's public-sector unions—notified each of the statewide unions that the governor wanted to open negotiations concerning employee furloughs, in other words, unpaid leaves. But, in this case anyway, Cuomo's approach to negotiations would have made General Electric's old union-busting Lemeuel Boulware proud. Like Boulware used to do at GE, Cuomo made a single offer; his first was his last. The unions' quickly recognized that his "Boulwaristic" take-it-or-leave-it approach sought their consent to a state-imposed lock-out, and they refused to yield. After failing to get labor's acquiescence, Cuomo publicly announced that he would furlough state workers for five days without pay. Always the humanitarian, he characterized the furloughs as the humane way of responding to the fiscal crisis, for in the long run, he noted, the furloughs would save jobs.

Cuomo's post-election attack on public workers came on the heels of years of cuts that had drastically reduced services and forced most public workers to take larger case loads, or, as the governor said, echoing the mantra of balanced-budget conservatism, to do "more with less." Doing more with less, however, is just a transparent way of describing speed-ups. And speed-ups affected virtually every facet of the public workforce. By December 1990, for instance, despite the fact that rising unemployment is statistically accompanied by higher crime rates, and with the state's overcrowded prisons bursting at the seams, 300 prison guards were fired for budgetary reasons, leaving the remaining force charged with supervising a constantly growing prison population. Council 82 President Joe Puma expressed concern for the safety of the remaining officers. "It's their lives that are at stake," he commented. Rumors of slow-downs and even a strike abounded as angry security officers talked about the re-emergence of many of the conditions that had contributed to the uprising at Attica Prison in the 1970s.

The cuts hit all state agencies, including the State University of New York, which over a fifteen-year period had lost 10.5% of its staff while enrollments grew by 6%. SUNY had suffered close to a 20% loss in resources since the 1970s, leading to increased workloads for faculty and staff. Indeed, with fewer professional workers responsible for more students, SUNY faculty and staff faced larger classes, more student advisees, additional students demanding library and other services, more papers to grade, and less time to do the scholarly research required at the university level. One faculty member summarized the stressful conditions of work at SUNY:

> I have students who are unable to get their papers corrected from me because I just have so many I can't do them as fast as they should be done...This can't continue and the university refer to itself as a premier institution.[10]

Movements began appearing on some campuses for faculty and staff to resist speed-ups, and the United University Professions held workshops around the state on workloads and the Taylor Law—the law that sets the parameters for collective bargaining in the public sector and that provides public workers in New York with the right to organize.

SUNY employees were not the only people affected. Admission standards jumped to record-high levels as thousands of qualified students with high-school grades of B or better were denied admission to the college of their choice; those students fortunate enough to gain admission felt the sting of thousands of class cancellations, making it extremely difficult to graduate in less than five years' time. In fact, the budget cuts made admission to SUNY more difficult than admission to the state's private colleges and universities, as SUNY's senior colleges and university centers accepted only slightly more than half of all applicants to its freshman class, down from 62% a decade earlier, compared to the almost two-thirds acceptance rate in the state's private sector. SUNY's plight was best summarized in a story in *Empire State Report:*

> Crumbling campuses and state-encouraged exodus of veteran faculty members is testimony to the enormous cutbacks in state funds for public education.[11]

Students organized protests against the cuts; some even publicly opted for higher tuition rates as a solution to the university's plight, even though there is an inverse relationship between tuition and college attendance, and others demonstrated against tuition hikes. Organized as a tuition-free university to provide education for all qualified New Yorkers, SUNY was becoming exclusive and expensive. Within two years, its tuition doubled, as state financing of the university dropped from 54.4%, when Cuomo took office, to 41.2% in 1992. The university's public mission, weakened decades earlier with the imposition of tuition, was under attack to such a degree that SUNY's chancellor began to talk publicly about the unspeakable: he raised the possibility of permanently closing some campuses.

Social-service and health-care workers also weathered the brunt and despair of speed-ups. Social-service workers, for instance, who care for their clients for fourteen or fifteen years on the average, according to then Public Employees Federation (PEF) President Rand Condell, lost their jobs in droves, as $4.5 billion of the proposed cuts were directed at prisons, education, and social services. The gaps were filled by increasing the workloads of remaining employees, allowing each to spend less time with individual clients and weakening if not destroying the care-giving relationship between provider and client.[12] This is particularly important, for most case workers fall within the category of public workers, who, in Andre Gorz's terms, perform "activities which meet a need for care...or help."[13] With the cutbacks, recipients of services faced longer lines, more delays, and less personal treatment. Rather than giving clients the quality care they need, case workers are now frequently forced to process human clients as widgets on an unending assembly line, losing sight of their individual uniqueness and treating them as faceless statistics that demonstrate how state workers can indeed increase their productivity by doing more with less, even if they humiliate and neglect clients in the process. This is, in fact, exactly what happened. When Barbara Sabol, the head of New York City's Human Resources Administration, sought to experience the bureaucracy she heads by posing as a welfare recipient, her worst fears were realized. She was treated shabbily, her documents were misplaced, no one recognized her unique talents, she waited in long lines and in roach-infested waiting rooms, and she felt humiliated throughout the entire process. Sabol summarized her experience in terms descriptive of the decaying process. "I ceased to be," she observed, and could have added that the process depersonalizes everyone it touches, converting them into non-persons. [14]

The lengthy recession increased workloads even more, as more people joined the ranks of the unemployed and sought refuge in the state's social welfare system. Mental health-care workers were hit the hardest, with case loads sometimes doubling in size for the remaining workers. Reports of worker burn-out increased, as state workers felt pressures similar to those expressed in Charlie Chaplin's film, *Modern Times*. Social workers faced such large case loads that personal treatment of clients became virtually impossible. The assembly-line approach to human services involved asking standard bureaucratic questions of all clients, regardless of situation and differences. The impact at the workplace of years of budget cutting was becoming crystal clear: public workers were burning out as recipients of services were channelled through a new assembly-line process of human-service delivery.

Demonstrations and protests by state workers proliferated, as employees tried to slow the assembly line and stop additional layoffs. The list of speed-ups and its consequences could go on *ad infinitum,* but the point of all this is that public workers were fed up. Working harder than ever, many faced the loss of their jobs, and if they were fortunate enough to avoid being fired, they would still lose five days' pay. Cuomo's proposed "lock-out" was the last straw. Public workers were ready to fight back.

A Show of Solidarity

Cuomo's lock-out proposal and proposed budget cuts galvanized public-sector unions to put their differences aside and fight the battle collectively. They began by forming a coalition of four of the largest unions to lobby Cuomo and the state legislature. The unions' efforts seemed to work, as Cuomo backed away from his announced lock-out. But the legislature, responding to the urgency of the fiscal crunch, introduced a program of its own called a "lag pay" that would temporarily withhold five days' salary. In other words, the workers would not be locked out. They would work, but the legislature's bipartisan definition of "temporary" raised some eyebrows. State employees would get their money back only when they left state service—dead or alive!

The lag-pay plan fueled the fires of labor solidarity, leading the unions, in a show of solidarity, to take what their leaders described as historic action. Recognizing that the legislature's unilateral withholding of five days' pay without negotiations was a contractual violation that threatened to undermine their organizations' *raison d'etre,* leaders of the statewide unions united in bringing their case to the public. They held a well-publicized joint press conference in Albany and marched to Cuomo's office, where they presented him with a copy of their collective grievance against the state. They cooperated as never before, jointly filing improper labor practice charges under New York's Taylor Law and collectively taking their cases to the courts. As the new year approached, an angry and unified public-sector labor movement stood prepared to resist further efforts to reduce the size and scope of government services.

The public-sector unions, however, did not always have the unequivocal backing of the New York State AFL-CIO. Sometimes the state federation and public-sector unions found themselves on different sides of the same issue. One important disagreement involved the AFL-CIO's waffling over public unions' challenge to Cuomo. Following the imposition of the lag on public workers' wages, public unions approached the state AFL-CIO with a resolution warning elected officials that unilateral reduction of public workers' pay would endanger potential endorsements for national office. This was designed to warn Cuomo that the lag scheme could cost union support in his quest for the presidency. But AFL-CIO President Ed Cleary responded initially by denying the existence of the resolution. He later admitted that it did exist, but then disregarded it by announcing that the AFL-CIO would back Cuomo anyway. The situation became more confused later on when Cleary reversed himself and strongly endorsed the anti-Cuomo idea. But maybe Cleary's initial position was more prescient than public labor's after all, for once the state AFL-CIO backed the resolution, Cuomo seized the opportunity to show the public that he was not the captive of "special interests" such as labor. He did this by publicly stating that he had to attack unions, even if he did so reluctantly. "Now they're filing resolutions at the AFL saying if this guy runs for president, you can't support him," Cuomo said. "It's a question of doing what you have to do even if its unpopular telling the unions no raises, laying off people. I've lost all union support," the governor boasted.[15]

Things worsened for public workers and their unions as mounting deficits enabled business interests to keep the need for additional budget cuts at the top of the state's political agenda. In fact, New York's fiscal situation was so bad that in January 1991, the state borrowed $900 million just to finish the fiscal year. Not surprisingly, Cuomo's proposed budget for the fiscal year 1991-92 reflected the Business Council's commitment to diminishing the size of government and rolling back taxes. As noted in the previous chapter, Cuomo's budget proposal, based on a projected $6 billion shortfall, contained the largest cutbacks in state history. It sought to fill the $6 billion gap by laying off 18,000 workers; it bought into the Business Council's provision for a wage freeze for public workers and cut deeply into school aid ($891 million), social services ($175 million), Medicaid ($875 million), and a wide variety of other programs, including a 10% decline in revenue-sharing to local governments. According to estimates made by the New York State AFL-CIO, Cuomo proposed to fill 75% of the $6 billion shortfall by cutting services and reducing the size and scope of government.[16]

In addition to the huge cutbacks in public services, Cuomo's budget also imposed a series of regressive new taxes, including a ten cent-per-gallon charge on gasoline and a five-dollar levy on tires. New York's governor clearly wanted to avoid the kind of "tax the rich" political battle that plagued New Jersey's Florio. Consequently, Cuomo's proposed budget failed to address the issue of restructuring corporate taxes and the personal income tax. It did, however, again defer the final phase of the income tax cut.

The Business Council, joined by other critics of state spending, hailed Cuomo's budget, claiming that the $6 billion-plus deficit was attributable to the state's profligate spending over the years. Once again the Council was shaping the political agenda with little resistance: discussion of tax reform was virtually non-existent, and the conventional wisdom, at least according to most of the media, viewed cutbacks in public spending as the best way to resolve the state's fiscal problems. New York's public sector was again under attack without any extended discussion or discourse on its merits and the consequences of massive public-sector retrenchment.

The Business Council's unchallenged position triggered another effort at collective action from organized labor. AFSCME took the lead this time by creating the Fiscal Policy Institute (FPI), a labor think tank charged with responding to the Council's anti-statist political propaganda. Although created by AFSCME, the FPI was an umbrella group of some thirty-seven labor and community organizations, including the major statewide public unions—CSEA and District Councils 37 and 82, all affiliated with AFSCME, PEF, UUP, and community organizations such as the New York Council of Churches, Community Services Society of New York (CSS), and the Statewide Emergency Network for Social and Economic Security (SENSES). The Appendix lists the Institute's entire membership. Significantly, missing from the FPI's membership roster was one of the most powerful unions in the state— the New York State United Teachers (NYSUT). On the assumption that they had the resources to wage a successful campaign without yielding control on key issues, NYSUT cooperated with the FPI, but decided to fight anti-tax sentiment on its own.

FPI sought to overcome the institutional differences, past turf battles, and other modes of conflict that characterized much of the history of public-sector unions in New York and fragmented the public-sector labor movement. [17] By inviting community groups to join, the FPI gave labor an institutional mechanism to launch an offensive against the Business Council's propaganda and to inform the public that almost all the recent levies in regressive taxes had resulted from tax breaks favorable to the wealthy in the 1987 tax reform. Potentially, New York State would have what California and New Jersey lacked, an institution-alized "fair tax" forum capable of building a viable political coalition between labor and community groups. But public employees had their work cut out for them. Not only did they have to confront business's collective political resources, including its important structural power— the need for jobs and a growing economy—but public unions also had to take on the complex ideological issues surrounding the tax cuts of 1987. For the cuts of 1987 favored the state's wealthiest individuals and contributed to growing state deficits, deficits that were met in part by the imposition of new regressive taxes, a series of sales and excise taxes that placed a heavy burden on poor and middle-class wage earners. The proliferation of regressive taxes that affected the bulk of the population contributed to a growing anti-tax sentiment that made it increasingly difficult to initiate rational public discourse on the tax issue.

The Orwellian Tax Debate

Public opinion pollsters, as noted in Chapter Five, found that large segments of the population support tax breaks and smaller government because they believe the government has to trim waste. They are not necessarily opposed to public services. In fact, the polls indicate that when public services are threatened, a majority often prefer tax increases to the loss of services. This is particularly true in the area of education.[18] In short, polls indicate that people are more opposed to taxes than government services, which suggests that they do not understand that government costs money.

The failure of the population to understand the necessary cost of government says much about the mystification of the role of the state in capitalist society. The literature analyzing the direct relationship between capitalist development and the rise of the positive political state is voluminous.[19] Much evidence exists suggesting that capitalism is incapable of reconciling its inherent contradictions without state intervention. Early twentieth-century U.S. capitalism, for instance, revealed the problems capital faced from excessive competition, eventually leaving it to the political state to work out the differences facing different units of capital.[20] The Depression of the 1930s and the constant crises of post-World War II monopoly capitalism all attest to the need for state intervention.[21] What Nicos Poulantzas called the "relative autonomy of the state,"[22] or what others accept as the need for regulation of the economy, is itself part of the logic of capitalist political economy and plays an essential role in promoting profitability by socializing the costs of production and ensuring what Paul Baron and Paul Sweezy call the absorption of surplus.[23] This indeed is a dilemma of corporate capitalism and its latest ideological "veil" balanced-budget conservatism. State spending is essential to the health of private enterprise, but spending requires taxation, a policy opposed by balanced-budget conservatives.

The role of the state in promoting capitalist development is equally applicable to the development of the welfare state. The welfare state is not rooted in the political benevolence of the ruling classes. Rather, it arose out of real struggles initiated by the social and economic consequences of capitalist production, for example: unemployment, low wages, environmental degradation, lack of health care, inadequate pensions for the elderly, an educational system incapable of providing a trained workforce, and so on. Without some form of a social safety net, the state may lose its political legitimacy, leading to massive social unrest and even social and legal breakdown.[24] The recent riots in Los Angeles provide a good case in point.

Yet despite the private economy's dependence on state intervention, both direct and indirect, attacks on New York's public sector gained momentum. The state's organized business interests, for instance, playing on the anti-tax fears generated by balanced-budget conservatism, took one facet of the polls—the fear of waste—and used it to justify new attacks on high taxes and the public sector. The idea of overpaid, unaccountable bureaucrats wasting taxpayer's money, bad enough during ordinary times but unacceptable to increasingly larger segments of the population during fiscally hard times, paved the way for business' campaign for a smaller public sector and lower income and corporate taxes, even though most government agencies had by now been stripped of any fat. In this sense, the fiscal crisis was reproducing both real and ideological animus against tax reform and the public sector. The ideological and political difficulties in bringing clear dialogue before the public on the need for and the role of the public sector were buried in the often uncritically accepted belief that government simply could not be sufficiently small or efficient. Public acceptance of Reagan's dictum that government was the problem played into the hands of the Business Council and worsened the fiscal crisis. Created in large part by the restructuring of the state's tax system, which itself was grounded in the ideology of balanced-budget conservatism, the fiscal crisis allowed the Business Council to attack the public sector from still another angle. Pointing to the high taxes most of the population pay, the Council called for reduced public spending and additional tax rollbacks. Needless to say, just as they overlooked the increasing insignificance of waste in government, business representatives conveniently ignored the fact that almost all of the recent levies in regressive taxes resulted from tax breaks favorable to the wealthy in the 1987 tax reform. Indeed, the data reveal a close link between cuts in the personal income tax and the imposition of regressive taxes to fill part of the budget gap. Between fiscal 1988 and 1990, for instance, elected state officials constructed budgets based on revenue shortfalls totaling $6.9 billion. They subsequently filled the shortfalls by a combination of cuts in public services and new regressive taxes. In a study for NYSUT, the American Economics Group identified 120 new taxes and fees introduced to fill the budget gaps.[25] The new levies raised about $4 billion. The fact that the bulk of the population was hit hard by the regressive taxes reminded people of the high taxes they paid in New York and, in an Orwellian twist of both logic and history, gave impetus to the spread of additional anti-tax sentiment. The apparent enigma of the income tax cut, then, is that for most people it increased taxes and created huge budget deficits, while it gave large breaks to a small proportion of the population. Those wealthy individuals receiving the benefits of income-tax reductions could then point to the higher taxes paid by about 95% of the population as a reason to keep taxes, specifically personal income taxes, down.

Upon reflection this is not an enigma at all, for it reflects the distribution and structure of power in New York, indeed, in the United States, where the costs of production are socialized among the populace while profits remain private. The fact that this is done under a logic that decries taxation while opting for more regressive taxation says much about the business community's power to shape and frame the political agenda. In short, this results in a world of politics where proponents of progressive taxes experience a reality where an income tax cut is a veiled tax increase and an income tax increase for the wealthy serves as the foundation for a tax cut for the rest. As public-sector unions soon discovered, getting this complex message across to the average citizen is not a simple task.

The Fiscal Policy Institute launched a statewide educational program to take on the logic of New York's taxes. The tactics used to realize this strategy varied, but the message was essentially the same: the state's fiscal problems stem from ill-conceived tax cuts beneficial to the wealthy, not from overspending, as the Business Council would have the populace believe. The Institute made this point at a number of mass political rallies across the state. FPI inundated the media with press releases and, in May 1991, launched a fair-tax postcard campaign that sent more than 90,000 postcards to Cuomo.

The backbone of the FPI campaign, however, was its educational efforts. Founded to respond to the Business Council's stronghold on information that blamed "big spending" for the state's fiscal woes, the FPI sought to demonstrate that revenue losses brought by the 1987 tax cuts were responsible for the state's problems. To do this it released a number of studies illustrating the damaging effects of the tax cuts on most of the state's population, including a document showing that state spending as part of the General Fund as a percentage of personal income had decreased annually since 1988. In that year, for instance, General Fund spending peaked at 8.3% of personal income, but has since fallen annually to below 7.3% in 1992. Significantly, FPI noted that when New York's General Fund spending is compared to the federal government and other states, New York is spending proportionally less. Over the last two years, General Fund spending in all states grew by 9.8%, growth for the federal government reached 20.2%, but for New York, General Fund spending jumped only 2.1%. Clearly, according to FPI, the reality of spending in New York is just the opposite of popular political perceptions. [26]

Solidarity Brings Fragmentation

Representing a major step toward labor solidarity on the political front, the Fiscal Policy Institute gave public labor a voice in opposition to the Business Council. The Institute was the most visible collective organization, but it was not alone. The severity of the fiscal crunch prompted public-sector unions to take other collective actions, including several informal arrangements designed to resist further cuts. Collective lobbying provides one good instance of unions' cooperation with each other. Recognizing that their very existence was at stake, New York's largest statewide public unions, CSEA, PEF, Council 82, and UUP combined forces to resist Cuomo's 1991-92 budget proposal. Jointly walking the halls of the Legislative Office Building in Albany, leaders of the four unions put together collective political lobbying efforts, demonstrating to elected officials that their organizations could work together in solidarity for the cause of jobs. Emulating the tactics of the struggles waged by their sisters and brothers in California over Propositions 8 and 13, the unions' lobbying efforts focused on the theme "Save Our Jobs!" Union leaders echoed the FPI's fair-tax approach, arguing that slight adjustments in the top rate of the personal income tax and some moderate changes in corporate taxes would produce the revenue to pay for the maintenance of existing jobs and services.

Lobbying was an important part of labor's collective efforts to reshape New York's political agenda, but the center of the offensive against the proposed cuts was a mass rally sponsored by statewide public unions to protest job cuts. The unions believed that a mass rally would bring two distinct benefits to a labor movement under the gun. First, a large demonstration would involve massive numbers of rank-and-file unionists, thereby giving them an outlet for their anger, an opportunity to vent their frustration, while letting union members know that their union was doing something to save their jobs. Second, a well-attended public rally might even work. Indeed, it potentially could galvanize public officials to seek new solutions—such as tax restructuring—to the state's fiscal problems. In any case, rally organizers hoped to bring 10,000 protestors to the capital. And they were not disappointed. Workers' anger and frustration over years of budget cuts, the threat of no pay increases, and the loss of five days' pay brought 20,000 people into Albany, making the February 5, 1991 demonstration one of the largest in the city's history.

Ironically, the labor demonstration began at the Albany armory, a building originally built to house National Guard troops charged with crushing strikes at the turn of the century. After rallying in the armory, demonstrators took to the streets *en masse* and marched to the governor's mansion chanting, "New York works because we work." On the surface, it appeared to be a rank-and-file demonstration, a collective show of mass support against the dismantling of the public sector. In some ways it was.

Public labor's efforts at solidarity were new and historic. Never had the state's major unions jointly participated in a political venture of this magnitude. The rally brought participants from all the major unions and from every corner of the state. Rank-and-file unionists joined their elected leaders when they challenged Cuomo to respond to their demands. The unions received widespread press coverage and attracted a great deal of public attention. But it was becoming crystal clear that their collective activities, while a step in the right direction, failed to transcend California's experience. Just as public unions in California more than a decade earlier had failed to go beyond what Selig Perlman called "job consciousness," New York's public unions made the same mistake.

The fear of job loss and retrenchments was the glue that held the coalition together. But the jobs-first approach had important political consequences, most of which were ultimately divisive. By framing the debate in terms of "job consciousness" rather than the more general issue of the need for a strong public sector, the unions exposed their vulnerability.[27] On the most immediate level, an argument in favor of a strong public sector is less self-serving and, most importantly, more likely to generate public support, including coalition-building with recipients of public services. By demanding budget restorations primarily to save jobs, labor presented itself to the public as selfish and self-serving. In this sense, the "Save Our Jobs" theme plays into the hands of anti-statists by depicting public employees as a special interest that would exacerbate the fiscal crisis by robbing more for themselves. In the eyes of many segments of the population, public workers have come to personify William Vanderbilt's "the public be damned" attitude. In short, political change in the epoch of balanced-budget conservatism requires public support, and the "Jobs First" approach projects an image offensive to large segments of the public, an image that often reinforces negative attitudes about public workers and their unions.

If public unions had emphasized the quality and type of goods and services they deliver, they would have had at least an ideological veneer illustrating how their particular interests coincide with the general good. This is critical. For, as social critic Franz Neumann lucidly demonstrated, since in a democracy groups compete for votes, political debate in a democracy must always be ideological. Under conditions of formal democracy it is important for each group in the political arena to demonstrate why the policies it espouses are in the best interest of the larger social whole, to put it more bluntly, why the particular interests of one bloc represent the interests of all. This, in fact, is what makes democratic politics ideological: the groups that win must convince voters, as a former Cabinet officer once observed, that the interests of General Motors and the United States are one and the same. [28] Public-sector unions lost the ideological struggle when they framed their demands in narrow job-consciousness terms. By avoiding public discussion of what needs government should fulfill, a debate that the dominant ideology of fiscal conservatism has stifled, the unions tacitly acquiesced to the ideology of balanced-budget conservatism, and they tacitly accepted the dominant ideology in a way that made them appear selfish and unconcerned with the public good. In essence, they missed an opportunity to show that their interests are not necessarily narrow or self-serving.[29]

Discussion of public needs and the quality of public goods has the potential to do more than give public workers an effective ideology necessary to open a much needed political dialogue. Strategically, it places public workers in a better position to form coalitions with their clients, who have a mutual interest in the production of high-quality goods and services. Public employees and recipients of public services often have interests sufficiently alike to form political coalitions. [30] Both workers and clients could jointly make a pitch for increased assistance by appealing to their version of the public interest. When they chose to stress job security, public unions subordinated the needs of recipients of public services to a position beneath their need for job security—not a good strategy to win friends among the people served, many of whom are already fed up with dealing with public-employee burnout and the declining quality of services. If, as Jeremy Brecher and others contend, the future of labor is outside the organized labor movement, emphasis on job security is likely to weaken the labor movement in the long run.[31] In short, as growing numbers of workers are outside the organized labor movement, it becomes increasingly important for unions to develop strategies to gain their support.

Union Cannibalism

Still, from the perspective of labor organizations, the "jobs first" approach is not without merit. In fact, it is attractive because of the obvious importance of jobs to union members and elected leaders. Without jobs there are no workers and without workers there are no unions. Elected union officers who want to stay in office must take actions that both save jobs and tell the membership that they are doing something. This is what makes the job-security approach attractive to union leaders in the first place. Its message is clear and simple, and the rank-and-file can easily and readily participate, venting their energies in common struggle. Unfortunately, it also encourages cannibalism among competing public-sector unions. For once the dialogue shifts from the need for a strong public sector and the kind and quality of goods produced by the public to the need to save workers' jobs, the possibility of one union working to save its members' jobs at the expense of others increases. Historically, this possibility becomes real all too often, as when college professors point to clerical workers as the place to cut, or when security guards point their finger at mental-health workers, and so on. Indeed, at the very juncture that New York's unions were uniting against layoffs, lock-outs, and other attacks, CSEA backed legislation that would move UUP members from their bargaining unit and put them into CSEA. The struggle to enlist dues-paying members sometimes clouds the commitment to solidarity, and when this occurs, in whatever variety, state officials and negotiators, of course, encourage it, seldom missing an opportunity to play one union against another.

The question of union cannibalism is particularly important in New York State. New York has a long history of jurisdictional battles within the public sector and between public and private unions. While it is beyond the scope of this chapter to present a history of public-sector jurisdictional battles, for purposes of illustrating the difficulty in building an effective level of union solidarity, it is worthwhile to note that PEF developed out of what many characterize as a union raid on CSEA by the New York State United Teachers (NYSUT) and the Service Employees International Union (SEIU). The formation of PEF took some 45,000 CSEA members out of the professional, technical, and scientific bargaining units, leaving CSEA to eventually merge with AFSCME, an AFL-CIO union, because an AFL-CIO rule prohibits affiliates from battling for representation rights. By joining the AFL-CIO through its merger with AFSCME, CSEA protected itself against raids by other public unions.

There is also an institutional basis for public-sector union competition in New York State. A primary cause of internecine union squabbles is the role played by the Public Employment Relations Board (PERB). Established to administer New York's Taylor Law, PERB divided the public labor force into five distinct units: institutional, operational, professional, scientific, and technical services. Representation elections are based upon the appropriate community of interest. In other words, the Taylor Law ensured that the industrial union model of one large union would not apply to the state's public labor force. Instead, the law organized public workers into several unions based on functional interests it identified as a "community of interest." In this respect, the Taylor Law's PERB has effectively institutionalized fragmentation and conflict within the state's public sector.[32]

Despite the potential for fragmentation, the February 5, 1991 rally projected an image of solidarity, though one based on self-serving motives. Another rally at the capital, however, did not. In fact, the latter rally, in addition to illuminating a negative image of public workers, also revealed new gaps in labor's solidarity. A second major demonstration, held one month later, brought some 20,000 protestors to Albany. But the March demonstration was different. Organizationally, it did not evolve from the efforts of public unions, although they participated. Instead, it was precipitated by African-American and Latino officials who criticized Cuomo for backing cuts in social services and health care while rejecting increases in personal and corporate taxes. Arthur Eve, deputy majority leader of the New York State Assembly and a leader in the Black and Hispanic Caucus, put the cuts in perspective when he characterized New York as "the most racist state in the union." Racist, he added, because they strike most harshly at services provided to people of color who live in the state's largest cities, people who have been ghettoized and excluded from the job market and are dependent on public services to eke out meager existences.

Organized by members of the Assembly's Black and Hispanic Caucus, the demonstration attracted large numbers of recipients of social services, many of whom were people of color. Once in Albany, their anger exploded when some threw furniture through a window of the governor's mansion. The press focused on the angry crowd's behavior and the protestors' "selfish" appeal for job security and the protection of public services. The rally, a success in bringing thousands to the capital, received hostile reviews and was ultimately seen as a public relations failure.

As anti-statists pointed to the March rally as an example of special interests gone amok, some supporters of public workers began to distance themselves from the cause espoused by both rallies. Perhaps worse than the developing negative public image, an image enhanced and exploited by the media, was the fact that the two demonstrations were only marginally related to each other. They both took narrow, "selfish" approaches by arguing for immediate self-interests. The February rally sought job protection; the March demonstration aimed at maintaining jobs and public services, particularly for the poor people and people of color. In short, neither group addressed the larger issue of the need for a public sector and how a vibrant public sector helps the economy and improves the quality of life, even if not equally for all races and ethnic groups. The March demonstration at least raised the issue of institutionalized racism by focusing on the disproportionate impact of the cuts on people of color. But the failure of both rallies to address the role of the public sector as a larger public issue constituted tacit consent to anti-statist, anti-taxist sentiment and missed the opportunity of cutting through the ideological veneer of balanced-budget conservatism. On this level, labor missed an important opportunity.

Aside from the general problem of failing to publicly discuss the role of the public sector, the two demonstrations revealed a gap in labor's solidarity network. The February rally was sponsored by public labor unions, and the participants were largely white. The March demonstration consisted primarily of people of color, large numbers of whom were recipients of social services dependent on public workers for delivery of these services. Issues such as the need for adequate health care, housing, and human services played a key role among the latter group, while the question of job security prevailed among the former. The rallies revealed the different dynamics of the two groups and suggested that the possibility of joining forces was somewhat limited. Yet, despite this, organizers of the March rally viewed the demonstration as the first step in a new effort to build a grassroots progressive organization "to pressure New York State government to deliver a fair and equitable state budget." Consequently, they formed a new progressive organization, The Coalition for Social and Economic Justice (CSEJ). CSEJ sought to build a broad-based constituency tied to labor and religious institutions. It met with limited success. The statewide public-sector unions that had arranged the February rally, rather than joining forces with their natural allies, were conspicuously absent from the March demonstration and tended to view the new coalition with suspicion and distrust.

Discussions with activists and personal observations as a leader in organizing the February event suggest a number of reasons for the failure to connect in a real way with the new Coalition for Social and Economic Justice. The first and most conspicuous is the issue of control. Union leaders were facing a major political crisis. Their organizations were under attack, workers were getting fired, and rank-and-file members demanded strong and decisive action. The fact that the presidents of several public unions faced tough re-election bids in Spring 1992 made it even more imperative for them to take visible leadership roles. In short, while all leaders wanted substantive results, the appearance of their actions to the membership was also a crucial consideration. They had to appear active and in command. Joining forces with a group led by a charismatic and controversial leader could create unnecessary controversy while simultaneously removing elected union officials from a favorable political limelight. Indeed, the controversy generated by Arthur Eve's reputation as a radical, his public confrontations with Cuomo, and his strident commitment to work with the poor and recipients of social and human services could weaken the image of "responsible" labor leaders. All this was in addition to the usual turf battles that cause public-sector unions to approach each other distrustfully.

Political pressure on public unions, both internal and external, allowed an opportunity to create and promote a coalition between providers and recipients of public services to pass. Despite the formation of the FPI with its emphasis on solidarity among public-sector unions and their clients, the experience of the winter demonstrations and the emergence of the CSEJ suggests that organized labor in the public sector and its clients were apparently marching to different drummers. Solidarity was at a very nascent stage; there was still a long way to go.

Matters continued to worsen for public employees as a new rift appeared between public- and private-sector unions. In 1989, the New York State AFL-CIO had provided organized labor with an umbrella organization—the Committee on Economic Priorities—to stop the last phase of the income tax cut. After achieving this goal, at least temporarily, in 1990 the AFL-CIO committee disbanded. But the worsening of the fiscal crunch and the increasingly hard hits taken by the public sector brought the state AFL-CIO back into the tax fray again. This time, however, public-sector unions did not receive the state federation's position with open arms.

Problems stemmed from the AFL-CIO's position paper on tax equity, "Taxes We Can Live With—Designing a System to Meet Future Needs." The paper articulated a position significantly different in one respect from the FPI's tax program and revealed a major break in strategy between public- and private-sector unions. Public-employee unions, led by the FPI, sought to restore progressivity in the personal income tax, backed the imposition of sales taxes on services consumed by upper-middle-income earners, and wanted an increase in corporate taxes. The AFL-CIO tax position agreed with the FPI program with one major exception. Responding to the needs of private-sector unions and their fear of corporate flight, the New York State AFL-CIO refused to support hikes in corporate taxes, arguing instead that "it would be unfair to increase taxes on all business."[33] Although the AFL-CIO report accepted the findings of numerous studies, including one sponsored by *Fortune* magazine, that taxes "are not dominant in location decisions," the AFL-CIO ultimately accepted the jobs-at-any-cost approach and, in so doing, acquiesced to the Business Council's and CHANGE-NY's warning that high taxes lead to corporate flight. The AFL-CIO position on corporate taxes took into account the perceptions of the state's private-sector unionists who had experienced plant closings and corporate flight throughout the past decade. Having suffered greatly over the years, private-sector workers were not going to accept the findings of studies that contradicted their experience. Once the state federation refused to support corporate tax hikes, however noble its motives or democratic its procedures, it gave credibility to business' ideological offensive connecting corporate interests with the general interest through the need to preserve jobs, and made it increasingly difficult for public workers to join forces with private-sector unionists. The divisive facet of the jobs-first approach had once again surfaced, this time through the rejection of corporate taxes. The structural power of capital, illuminated by the threat of corporate flight, replaced union solidarity with another version of conflict and cannibalism.

Labor Leaders Face the Voters

Labor's semi-successful attempts at solidarity and the deepening fiscal crisis, with its attacks on public workers, including layoffs, pay freezes, and speed-ups, made it a risky political year for elected union officials. By the time the state budget for fiscal year 1991-92 was finally passed in July 1991, a record-setting delay for the second straight year, one union president had lost his re-election bid and a second won by the narrowest of margins.

The leaders of public unions (CSEA, PEF, and UUP) that had endorsed the governor during his 1990 re-election campaign felt the anger and frustration of their members at the polls. CSEA's President, Joe McDermott, although critical of Cuomo and aware of his members' anger toward the governor, had still backed Cuomo in his 1990 re-election bid. It almost cost McDermott his job. He squeaked through a surprisingly close election by a margin of 1,258 votes of the almost 43,000 cast, beating his insurgent challenger, Pat Mascioli, 21,544 to 20,286. Mascioli had taken a strong anti-Cuomo stand, attacking Mc-Dermott for being "too cozy" with Cuomo even though CSEA was working without a contract. Playing on this theme, Mascioli said, "Nine years ago, it was the unions that put Cuomo where he is...I'm not saying he should give us the store, but he should be able to sit down and listen."[34]

PEF's Rand Condell was not as lucky as McDermott. Engaged in a campaign similar to McDermott's, where the key issue was PEF's support of Cuomo, Condell, despite his public Cuomo-bashing, was soundly beaten by challenger Howard Schaeffer, who based his campaign on Condell's endorsement of Cuomo.

President John "Tim" Reilly of UUP, who had run unopposed two years earlier, faced an oppositional candidate, whom he beat handily. But here the message was the same. The results of elections in the largest statewide unions, CSEA, PEF, and UUP, sent a clear message to labor leaders: the social and political forces that moved Governor Cuomo were unimportant. Public workers were interested only in the facts, not the factors that made the facts, and the facts, as far as their jobs were concerned, did not instill confidence in elected leaders. They blamed Cuomo for their plight, and unions would have to take a more militant posture.

Solidarity Breeches Surface Again

Rank-and-file unionists expressed their anger in the union elections of Spring 1991. But by the following spring, things had deteriorated further. As noted in Chapter Six, the budget for fiscal year 1992-93 was another bad one for public workers, cutting an additional 5,000 jobs for a total workforce reduction of 14% over a two-year period. With no wage increases on the horizon, working without a contract since the spring of 1991, having lost about 2% of members' salaries to the five-day lag, and, looking at additional layoffs, the future did not augur well for public-sector unions. Things worsened in late May 1992 when the FPI's director suddenly resigned. FPI drifted in search of a new leader for over six months, losing vital time in the struggle to change New York's tax structure. Worse yet for public unions, solidarity breeches began to surface over contract negotiations with the state.

In late Spring 1992, CSEA reached an agreement with the state. The agreement came without warning or deliberations with some of the other public unions. Discussions with other public-sector unions are crucial because CSEA, the largest of the statewide unions, sets the standard for pattern bargaining. That is, what CSEA gets at the bargaining table generally determines the pattern for what the other unions get, barring drastic actions on their part. Leaders of some of the other statewide unions were not impressed with CSEA's contract. UUP's Reilly openly criticized the CSEA agreement for negotiating away the lag-pay lawsuit—part of the unions' solidarity efforts—in return for financial remuneration. CSEA unit members would not receive across-the-board pay increases for two years, just as the Business Council recommended, and there were some significant give-backs, including a major change in workers compensation payments.[35]

Once CSEA was in line and the pattern established, Cuomo issued an ultimatum. If the other statewide unions failed to reach an accord by June 24, 1992, he would pull all proposed pay raises from the table. Public-union leaders attacked Cuomo's tactics; more even publicly criticized CSEA's unilateral action. They were in a bad spot. For most of the unions a year or more had passed since the expiration of their contracts. Now that CSEA had reached agreement, members of that bargaining unit would eventually receive raises while colleagues who belonged to other unions would not. This increased the pressure to agree. And that is what happened. Once the rhetoric and anger cleared, the other unions, with the exception of PEF, came to terms. Terms of the agreements were similar to CSEA's, with the major difference being the schedule worked out for repaying the lag pay.

PEF did not reach an accord with the state until Spring 1993, as its newly elected president publicly feuded with Cuomo. But PEF was not alone in not agreeing. The New York State Troopers union did the unexpected. After their leadership reached a tentative agreement with the state, the rank-and-file voted it down, thereby feeding the fear that the membership would not ratify other contracts. Despite the Troopers' rejection, this did not happen. Members of the other unions bit the bullet and voted for ratification. The Troopers and PEF eventually signed, as the governor's office issued threats and ultimatums.

Amidst all this, the governor announced new deficits in the Fall of 1992, making additional cuts in government services a certainty for the 1993-94 fiscal year. As discussion of the latest round of cuts accelerates and as public workers brace for another round of attacks on their jobs, one thing is clear: public unions are not in a position to stop major new cuts. There is still time to slow or stop the attacks, but only if the unions learn from their most recent experience.

Conclusion

Public labor's dilemma is multi-faceted. On the one hand, public workers experience the pain of global economic competition and recession, and competition among states exacerbates things further. Plant closings, corporate flight, and massive layoffs increase the need for social spending at the same time that taxes and other government revenues are falling. [36] When, as in the case of New York, business interests hurt by global restructuring and the recession use these same crises to launch new, aggressive campaigns for lower taxes, the entire situation is aggravated. In New York State, as elsewhere, the economically weakened but politically vibrant business community attained its sought-after tax breaks, forcing public revenues to plummet. Politicians, then, turned to the public sector for relief. Led by Cuomo, who by 1992 had the ill-fated tax revolts of New Jersey and California past him, politicians initially sought the relief through attacks on waste in government; later on they downplayed the waste side of the attack and just called for smaller government, tightening the squeeze from the top. As cutbacks in public services and balanced budgets became the operational terms of the day, Cuomo sidestepped the political minefields that had exploded on Brown and Florio. Cuomo was more astute. The governor compromised with the anti-tax right, but he still held control. Unions are limping, not broken; the Republican Right has disproportionate influence, but, as the CHANGE-NY attacks on Ralph Marino attest, the far Right does not hold the trump card. In other words, things could have turned out worse.

The fact that Cuomo may have kept a very bad situation from getting even worse does not reassure those who have lost their jobs or the thousands of others who feel the real threat of eventual unemployment. Nor does it assuage the victims of speed-ups, workers and clients alike. Indeed, as the axe of additional cutbacks hovers above public workers, morale plummets, and the stress from doing more with less takes its toll on public employees.

New York's public unions might have pushed Cuomo to the Left had they built a real solidarity movement. But this is not an easy task. The forces in favor of balanced-budget conservatism have the upper hand. In responding to balanced-budget conservatism, New York's public-sector unions had to react to the recession, the restructuring of the global economy, and business' collective assertion of its political power—its willingness to downplay traditional differences and act more coherently as a class. Try as it might, public labor has still not met this challenge in New York. Attempts at solidarity failed to realize their full potential for a number of reasons. The Taylor Law's forced fragmentation of public unions and prevention of a single public-workers' organization based on the industrial unionism model hurts solidarity efforts.[37] Competition among public unions, then, is structured into the legal foundations of the state's public-sector unions, and the long history of turf battles attests to the significance of this issue.

The question of different interests, promoted in the public sector by the Taylor Law, exists structurally, at least in the short run, between New York's public- and private-sector unions. Private unions in New York State, fearful of contributing to corporate flight, rejected proposed increases in business taxes. In order to save jobs, they sided with the corporate sector against their sisters and brothers in the public sphere. The fact that investment decisions are only peripherally related to state and local taxes attests to the ability of the business community to define the political agenda and instill fear among unionists. The structural power of business has intimidated unionists in the private sector who buy into the business agenda in an effort to forestall what is rapidly becoming inevitable—plant closings and corporate flight. Deferring the inevitable as long as they may, they fearfully await the day when corporate flight takes their jobs.

Plant closings and corporate flight mean less revenue, as do lower business taxes, a need successfully attained by New York's business community. This closed circle of corporate flight, reduced public revenues, and diminished government spending reinforces itself, further aggravating the crisis and ultimately reducing public revenues even more. Public unions have tried to break the cycle by transcending the fragmentation institutionalized by the Taylor Law. They cooperate in a number of ways to reverse the ongoing cycle of deficits and retrenchments. Sometimes the cooperation is informal, as in the case of joint lobbying; sometimes cooperation is institutionalized, as in the case of FPI. But there are a number of forces other than the Taylor Law obstructing the emergence of real solidarity.

The old principle of business unionism—getting more for members in terms and conditions of employment while avoiding larger, more abstract, and potentially divisive social and political issues—allows state negotiators to sometimes play one union against another, rewarding the winner with a special benefit not available to all. Contract negotiations and the use of state sanctions against recalcitrant unions are the forums where this scenario usually unfolds. There are no winners when this happens. One union may benefit at the expense of another, but that weakens the labor movement as a whole. Mistrust and suspicion replace cooperation and collaboration, allowing state managers and politicians to watch quietly as their adversaries devour each other. The effects of business unionism are at play in today's crisis, as solidarity efforts are displaced by conflicting strategies over negotiations and the general tendency to grab as much as possible for the membership.

Part of the question of business unionism is the need for union officers to protect their members. Failure to do this—or at least the perception of failure—may lead to an electoral loss. Consequently, many leaders take actions designed to appear effective; they may gear programs to give members a sense of participation and power rather than actually giving them power. This is not to suggest that union leaders always engage in smoke-and-mirror policies of deception. That hardly ever happens. But the simple point is that they are elected by the rank-and-file and therefore they must give their constituents a sense of empowerment and participation in their union. Results are always important, but so is the feeling of empowerment. At times this leads some officials to avoid working with other unions or leaders outside organized labor. It even contributes to a leader's verbal attacks on the work of other unions. More often than not it obstructs rather than promotes solidarity. Some unions see a solution to this problem, a solution that is worse than the disease it cures: reducing democratic rank-and-file involvement so that leaders have the freedom to move with minimal levels of interference from well-meaning but "ignorant" members.

Limiting democracy and restricting rank-and-file participation may increase leaders' flexibility, but it surely weakens the union. Exclusion of the rank-and-file restricts and even alienates large segments of the membership. Organization as a source of power requires dedicated members, lots of them. Exclusion creates alienation by fueling the belief that the union is something other than its membership. This reified attitude is expressed frequently, most often when members are asked to show their numbers in a demonstration of strength. Only on the rarest occasions does this successfully happen, and even then it is usually not sustained. The experience of the fiscal crunch in New York suggests that more, not less democracy, is what New York's public unions need.

These problems are all serious. But public-sector unions might have transcended them if they had approached the crisis with unifying rather than divisive strategies. As noted above, by defining the issue in terms of job consciousness, the unions appeared narrow and selfish in their claim for justice; not only is this approach likely to galvanize public resistance, but it also offends and alienates large blocs of potential allies, that is, the clients who receive public services. This, of course, is the underside of the public labor squeeze. Rather than working together in common interest, the unions downplay the needs of the clients who receive lower-quality services virtually every time large numbers of public workers are laid off.

Of equal importance, emphasis on job security obstructs the development of public dialogue on the nature of the public sector. What should government do? Why does government grow? Should it continue to do so? By avoiding these questions, public unions have tacitly accepted the public philosophy of balanced-budget conservatism.

The fair-tax approach has helped unify the disparate segments of organized labor. But, as author Nick Salvatore argues, it never overcomes the problems of the "jobs first" tactic. The struggle for fair taxes identifies something that is true—tax laws are unfair—but it overlooks the larger social issues and economic undercurrents that created the recession and gave political justification for tax breaks in the first place, issues that emphasize the commonality and interdependence of all working people. [38] Cries for help by middle-class teachers, college professors, and other state professionals are unlikely to generate sympathy from the public or the recipients of public services. Discussion of the root causes of the crisis, why the downturn in the economy occurred, for example, and how it affects all working people, provides an understanding of how a society is organized and of, to use Robert Lynd's term, its generating source of power. [39] Recognition of the larger structural causes of recession and fiscal crisis could potentially unite the various segments of New York's working population. Again, labor took some significant steps toward solidarity in fighting for fair state taxes, but the focus on taxes as the problem rather than a symptom of a more general malaise let an important opportunity pass—an opportunity to build a large coalition organized around issues beneficial to unorganized as well as organized workers.

Organized labor faces the crisis of its existence. A politically resurgent business community has used the global restructuring of capital to create a brave new corporate order in New York State, an order once characterized by a progressive tradition running the gamut from the Democratic Al Smith and Franklin Roosevelt to the liberal Republicanism of Nelson Rockefeller has become an order where the philosophy of balanced-budget conservatism has forced a progressive Governor to reject much of the state's progressive tradition in favor of a harsh version of fiscal conservatism. Whatever the limitations of New York's progressive tradition—and they are many and severe—the problem today is that even this is disappearing. Sadly, at this juncture, organized labor in New York is not up to meeting the challenge. But all is not lost. Perhaps the current crisis will provide the opportunity to create a new and more democratic order for the twenty-first century. The concluding chapter explores the possibilities for an emergent new progressive movement outside the ideological parameters of the political party system that has become submerged in the politics of balanced-budget conservatism.

Appendix

Fiscal Policy Institute Members

American Federation of State, County, and Municipal
Employees/New York State, AFSCME/NYS
Brooklyn-Wide Interagency Council on the Aging
Citizen Action of New York State
Citywide Welfare Advocacy Network
The City Project
Civil Service Employees Association, CSEA
Community Service Society
Council of Senior Centers & Services of New York City
District Council 35-AFSCME
District Council 37-AFSCME
District Council 66-AFSCME
District Council 82-AFSCME
Hunger Action Network of New York State
Housing Patrolmen's Benevolent Association of New York City
Health & Welfare Council of Nassau County
Local 375-District Council #37
Local 1199
Local 1549-District Council #37
Local 1931-District Council #37
Municipal Labor Committee
Non-Profit Resource Center
New York Public Interest Research Group
National Association for the Advancement of
Colored People, NAACP
National Education Association, NY
New York City Coalition Against Hunger
New York City Labor Council for Latin American Advancement
New York State Child Care Coordinating Council
New York State Conference of Mayors and other Municipal
Officials
New York State Council of Churches
Public Employees Federation, PEF
Public Utility Law Project
Rockland Community Action Council
Statewide Emergency Network for Social and Economic Security
Service Employees International Union
Statewide Youth Advocacy
United University Professions

Chapter Nine

WHOSE DEFICIT, WHOSE PLAN, WHOSE POWER?

The architects of power in the United States must create a force that can be felt but not seen. Power remains strong when it remains in the dark; exposed to the sunlight it begins to evaporate.

Samuel P. Huntington[1]

But what is clear throughout the conservative tradition is its motivation by fear and by anxieties in which civil war or urban crime are themselves mere fissures for class struggle. The market is thus Leviathan in sheep's clothing: its function is not to encourage and perpetuate freedom [let alone freedom of a political variety] but rather to repress it.

Fredric Jameson[2]

Material Directions

It says much about the age of balanced-budget conservatism that Governor Mario Cuomo's greatest political achievement was a non-event. Unlike California and New Jersey, New York State politics under Cuomo did not crash and burn in a tax revolt. New York State also escaped a Rightwing takeover of its government. That Cuomo managed to hold off taxpayer militance and the Right despite raising taxes on ordinary New Yorkers is a political performance worthy of respect. And when you consider that he also fired thousands of public employees, a policy that reduced both the quality and quantity of state services while raising their price, the achievement is all the more impressive. George Bush had good reason to fear a Cuomo candidacy: here was a liberal who knew how to move Right, speak Left, and hold the center.

In New York State, Governor Mario Cuomo rode the wave of taxpayer militance by translating the mass politics of tax discontent into a corporate liberal politics of private growth and investment at the cost of public spending and social progress. New York's pay-as-you-go liberal governor cut thousands of state jobs, reduced state aid to the localities, imposed a series of regressive taxes and fees, cut the state income tax for the richest income earners, and extracted significant give-backs from public-sector unions while instituting a two-year pay freeze. Cuomo's record would make any balanced-budget conservative envious, and he won three terms as a liberal.[3] Cuomo succeeded by exhibiting unusual political versatility. He had the ability to move grudgingly but convincingly against his own ideological beliefs as well as the interests of his base constituents. Indeed, as we saw in the last two chapters, Cuomo succeeded by punishing his constituents. This treatment was not laudable, Cuomo repeatedly explained, but necessary. The economy made him do it. Like any smart political executive in the grip of balanced-budget conservatism, Cuomo looked to the iron law of fiscal integrity to excuse otherwise unacceptable political decisions.

As our case study of New York shows, skillful liberal leaders are more likely to manage the repressive consequences of balanced-budget conservatism than to transcend the rules of fiscal domination. Not even Mario Cuomo, the nation's most outspoken liberal, could overcome the power of private economic institutions to dictate public agendas and choices. As market rationality successfully substituted for democratic politics even in liberal New York, we must conclude that though George Bush lost the White House, "the new class war" started by Ronald Reagan is still on.[4]

The Ideological Fog of Debt

The difference is that now conservatives dominate the public agenda not by proposing weird economic miracles based on something-for-nothing, but, more ruthlessly, by making government officials the captives of debt. Mystified by abstract bookkeeping, the real issues of power and political economy remain where Samuel Huntington says they belong, hidden "in the dark."

Having pushed questions of high taxes and unbalanced budgets to the top of all U.S. political agendas, balanced-budget conservatism now keeps a tight muzzle on issues of economic health and well-being. Questions of stagnation, growing inequality, the future of full-time work, the economic squeeze on state and local government, conversion of the war economy, recovery of the lost cities of the Rust Belt, and a generation of poor urban youth, each get little hearing. Although Bill Clinton read the polls and catapulted the issue of economic directions to the forefront of his campaign, his administration, like Cuomo's and Florio's, was immediately preoccupied with debt. His promised middle-class tax cut soon disappeared, as did the political muscle to push even a small economic stimulus program through the Senate.

Confused about Clinton's direction and angry about their prospects in a slow-growth economy that erodes job security and real-estate values, the discontented middle class shows its own signs of rising class resentment against the super-rich and the politics of evasion. Not even the suburban fortress, after all, can keep stagnation at bay. Income surveys suggest that, compared with capital's golden age in the 1960s, middle-income groups have "thinned by eight to fifteen percentage points of the nation's population" and now encompass only approximately 45% of the total. [5] The economic majority of Americans is no longer "middle class" even in the loose sense of measurement by income distribution. As the decade-long attack on working people makes its inroads into suburbia, once economically secure voters now feel that they too are victims of a class rip-off. More than half of a recent survey, 55%, told *Fortune* that "millionaires have gotten where they are by exploiting others," while a third said the country would be better off without millionaires altogether. A majority of citizens favors increased taxation on the corporate rich. More than half of the people now wish for a third party to hold the major parties' feet to the fire. Millions of people sense a need for an expanded range of alternatives, and they are searching for new ways to bring the political system under public control.[6]

But mainstream politics offers few outlets for popular anger to link up with effective means of change. Conservatives have thrown people the bone of the state debt to chew on, while the notable "third party" candidate of 1992 was a billionaire populist who named the debt as issue Number One. Thus, angry voters have largely channeled the mass political rage of the early 1990s into struggles for political reforms, such as limits on state and local legislative terms, which punish the levels of government already most constrained by market forces, or on self-defeating tax limitation measures, which only compound the public-service squeeze.

Overall, the constant harping on deficits has produced a politics that denies the existence of social surplus, mystifies the irrationality and coerciveness of market forces, impoverishes the public sector, and aggravates social divisions. The new fiscal politics denies people a chance even to consider the possibility of collective democratic means to drive the forces of production toward socially useful purposes. In all these ways balanced-budget conservatism preempts a general debate about how society as a whole might choose to use the available forces of production for the good of the whole. It is not too much to say that the deficit obsession has begun to sour people on the whole idea of democratic rationality. After all, if democracy cannot even balance the books, how can it manage anything else?

What is astonishing is the ability of corporations and markets to evade responsibility for the wider economic disarray. Despite their obvious failure to improve average living standards, provide good jobs, reduce poverty, eliminate ghettos, or create urban opportunity, the market reigns triumphant. Economic rationality and the price system now prevail more than ever as the exclusive standards for measuring the worth of public need as well as private action. The market, an invisible control system that currently transmits economic coercions more than pecuniary incentives, has left much of the United States in shambles, but we are told it is wrong for society to defend itself, unwise to adopt qualitative standards for appraising action, using resources, or identifying needs. It is too dangerous to meddle with the natural economic impulse. The market, we are told, will not tolerate experiments in economic organization. Attempts to explore alternative forms of social decision are *verboten*. Stabs at political regulation or community self-defense are out of the question.

In fact, what passes for the market is really a system of irresponsible economic controls that protrudes from the decision-making centers of the world's multinationals, and it demands a world shaped exclusively in its image. The market is our new world government, and it must have everything its way. It is not enough for the market to predominate, to hold sway; it must have exclusive and total obedience. It will not tolerate pluralism of economic ways and means. We may have no other gods.

This one-world government of economic rules and regulations has reduced democratic politics to "the care and feeding of the economic apparatus." [7] What follows is a trend toward fiscal starvation of government. Democracy is slowly collapsing into a debt that was run up to save capital from itself.

The Drift Toward Oligarchy

Is there a democratic way out of the blind alley? Candidly, the odds are against it. The main drift is now unmistakably toward some more opaque and mystified form of oligarchy. Bertram Gross calls this trend "Friendly Fascism," Andre Gorz foresees "a totalitarian society run by a technocracy," and Alain Touraine writes of a "Programmed Society." [8] The terms vary more than the content. For each of these writers, democracy is fast losing ground to a system of multinational capital whose means of technical manipulation now extend deep under the skin of late capitalist culture. Aided by a weird and terrifying combination of magical commodities, celebrations of political decentralism, cooptive sponsorship of multiculturalism, and selective but extreme applications of economic pressure, the new system of controls makes mincemeat of an effective mass politics. The chances for a renewal of serious national politics may be little better than those favoring a revival of urban political machines.

Democracy and Disorganization on the Left

As we have seen in previous chapters, popular resistance is now mainly disorganized, unfocused, divided, and, as often as not, misguided and self-defeating. Too often, no one offers resistance. Some have fought back, of course. Near Pittsburgh, for example, steel workers have formed a state-backed regional industrial authority to reclaim abandoned plants. And the people of Flint, Michigan, recently dared to demand that General Motors repay the town for its tax abatements when the company closed the plant for which the town had given incentives. A local Michigan court boldly proclaimed that the folks of Flint indeed had a right to do just that. The public-employees unions of New York State have also made some inroads on unity, as we have seen, but has largely overlooked potential links to community organizations. Overall, the larger pattern of mass response to "the new class war" has not been one of militant resistance. Certainly, no mass popular movement exists to demand the reorganization of work or the social responsibility of capital. As economic coercions move from the corporations to Washington, D.C., and from there down to the states and cities, outcroppings of resistance have aimed at individual tax increases, cutbacks in the provision of specific public goods, the squeeze on particular groups of government workers, and, as noted above, the recent efforts to punish local and state officials.

As we shall see, for reasons connected to the very nature of capital itself, the Left is more and more reduced to fights and struggles of scattered and fragmented resistance. Some on the Left now champion this very diversity of struggles as a sign of healthy radical pluralism. Localized resistance, however, cannot stop the current drift. Without a mass mobilization of the economic majority, the leaders of this society will almost certainly not take renewed interest in repairing the wreckage and waste of an industrial order that no longer serves their purposes.

But perhaps the power elite's very indifference to real economic issues has created a strategic opening, a systemic vulnerability to a politics of democratic change. Perhaps mainstream politics has created a gap in responsiveness to the concrete problems faced by most people in their everyday lives that action from below can yet fill. Out of elite indifference, after all, grows tangible anger. This anger is more populist than radical; it is more preoccupied with deficits and taxes than social needs and corporate accountability. But the fact remains: millions of people are frustrated and impatient with the status quo. In poll after poll, huge majorities declare that the country is moving in the wrong direction, that neither of the major parties is willing to act, that something has to change. People are growing impatient with things as they are; they are developing a rough-hewn, embittered common sense that the rich have had it too well, that government does not care, and that somehow people have to take politics into their own hands. When Republicans tried in 1992 to lure people from common sense with appeals to "patriotism" and "family values," the strategy fell on its face. The economy hurts, and people know it.

Unfortunately, the political Left in the United States is anything but ideally positioned to channel this resentment into progressive change. The Left has a small base; it is poorly financed and lacks regular access to national media. The healthy diversity of radical journals is read by the same relatively small group. Moreover, many of the various Left organizations are barely on speaking terms. Labor unions in particular have generally kept their distance from peace, civil liberties, consumer, environmental, women's rights, and neighborhood protest groups. Nor are the unions or any other cluster of Leftist organizations themselves strongly united by a dominant interest or program. Increasingly, the Left seems engulfed by divisions between groups oriented to the economy and those preoccupied by questions of culture and identity. For all these reasons, the Left has virtually no influence in shaping national economic agendas or priorities.

Yet the Left may still influence future developments. Even now, on key legislative battles, labor, civil rights, consumer, and other groups form vocal coalitions. Through such coalitions, the Left maintains some veto power in U.S. politics. A broad labor-led effort, for example, was extremely effective in stopping a balanced-budget amendment from passing Congress in 1992. This was a major victory. And in 1986, a different kind of Left coalition successfully blocked the nomination of conservative judge Robert Bork to the Supreme Court.

The Left has some power to block action; what it really lacks is the ability to influence national agendas, to move action, to build a constituency for limits on the market and a liberation of public policy to meet social needs. Yet with its organized footholds in labor unions, universities, urban neighborhoods, and suburban green movements, even in segments of the Democratic Party, the Left does have some resources to communicate its ideas to people at the grassroots. Moreover, the activist Left is experienced in the ways and means of mounting an opposition. Left activists understand the dynamics of movements, confrontational politics, and protest. Many remain strongly committed to the interests of working people of all types; they are prepared to do what they can. The question is, can the Left take advantage of its resources to turn the mounting populist anger toward the goals of social justice and an economy of needs? Can it can have some kind of general programmatic impact on mass politics?

Theorists of the Left, such as Richard Flacks, think not. For him, it is high time Leftists acknowledge that most Americans do not share their radical vision of activist democracy. Inasmuch as oppositional movements of ordinary people tend to aim at restabilizing threatened lives and communities, not at transforming society, the Left plays its most important role by supplying field organizers to support popular resistance wherever it erupts. In Flacks' words,

> What the organized left has been able to do is to nourish capacities for collective action and organization at the grass-roots by encouraging adherents to develop themselves and by fostering in the wider population awareness of shared threat, collective possibilities, and responsibilities. The authentic mission of the American left has always been "socialization"—not of the economy but of the people it has been able to touch.[9]

Flacks views the activist Left as adding more to the psychic and cultural income than to the economic income of working people. Its contribution is more symbolic than material. In a similar vein, Carl Boggs celebrates the influence that "New Left" activists of the 1960s have had on community-based political movements in the '70s and '80s. Aging '60s rebels, he argues, have helped greatly to foment and organize a variety of new, locally based movements of community self-defense, ecological and feminist awareness, gay rights, and minority empowerment. Like Flacks, Boggs describes the Left's contribution as essentially counter-cultural and psychological. The new movements of feminism and ecology, he writes, "ideally embellish not only democratization but a recovery of the self in a world in which politics has been deformed."[10]

In effect, following on the heels of the important work of Left social commentators Francis Fox Piven and Richard Cloward, Flacks and Boggs reasonably argue that radical action grows out of immediate experiences of grievance, not out of ideological condemnation. Pain is what moves people, not philosophy.[11] The trouble is, according to current theorists of capital and power, that the systematic infliction of economic pain is bound to become even more localized, finely grained, and dispersed in its effects than ever before. Such trends auger badly for class action and systemic reform.

The Politics of Cooptation and Repression

Capital is intensifying its splintering and decentralizing of political and cultural power. It is creating ever more discrete communities (e.g., edge cities, the insulated downtown and suburban corporate zones, the rural hamlets from which technocrats wire their messages to corporate headquarters, the abandonment of working-class cities). It is differentiating, marginalizing, and stigmatizing socially unnecessary labor (women, immigrants, surplus manual workers, the layers of unemployed managers, part-time and temporary labor). It is increasingly refining and specializing marketing (e.g., cable TV, direct mail) and commodifying ideas, images, spectacles, and diverse cultural forms (e.g., everything from the Superbowl, Michael Jordan, and rap, to video games, virtual reality machines, movie spectaculars, self-help books, the new literary criticism, and the great political correctness debate).

In a powerful observation that illuminates the deep connections between the decentralizing thrust of balanced-budget conservativism and the wholesale shift in social-control patterns typical of advanced technocratic capitalism, Alain Touraine declares that "integration no longer comes from the top, from the center of decisions, but from the bottom: consumption sets up hierarchies and achieves integration by multiplying indices of social standing." [12] The political manifestations abound, not least in respect to liberal opportunities for women and people of color. Bill Clinton, for example, joins conservative theorists like Jack Kemp in offering ghetto "empowerment zones" to bribe capital by eliminating taxes and regulations. Likewise, affirmative-action programs encourage talented women and minorities to serve established institutions, colleges and universities coopt the more radical women and minorities by giving them control of separate multicultural and feminist academic departments, and Republicans cheerlead minority efforts to create single-race legislative districts that sustain racial animosities. In all these ways, capital and the state preserve themselves through the most subtle and engaging forms of segmentation and cooptation. These are the smiling, receptive faces of a control system sensitive to our aspirations.

But this type of social control has meaner expressions too: the deepening and brutal segregation of unneeded labor. Andre Gorz is an all too eloquent guide to this side of late capitalism.

> The regimentation and segregation of non-workers has already begun…How authoritarian this segregation will become depends on the political form and traditions of individual regimes: apartheid, gulags, compulsory paramilitary service; shanty towns and North American-style urban

ghettos, crowding people together who are mostly unemployed; or gangs of unemployed youth, subsidized eternal students and endless apprenticeships, temporary, holiday, and seasonal workers, etc.[13]

In this world, life for the surplus proletariat is anything but a matter of "recovery of the self." It is a bitter, often failed struggle to survive. This is Hobbes' world of the war of each against all, overarched, as Fredric Jameson says in the epigram to this chapter, by the market as Leviathan. Political scientist Manning Marable vividly describes the brutal impact on the ghetto. "This crisis," he observes, "can be characterized by a deep sense of fragmentation and self-doubt, rooted in group consciousness and social existence. The symptoms of this internal crisis [are] the widespread drug epidemic, black-against-black violence, the growth of urban youth gangs, and the destruction of black institutions."[14] This living tragedy speaks to the emergency conditions the poorest people of this and other societies now face. Moreover, it points squarely to the even greater and more widespread emergency looming from the unmitigated deregulation of the market. More economic barbarism lies ahead.

But a cultural, politically de-centralized Left, one that conceives of and champions radical opposition to local grievances as the new essence of democracy, runs the great risk of answering capital's need for a resistance that confirms the system's claim to pluralism. Such an opposition is legitimating more than disturbing. It conforms to capital's ability to diffuse oppression.

Perhaps, as Flacks says, the rise of a majoritarian economic Left is itself a Leftist delusion. We plead guilty to the dream. But the present situation makes the older majoritarian hope more than romantic; it is indispensable if anyone is to temper the logic of economic coercion, not to mention reverse it. Indeed, Flacks himself suggests as much when he observes that today's variegated social movements "must turn the national government into a vehicle for societal democratization." [15] But what kind of politics will draw the urban movements toward the nation-state? And will they find enemies or allies among the workers and frightened people of the suburbs?

Unless the large body of working people find ways to channel their anger across the divide of sectarian identities and diverse movements, unless they identify their interest in terms of what Marx preferred to call "the immense majority," it seems doubtful to us that popular forces will retake the political system, take on the systemic logic where it is most vulnerable to regulation and control, or avoid the Gorzean nightmare state of more gulag ghettos. Consider that U.S. prisons already harbor a large fraction of African American males under thirty, that the South Central Los Angeles riot of 1992 did not win so much as a cursory symbolic response from elites of either party, that elites now delay the broadcast of potentially volatile verdicts in order to prepare the appropriate mobilizations of military force, that a smiling Bill Clinton now offers a frightened society the prospect of "boot camps" for the oncoming generation of "youthful offenders." As the repressive potential grows, the chance for democracy needs a broad-based mass politics, one whose first task must be to change the terms of the present debate, to dislodge the grip of balanced-budget conservatism, and to demand a political framework in which the public has a say in economic action.

"It's Not the Deficit, Stupid!"

Nothing will change for the better for working people until they liberate public debate from the shackles of balanced-budget conservatism. For us, the economic majority, to have a future, we have to demand a politics that busts out of the ideological prison of budgets and retrenchment. To help this happen, we must be absolutely clear about the systemic roots of deficit politics. The Left needs to explain how and why the deficit, which once unified the political economy and furthered corporate management of class peace, has now become an obsession of elites, who are today less fearful of conflicts below.

The myth of balanced-budget conservatism is that government deficits are inherently evil. For more than forty years, however, national policy ran on the opposite principle. Elites believed that deficits were necessary to expand the economy. Because corporate capitalism failed to guarantee people and technology full employment, governments of both parties spent borrowed money in droves to prop up demand and prod investment. They correctly bet that chronic stagnation would not cure itself. In fact, their public borrowing helped increase consumption, investment, and production; it absorbed surplus, moderated the pain of stagnation, enlarged the material base, and expanded the system's ability to satisfy human needs. Most of this satisfaction was, as we have argued, distorted through a social structure divided by class and race. It aided Fortress Suburbia and systematically abandoned the surplus populations of cities. Most important, though, deficit spending kept economic crisis at bay; it prevented a political crisis that could threaten the regime itself.

At the same time, deficit spending also imposed on government the chief social responsibility for maintaining economic progress. From the New Deal forward, corporations responded to an economic climate that was no longer spontaneously created by market forces. Through its powers to influence demand, employment, and inflation, central government now deliberately managed economic conditions. By the same token, though, public economic leadership meant that private power was no longer to blame for economic crisis.

In these ways, the public function of economic management both absorbed and mystified the crisis tendencies of capitalism; politics now took place, as Habermas notes, "on the basis of a processed and repressed system crisis."[16] Government management helped capital avoid crisis, but it did not eliminate the tendency toward crisis. This state economic responsibility meant that, as the underlying conditions of world accumulation changed for the worse after 1973, the public would look to government for answers, not to the corporations.

Since 1973, extraordinary changes have occurred between labor and capital; global competition has taken on hurricane dimensions. Everywhere, not only in the United States, the power of states to manage economic conditions has shrunk. But the weakened state still has its responsibilities. It cannot fall back in hopes of self-correcting adjustments from the global market. For those adjustments only bring more unemployment, factory shutdowns, lower wages, and inflation. As we saw in Chapter Two, the last twenty years have brought economic insecurity to everyone but the highest income groups, and real devastation to the poorest members of society. In this environment, the chances for a market-led fix favoring fast growth and full employment are about as good as for a comeback of the Model T.

Yet deficit spending can no longer moderate what is now a transformed economic crisis. The problem facing governments is not simply inadequate demand for corporate output. The social, technical, commercial, and spatial relations of capital have fundamentally changed. At bottom, the dynamic of capitalist technical progress has reduced the need for labor while vastly expanding and accelerating the circulation of capital. The resulting surplus has exploded in unprecedented financial speculation, commercial waste, and disinvestment. Workers have lost good jobs and become poorer while the managers of capital have gorged on its ever-faster circulation.

The Reagan Administration operated on the assumption that deficit spending was simply the easiest, most politically popular way of postponing a confrontation with real economic crisis. At least the rising deficit spurred demand, just as the downward draft of real wages was moderated by the steady upward lift of entitlements. The economic needle barely stayed in the groove, but did not collapse.

Just as important, deficits carried the secondary ideological advantage of reinforcing Reagan's conservative anti-governmental political message. Reagan thus inaugurated the new Orwellian political economy of balanced-budget conservatism. Beginning in the 1980s, the very government that used deficits to forestall crisis began to abuse itself for doing so.

By now, of course, politicians preach to us, waving tables showing current and future deficits in bright red ink. Third-party gadfly Ross Perot has made crimson-colored graphs the icon of choice in the age of balanced-budget conservatism. Democratic President Bill Clinton rests the fate of his administration on a gently downward sloping line of federal borrowing. Senate Republican Minority Leader Robert Dole makes political points by insisting that the line drops too gently at the cost of higher taxes.

Statistical scare tactics and bizarre forms of numerical manipulation now dominate debates over economic policy. Leaders of both major parties use titanic numbers to intimidate and confuse people and to justify a lowered social wage. In the process, economic realism has disappeared. The mystique of the deficit overpowers public reason.

In light of the anti-credit hysteria, one wonders how Americans ever dare to risk taking out a thirty-year mortgage to purchase their house. But then, if banks printed full repayment prices at the top of every page of the mortgage in bold red ink, many people, confronted with such endless reminders of the full cost, might well forgo the purchase. For average homebuyers, though, who face interest costs that greatly inflate the real price of their house, the key issues are whether the total charge is within the reach of their long-term earning power, and whether the house serves their family's long-term needs.

In the same way, the key issue of the deficit is not its current or even projected size. The issue is whether the government uses federal borrowing to enhance the society's future economic capacity and social needs. This is one clue to a unifying theme for new progressive strategies.

Even those mainstream economists who agonize over the federal deficit acknowledge the truth of this principle. David Calleo counts himself among the biggest worriers over the nation's borrowing practices, yet even he admits that "the practice of borrowing is not intrinsically harmful, even in purely economic terms. If the government's borrowing results, overall, in commensurately greater economic growth for the whole economy, then the deficit can be considered an investment in the future." [17] For Calleo and other serious critics of the deficit, its crisis potential concerns not so much its size as its political misuse. For them, the issue is whether current borrowing is used for long-term and rational economic purposes or sunk down a rat hole. Will the political economy be able to pay off the debt it accumulates?

If the government borrows, even massively borrows, to refurbish an aging economic base, or to create a social infrastructure of schools and laboratories that will generate sustained growth in productivity, then borrowing makes sense, even on quite capitalistic grounds. But if government borrows simply to pay off the cost of more borrowing (i.e., the rising interest costs of the debt), or to preserve an excessive defense establishment that adds nothing directly to the civilian production base, or to feed the finance charges and oligopoly profits of an exceptionally inefficient health-care system, then mounting deficits are fiscally and socially destructive. They waste tomorrow's taxpayers' money, eat away at the capital for needed public investment, erode the financial system, and ultimately threaten the political system's very viability.

With the examples just noted, each of which is a major component of today's federal deficit, the problem is not the aggregate deficit itself, but its irrational and wasteful components, the distorted uses of public capital in the budget and the institutional biases that drive such uses. The deficit is troublesome, in other words, not because it has reached some arbitrary volume or growth rate, or because the red lines on a graph point up rather than down, but because its specific underlying forces do not increase the future well-being of this society or its economic potential; in fact, it is the major uses of deficit spending that now contribute even more to subverting society's potential for progress. In short, the social composition of the deficit, not its size, should worry people.

But how did the deficit come to represent such distorted priorities? Apart from the political charade of the Reagan years and the deep-seated distortions encompassed by the military and health political economies, two even more fundamental factors stand out.

First, as we have already stressed, the deficit began in the 1930s as a systemic solution to the problem of chronic stagnation. The existing arrangement of capitalist economic power forbade society to use the nation's economic potential fully. Deficits helped to reclaim some of that potential in ways that preserved the system of power, for example, through the build-up of the warfare state. But the deficit did not change the system that allows corporations to use, abuse, or not use their capital, as they see fit. It did not change the basic forces creating stagnation. Those forces remained in place, only to be aggravated by the growth of global capitalism.

Thus, the deficit developed in distorted ways. In part, this was because its function was to preserve the private power network that kept capital from meeting social needs. It helped prolong the day when the present organization of society might yield to a less repressive, more liberated social order founded on a rational aligning of economic forces and social relations. Later, the increasingly strained relationship between social relations and productive forces in effect exacerbated the deficit, and it became a quantitative expression of this breakdown. The deficit is the rising price that elites imposed on society to maintain their social system and keep their power. But even this crucial aspect of the deficit only partly explains why it has been spent so irrationally.

Preserving power through borrowing is one thing; spending the deficit rationally is quite another. This suggests the second main factor of distortion in the deficit. At the very least, a rational plan of spending requires a fairly centralized political system to outline and coordinate public investments. The U.S. political system does not remotely satisfy this condition. From the start, the U.S. political system was poorly fitted to ration public spending in accordance with public need, much less to control large deficits. Separation of powers, checks and balances, the preoccupations of congresspeople with issues in their home districts, the non-centralized bureaucracy, all coupled with the diffuse but powerful array of private interest groups, all contribute to the sprawling, discombobulated nature of federal spending. The structure of the political system all but dictates that government spend in response to organized power, not social need.

After World War II, when deficits expanded the pie, interest groups, warmly encouraged by the Democratic Party, lined up and hitched their political wagons to the government's new money machine. The result was what C. Wright Mills called "the governmentalization of the lobby"; Theodore J. Lowi later named its covering ideology "interest group liberalism." [18]

Whatever the name, the group takeover of the budget implied big spending, and it rested on minimal planning. Private pressures to plunder the state by spending public money mounted through the fragmented system of absentee democracy, and the disjointed processes of budget-making ensured that such spending reflected narrow, unplanned purposes. Although Washington did attempt over the years to rationalize executive and congressional budget-making, most recently when Congress passed the Budget Reform Act of 1974, none of the reforms altered the basic interest-group-driven pattern of uncoordinated expenditure. Each separate interest group and constituency kept making its bid for public spending, and compliant legislators usually responded in kind.

We see no easy remedy to these institutional defects in the U.S. political design. Indeed, as far as private power is concerned, such patterns are not defects at all. They constitute a set of rules and institutions that we have called absentee democracy because they deny majority rule by the people as a whole. The nation's founders designed such rules to over-produce and over-represent private power in public government and to weaken the majority's capacity to use public power. Absentee democracy expresses the original ruling-class preference to limit labor's power to change society comprehensively through legislation. Property never wanted the mass of ordinary people to self-consciously rule in their own behalf. Institutional fragmentation was a way to keep the people at bay. The founders understood that democracy—rule of the many—and oligarchy—rule of the few—represent opposite principles. Thus, they fashioned a republic that tried awkwardly to mix the two, in the end creating a system that mainly fractured mass democracy and disorganized mass political power without preventing the excessive power of narrow private interests.

When this awkward political system attempted to overcome the first great crisis of stagnation in the 1930s, it simply wed its patterns of fragmented policy-making to a government that begged for but never got the equipment to plan. It is now clear that even so modest a form of planning as Keynesian fiscal policy demanded more than the U.S. government could give. When the second big wave of stagnation hit in the 1970s, the government's job was made all the harder by massive global economic changes. Technical transformations of production and the arrival of a conservative political elite that despised the idea of a muscular democratic government that could think for itself added to government's difficulties. As conservative commentator Kevin Phillips notes in his 1993 book *Boiling Point*, during the Reagan years, as "the effectiveness of government degenerated…economic interest groups fattened on the fragmentation of power and achieved leverage unmatched since the Gilded Age."[19]

The obliteration of the Cold War denied Washington its only major outlet of government spending that allowed it any explicit, deliberate planning. Now that government lacks even this, budgeting becomes sheer plunder. Washington simply has no unifying principle, not even a repressive one, left to frame priorities. Powerful claims run rampant, and the deficit keeps growing, although bipartisan elites remind us that there is not enough to go around.

The mainstream debate about how to revive the U.S. system naturally tries to avoid implicating its structural weakness. But such a debate can never restore a system whose material progress and tensions have far outgrown its means of political action. On the one hand, in the name of free markets and pained taxpayers, balanced-budget conservatives enforce a version of competitive rationality on the system. To use the apt and pungent phrase of C. Wright Mills, theirs is the "crackpot realism" of an elite that renounces any obligation to society whatsoever. Offering more enlightened prospects, faithful liberals plead for a lessening of hysteria and a strengthening of leadership. Authors such as Donald Kettl dispassionately invoke elitism as the answer to the regime's internal dilemmas. "The battles of the deficit," he declares, are best seen as "challenges to our political leaders." The high officials will resolve the nation's difficulties when finally they offer "a broad vision for where society will go." A more anxious David Calleo also looks to "an exceptionally determined and principled political leadership" to furnish "a well-thought-out and coordinated set of policies." [20] Reform can be had, liberals believe, if only the nation's political leadership would muster the nerve to identify the crisis, develop the partisan muscle to advance and coordinate appropriate reforms, and inspire mass belief in the moral rightness of their approach. The nation, however, has waited more than thirty years for this leadership, and like Godot, it never comes.

No leader has ever defined the crisis because a definition would challenge the very nature of the regime; it would upset the powers that benefit from its present organization. No leader has marshalled the political strength to overcome private power because, short of a sudden calamity of the 1929 or 1941 type, the system is organized precisely to over-produce private power. And none has sustained public confidence for their plans because they have produced no plans adequate to the problem. What liberalism cannot face is the terrible reality that the deficit, the omnivorous red spiral, is now the most powerful symptom of the self-expanding irrationality of its own attempt to save capitalism from itself.

We cannot avoid the systemic roots of the problem. Capitalist political economy in the United States is a system of private, unplanned investment for profit. By its very nature it imposes huge penalties on society. How we pay these penalties, however, is not subject to the nation collectively and rationally deliberating national interests, nor is private irrationality acknowledged as the source of the costs. Instead, open-ended, fragmented, undirected political processes settle the questions of the appropriate level and direction of social payments. The pluralism that political science championed, a product of an absentee democracy designed to cripple labor's political power, distorts deliberative rationality. Conservatives then point shamelessly to this distortion of their own making as evidence of why the state cannot plan.

In sum, the deficit grows according to its own self-expansive logic because private rationality produces social irrationality; because society is unable to compensate except by way of the same blind competitive rationality—now applied to politics—that itself generates the problem in the first place. We can see that there is a direct connection between the competitive private process that raises costs to society as whole and the disorganized political process that regularly generates pressures toward unplanned overspending and under-taxation. Waste, duplication, and undirected spending mount up on the output side while revenues are held down on the input side. The entire process unfolds independent of any unified democratic assessment of the needs of society as whole. The problem is far from one of excessive political power, of too much democracy; it is one of a handicapped system of absentee democracy in thrall to irresponsible private powers.

Above all, we must emphasize, the federal deficit is not a sign of objective impoverishment. If this society is poor, it is in the organized capacity for democratic power, not in its wealth, material resources, or technical forces of production. As liberal economist Benjamin Friedman argues, even assuming that the society wanted to maintain the overall public spending priorities of the 1980s—6% of national income going to defense, 11% for entitlements and 3% for all other federal civilian functions—"America remains a strong and affluent country, well able to afford its current level of government if that is what its citizens choose." [21]

The deficit is a problem because society as currently organized is democratically incapacitated; its social-class structure, its relations of production and power, do not now permit the population as a whole to demand the full use of the nation's resources. The social structure is undemocratic, the economic forces are under the control of the few, and the public political order is thwarted at every turn by private vetoes of class, market, and property. To massively redirect economic policy through existing arrangements seems virtually impossible. To attempt the needed alteration of the political and economic institutions presupposes the very political power that is missing. The fearsome problem was never better stated than by Robert S. Lynd: "To attempt fundamental change in institutions, of a kind that affects the basic character of organized power in a given society, without changing the social structure of that society is like trying to drive a car forward with the gears set in reverse." [22] Is it yet possible to get at and reform Lynd's social structure?

The advantage of Lynd's formulation is that it states both the difficulty and the possibility of structural change through existing institutions. The prevailing institutions were designed to preserve not only existing society but its characteristically ponderous forms of political change. In the United States, a fragmented system for making political changes has been hitched to the fastest moving market system in the world. The localization and fragmentation of political power is, in this sense, one of the prime conditions for the mobilization and acceleration of domestic corporate power. As we have stressed throughout this book, the political strength of capital has depended on the political weakening of labor. In this sense, social structure and political institutions are anything but separate phenomena. The social structure of power has made itself felt in the very organization and disorganization of political institutions. The U.S. political system has simply left a huge vacuum of social capacity for managing capital either from above or below.

Balanced-budget conservatism now makes the effort to dismantle what little effective democratic power was channeled into the economy by the warfare-welfare state. It aims to re-institutionalize political decentralization as a means for speeding up and diffusing the market's power to incorporate, dominate, change, and even abandon large parts of U.S. society, and to accomplish this without mass opposition. The whole approach, as we have argued from the outset, rests on destroying the never more than tenuous institutional links between labor and national government. Following Lynd's formulation, however, it is not impossible to conceive of possible responses.

Institutional strategies of "fundamental" social change are not out of the cards, as long as such strategies take aim at vital institutional points. The key for the Left is to intercept and demand change in anti-majoritarian political institutions at points of maximum vulnerability to democratic pressure. In other words, the Left needs to aim at the more vital intersections of social structure and institutions, especially those which directly distort the majority's ability to organize and think for itself. Our proposal is to channel mass discontent with the political economy into a nationally oriented program of political democratization and democratic public-expenditure planning that is coupled to a re-energization of local publics as the spontaneous, independent voices of grassroots demand.

As noted above, we think that our proposal is a longshot at best. Moreover, we are all too aware of its weaknesses, especially in the context of a world capitalism with such enormous power to de-center politics and warp dissent itself into a means of legitimation and social control. But as long as capital continues to need centralized political power for its aid in administration, rationalization, and legitimacy, the central state remains a potentially democratic lever to control, maybe even to change, the national economic dynamic. What follows, then, rests on two interconnected trends: the continued relevance of national power to capitalist power, and thus, the continued vulnerability of capital to a nationally empowered democracy.

The starting point for any hope of change is as always the discontent of ordinary people with the status quo, and there is plenty of that around. Millions of people now do feel that there is something wrong with "the system." As people fight their numerous localized battles against taxes, distorted spending priorities, and the squeeze on public services, many have come to sense disjunctions between the limited responsiveness of available arenas and the fact that real power seems to come, as Lynd describes it, "from somewhere behind or beneath institutions." [23] People sense that such unseen power compromises democratic power at all levels, and yet is immune to popular control. The poll data of mass alienation from politics clearly reflects suspicions of this sort. A June 1992 study discovered, for instance, that 54% of Americans believe that the political system needs either "major changes" or "a complete overhaul." Similarly, a series of detailed discussions with citizens around the country convinced the Kettering Foundation that many Americans now "believe they have been squeezed out of politics by a 'system' made up of lobbyists, political action committees, special interest organizations, and the media." [24] And the decline in confidence does not stop at public anger at the political system. As Republican political strategist Kevin Phillips reports, there is in the shrinking middle class of the 1990s a "gathering anger at the rich," reflected in outrage at the super-salaries of the corporate elite, their 1980s tax holiday, and Wall Street's speculative binge. These attitudes, rife in U.S. politics today, provide a fragile tap root of mass support for a democratic program of economic and political reconstruction. A key factor in deciding the outcome will be whether progressive organizers, working with their bases in urban ghettos, suburban environmental movements, and labor unions, among other places, can thoughtfully link the grievances of residence and workplace to the discontents that now plague the larger systems of power. In short, the Left can make significant change through institutions as long as the institutional change is tied to some larger "public" issue.

From Protest Groups to Publics

Two clear-headed radicals, Joe Kling and Prudence Posner, offer one sensible line of thinking. Kling and Posner argue that organizers can make such connections by developing programs with class content to transform organized eruptions of local grievance into wider, more effective "publics." [25] Publics, they believe, draw on, but go a step beyond, the more familiar organs of popular opposition on the Left, the numerous community organizations, local self-help associations, and labor unions that are today embattled on so many fronts. In a crucial sense, Kling and Posner argue, publics can transform protest groups into wider democratic forces with added class content.

Kling and Posner recognize, with Flacks and Boggs, that existing Left protest groups can generate effective veto power when their memberships understand the social grounding of their grievances. They can block unwanted development projects, resist tax or wage cuts, remedy specific abuses of people's civil rights, and even work more positively to improve housing or other local social services. At this level Kling and Posner agree with Flacks and Boggs that Left organizations play a vital role in helping people transform their private troubles into social issues.

Protest organizations become "publics" when organizers help people see their grievance and its solution in broader "public" terms; they see that "others, outside their immediately identified peers, suffer the same treatment." [26] In other words, publics experience grievances not as a particular or localized problem but as a more generalized one. They see people from outside the local milieu enduring similar patterns of exploitation, inequity, or oppression. In this way, publics begin to do two things that many existing protest groups tend not to do.

First, the organizers of publics regularly urge their members to develop a sympathetic identity that cuts across established social and political divisions and boundaries. Publics try to link constituencies, which tend to focus on their specific problems and local jurisdictions, into a common constituency for change. They strive to bridge the divisions and gaps created by the localized base of absentee democracy and the narrowness of membership organizations such as unions. In this way, publics serve as a surrogate for class action in a federal system that divides interests.

Consequently, having invoked an enlarged scope of suffering and grievance, publics logically insist upon "some form of broad-based collective action," some kind of multi-jurisdictional, trans-federal, or national program, to produce policies that can effectively overcome the sources of frustration in many different places at once. [27] The conscientious development of programs favoring national enforcement thus becomes a key moment in the hard transition from protest group to public. Such programs have the potential to give mass democratic content to social change. Kling and Posner are worth quoting at length on this point. Organized publics, they argue,

> function as social movements, but as movements that link constituent- and community-based social action groups to policies and programs that can have class content and orientation. The organized public describes social movements that seek to reshape rules in broader democratic directions and that have core structures rooted in any kind of social base, whether class, constituency, or community. [28]

The labor movements of the 1930s and the Civil Rights movements of the 1960s are powerful examples of social movements that became publics. Workers in the 1930s demanded from the national government not this or that benefit, but a new framework of rights within which to battle for their grievances in general, a framework that would enhance labor power in the public and private sectors all at once. Through a fight for broad political and economic rights at the national level, the old labor movement used its political power to change the direction of national policy toward the working class. The effect was to modify or move, however slightly, Lynd's social structure of unequal classes in the direction of greater equality. Much the same could be said for the old Civil Rights Movement and its demand for the use of federal power to recast historic relations of racial dominance. When today's women's movement makes the call for an "equal rights amendment," it acts as a public.

Although the Left, not to mention the black poor, is understandably disappointed that the Civil Rights Movement failed to make a successful transition from political to socio-economic demands, the fact remains that the mass protests of the 1960s did move the country in the right direction, toward greater equality and democracy, a direction that conservative rule has halted since 1968. [29] Today, the most important thing that the Left can contribute to national politics is to apply as much pressure as possible to reset the nation's direction back toward democracy. In this fight, protest against specific grievances and threats at all levels is essential. But precisely because the readily available channels of action overwhelmingly favor local, communal, or limited types of mobilization, it is imperative for activists to move their groups in the direction of more "public" organization and frame their purpose through national political change.

Organizers need to take this political chance, to frame their issues so that local anger conceives of grievance not as an isolated incursion against "us," but as part of a larger political assault against other people like "us" who may well live and work in other places. Below, we offer one stab at a program that places the accent on unifying the broad economic majority into an effective national political majority. Further, we argue that public-employee unions have the make-up, resources, and skills to help lead the fight for unity among all segments of the economic majority.

A Plan for a National Majority

Our critique of the deficit stresses that balanced-budget conservatism can be combatted by focusing on the potential wealth of the country and the need for democracy to gain rational control over public resources. In line with that analysis, we base a solution to the deficit on three, inter-connected steps. First, we need a collective agreement on a particular structure of national public investments that meets the nation's social needs. Second, we need to strengthen the government's ability to direct public investment toward social needs. Third, we need a majoritarian politics willing and strong enough to back such a program and claim the taxes necessary to finance it. The answer to balanced-budget conservatism, in other words, requires working to make the present political system more democratic. Only then will the economic majority even have a chance to make its own voice loud and clear on economic policy.

Toward this end, we outline important and attainable goals for change, a broad-based agenda that has a chance, might do some good, and, most importantly, puts the focus on national democratic power.

1. A public plan should be created to guide long-term federal expenditures toward meeting democratically chosen public needs.

2. A knowledge and information base should be developed in the federal government to provide a public-needs inventory as the basis of debates about alternative plans to balanced-budget conservatism. Later, such an inventory should be extended to include systematic knowledge of corporate capacity.

3. To protect local governments from the economic coercion of credit markets, Washington should provide full faith and credit backing of local bonds for projects developed to meet regional and national development goals.

4. To enhance representation of the national majority, the government must have direct election of the president. In addition, the government should extend the terms of House members to four years and consider adding a number of new at-large national seats, perhaps as many as ten, to the Senate.

5. To neutralize private economic power in the electoral process, the government must completely finance Congressional election campaigns, abolish Political Action Committees, and mandate free air-time to candidates for all federal elections. It should prohibit the purchase and sale of television and radio time for political advertisements.

These steps are basic and interconnected, and neither in spirit nor form are they foreign to the history of U.S. political debates. First, we suggest the need for more explicit coordination and planning of public spending in relation to a scheme of democratic social priorities. As the terms of public discourse stand now, this is impossible. The starting point for balanced-budget conservatism is cost, not need. Narrow budgetary considerations drive policy, making broad-based social planning impossible. This debate excludes alternatives to balanced-budget conservatism. By shifting the debate from costs to social needs the possibility, indeed, the likelihood, of transcending balanced-budget conservatism emerges. The focus shifts to tapping existing wealth to pay for social needs, and this raises the possibility of planning. This sounds like an easy task, but it's not. We can only make this transition through the full-scale representation of the national economic majority in the political process and by de-throning private economic power in the electoral process.

The system desperately needs an enlarged institutionalized base for democratic, collective social rationality. In a word, it needs to plan. And Theodore Lowi is right to claim that planning demands a strong government, or what he describes as "the authoritative use of authority." [30] What is imperative about such authority is not merely that it has sufficient strength, but that its roots and direction be solidly and massively democratic. A strong government capable of planning for social needs must directly answer to the national majority, not simply to the scattering of parcellized state and local majorities, but to the majority of the people as a whole. The national majority must be the political system's main directive and unifying force, the clear inspiration of what Lowi calls the "choice, priorities, moralities" that guide and channel planning. [31] Only when the majority gains this collective electoral expression can it form new independent political organizations and public movements to represent and project its will. Only then can it empower public government to realize the social potential of mass democracy, what Franz Neumann once described as "the execution of large-scale social changes maximizing the freedom of man."[32]

The existing federal budget serves as the natural starting point of such a plan. It represents where we are. What we need in addition to the budget is a statement of unmet needs and priorities to guide the direction of future spending patterns and the political capacity to achieve it. Here is where the difficulties begin. At present, the federal government has no centralized means of gathering and assessing information about alternative public needs. No unified social report matches the macro-economic analyses provided by the Office of Management and Budget, Council of Economic Advisors, the U.S. Treasury, and other agencies. Instead, federal agencies publish numerous scattered reports and studies largely to justify their own programs. And then, of course, we have the endless, self-serving interest-group studies.

Minimally, the federal government needs to create an agency to produce and/or coordinate measurements and indicators of social needs. This document could provide the basis for more rational and informed political debates about where and how to allocate public funds in areas such as public housing, public education, public transportation, public health. A central-planning agency could emerge as the appropriate capstone for regional, state, and local planning bodies, with roots in the needs of regional majorities. Linking national and regional needs-inventories would lend a grassroots tone and shape to a document that the federal government cannot and should not author alone from on high.

The proposal to put federal financial backing behind local bonds fits here too, and it is equally important. [33] As we have seen, grassroots democratic efforts to reclaim neighborhoods, abandoned industrial facilities and to remake infrastructure are handicapped by the hegemony of the credit agencies and fiscal watchdogs of Wall Street, not to mention the competitive bidding of states and cities that offer tax abatements and other lures to business. Federal credit backing for local projects would take the gun of cutthroat competition out of the arsenal of balanced-budget conservatism. Moreover, it might actually give regional development plans, neighborhood groups, and local councils a real economic chance to rebuild the lost cities of the Rust Belt. Planning federal expenditure makes such a proposal a matter of sound social economy as well as an indispensable tool for grassroots democratic planning.

Without a national economic majority politically organized and empowered to support and fight for social needs, however, any social-needs inventory, even if established, would quickly lose to the demands flowing from the uneven pluralism of interests that currently prevails.

National planning requires a national majority, a majority prepared to assent to an overall scheme of priorities, investments, and commitments. To exist, this potential majority needs political reforms to nationalize the electorate, forging a constituency capable of bringing the demands of the economic majority as a whole directly into the system. One obvious and popular move would be to rejoin the fight for direct election of the president. Indeed, in one formulation recently urged by Steven J. Rosenstone, such a change could have the added benefit of breaking the current two-party monopoly of national elections. "If we were to abolish the Electoral College altogether," Rosenstone argues, "replace it with the direct, popular election of the president, and require that the president win an absolute majority of the popular vote, the two-party monopoly would be broken." [34] In the opening round of such an election, a reasonably strong third-party bid would deny an absolute majority to one of the two major parties, leaving the third party with a loud voice in the campaign and influence in the runoff. Direct election would thus help both to nationalize the electorate, create a more solid basis for a majoritarian consensus to gather around a spending plan, and also give more of a chance to a serious third-party effort, including one from the Left. Obviously, a more conservative third candidate could also benefit, such as Ross Perot; but we think that, on balance, the economic majority has more to gain than to lose from the generalization of its power.

In a similar vein, increasing House terms by two years would solidify the president's majority base. The notion of adding at-large national seats to the Senate may strike some as wild, but we must do something to enhance representation of national needs in the Senate. With its staggered terms, equally empowered state constituencies, and rules favoring minority control of political debate, the Senate remains much too stubbornly representative of the eighteenth-century spirit of absentee democracy. In an even more outrageous thought, perhaps it is even time to consider abolishing it altogether; democracy, after all, should concern itself with representing people, not arbitrary territorial jurisdictions, especially those that give underpopulated areas disproportionate legislative power to control the will of the majority. Perhaps readers can generate better alternatives, but this issue needs thought.

In the spirit of such reforms, the Left is now debating whether it is time to pressure the system through a third-party effort. Former union head Tony Mazzochi of the Oil, Chemical and Atomic Workers has organized a pre-party organization, Labor Party Advocates, which is building the case for a new labor party; Joel Rogers, a progressive political scientist at the University of Wisconsin, is working along somewhat different lines to create what he calls "the New Party," with a broader participatory democratic focus. The Left should pay careful attention to these moves, but without a national constituency for working people to control, any new third-party effort is bound, like so many earlier efforts along these lines, to flounder on the shoals of federalism. Moreover, given the current system of campaign finance and media power, it is difficult to see how a Left party could successfully compete.

As it is, the program we are recommending probably has to find its first voice in the national Democratic Party, for there is no other current mechanism to challenge its monopoly of the Left, and we are too familiar with the limits of the Democrats as the party of democracy. But what choice is there?

If electoral politics in the United States is to become a regular part of the ongoing struggle of working people to get a government that represents their interests, then people will have to disengage it from the grip of private economic power. At every level of politics, including state and local government, Left groups need to make part of their platform abolishing large-scale, private financing of public elections. Such a development might even uncover latent democratic potential amongst the Democrats. In any event, electoral politics in a democratic society must serve not the money of interests, but the ideas of publics.

In this sense, among the chief unmet public needs for which our society needs to plan is a political framework encouraging independent political organization and discussion, a public sphere for publics that thrives outside the formal governmental network and its appendages of political parties and governmentalized interest groups. In other words, we need to plan the re-formation of a free, open sphere of publics that are equipped to think, talk through, and make claims for their needs. Gorz makes the key point when he insists that "politics should never be confused with executive power, with administration, with the state. If it is not a means of expression that transmits the aspirations of civil society to the government and challenges the latter in the name of the former and, conversely, the former in the name of a coherent overall view, then politics loses its autonomy, and goes into decline."[35]

Political parties and interest groups tend to focus on the interior processes of administration and legislation such that, even if the Left were successfully to form a mass party, the party would not suffice for democratic needs. People must be capable "of spontaneously organizing" themselves for action. As Franz Neumann's classic essay on "The Concept of Political Freedom" reminds us, democracy requires two quite distinct things: both the free election of representatives and the room for spontaneous public responsiveness to the decisions.

Planning is democratic when it answers to the will of the majority and guarantees the right of the minority to make its voice heard. But the majority will not just arise like some automatic reflex of an election, not even a direct election for president. As De Toqueville insisted, people will not participate in processes of power if they feel their views do not count. Just the same, they are unlikely to participate in electoral activities unless they come to have an experience of democratic reason and power. We are not talking here about some imaginary return to Athenian democracy, nor do we mean an everyday life dominated by civic meetings and public discussions. We are talking about the numerous community, labor, and social-cause groups that now exist, and the role that organizers can play in giving broadened public meaning to their discussions of issues and strategy.

In other words, the majority already has a multiplicity of organizational types to give it breathing room and life. It certainly needs national parties to frame competing options, to articulate varying conceptions of social needs, to help bridge differences and enlarge the bases of majoritarian unity. But the majority is, as Flacks and Boggs make clear, already a heterogenous grouping of diverse groups. Such diversity need not be divisive, if group members and leaders engage themselves in the kind of thinking and action that invites coalition and unity rather than backbiting competition. Obviously, the history of the Left offers all too many examples of backbiting and not nearly enough illustrations of solidarity. Perhaps we are whistling in the wind, but, as we stressed in the beginning of this study, people are still relatively free to make choices about goals and strategies, about ends and means. The only alternative to despair is the faith that experience and reason can still make themselves felt as democratic resources. It is still possible to bring such things to bear in the making of publics. In the final analysis, of course, it will not be organizers, leaders, and academics who will decide the outcome. It is left to the many strains of the economic majority to decide whether, how, and for what purposes it may bring itself into being.

For decades, of course, we in the United States have been told that democratic planning is impossible, that markets offer the only rational guide to rational economic behavior, that big government has no business wasting people's money financing campaign expenditures. The collapse of the Soviet system seems on its face to substantiate the case against planning. But history is as cunning as it is cruel. Even as it seems to deprive humanity of the socialist promise, history now forces the greatest capitalist nation on earth to confront the irrational and unplanned nature of its own system. The fact is, planning is not an option for the United States; just to maintain itself as a system of private power, the regime will find it structurally necessary to plan. The national government simply cannot go on spending aimlessly, failing to meet more and more social needs, and offering no real promise of economic revival.

Today, the ideological suspicions of planning are themselves archaic; they matter only at the level of pure ideology. For one thing, such arguments are irrelevant to the conditions of public spending; the federal budget is already a vast, if uncoordinated, planning document. Its spending equals more than 20% of Gross National Product annually. Second, the fragility of the world financial system, its utter dependence on the strength of the U.S. economy, will inevitably make public planning part of multinational capital's U.S. agenda. U.S. business would certainly prefer to avoid this, and it will strive mightily to fight against a move toward democratic financial planning, but in light of the waning military focus to spending, some kind of alternative financial planning guide is now inevitable. Is it inevitable that corporate elites will dominate such a state planning mechanism? Not inevitable, perhaps, but likely, especially if Left organizations of all types do not engage the issue.

Public Employee Unions as a Lead Public

In the fight for a democratic program, we think public-sector unions could play a particularly important role. For one thing, their memberships straddle the most dangerous and difficult divisions of the economic majority, the separations of race and residence. Public employees include working people who live in cities and suburbs, women and men, people of all colors. For all the limits and shrinkage of unions, public-sector unions are growing; they are among the most inclusive and dynamic organizations of the economic majority. This means that public-sector unions enjoy one of the best available platforms for making common political and economic appeals across the key divides of the economic majority. The very fact that unions are legitimate contenders for power in the system gives their leaders access to the mass media. But, more important, the fact that public employees can readily speak the language of public needs gives them a central role in identifying needs, resources, and possibilities.

Moreover, public-sector unions are right on the economic firing line of capital's class attack. More than any other social group, public-union members and leaders have the clearest insight into those changes in the administrative processes that now distort the state. Thus, labor is best positioned to develop and articulate alternatives to the current organization and distribution of public services, including how best and most efficiently to utilize the available means of public production for social benefit.

Third, because their memberships live in and serve neighborhoods that are feeling the effects of public budget cuts, public-employee unions are well placed to build alliances with neighborhood-based organizations, and to help frame such alliances in terms of broad, publicly oriented, class-wide solutions. Indeed, precisely because public employees are often the most immediate targets of balanced-budget conservatism, they have the greatest immediate interest in shifting the terms of the current debate. Their leaders and members have a special responsibility to demonstrate solidarity between the services of the state and the needs of citizens.

Fourth, because public-employee unions represent workers in local and state governments as well as the national government, they have a unique ability to address inter-governmental competition, the universality of fiscal domination, and the false promise of beggar-thy-neighbor economic development policies. Public-employee unions have the power to frame inter-governmental alliances of workers and consumers to demand equality through uniform federal standards for delivery of services. Public-sector unions can build, both within the states and nationally, a movement to resurrect an understanding of how indispensable the national government is to overall economic management. Police, firefighters, teachers, sanitation workers, and the host of other public employees know better than anyone else what fiscal domination does to the conditions and provision of public service. No sector of the Left is better able to make the case for re-distributive federal economic policies than the employees left holding the bag of fiscally strapped local governments.

Unions, public and private, have a long tradition of supporting civil liberties and civil rights; they understand how important the federal government is to assuring the collective bargaining rights of workers, rights to dissent, picket and strike, and oppose the powers that be. Moreover, labor's historic commitment to the cause of social justice, its belief in the use of federal power to achieve broad public purposes for the interests of working people, and its commitment to make the public sector serviceable to the needs of society as a whole make it an ally of all groups who yearn for equal treatment.

If it means anything, the main implication of the critique of balanced-budget conservatism is that working people cannot overcome the forces depressing their living standards and marginalizing their lives if the deep fracturing of the political economy prevails. The power to dispose of the social surplus for public uses and social needs is available only to a unified democracy empowered by an economic majority. Under current conditions, as the forces of production ever more exceed the prior limits of the old industrial work relations, the deepest threat to freedom lies in what Neumann described as "the growing antagonism between the potentialities of our historical situation and their actual realization." [36] That elites need to preserve an economic order that no longer even pretends to serve workers means that increasingly, elites use their power not to produce value, but only to preserve themselves. As Gorz warns, "We are much closer to a totalitarian society run by a technocracy with a quasi-military hierarchy than to a perfect bourgeois capitalist society." [37] We are indeed closer, but we are not there. The question is, will the forces of democracy or those of the emerging techno-oligarchy embrace the necessity of planning first?

Notes to Chapters

Chapter One

1. "Clinton Sees Need to Focus His Goals and Sharpen His Staff," *The New York Times,* 5 May 1993, pp. A1, B9; John Kenneth Galbraith, "Recession? Why Worry?" *The New York Times,* 12 May 1993, p. A19.

2. "Clinton Sees Need to Focus His Goals and Sharpen Staff," *The New York Times,* 5 May 1993, pp. A1, B9.

3. "Service Jobs Fall as Business Gains," *The New York Times,* 18 April 1993, pp. 1, 43.

4. For general trends in work and income, see Bennett Harrison and Barry Bluestone, *The Great U-Turn: Corporate Restructuring and the Polarization of America* (New York: Basic Books, 1988); Robert Reich, *The Work of Nations* (New York: Random House, 1992); Frank Levy, *Dollars and Dreams: The Changing of American Income Distribution* (New York: Norton, 1988). Also see below, Chapter Two, *passim.*

5. Richard Rothstein, "The Myth of Public School Failure," *American Prospect,* Spring 1993, p. 22; "How Much Good Will Training Do?" *Business Week,* 22 February 1983, pp. 76-77.

6. "Jobs, Jobs," *Business Week,* 22 February 1993, p. 68; "Tall Order for Small Businesses," *Business Week,* 19 April 1993, p. 114; Adam Smith, "The Shape of Things to Come," review of Peter Drucker, *Post-Capitalist Society* (New York: Harper-Collins, 1993), *The New York Times Book Review,* 11 April 1993, p. 8; Paul Starobin, "Small Talk," *National Journal,* 6 March 1993, pp. 554-555.

7. Jeremy Rifkin, "Watch Out For Trickle-Down Technology," *The New York Times,* 24 February 1993, op. ed.

8. Andre Gorz, *Critique of Economic Reason,* trans. Gillian Handyside and Chris Turner (London: Verso, 1989), p. 7. See also Gorz, *Paths to Paradise, On the Liberation from Work,* trans. Malcome Imrie (Boston: South End Press, 1985).

9. "Tall Order for Small Businesses," *Business Week,* p. 115; Starobin, "Small Talk," p. 554.

10. "Tall Order for Small Businesses," *Business Week,* pp. 114-117.

11. "Reich's Return to Those Thrilling Days of Yesteryear," *Business Week,* 12 April 1993, p. 45. In a similar vein, one business writer, Jane White, recently complained about Secretary of Labor Robert Reich's appointment of Joyce Miller, a former AFL-CIO official, to head up President Clinton's Glass Ceiling Commission, a body appointed to help remove barriers to high-level corporate promotions of women and minorities. In White's view, Reich's appointment reflects "his fantasy of turning the clock back to a labor-intensive industrial age when jobs were virtually guaranteed to everybody." White

warned, however, that "a reality check is in order." Letter to the Editor, *The New York Times,* 2 May 1993, sec. 3, p. 36.

12. Robert Kuttner, "Training Programs Alone Can't Produce $20-An-Hour Workers," *Business Week,* 8 March 1993, p. 16; Reich, *Work of Nations,* pp. 171-184.

13. "Clinton Outlines Spending Package of 1.52 Trillion," *The New York Times,* 9 April 1993, pp. 1, 16; "President Throws Down Gauntlet," *Congressional Quarterly,* 20 February 1993, pp. 335-359. Just as important, Clinton's proposed $16.2 billion temporary stimulus package, which Republicans successfully stopped in the Senate, would have created 200,000 mainly low- and medium-wage traditional jobs, in fields such as construction, social services, and riot-prevention make-work for inner-city teens. Interestingly, the plan's major high-technology component, a $64 million plan to construct an "information superhighway" and improve telecommunications, would have added just thirty jobs. See "White House Hints a Deal Is Possible on Its Jobs Plan," *The New York Times,* 6 April 1993, pp. 1, 20.

14. Donald F. Kettl, *Deficit Politics, Public Budgeting in Its Institutional and Historical Context* (New York: Macmillan, 1992), p. 1. Kettl himself is somewhat critical of this anti-government attitude, though he makes no plea for a refocusing of the issue on political economic structures.

15. James D. Savage, *Balanced Budgets & American Politics* (Ithaca, New York: Cornell University Press, 1988), p. 48. It is especially worth remembering in this context that in Reagan's early days, his Democrat-like penchant for deficits did not go over well on Wall Street. For example, as the budget-busting implications of Reagan's economic plan became obvious as early as 1981, interest rates kicked up and the stock market slid 125 points during the summer of 1981. The stock traders were not happy. As one financial executive noted at the time, "The question is no longer whether the Administration can balance the budget—it's now doubtful that a balanced budget could be achieved by 1984—but whether the whole supply-side concept will ultimately work." But when Wall Street complained, it was the Republicans in Washington who replied with Democratic-sounding warnings that if the financial markets did not show more faith in the president's program, "The Street" might soon be facing credit controls and windfall profits taxes. As Republican Majority Leader Sen. Howard Baker bluntly told Wall Street, "It's time indeed that the financial markets realize they're playing a dangerous game." See "Wall Street Blames Reagan Budget for Stock Slide," *The New York Times,* 26 August 1981, Business Section, p. 1; "2 Republican Legislators Threaten Wall Street With Tighter Controls," *The New York Times,* 10 September 1981, p. 1.

16. Benjamin Friedman, *Day of Reckoning, The Consequences of American Economic Policy* (New York: Random House, 1989).

17. Ross Perot, *United We Stand: How We Can Take Back Our Country* (New York: Hyperion, 1992), p. 8.

18. For detailed reviews of the Gramm-Rudman laws and related budgetary charades see Kettl, *Deficit Politics;* Allan Schick, *The Capacity to Budget* (Washington, D.C.: Urban Institute Press, 1990). According to the Congres-

sional Budget Office, the 1990 Budget Enforcement Act has helped restrain spending, although such restraint has not brought the deficit down. Due to "the deterioration of the economy and technical re-estimates of revenues and spending, especially for Medicare and Medicaid," the deficit continued to climb. Congressional Budget Office, *The Economic and Budget Outlook: Fiscal Years 1994-1998, A Report to the Senate and House Committees on the Budget* (Washington, D.C.: U.S. Government Printing Office, 1993), p. 86.

19. "Fiscal Reconversion," *The New York Times,* 21 May 1982, p. 16.

20. William Crotty, "Who Needs Two Democratic Parties?" in James MacGregor Burns, et al., eds., *The Democrats Must Lead: The Case for a Progressive Democratic Party* (Boulder, CO: Westview, 1992), p. 67.

21. Donald F. Kettl, *Deficit Politics,* p. 15.

22. Quoted in Robert Guskind, "The New Civil War," *National Journal,* 3 April 1993, p. 817.

23. "Many Northern Firms Seeking Sites in South Get Chilly Reception," *The Wall Street Journal,* 10 February 1978, pp. 1, 29.

24. Guskind, "The New Civil War," p. 817.

25. Reich, *Work of Nations,* p. 281.

26. Sarah Ritchie and Steven D. Gold, "State and Local Employment in the 1980s: How Did It Grow," *State Fiscal Briefs,* 7 November 1992, pp. 1-2; Reich, *Work of Nations,* p. 269.

27. Harold W. Stanley and Richard G. Niemi, *Vital Statistics on American Politics,* 2d. ed. (Washington, D.C.: Congressional Quarterly Press, 1990), pp. 299-300; Reich, *Work of Nations,* p. 272.

28. John Kenneth Galbraith, *The Affluent Society* (New York: Mentor, 1958).

29. "Transcript of Clinton's Address to a Joint Session of Congress," *The New York Times,* 18 February 1993, p. 20.

30. C. Wright Mills, *The Power Elite* (New York: Oxford University Press, 1956), p. 28.

31. Zack Nauth, "Taking on the Tax Burden," *In These Times,* 11 January 1993, p. 24.

32. Jerry Kloby, "The Growing Divide: Class Polarization in the 1980s," *Monthly Review,* p. 6, Table 4.

33. All the tax data in this paragraph are culled from Congressional Budget Office, *Economic and Budget Outlook: Fiscal Years 1994-1998,* Table E-5, p. 127.

34. James O'Connor, *The Fiscal Crisis of the State* (New York: St. Martin's Press, 1973), p. 203.

35. In his important study of the symbolic and real politics of balanced budgets, James D. Savage makes the point that in U.S. history, demands for balanced budgets originated from Jeffersonians who wished to preserve a small-scale agricultural political economy against the oligarchic and militaristic implications of a Hamiltonian state run by financiers, central bankers, and generals, elites with vested interests in a big state debt. As we argue throughout, and especially in Chapter Three, modern economic conservatives have borrowed, transformed, and manipulated the anti-deficit Jeffersonian impulse to

serve undemocratic corporate purposes. See Savage, *Balanced Budgets & American Politics,* pp. 85-120.

36. Richard A. Epstein, *Takings, Private Property and the Power of Eminent Domain* (Cambridge: Harvard University Press, 1985), p. 15.

37. For Epstein, the presence of force does not mean that we have abandoned the realm of voluntary exchange relationships, but that the state must be forced to abide by the norm of equal exchange. Yet the very presence of force implies the existence of a communal authority that defines general interests apart from particular private interests. Under democratic conditions, this authority carries the legitimate mantle of majority will. And such authority may well compel individuals to share in the financial obligations of collective public betterment. The alternative democratic principle is, as Marx stated it, "From each according to his ability; to each according to his need."

38. Epstein, *Takings,* pp. 333-334.

39. *Ibid.,* p. 17. For a powerful critique of the anti-labor implications of Locke's thought, see C. B. Macpherson, *The Political Theory of Possessive Individualism: Hobbes to Locke* (New York: Oxford University Press, 1962).

40. Quoted in Kevin Phillips, *The Politics of Rich and Poor: Wealth and the American Electorate in the Reagan Aftermath* (New York: Random House, 1990), p. 32.

Chapter Two

1. *Business Week,* "Egalitarianism: threat to a free market," 1 December 1962, p. 62; Thorstein Veblen, *The Theory of the Leisure Class* (New York: Penguin, 1979), p. 98.

2. Herbert Marcuse, *One-Dimensional Man, Studies in the Ideology of Advanced Industrial Society* (Boston: Beacon Press, 1964); C. Wright Mills, *The Power Elite* (New York: Oxford University Press, 1956); *The Sociological Imagination* (New York: Grove Press, 1959), pp. 174-175.

3. Marcuse, *One-Dimensional Man,* p. 2.

4. Jurgen Habermas, *Legitimation Crisis,* trans. Thomas McCarthy (Boston: Beacon Press, 1973).

5. Senate Committee on Governmental Affairs, *Structure of Corporate Concentration, Institutional Shareholders and Interlocking Directorates Among Major U.S. Corporations,* Staff Study, vol. 1, 96th Cong., 2nd sess., December 1980.

6. House Committee on the Judiciary, *Investigation of Conglomerate Corporations,* A Report by the Staff of the Antitrust Subcommittee, 92nd. Cong., 1st. sess., 1 June 1971, p. 29.

7. Douglas Dowd, "The Centralization of Capital," in Ralph C. Edwards, Michael Reich, and Thomas E. Weisskopf, eds., *The Capitalist System,* 2nd ed. (Englewood Cliffs, New Jersey: Prentice-Hall, 1978), p. 130; Judiciary Committee, *Report on Conglomerates,* p. 28.

8. John Blair, *Economic Concentration, Structure, Behavior and Public Policy* (New York: Harcourt, Brace, Jovanovich, 1972), p. 471.

9. "Why Detroit can't cut prices," *Business Week,* 1 March 1982, pp. 110-111.

10. "Prices Rise in Spite of Spare Capacity," *Business Week,* 21 March 1977, p. 120.

11. *Ibid.*

12. Paul Baran and Paul Sweezy, *Monopoly Capital, An Essay on the American Economic and Social Order* (New York: Monthly Review Press), p. 14.

13. Thorstein Veblen, *The Theory of Business Enterprise* (New Brunswick, New Jersey: Transaction Books, 1978).

14. *Business Week,* "Why Detroit can't cut prices," p. 111.

15. Baran and Sweezy, *Monopoly Capital,* chap. 3.

16. In theory, of course, government might have used anti-trust laws to break up concentrated industries, but for reasons of power, long codified in legal opinions that held "bigness in itself is not bad," none of the major post-World War II oligopoly industries faced a state order to dismantle itself until after the most recent era of stagnation began in 1973. Once the seriousness of the economic slowdown became clear to the power elite, Democrats led by Jimmy Carter pressed the break-up of a handful of major sectors, including telephone communications (ATT), finance (banks and S&Ls), airlines, and trucking. Certainly in the case of the first three industries, increased competition has by no means led to lower prices or better service, and in the case of the S&Ls, deregulation turned out to be a financial disaster. As one student of the period has commented, the timing of this spurt of deregulation "could not have been worse, as the threat of massive debt defaults, the trend toward recession in the largest capitalist economies, a free fall of commodity prices, and the dangers of de-flation all moved the economy closer to breakdown." Joyce Kolko, *Restructuring the World Economy* (New York: Pantheon, 1988), pp. 236-237.

17. Quoted in David Vogel, *Fluctuating Fortunes, The Political Power of Business in America* (New York: Basic Books, 1989), p. 24. The same issue of the *Harvard Business Review* also reported an uptick since 1960 in business' sense of its power in Washington, this despite the shift in executive power from the Republican Eisenhower to the Democrats, Kennedy and Johnson. But then, business commands access in government no matter which party holds the formal reigns of power, a tendency noted by the tougher-minded founders of modern pluralist political science. See David Truman, *The Governmental Process* (New York: Knopf, 1962), pp. 247ff.

18. Harry Magdoff and Paul Sweezy, "Review of the Month," *Monthly Review,* April 1984, p. 3, table 1.

19. Paul Baran defines the concept of potential economic surplus as "the difference between the output that could be produced in a given natural and technological environment with the help of employable productive resources, and what might be regarded as essential consumption," or the satisfaction of socially necessary needs. Among the various forms of such potential in the actual economy are excess consumption by upper-income groups; output lost to the business need for unproductive workers, such as advertising staffs; waste inherent in the existing organization of production, such as devotion of resources to the control of labor; and finally, lost output resulting from unemployment, insufficient demand, and the overall anarchy

of capitalist economic organization. See *The Political Economy of Growth* (New York: Monthly Review Press, 1957), pp. 23-24. Cf. also the discussion of "waste" by Veblen in *Theory of the Leisure Class,* pp. 97-99.

20. Michael Dawson and John Bellamy Foster, "The Tendency of the Surplus to Rise, 1963-1988," *Monthly Review,* September 1991, p. 48. Also see Joseph D. Phillips, "Estimating the Economic Surplus," in Baran and Sweezy, *Monopoly Capital,* pp. 369-389; John Bellamy Foster, *The Theory of Monopoly Capitalism: An Elaboration of Marxian Political Economy* (New York: Monthly Review Press, 1986), pp. 11-50. Dawson's and Foster's calculus of surplus includes the following indicators: adjusted corporate profits, profits of unincorporated businesses, rental income, net interest, business contributions to social insurance, surplus employee compensation (i.e., salaries in such fields as finance, insurance, real estate, and legal services), advertising costs of corporations, profit in corporate officer compensation (as a disguised form of profit), gross business depreciation, indirect business tax and non-tax liabilities, and estimated taxes on wages and salaries. As these authors acknowledge, this is an accounting of what might be termed the "positive" surplus, the wealth produced by the corporate system minus socially necessary costs, especially workers' wages. This sum does not include what might be termed the "negative" surplus, the payments capital avoids by shifting social costs onto labor and society, everything from unemployment, to environmental abuse, to the wasted effort and resources that enter into the design of products for purely commercial reasons. For an excellent discussion of what a full-scale accounting of this "negative" surplus might look like, see K. William Kapp, *The Social Costs of Private Enterprise* (New York: Schoken, 1971).

21. Harold W. Stanley and Richard G. Niemi, *Vital Statistics on American Politics,* 2nd ed. (Washington, D.C.: Congressional Quarterly Press, 1990), pp. 398-399.

22. *Ibid.,* pp. 381-382.

23. These figures are calculated from data in Dawson and Foster, "Tendency of the Surplus to Rise," p. 46.

24. Lawrence Mishel and David M. Frankel, *The State of Working America,* 1990-1991 ed. (Washington, D.C.: Economic Policy Institute, 1990), pp. 58-59.

25. *Ibid.*

26. *Business Week,* "Cash Management, the new art of wringing more profit from corporate funds," 13 March 1978, p. 62.

27. Kolko, *Restructuring the World Economy,* p. 221.

28. House Committee on Banking, Finance and Urban Affairs, *Forging An Industrial Competitiveness Strategy,* 98th Cong., 1st. sess., November 1983, pp. 5-6.

29. *Ibid.,* p. 221.

30. Samuel Bowles, David M. Gordon, and Thomas E. Weisskopf, *After the Wasteland: A Democratic Economics for the Year 2000* (Armonk, New York: M.E. Sharpe, 1990), p. 63.

31. Kolko, *Restructuring the Wold Economy,* p. 73.

32. *The New York Times,* "Faltering Companies Seek Outsiders," 18 January 1993, p. D4.

33. Kolko, *Restructuring the World Economy,* p. 68.

34. Stephen B. Shepard, "The End of the Cowboy Economy," *Business Week,* 24 November 1973, p. 62.

35. Kolko, *Restructuring the World Economy,* p. 309; *The New York Times,* 18 January 1993.

36. Bennett Harrison and Barry Bluestone, *The Great U-Turn: Corporate Restructuring and the Polarizing of America* (New York: Basic Books, 1988), p. 37.

37. Kolko, *Economic Restructuring of the World Economy,* p. 310; Harrison and Bluestone, *Great U-Turn,* pp. 39-40.

38. Thomas B. Edsall, *The New Politics of Inequality* (New York: Norton, 1984), pp. 151-156; Vogel, *Fluctuating Fortunes,* pp. 150-159.

39. Edsall, *New Politics of Inequality,* p. 159.

40. Harrison and Bluestone, *Great U-Turn,* p. 45.

41. Francis Fox Piven and Richard A. Cloward, *The New Class War: Reagan's Attack on the Welfare State and Its Consequences* (New York: Pantheon, 1982), p. 2.

42. Harrison and Bluestone, *Great U-Turn,* p. 26.

43. *Ibid.,* pp. 29-30.

44. Robert B. Reich, *The Work of Nations* (New York: Random House, 1991), pp. 210-211.

45. Kolko, *Economic Restructuring of the World Economy,* p. 59.

46. Wallace C. Peterson, "The Silent Depression," *Challenge,* July-August 1991, p. 30; *Business Week,* "Business Outlook," 14 September 1992, p. 21.

47. Stanley and Niemi, *Vital Statistics in American Politics,* Table 13.2, p. 382-384.

48. These data, from the U.S. Census Bureau, were reported in "Pay of College Graduates is Outpaced by Inflation," *The New York Times,* 14 May 1992, p. 1.

49. Peterson, "Silent Depression," p. 30; "Ranks of U.S. Poor Reach 35.7 Million, The Most Since '64," *The New York Times,* 4 September 1992, p. 1.

50. "Report, Delayed Months, Says Lowest Income Group Grew Sharply," *The New York Times,* 12 May 1992, p. A15.

51. Harrison and Bluestone, *Great U-Turn,* pp. 70-71; Aaron Bernstein, "Commentary: What's Dragging Productivity Down? Women's Low Wages," *Business Week,* 27 November 1989, p. 171; Reich, *Work of Nations,* pp. 215-219.

52. "House Data on Incomes Sets Off Debate on Fairness in America," *The New York Times,* 22 May 1992, p. 16.

53. "The Recovery: Why So Slow?," *Business Week,* 20 July 1992, pp. 62, 66. "In 1988...the median family income of black Americans was only $18,098, compared with $32,274 for whites. Thirty-three percent of blacks, but only 11% of whites fell below the poverty line. Hispanics are not much better off than blacks, with a median family income of $20,306 and with 28% below the poverty line." See Edward S. Greenberg and Benjamin I. Page, *The Struggle for Democracy* (New York: Harper-Collins, 1993), p. 555.

54. "Business Outlook," *Business Week,* 14 September 1992, p. 21.

55. Gabriel Kolko, *Wealth and Power in America* (New York: Praeger, 1962), p. 15.
56. Mills commented that "with the expansion of the state, economic powers are now often defensive and limited, and...they are not the all-sufficient key to the understanding of political power or to the shaping of social structures." C. Wright Mills, *The Marxists* (New York: Dell, 1962), p. 125. As this and later chapters argue, capital has now very much gone on the offensive and successfully released itself from overarching supervision by the state.
57. Jerry Kloby, "The Growing Divide: Class Polarization in the 1980s," *Monthly Review,* September 1987, p. 7.
58. "The Flap Over Executive Pay," *Business Week,* 6 May 1991, p. 90; also see "CEO Disease," *Business Week,* 1 April 1991, pp. 52-60.
59. Mishel and Frankel, *State of Working America,* p. 30.
60. Kloby, "Growing Divide," p. 6.
61. "The Casino Society," *Business Week,* 16 September 1985, pp. 78-90; Robert Reich, *The Next American Frontier* (New York: Times Books, 1983).
62. Thorstein Veblen, *The Theory of Business Enterprise* (New Brunswick, New Jersey: Transaction Books, 1978), p. 24.
63. Dawson and Foster, "Tendency of the Surplus to Rise," pp. 48-49.
64. For useful reviews of this period, see David P. Calleo and Benjamin M. Rowland, *America and the World Political Economy, Atlantic Dreams and National Realities* (Bloomington, Indiana: University of Indiana Press, 1973); Bowles, Gordon, and Weisskopf, *After the Wasteland,* pp. 47-79. As early as 1969, the Johnson Administration saw the handwriting on the wall. In his budget message to the Congress that year, this most liberal of recent U.S. presidents warned that "faced with a costly war abroad and urgent requirements at home, we have to set priorities...*We cannot do everything we would wish to do.* And so we must choose carefully among the many competing demands on our resources." Quoted in Allan Schick, *The Capacity to Budget* (Washington, D.C.: Urban Institute Press, 1990), p. 53 (emphasis added).
65. J. Kolko, *Restructuring of the World Economy,* p. 101.
66. *Ibid.*
67. William Greider, *Secrets of the Temple, How the Federal Reserve Runs the Country* (New York: Simon and Schuster, 1987), offers an exceptionally lucid discussion of these developments. See esp. "Part Four: The Restoration of Capital."
68. Harry Magdoff and Paul Sweezy, "Review of the Month," *Monthly Review,* June 1984, p. 10; *Business Week,* "The Casino Society," p. 79.
69. "The S&L Mess—And How to Fix It," *Business Week,* 31 October 1988, p. 131.
70. *Ibid.,* p. 81.
71. Washington insider Edward Bennet Williams, an attorney who once defended the likes of mobster Frank Costello, Teamster strongman Jimmy Hoffa, and arch-Cold Warrior Senator Joseph McCarthy, bluntly described the ethics of the raiders and their banker allies: "The worst charlatans I've found in my old age, absolutely nadir to the morality of economics, are those investment bankers...Those fuckers, they are the worst. They go out there

and sell glass insurance to greenhouses while they break windows. You know, they'll say, 'You're ripe for a takeover.' That's the way the gangsters used to do it: 'You're ripe for a takeover.'" See Haynes Johnson, *Sleepwalking Through History, America in the Reagan Years* (New York: W.W. Norton, 1991), p. 227.

72. "Learning to Live With Leverage," *Business Week,* 7 November 1988, p. 138; John B. Shoven and Joel Waldfogel, eds., *Debt, Taxes & Corporate Restructuring* (Washington, D.C.: Brookings Institution, 1990).

73. Mishel and Frankel, *State of Working America,* p. 160.

74. C. Eugene Steuerle, "Federal Policy and the Accumulation of Private Debt," in Shoven and Waldfogel, eds., *Debt, Taxes & Corporate Restructuring,* p.22; "Casino Society," *Business Week,* p. 79.

75. "Learning to Live with Leverage," *Business Week,* p. 138.

76. Quoted from *Barron's,* 8 November 1982, in Magdoff and Sweezy, "Review of the Month," *Monthly Review,* p. 1.

77. Congressional Budget Office, *The Economic and Budget Outlook: Fiscal Years 1994-1998, A Report to the Senate and House Committees on the Budget* (Washington, D.C.: U.S. Government Printing Office, 1993), Table E-3, p. 125.

78. Donald F. Kettl, *Deficit Politics, Public Budgeting in Its Institutional and Historical Context* (New York: Macmillan, 1992), p. 16.

79. Stanley and Niemi, *Vital Statistics,* Table 13.1, p. 381.

80. "Answer: Cut Entitlements. Question: But How?," *The New York Times,* 8 June 1993, p. 22 (emphasis added).

81. Congressional Budget Office, *Economic and Budget Outlook,* 1994-1998, Table E-9, p. 131. Defense spending equalled 5.2% of GDP in 1992; non-entitlement domestic spending equalled 3.7%.

82. Schick, *Capacity to Budget,* p. 80.

83. Greenberg and Page, *Struggle of Democracy,* pp. 619-623; Benjamin Friedman, *Day of Reckoning, The Consequences of American Economic Policy* (New York: Random House, 1989), pp. 285-286.

84. Robert Heilbroner and Peter Bernstein, *The Debt and the Deficit: False Alarms and Real Possibilities* (New York: Norton, 1989), p. 132.

85. Congressional Budget Office, "The Economic and Budget Outlook: Fiscal Years 1994-1998," A Report to the Senate and House Budget Committees on the Budget (Washington: U.S. Government Printing Office, 1993), Table E-6, p. 128.

86. John Judis, "The Disappearing Rabbit of American Politics," *In These Times,* 19 August-1 September 1992, p. 8.

87. Magdoff and Sweezy, "Review of the Month," *Monthly Review,* p. 1.

88. The federal government through various accounts owes about 30% of the national debt to itself, while state and local governments hold another 18%. Kettle, *Deficit Politics,* p. 27.

Chapter Three

1. Ross Perot, *United We Stand: How We Can Take Back Our Country* (New York: Hyperion, 1992), p. 8; Robert Heilbroner and Peter Bernstein, *The Debt and the Deficit: False Alarms and Real Possibilities* (New York: Norton, 1989), pp. 133-134.

2. George E. Peterson, "Federalism and the States, an Experiment in Decentralization," in John L. Palmer and Isabel V. Sawhill, eds., *The Reagan Record* (Cambridge, Mass.: Ballinger Publishing Co.; The Urban Institute, 1984), p. 247.

3. Richard P. Nathan, "The Role of the States in American Federalism," in Carl E. Van Horn, ed., *The State of the States,* 2nd ed. (Washington, D.C.: Congressional Quarterly Press, 1993), pp. 24-25.

4. Henry J. Raimondo, "State Budgeting in the Nineties," in Van Horn, ed. *State of the States,* p. 34, Table 3.2.

5. Franklin James, "City Need and Distress in the United States: 1970 to the Mid-1980s," in Marshall Kaplan and Franklin James, eds., *The Future of National Urban Policy* (Durham: Duke University Press, 1990), pp. 14-31; "80s Leave States and Cities in Need," *The New York Times,* 30 December 1990, p. 1.

6. Roy Bahl, William Duncombe, and Wanda Schulman, "The New Anatomy of Urban Fiscal Problems," in Kaplan and James, eds., *Future of National Urban Policy,* p. 55.

7. "States and Cities Fight Recession with New Taxes," *The New York Times,* 27 July 1991, p. 1; *The Economist,* 22 June 1991, pp. 25-26, 81.

8. "In a Time of Deficits, Florida Ponders the Unpopular Idea of an Income Tax," *The New York Times,* 10 December 1991, p. A22.

9. "California Forced to Turn to I.O.U.'s," *The New York Times,* 2 July 1992, p. 1.

10. "63 Days After Its Cash Ran Out, California Passes Austere Budget," *The New York Times,* 3 September 1992, p. 1; "'We Haven't Hit Bottom—And Won't Until 1993,'" *Business Week,* 14 September 1992, p. 27; Paul Starobin, "Is the Dreamin' Over?" *National Journal,* 26 September 1992, pp. 2166-2172.

11. "Recession Leaving State Governments More Efficient," *The New York Times,* 22 April 1992, p. 14; "As Washington Lives on Credit, States Live on Gruel," *The New York Times,* 6 September 1992, sec. 4, p. 1.

12. "Michigan Faces Painful Choices in Cutting Budget," *The New York Times,* 23 January 1991, p. 14; "Weld Denting Massachusetts' Liberal Framework," *The New York Times,* 17 October 1991, p. 18.

13. "80s Leave States and Cities in Need," *The New York Times,* 30 December 1990, p. 1; "New York City Given Stern Warning by a Fiscal Monitor," *The New York Times,* 7 February 1991, p. 1.

14. "State Legislators Are Leaving Office in Record Numbers," *The New York Times,* 2 August 1992, p. 1.

15. "National Recovery Fattening Tax Revenue in Many States," *The New York Times,* 17 February 1993, p. 1; "Like U.S., States Look to the Affluent to Pay More Tax," *The New York Times,* 21 March 1993, p. A28.

16. Thad L. Beyle, "New Governors in Hard Economic and Political Times," in T. Beyle, ed., *Governors & Hard Times,* p. 9. As liberal economist Robert M.

Solow has lucidly noted, "It is a standard conservative ploy to say that the states should do more because they are closer to the people, while at the same time failing to suggest where the states are to get the financial and intellectual wherewithal to carry out their greater responsibilities. That is not an oversight: the conservative goal is not to redistribute the economic functions of government but to diminish or eliminate them." See "Dr. Rivlin's Diagnosis & Mr. Clinton's Remedy," *The New York Review of Books,* 25 March 1993, p. 12.

17. Quoted in Richard S. Williamson, "A Review of Reagan Federalism," in Robert B. Hawkins, ed., *American Federalism: A New Partnership for the Republic* (New Brunswick, New Jersey: Transaction Books, Institute for Contemporary Studies, 1982), p. 100.

18. John Shannon, "The Return to Fend-for-Yourself Federalism: The Reagan Mark," *Intergovernmental Perspective,* Fall 1987, pp. 34-37, cited in Beyle, "New Governors," pp. 8-9.

19. Thodore J. Lowi, *The End of Liberalism: The Second Republic of the United States,* 2nd. ed. (New York: Norton, 1979), p. 272.

20. See Paul Peterson, *City Limits* (Chicago: University of Chicago Press, 1981), whose analysis of the economic limits on cities applies equally well to the states. David B. Robertson and Dennis R. Judd, in *The Development of American Public Policy: The Structure of Policy Restraint* (Glenview, IL: Scott Foresman, 1989), build their excellent critique of U.S. policy in large part on the premise that "interstate economic competition" represents a major "drag" on progressive social policy at the state and local levels. See especially pp. 12-14, 31-32.

21. Robert Bork, *The Tempting of America: The Political Seduction of the Law* (New York: Simon & Schuster, 1990), pp. 248-249; E.S. Savas, *Privatization: The Key to Better Government* (Chatham, NJ: Chatham House Publishers, 1987), pp. 290-291; Vincent Ostrom, Robert Bish, and Elinor Ostrom, *Local Government in the United States* (San Francisco: Institute for Contemporary Studies, 1988). For a concrete application of Bork's principles, see the U.S. Supreme Court's decision in *Bowers vs. Hardwick,* in which the court upheld a Georgia law that makes it a crime for any persons to engage in oral or anal sex. Although technically the law applies to all persons, including heterosexuals, it was used to prosecute homosexuals. See "High Court, 5-4, Says States Have The Right To Outlaw Private Homosexual Acts," *The New York Times,* 1 July 1986, pp. 1, 18.

22. George Gilder, *Wealth and Poverty* (New York: Bantam Books, 1981), pp. 267-268; Jude Wannisky, "Blame Bush for the Recession," *The New York Times,* 12 November 1991, Op Ed page; Paul Craig Roberts, "Bush Is Burning the Mantle He Inherited from Reagan," and "You Might Call It the Bush-Whacked Economy," *Business Week,* 22 October 1990, p. 18; 2 September 1991, p. 12.

23. Allan Schick, *The Capacity to Budget* (Washington, D.C.: Urban Institute Press, 1990), pp. 2-3.

24. See Arthur MacEwan, "Why the Emperor Can't Afford New Clothes," *Monthly Review,* July-August 1991, p. 89.

25. The view taken here departs from that of James D. Savage in his excellent analysis, *Balanced Budget and the American Politics* (Ithaca, NY: Cornell University Press, 1988). Savage identifies the roots of the balanced-budget preoccupation in U.S. politics with eighteenth-century classical republican fears of corruption of the state by a debt-driven financial oligarchy, a banking elite with ties to foreign lenders. This is a crucial insight, and it adds enormously to an understanding of the anti-oligarchical, pro-democratic strain in U.S. political thought. Nonetheless, we think that much of what passes for the classical republican celebration of the yeoman farmer as the best citizen, is, in the eighteenth-century U.S. context, inextricably intertwined with classical liberal, Lockean ideals of hard work, property ownership, and anti-taxism, ideals that owed much to Calvinism and the Protestant ethic, which is why we stress these ideas here. In any event, as Savage himself realizes, the classical republican strain in current debates over budgeting is less visible today than the fiscal conservatism of the Republican Party.

26. Readers interested in tracing the remarkable continuity of such ideas, extending even into the age of credit-card capitalism, might look at the following: Benjamin Franklin, *The Autobiography of Benjamin Franklin* (New Haven: Yale University Press, 1964); William Graham Summner, *What Social Classes Owe To Each Other* (Caldwell, Idaho: The Caxton Printers, 1986); Edward C. Banfield, *The Unheavenly City Revisited* (Boston: Little, Brown & Co., 1974). For Daniel Bell, the contradiction between the ethic of saving and the ethic of consumption, the latter of which is systematically propagated by modern capitalism, is a destructive factor in the moral culture of bourgeois society. But it is one which the economic system cannot help; capitalism now lives on credit and the sales effort, and there is simply nothing capital can do about it, except to criticize the state for it. Daniel Bell, *The Cultural Contradictions of Capitalism* (New York: Basic Books, 1976). For Marx's pithy comments on "original sin" in economic theology, see Frederick Engels, ed., *Capital, A Critique of Political Economy,* Vol. I (New York: International Publishers, 1967), pp. 713-714.

27. Lenders therefore also come in for their share of abuse: "Jewish money lenders" are an obvious example, but black-suited bankers have never ranked high in the esteem of Main Street America either. "The folk wisdom feared debt, yet future prosperity depended on it." William Grieder, *Secrets of the Temple, How the Federal Reserve Runs the Country* (New York: Simon & Schuster, 1987), pp. 64, 25. Populist suspicions of bankers are one aspect of the anti-oligarchical strain emphasized by Savage, *Balanced Budgets and American Politics.* See note 25 above and note 34 below.

28. John Kenneth Galbraith, *The Affluent Society* (New York: Mentor Books, 1958, 1969), p. 197; Emma Rothchild, "The Real Reagan Economy," *The New York Review of Books,* 30 June 1988, p. 47.

29. "Quayle Criticizes New York as Proof of Welfare's Ills," *The New York Times,* 28 February 1992, p. 1, 18. In fact, this childlike, minimalist view of the state has never been adequate to explaining its broad role in the development of capitalism. "The liberal state has always been as strong as the political and

social situation and the interests of society demanded," writes Franz Neu-
mann in "The Change in the Function of Law in Modern Society," in F.
Neumann, *The Democratic and the Authoritarian State: Essays in Political and
Legal Theory,* ed. Herbert Marcuse (New York: The Free Press, 1957), p. 22.

30. Milton Friedman and Rose Friedman, *Tyranny of the Status Quo* (New York:
    Avon Books, 1984), p. 47.

31. *Ibid.,* p. 45. In the next chapter we shall revisit such arguments in the claims
    of late nineteenth-century anti-political machine reformers.

32. There are, of course, additional conservative benefits in federalism. As we
    argue throughout this study, keeping most governmental power locked away
    beneath the national level means that the national economic majority is split
    up into much smaller units of political power and is therefore more easily
    managed by anti-tax interests who live increasingly inside their own jurisdic-
    tions. As we argue in Chapter Four, Fortress Suburbia has its roots in a class
    effort to create taxpayer majorities in municipalities separate from pro-spend-
    ing working-class majorities. In addition, the wealth of state and local gov-
    ernments depends almost exclusively on the extent of private business
    activity or the value of residential real estate within their borders. States and
    cities are therefore much safer bets not to bite the hand that feeds them.

33. Alvin Rabushka and Pauline Ryan, *The Tax Revolt* (Stanford: Hoover Institu-
    tion, Stanford University Press, 1982).

34. James D. Savage, *Balanced Budgets & American Politics* (Ithaca: Cornell
    University Press, 1988), pp. 93-95, 106-107. Jefferson held a spirited republi-
    can contempt for national debt because, not incorrectly, he saw how it
    encouraged the centralization of financial power, tightened interconnections
    between big banks and the nation-state, provided economic fuel for the
    growth of dangerous military power along with the propensity to use it, and
    offered ample enticements to corruption. In other words, Jefferson's hostility
    to debt was fundamentally anti-oligarchical and had little to do with a faith in
    budgetary balance for its own sake. Indeed, like other classical republicans,
    Jefferson supported deficit spending by the states to encourage economic
    development. Because state officials were closer to the democratic pull of
    popular accountability, the chances for corruption and financial excess there
    were much smaller. In fact, in the years before the panic of 1837, to stimulate
    canal and road construction, a number of state governments borrowed way
    over their heads from English and other European banks, and ended up
    going bankrupt when the expansionist bubble burst. It was after this experi-
    ence that balanced-budget rules were incorporated in state constitutions. See
    also Chapter Four, on how the financial panic of 1871 in New York City
    brought down the Tweed Ring machine.

35. "The Debt Economy," *Business Week,* 12 October 1974, p. 45. Remarking on
    what it called the nation's already "ominously heavy burden" of debt, $2.5
    trillion in 1974, *Business Week* wondered nonetheless whether the economy
    would be able to "add enough debt to keep growing at anything close to the
    rate of the postwar era." Apparently not.

36. Thorstein Veblen, *Absentee Ownership: The Case of America* (Boston: Beacon
    Press, 1967), p. 326.

37. Ross Perot, *United We Stand: How We Can Take Back Our Country* (New York: Hyperion, 1992), p. 4 (emphasis added).

38. Friedman and Friedman, *Tyranny of the Status Quo,* p. 48.

39. Friedreich A. Hayek, *The Road to Serfdom* (Chicago: University of Chicago Press, 1944); Ludwig Von Mises, *Bureaucracy* (New Haven: Yale University Press, 1944).

40. Thus, for Milton Friedman, "The most important fact about enterprise monopoly is its relative unimportance from the point of view of the economy as a whole." *Capitalism and Freedom* (Chicago: University of Chicago Press, 1962), p. 121. And the only mention of the term "corporation" in the index of the Friedmans' more recent work consists of a reference to "corporate taxes." See *Tyranny of the Status Quo,* p. 176.

41. For example, upon hearing that the top job at his chief competitor IBM had gone to Louis V. Gerstner, former head of R.J.R. Nabisco, Scott McNeally, chair of Sun Microsystems, commented that a man with experience in the baked-goods industry should have no trouble heading the world's largest computer company, "After all, the shelf life of biscuits and technology is about the same." Quoted in "In Silicon Valley, Raised Eyebrows," *The New York Times,* 27 March 1993, p. 45. Also see Robert Hayes and William Abernathy, "Managing Our Way Toward Economic Decline," *Harvard Business Review,* July-August 1980, p. 68; Thorstein Veblen, *The Theory of Business Enterprise* (New Brunswick, New Jersey: Transaction Books, 1978); *The Instinct of Workmanship and the State of the Industrial Arts* (New Brunswick, New Jersey: Transaction Books, 1990).

42. See Chapter Four.

43. See, e.g., Alfred D. Chandler, *The Visible Hand: The Managerial Revolution in American Business* (Cambridge: Harvard University Press, 1977), pp. 466-468; Raymond Seidelman with the assistance of Edward J. Harpham, *Disenchanted Realists: Political Science and the American Crisis, 1884-1984* (Albany, NY: State University of New York Press, 1985), pp. 62-63.

44. David Stockman, *The Triumph of Politics: The Inside Story of the Reagan Revolution* (New York: Avon, 1987), p. 37. The bee keepers' subsidy reference is taken from Congressional Budget Office, *Reducing the Deficit: Spending and Revenue Options, A Report to the Senate and House Committees on the Budget* (Washington, D.C.: U.S. Government Printing Office, 1993), pp. 252-253.

45. H.H. Wellington and R.K. Winter, *The Unions and the Cities* (Washington, D.C.: Brookings Institution, 1971).

46. *Statistical Abstract of the United States, 1991* (Washington, D.C.: U.S. Government Printing Office, 1992), Table 465, p. 279.

47. Ester Fuchs, *Mayors and Money: Fiscal Policy in New York and Chicago* (Chicago: University of Chicago Press, 1992); Alberta M. Spragia, ed., *The Municipal Money Chase: The Politics of Local Government Finance* (Boulder, CO: Westview Press, 1983).

48. "A Downgraded Detroit Cries Foul," *The New York Times,* 3 December 1992, pp. D1, 4.

49. "New Jersey Counties Retain Above-Average Credit Ratings," *The New York Times,* 19 November 1992, p. B1.

50. In Chapter Four, we will discuss how the politics of local boundary lines, balanced-budget conservatism, and economic-minority rule fuse together to form Fortress Suburbia. In Chapter Five, we will investigate what happened when Governor James Florio of New Jersey attempted to violate the economic expectations of Fortress Suburbia in his state.

51. *The New York Times,* 20 October 1992, p. 20.

52. Citizens for Tax Justice, "A Far Cry from Fair," cited in Lawrence J. Hass, "Taxing Democrats' Wits," *National Journal,* 4 May 1991, p. 1080.

53. "Searching for New Jobs, Many States Steal Them," *The New York Times,* 25 November 1992, pp. 1, 19; "No More Nonaggression: Albany Vows to Fight New Jersey on Jobs," *The New York Times,* 1 December 1992, p. 1; "Promises Aside, States in Region Fight With One Another for Jobs," *The New York Times,* 30 November 1992, p. 1. New York and New Jersey have also fought bitterly over sales taxes. When, during the Christmas 1992 shopping season, several New Jersey towns temporarily lowered their sales taxes to lure New York shoppers, New York State sent tax investigators to prowl shopping malls on the New Jersey side of the Hudson in search of New York license plates. For a good review of this phenomenon, see Robert Goodman, *The Last Entrepreneurs: America's Regional Wars for Jobs and Dollars* (New York: Simon & Schuster, 1979).

54. John R. Logan and Harvey L. Molotch, *Urban Fortunes: The Political Economy of Place* (Berkeley: University of California Press, 1987); Sidney Plotkin, *Keep Out: The Struggle for Land Use Control* (Berkeley: University of California Press, 1987).

55. Peter Bachrach and Morton Baratz, *Power and Poverty, Theory and Practice* (New York: Oxford University Press, 1970), p. 44.

56. Arthur MacEwen, "Why the Emperor Can't Afford New Clothes," *Monthly Review,* July-August 1991, p. 87.

57. Theodore J. Lowi, *The End of Liberalism: The Second Republic of the United States,* 2nd ed. (New York: W.W. Norton, 1979), p. 92.

58. "Political thought is really *political* thought in the sense that the thinking takes place within the framework of politics. The clearer and more vigorous political thought is, the *less* it is able to grasp the nature of social evils." Karl Marx, *Selected Writings in Sociology and Social Philosophy,* ed. T.B. Bottomore and Maximilien Rubel (New York: McGraw-Hill, 1964), p. 217.

59. The analysis here draws on a number of key works, including Herbert Marcuse, *One-Dimensional Man: Studies in the Ideology of Advanced Industrial Society* (Boston: Beacon Press, 1964); Andre Gorz, *Critique of Economic Reason* (New York: Verso, 1990); Jurgen Habermas, *Legitimation Crisis* (Boston: Beacon Press, 1975); Daniel Bell, *The Cultural Contradictions of Capitalism* (New York: Basic Books, 1978).

60. Lowi, *The End of Liberalism.*

61. Fredric Jameson, *Postmodernism, or The Cultural Logic of Late Capitalism* (Durham: Duke University Press, 1990), p. 271.

Chapter Four

1. Democratic capitalism is an oxymoron because capitalism is not democratic and democracy is not capitalistic. Democracy rests squarely on the principle of equality, that each and every citizen has a right to participate in public decisions. In principle, democracy places no necessary limit on the scope of "public" concern. In principle, democracy can involve itself in matters stretching all the way from the intimate sphere of marriage and the family to the organization and running of the economy. Capitalism rests on the diametrically opposite principles of inequality and privacy. Capitalist economic organization is based on unequal economic classes of owners and workers, and it demands strict limits on the scope of public "intervention" in the economy. The term "democratic capitalism" as used in the text refers to the conventional idea that the governmental system is controlled by a political majority that refuses to use its potential for economic control. Of course, at some later date, the term might come to have an alternative meaning: a majoritarian political system that uses its political power to make private power systematically answerable to public purpose. How far this is possible or workable within an economy that still might be called "capitalist" is debatable, but it would take a much more unified working class to even raise the issue. Capital, of course, would prefer that the issue not be raised, which is the point of divide and rule.

2. Alexander Hamilton, James Madison, and John Jay, *The Federalist Papers,* ed. Clinton Rossiter (New York: Mentor Books, New American Library, 1961), p. 79.

3. Jennifer Nedelsky, *Private Property and the Limits of American Constitutionalism: The Madisonian Framework and Its Legacy* (Chicago: University of Chicago Press, 1990), p. 47.

4. Quoted in *ibid.,* p. 47.

5. Ralph Miliband, *Marxism and Politics* (New York: Oxford University Press, 1977), p. 17.

6. Madison, "Federalist #10," in Hamilton, et al., *The Federalist Papers,* p. 84.

7. Madison, *The Federalist Papers,* pp. 81, 79.

8. Winston U. Solberg, ed., *The Federal Convention and the Formation of the Union of the American States* (New York: Liberal Arts Press, 1958), p. 176.

9. *Ibid,* p. 79.

10. Richard Flacks, *Making History: The American Left and the American Mind* (New York: Columbia University Press, 1988), pp. 71-72.

11. Madison, *The Federalist Papers,* p. 81.

12. Gerald E. Frug, "The City as a Legal Concept," *Harvard Law Review,* April 1980, p. 1062. There is another extremely important political point lurking here, one whose implications would not be fully clear for another century. The utter subordination of local government to state government means that beneath the level of the state, there is an extraordinarily wide-open field for the creation and manipulation of political boundaries available to any interests powerful enough to take advantage of it. In the words of John Dillon, who wrote perhaps the most influential legal treatise on urban political power in U.S. history, state power "is supreme and transcendent: It may erect,

change, divide, and even abolish, at pleasure, as it deems the public good to require." Cited by Frug, *ibid.,* p. 1112. As we shall see below, Dillon's analysis legitimates the build-up of Fortress Suburbia.

13. Madison, *The Federalist Papers,* p. 324.

14. Quoted in Hal Draper, *Karl Marx's Theory of Revolution, Vol. I: State and Bureaucracy* (New York: Monthly Review Press, 1977), p. 316.

15. David R. Roediger, *The Wages of Whiteness, Race and the Making of the American Working Class* (London: Verso, 1991). The phrase "truly disadvantaged" is borrowed from William Julius Wilson, *The Truly Disadvantaged, The Inner City, the Underclass, and Public Policy* (Chicago: University of Chicago Press, 1987).

16. Ira Katznelson, *City Trenches, Urban Politics and the Patterning of Class in the United States* (Chicago: University of Chicago Press, 1981), ch. 3. We should stress that white male workers did have to fight for the vote; the ruling elites in the various states did not hand labor the right to vote on a silver platter. In the most glaring illustration of this popular need to battle for the vote, in the state of Rhode Island it took virtually "a military assault of the state capitol"—the so-called Dorr Rebellion, named for its leader Thomas W. Dorr—before the state's political directorate was willing to concede voting rights to white males in the economic majority. Dorr's rebellion was an extreme instance of a broader popular struggle by workers, one which had to be made state by state. Just as Madison hoped, the price of expanded democracy for white labor was to go through the salami slicer of federalism. See Sean Wilentz, "Property and Power: Suffrage Reform in the United States," in Donald W. Rogers, ed., *Voting and the Spirit of American Democracy: Essays on the History of Voting and Voting Rights in America* (Urbana, IL: University of Chicago Press, 1990), p. 36.

17. Arthur Rosenberg, *Democracy and Socialism* (Boston: Beacon Press, 1965), p. 4.

18. What Nicos Poulantzas observed from a strictly theoretical standpoint is thus confirmed empirically and dramatically for the U.S. case: "The political field of the state (as well as the sphere of ideology) has always, in different forms, been present in the constitution and reproduction of the relations of production." See *State, Power, Socialism,* trans. P. Camiller (London: Verso, 1980), p. 17. Clearly, in capitalist societies, governments are active agents in the constitution and even in the confusion of working-class consciousness and identity.

19. Roediger, *Wages of Whiteness,* p. 13; W.E.B. Du Bois, *Black Reconstruction in the United States, 1860-1880* (New York: 1977); Thorstein Veblen, *The Theory of the Leisure Class* (New York: Penguin, 1979).

20. Katznelson, *City Trenches,* ch. 3.

21. Quoted in Grant McConnell, *Private Power and American Democracy* (New York: Vintage Books, 1966), p. 80. Also see Selig Perlman, *The Theory of the Labor Movement* (New York: MacMillan, 1928).

22. McConnell, *Private Power,* pp. 79-88.

23. *Workingman's Advocate,* 21 August 1869, quoted in Philip S. Foner, *History of the Labor Movement in the United States: From Colonial Times to the*

Founding of the American Federation of Labor, Vol. I (New York: International Publishers, 1947), p. 370; Melvyn Dubofsky, *We Shall Be All, A History of the IWW* (New York: Quadrangle Books, 1969).

24. This division of workplace and community politics was not universal. In smaller, isolated mining and factory towns, where workers were more likely to share bonds of ethnicity, language, and culture, labor militancy and political struggle often fused together, just as Madison's theory of communal activism would suggest. See, for example, Martin Shefter, "Trade Unions and Political Machines: The Organization and Disorganization of the American Working Class in the Late 19th Century," in *Working-Class Formation, Nineteenth-Century Patterns in Western Europe and the United States,* ed. Ira Katznelson and Ariste R. Zolberg (Princeton: Princeton University Press, 1986), pp. 197-276. But having noted this qualification, it is just as important to recognize that there is nothing automatic about the relationship between such factors as geographic isolation or social homogeneity and a propensity toward labor militancy. In some isolated areas, such as the East Kentucky coal fields, ignorance, alienation, personal and family feuds, and brutal corporate tactics repressed militant labor organization despite proximity and strong cultural ties. See, e.g., Harry Caudill, *Night Comes to the Cumberlands* (Boston: Atlantic Monthly Press-Little, Brown, & Co., 1963) and John Gaventa, *Power and Powerlessness: Quiescence and Rebellion in an Appalachian Valley* (Urbana, IL: University of Illinois Press, 1980). The larger generalization is, therefore, that in the big multi-ethnic industrial cities, where immigrant workers gravitated to local Democratic Party organizations to get help from local government while fighting for stronger unions in the workplace, the typical result was, as Ira Katznelson writes, "a politics of competition between ethnic-territorial communities from which capital was absent." *City Trenches,* p. 65.

25. As Amy Bridges notes, from about 1800 to 1840 or so, "Career politicians were lacking not only the wealth of earlier political leaders, but also the 'machinery' of the later party system. Their initial efforts at organization involved not only the forming of ward or citywide committees, but also an attempt to rely on organizations whose primary purpose was not the delivery of the vote. These organizations—the volunteer fire companies, militia companies, and gangs—were courted with donations, occasional patronage, or freedom (when it was necessary) from arrest." *A City in the Republic, Antebellum New York and the Origins of Machine Politics* (Ithaca: Cornell University Press, 1984), p. 75.

26. Dennis Judd, *The Politics of American Cities: Private Power and Public Policy,* 2nd ed. (Boston: Little Brown, 1984), pp. 54-55.

27. *Ibid.*

28. *Ibid.,* p. 36.

29. Steven P. Erie, *Rainbow's End: Irish-Americans and the Dilemmas of Urban Machine Politics, 1840-1985* (Berkeley: University of California Press, 1988), pp. 84-85.

30. Erie, *Rainbow's End, passim.*

31. For the case of ethnic rivalry in New Haven see Robert Dahl, *Who Governs?, Democracy and Power in an American City* (New Haven: Yale University Press, 1961). On divisions within the Jewish political community, see Lawrence Fuchs, *The Political Behavior of American Jews* (Glencoe, IL: The Free Press, 1956).

32. Katznelson, *City Trenches.*

33. Of this feature of the political system, Thomas B. Edsall writes, "In certain respects, the political system at all levels of government functions as a back-door antitrust mechanism, breaking up established power and allowing the entry of new groups into the political-economic system." *The New Politics of Inequality* (New York: Norton, 1984), p. 27.

34. George ran with the support of the city's Central Labor Union and the Knights of Labor, which together formed the United Labor Party. Winning proportionately more second-generation Irish votes than the machine, and running well in working-class German neighborhoods, George nonetheless lost the election, as Tammany simply tossed many of his votes into the city dump. This after the machine failed to bribe George to get off labor's ticket. See Shefter, "Trade Unions and Political Machines," in *Working Class Formation,* pp. 270-271; Erie, *Rainbow's End,* pp. 217-218; and Dennis R. Judd, *The Politics of American Cities* (Boston: Little, Brown, 1984), p. 71.

35. Erie, *Rainbow's End,* pp. 217-218.

36. Flacks, *Making History,* p. 113.

37. William L. Riordon, ed., *Plunkitt of Tammany Hall* (New York: E.P. Dutton, 1963), p. 19.

38. *Ibid.,* p. 37.

39. *Ibid.,* pp. 37, 3.

40. No one has written more brilliantly or caustically about the foggy ethics shared by the leading business and political elites than Thorstein Veblen. Businessmen and politicians, wrote Veblen, arise out of the same "raw material." "To be acceptable" to the powerful, therefore, aspirants for the top are advised to be "reliable, conciliatory, conservative, secretive, patient and prehensile. The capacities that make the outcome and that characterize this gild of self-made businessmen are cupidity, prudence, and chicane—the greatest of these, and the one that chiefly gives its tone to this business life, is prudence." For Veblen, a recent president's fondness for the latter term could not have been an accident. See *Imperial Germany and the Industrial Revolution* (New York: MacMillan, 1915), pp. 333, 336.

41. Erie, *Rainbow's End,* pp. 56-57.

42. Seymour J. Mandelbaum, *Boss Tweed's New York* (Chicago: Ivan R. Dee, 1990), pp. 77-78.

43. Martin Shefter, *Political Crisis: Fiscal Crisis, The Collapse and Revival of New York* (New York: Basic Books, 1987), p. 18. For discussions of similarities with the later fiscal crises in New York City, see also Ester R. Fuchs, *Mayors and Money: Fiscal Policy in New York and Chicago* (Chicago: University of Chicago Press, 1992) and Roger A. Alcaly and David Mermelstein, eds., *The Fiscal Crisis of American Cities, Essays on the Political Economy of Urban*

America with Special Reference to New York (New York: Vintage Books, 1977).

44. Quoted in David C. Hammack, *Power and Society, Greater New York at the Turn of the Century* (New York: Columbia University Press, 1987), p. 9.

45. Quoted in *ibid.*

46. *Ibid.,* p. 200.

47. Quoted in *ibid.,* p. 201. Specifically, the Tilden Commission proposed restricting the municipal voting class to "those with more than $500 in property, or those with annual rental payments over $250." See Francis Fox Piven and Richard A. Cloward, *Why Americans Don't Vote* (New York: Pantheon, 1988), p. 86.

48. Quoted in Hammack, *Power and Society,* p. 201.

49. Madison, "Federalist #10," p. 79.

50. Thomas Edsall, *The New Politics of Inequality* (New York: Norton, 1984), pp. 25-26.

51. For detailed discussions of the political ideology and technology of reform and especially its relation to changes in corporate capitalism, see Samuel P. Hays, *Conservation and the Gospel of Efficiency: The Progressive Conservation Movement, 1880-1920* (New York: Atheneum, 1969), as well as Hays' seminal article, "The Politics of Municipal Government in the Progressive Era," *Pacific Northwest Quarterly 55,* October 1964, pp. 157-166; James Weinstein, *The Corporate Ideal in the Liberal State, 1900-1918* (Boston: Beacon Press, 1968); Harry Braverman, *Labor and Monopoly Capital* (New York: Monthly Review Press, 1974); R. Jeffery Lustig, *Corporate Liberalism: The Origins of Modern American Political Theory, 1890-1920* (Berkeley: University of California Press, 1982).

52. Quoted in Frug, "City as a Legal Concept," p. 1110.

53. For detailed reviews of such reformist arguments, see Thomas E. Cronin, *Direct Democracy: The Politics of Initiative, Referendum, and Recall* (Cambridge: Harvard University Press, Twentieth Century Fund, 1989), especially ch. 3; James A. Morone, *The Democratic Wish, Popular Participation and the Limits of American Government* (New York: Basic Books, 1990).

54. Frug, "City as a Legal Concept," p. 1109.

55. It should be noted that in a handful of cities, notably Cleveland under Mayor Tom Johnson and Detroit under Hazen Pingree, upper-class reform leaders transcended this ideological milieu. They went beyond the elitist manipulation of procedures to lead battles for genuinely socially democratic policies of benefit to workers, such as public ownership of utilities, tax reform, and parks for everyone. See, for example, Melvin G. Holli, *Reform in Detroit: Hazen S. Pingree and Urban Politics* (New York: Oxford University Press, 1969) and Todd Swanstrom, *The Crisis of Growth Politics, Cleveland, Kucinich and Challenge of Growth Populism* (Philadelphia: Temple University Press, 1985), especially pp. 44-48. As Swanstrom writes of Tom Johnson, a self-made millionaire who became a true believer in Henry George's radical land theory, "Johnson was different, it is important to understand, from the typical good government Reformers of his day. For middle-class Reformers, the solution to municipal problems was to put the 'right men' into office. Johnson

attacked unjust institutions, economic privilege, not men." As Swanstrom rightfully emphasizes, men like Johnson and Pingree were exceptions to the prevalent elitism of reform.

56. Shefter, *Fiscal Crisis, Political Crisis;* Fuchs, *Mayors and Money.*

57. Robert Caro, *The Power Broker: Robert Moses and the Fall of New York* (New York: Vintage, 1975); Chester Hartman, *The Transformation of San Francisco* (Totowa, New Jersey: Rowman and Allanheld, 1984); John R. Logan and Harvey Molotch, *Urban Fortunes: The Political Economy of Space* (Berkeley: University of California Press, 1987).

58. Piven and Cloward, *Why Americans Don't Vote,* pp. 54-57.

59. Quoted in Judd, *Politics of American Cities,* p. 85. A key aspect of mid-nineteenth-century nativist fervor was the effort by xenophobes to limit the voting rights of immigrant workers by requiring no less than a twenty-one-year residency requirement on foreign-born citizens before they might vote. See Paul Kleppner, "Defining Citizenship: Immigration and the Struggle for Voting Rights in Antebellum America," in Rodgers, ed., *Voting and the Spirit of American Democracy,* pp. 43-53. Though such efforts failed, not least because the established parties wanted immigrant votes, they offer another illustration of anti-democratic rules manipulation to shrink the economic majority, and of division within the ranks of labor, for many among the xenophobic faction were themselves working- and lower-middle-class people. See, e.g., Kleppner, p. 50.

60. Quoted in Samuel P. Hays, *The Response to Industrialism, 1885-1914* (Chicago: University of Chicago Press, 1957), p. 100.

61. *Ibid.,* pp. 100-101.

62. David Gordon, "Capitalist Development and the History of American Cities," in *Marxism and the Metropolis: New Perspectives in Urban Political Economy,* ed. William K. Tabb and Larry Sawyers (New York: Oxford University Press, 1978), p. 43. On the general process of suburbanization and its connection to government restructuring, see Sidney Plotkin, *Keep Out: The Struggle for Land Use Reform* (Berkeley: University of California Press, 1978), ch. 4.

63. Paul Kantor with Stephen David, *The Dependent City* (Glenview, IL: Scott, Foreman, 1988), p. 108; Erie, *Rainbow's End,* p. 81.

64. Hammack, *Power and the City, passim.*

65. Kenneth T. Jackson, *Crabgrass Frontier: The Suburbanization of the United States* (New York: Oxford University Press, 1985), pp. 130-148.

66. Quoted in *ibid.,* p. 151.

67. Theodore J. Lowi, *The End of Liberalism, The Second Republic of the United States,* 2nd ed. (New York: Norton, 1979), p. 169.

68. *Ibid.,* p. 175.

69. In the words of a key U.S. Supreme Court decision, the suburb is a distinct civic institution, which has "powers of its own and authority to govern itself as it sees fit within the limits of the organic law of its creation and the Federal and State Constitutions." *Village of Euclid v. Ambler Realty Co.* 272 U.S. 365 (1926), in Charles M. Haar, *Land-Use Planning: A Casebook on the Use, Misuse, and Re-Use of Urban Land,* 3rd ed. (Boston: Little Brown, 1976), p. 201. This decision lent suburbs the constitutional right to zone their land

off-limits to the city. Indeed, as the Court's references to state and federal law make clear, the city has no place or legal standing in the suburb.

70. Plotkin, *Keep Out,* p. 158.

71. Suburbanization is thus an apt example of E.E. Schattschneider's observation that "A conclusive way of checking the rise of conflict is simply to provide no arena for it or to create no public agency with power to do anything about it." But then, as Schattschneider also keenly understood, "The best point at which to manage conflict is before it starts." *Semisovereign People,* pp. 69, 15.

72. Sidney Plotkin, "Democratic Change in the Urban Political Economy: San Antonio's Edwards Aquifer Controversy," *Texas Journal of Political Studies* No. I, Fall 1978, p. 14.

Chapter Five

1. See Kevin Phillips, *Post-Reagan America, People, Politics, and Ideology in a Time of Crisis* (New York: Random House, 1982); Thad Beyle, "New Governors in Hard Economic and Political Times," in T. Beyle, ed., *Governors and Hard Times* (Washington, D.C.: Congressional Quarterly Press, 1992), pp. 1-14.

2. William Crotty, "Who Needs Two Republican Parties?" in James MacGregor Burns, et al., eds., *The Democrats Must Lead: The Case for a Progressive Democratic Party* (Boulder, CO: Westview Press, 1992), p. 65.

3. John J. Harrigan, *Political Change in the Metropolis,* (Glenview, IL: Scott Foresman, 1989), pp. 251, 299.

4. Seymour Melman, "Military State Capitalism," *The Nation,* 20 May 1991, p. 666.

5. David B. Robertson and Dennis R. Judd, *The Development of American Policy: The Structure of Policy Restraint* (Glenview, IL: Scott, Foresman, 1989), p. 303.

6. Deil S. Wright, *Understanding Intergovernmental Relations,* 3rd ed. (Pacific Grove, CA: Broks/Cole, 1988), pp. 157-158; Robertson and Judd, *Development of American Public Policy,* p. 209; David B. Walker, *Toward a Functioning Federalism* (Cambridge, MA: Winthrop, 1981), pp. 163-165; Congressional Budget Office, *The Economic and Budget Outlook: Fiscal Years 1993-1997, A Report to the Senate and House Committees on the Budget* (Washington, D.C.: U.S. Government Printing Office, 1992), Table D-4, p. 116.

7. Thorstein Veblen, *Absentee Ownership: The Case of America* (Boston: Beacon, 1967), pp. 142-143.

8. Dean Tipps and Lee Webb, *State and Local Tax Revolt, New Directions for the '80s* (Washington, D.C.: Conference on Alternative State and Local Policies, 1980), pp. 35-53; Sara Fitzgerald and Patricia Meisol, "The 'Taxpayers Revolt' Takes to the States," *National Journal,* 3 June 1978, p. 873.

9. Thomas B. Edsall and Mary D. Edsall, *Chain Reaction: The Impact of Race, Rights and Taxes on American Politics* (New York: Norton, 1991), p. 228.

10. William Craig Stubblebine, "Revenue Reallocation in the Federal System: Options and Prospects," in Robert B. Hawkins, Jr., ed., *American Federalism:*

A New Partnership for the Republic (New Brunswick, NJ: Transaction Books, Institute for Contemporary Studies, 1982), p. 147.

11. Max Weber, *Economy and Society: An Outline of Interpretive Sociology,* eds. Guenther Roth and Claus Wittich (Berkeley: University of California Press, 1978), vol. 1, pp. 361-362; Sidney Plotkin, "Community and Alienation: Enclave Consciousness and Urban Movements," in *Breaking Chains: Social Movements and Collective Action,* ed. Michael P. Smith (New Brunswick, NJ: Transaction, 1991), pp. 5-25.

12. "Upscale locales hardly blinked when federal revenue-sharing dollars stopped flowing, but for some poor cities and rural hamlets, this program was a lifeline, not a luxury." W. John Moore, "Cutoff at Town Hall," *National Journal,* 11 April 1987, p. 862.

13. Alvin Rabushka and Pauline Ryan, *The Tax Revolt* (Stanford, CA: Hoover Institution, Stanford University, 1982), p. 1; David O. Sears and Jack Citrin, *Tax Revolt: Something for Nothing in California* (Cambridge: Harvard University Press, 1982), p. 3; Peter Schrag, "Why California Doesn't Work," *The Nation,* 12 October 1992, pp. 390-392.

14. Mike Davis, *City of Quartz: Excavating the Future in Los Angeles* (New York: Random House, Vintage, 1992), p. 182.

15. Rabushka and Ryan, *Tax Revolt,* p. 16; Sears and Citrin, *Tax Revolt,* p. 20. "Interestingly, in a 1973 poll, about two-thirds of the members of the International Association of Assessing Officers (a professional organization for tax assessors) sided with their critics by rating the overall quality of tax assessments as 'poor' or 'very poor.'" Diane Fuchs, "Property Tax Is Often Poorly Run," in Tipps and Webb, eds., *State & Local Tax Revolt,* p. 39.

16. Rabushka and Ryan, *Tax Revolt,* pp. 16-17.

17. Robert Lekachman, *The Great Tax Debate* (New York: Public Affairs Committee, 1980), p. 7.

18. Robert Kuttner, "The Property Tax: Homeowner Relief," in Tripps and Webb, eds., *State & Local Tax Revolt,* p. 65; Rabushka and Ryan, *Tax Revolt,* pp. 15-16.

19. Sears and Citrin, *Tax Revolt,* p. 20.

20. Davis, *City of Quartz,* p. 153. For a discussion of how such movements arise directly out of contradictions within capitalist property itself, see Sidney Plotkin, *Keep Out: The Struggle for Land Use Control* (Berkeley: University of California Press, 1987). On the concept of resistance movements generally, see Richard Flacks, *Making History: The American Left and the American Mind* (New York: Columbia University Press, 1988), pp. 92-93.

21. Even the state's popular conservative governor, Ronald Reagan, failed to win public support for a 1973 constitutional amendment that would have confined the annual growth of total state expenditures to the increase in state income, tightened restraints on local tax rates, and required a two-thirds majority in the state legislature to pass tax bills. Taxes and government spending were not yet widely experienced as key organizing themes of a new public order, and even the "Great Communicator" could not make them so. Sears and Citrin, *Tax Revolt,* p. 21.

22. Davis, *City of Quartz,* p. 181.

23. Sears and Citrin, *Tax Revolt,* p. 22.

24. By 1978, most states were benefitting from the recovery and inflation-driven rise in tax receipts. In 1977 alone, the state take in taxes rose above $100 billion, a 13% increase over the previous year. In this circumstance, the majority of states were finding it much easier to meet their balanced-budget requirements, and many even began to dream of surpluses and new spending programs. "Developing Trend by States Toward Balancing Budgets," *The New York Times,* 8 March 1978, p. 59.

25. Cited in Harrell R. Rodgers and Michael Harrington, *Unfinished Democracy: The American Political System* (Glenview, IL: Scott, Foresman, 1981), p. 185.

26. For a detailed account of the various tax-reform proposals considered by the legislature, see Dean C. Tipps, "California's Great Property Tax Revolt: The Origins and Impact of Proposition 13," in Tipps and Webb, *State & Local Tax Revolt,* pp. 73-74.

27. See Schrag, "Why California Doesn't Work," *The Nation,* p. 390.

28. *Ibid.,* pp. 76-77.

29. Sears and Citrin, *Tax Revolt,* p. 25.

30. Rabushka and Ryan, *Tax Revolt,* pp. 26-29.

31. *Ibid.,* pp. 15, 20.

32. Lekachman, *Great Tax Debate,* p. 5. For Sears and Citrin, Prop 13 promised a system of "plebiscitary budgeting" for California, the turning of basic decisions about the size of the public sector over to the taxpayers. On its face, this seemed very democratic. The taxpayers would now rule tax policy. But if the term "plebiscite" is taken at its root meaning—direct rule by the plebs, or common people—Prop 13 was in truth less an example of "plebiscitary" than "oligarchical" budgeting. Plebiscites are democratic elections governed by the principle of majority rule. But by requiring super-majorities to pass tax legislation at the state and local levels, Prop 13 truly empowered the most embittered minority in tax policy. Now one-third plus one vote could defeat the wishes of almost two-thirds of the state legislature or two-thirds of the local community. Just as balanced-budget conservatism nationally would soon come to rest on the belief that state and local taxpayers are the most discontented taxpayers, Prop 13 went a step further to greatly strengthen the hand of the angriest of the angry at the expense of the majority. In fact, Jarvis' empowerment of angry minority voices owed more to the cranky defensiveness of John Calhoun's theory of "concurrent majorities" than to any straightforward faith in simple majority rule.

33. James O'Connor, *The Fiscal Crisis of the State* (New York: St. Martin's Press, 1973). On corporate pressure to centralize state controls over the growth and development process, see Plotkin, *Keep Out.*

34. "California: Will It Choke Its Boom," *Business Week,* 17 July 1978, pp. 54-55; Rabushka and Ryan, *Tax Revolt,* p. 23.

35. Rabushka and Ryan, *Tax Revolt,* p. 22.

36. Davis, *City of Quartz,* p. 182.

37. Sears and Citrin, *Tax Revolt,* p. 123; Davis, *City of Quartz,* pp. 183-184. Further support for Davis' argument can be found in Sears and Citrin's studies of public opinion on Proposition 13. The authors discovered what they called an unmistakable tendency toward "symbolic racism" among supporters of

Jarvis-Gann, indeed they concluded that this was "a major factor in whites' support for the tax revolt." Basing their conclusions in part on a two-question scale that probed backing for an anti-busing amendment that appeared on the November 1979 California ballot, as well as the question of whether government should make special efforts to aid blacks and other racial majorities, these researchers concluded that "symbolic racism" was probably more influential on Prop 13 whites than partisan or ideological factors (Sears and Citrin, pp. 168-169, 239). And for an excellent discussion of suburban civic associations as a form of Rightwing democratic action, see Robert Fisher, *Let the People Decide: Neighborhood Organizing in America* (Boston: G.K. Hall, Twayne, 1984), pp. 61-89.

38. Jack Citrin, "Introduction: The Legacy of Proposition 13," in Terry Schwadon and Paul Richter, eds. and principal writers, *California and the American Tax Revolt: Proposition 13 Five Years Later* (Berkeley: University of California Press, 1984), p. 3.

39. Sears and Citrin, *Tax Revolt,* p. 158. And not all unionists were anti-Prop 13, in any case. The United Firefighters of Los Angeles City, Local 112, AFL/CIO, for example, voted to support Proposition 13, because, as the union's president explained, "the firefighters are first and foremost citizens and taxpayers...They felt government had been unresponsive to them." Besides, many members of Local 112 simply did not believe that Los Angles would ever lay off firefighters. See Fitzgerald and Meisol, "The 'Taxpayers' Revolt Takes to the States," *National Journal,* p. 875.

40. Paul A. Beck, Hal G. Rainey, and Carol Traut, "Disadvantage, Disaffection, and Race as Divergent Bases for Citizen Fiscal Policy Preferences," *Journal of Politics* 52 (1990), pp. 71-93; Gallup Poll, reported in *San Francisco Chronicle,* 31 August 1990; Ed McManus, "Whites Get Lower Levy Regularly," in Tipps and Webb, *State & Local Tax Revolt,* p. 43.

41. *Ibid.,* pp. 52-53. Such polls found, for example, that a majority of Californians felt acutely disconnected from their government. A majority (57%) trusted government to do what was right "only some of the time," and nearly two-thirds (64%) thought that government was run for the benefit of a few special interests, not for all Californians. Furthermore, strong and generalized distrust of government was coupled with related beliefs that governments at all levels wasted people's money, and did so in a big way. A Gallup Poll of October 1978 found that Americans believed that nearly half of every tax dollar was wasted by Washington, a third of every dollar went down the drain of state governments, and 25 cents of each local tax dollar bought absolutely nothing. Consistent with this level of mass belief in the existence of wasteful, inefficient government, many California taxpayers were convinced that existing or even higher service levels could be sustained at much lower levels of taxing and spending. Weeks before the vote, 54% of Californians told pollsters that state spending could be trimmed by as much as 10% without *any* effect on the level or quality of public services, and a minority more than large enough to block tax increases under the two-thirds rule of Jarvis-Gann—38%—said that even as much as a 40% cut in state spending would not hurt existing service levels. Similarly, many Californians saw the

pay scale of government employees as out of line with private-sector wages; as many as 35%—once again a minority large enough to stop a future tax increase—believed that state and local workers were paid more than they deserved compared to private workers, though fully 56% believed public employees were paid fairly or too little.

42. Davis, *City of Quartz*, p. 183. It was precisely in this sense that Sears and Citrin found the tax-cut fever to embody potent strains of "symbolic racism": a vote against taxes was a vote to de-fund poor blacks.

43. Robert Kuttner, *Revolt of the Haves* (New York: Simon & Schuster, 1980).

44. Fitzgerald and Meisol, "The 'Taxpayers' Revolt'," p. 876; "Nationwide Revolt on Taxes Showing No Sign of Abating," *The New York Times,* 5 August 1979, pp. 1, 38; Tipps, "California's Tax Revolt," p. 81.

45. Peter Kerr, "Read His Lips: More Taxes," *The New York Times Magazine,* 20 May 1990, p. 31; "Goals Similar, But Florio and Cuomo Split on Strategy," *The New York Times,* 13 July 1990, p. B1.

46. Robert Guskind, "Gloves-Off Guv," *National Journal,* 11 April 1992, p. 875.

47. *Ibid.,* p. 877.

48. "Poll Says Home Rule Could Bend to Ward Off Sprawling Growth," *The New York Times,* 18 March 1992, p. B5.

49. "Florio Defends Higher Taxes, Urging State to Face Reality," *The New York Times,* 16 March 1990, pp. 1-2; "Governor Urges Great Leap and Volunteers to Go First," *The New York Times,* 25 March 1990, sec. IV, p. 4.

50. "Governor Urges Great Leap," *The New York Times,* p. B4.

51. "Florio Plans to Balance Budget with $1.4 Billion Tax Increase," *The New York Times,* 15 March 1990, pp. B1, 4.

52. William Schneider, "Populist Policy, Not Populist Politics," *National Journal,* 21 July 1990, p. 1806.

53. O'Neill was but one of ten governors in 1990 who decided against re-election bids after having raised taxes. Among the others were Republicans George Deukmejian of California and Jim Thompson of Illinois, and Democrat Madeline Kunin of Vermont. See Dick Kirschten, "Targets of Discontent," *National Journal,* 10 November 1990, p. 2736; "Days of Rage: Florio and the Taxpayers," *The New York Times,* 27 April 1990, pp. B1-2.

54. "Florio Defends Higher Taxes"; "Governor Urges Great Leap"; "Days of Rage: Florio and the Taxpayers," *The New York Times.*

55. "Teachers Union and Bergen Democrats Attack Florio's Budget Proposal," *The New York Times,* 14 June 1990, p. B1; "Florio Faces Growing Anti-Tax Storm in New Jersey," *The New York Times,* 23 July 1990, pp. B1-2.

56. "Tax Rally Displays Petitions Against Florio," *The New York Times,* 24 September 1990, pp. B1, 4.

57. "New Jersey Anti-Tax Storm Growing as Rate Rise Precedes Benefits," *The New York Times,* 23 July 1990, p. B1.

58. "Florio Faces Growing Anti-Tax Storm"; "Tax Rally Displays Petitions Against Florio," *The New York Times,* 24 September 1990, pp. B1, 4

59. "Florio and Tax Protestors: Battle Could Be a Long One," *The New York Times,* 27 September 1990, p. B1. V.O. Key, Jr., with the assistance of Milton

C. Cummings, Jr., *The Responsible Electorate: Rationality in Presidential Voting, 1936-1960* (New York: Random House, 1966), p. 7.

60. Bradley, who kept a carefully measured distance from the state tax fight, ran on national themes; indeed, he was a main sponsor of the 1986 Tax Reform Act, which flattened rates in the U.S. income tax and even closed dozens of corporate tax loopholes. But, as Marx said, the people make their own history all right, though not necessarily under circumstances of their own choosing. The U.S. Senate election was the next available object of voter disaffection, so New Jerseyans used it. After all, elections are among the most powerful amplifiers people have in democratic societies, and when times are bad, any old election will do. So, despite a sterling national reputation, and having done nothing in particular to offend his constituents, Bradley just scraped by a virtually unknown opponent, Christine Whitman, with 51% of the vote. (Whitman would later run for the Republican nomination for governor in the 1993 election.) As nearly every commentator agreed, voters chose to deflate the Bradley myth as a way to get at more local Democrats. Similarly, next door in New York, Gov. Mario Cuomo won re-election in 1990 by a surprisingly small 53%-47% margin, this against an all but decimated Republican opposition that was fractured by a third-party conservative challenge. Cuomo's response to the challenge of fiscal crisis will, of course, be the central theme of the chapters ahead.

61. At the same time, as if betokening the Perot insurgency of 1992, HANJ co-founder John Budzash warned Republicans not to assume that tax protesters would automatically support the GOP. "What we want is accountability by *all* our elected officials," including Republicans, which is why the group made direct democracy, including term limitations, a major component of its program. "Leaders of New Jersey Tax Revolt Take Aim at Legislature," *The New York Times,* 22 November 1990, p. B6.

62. "Florio Needs $800 Million to Balance Budet for 1992," *The New York Times,* 11 January 1991., p B2; "Florio Approves a Rise in Tolls on the Turnpike," *The New York Times,* 29 January 1991, p. B2.

63. "Embattled Florio Says He'll Seek Guidance from the Voters," *The New York Times,* 13 November 1991, p. B1; *"New Jersey Officials Reach Pact on Taxes," The New York Times,* 6 March 1991, p. B4; "In Trenton, Senate Passes Sweeping Welfare Package," *The New York Times,* 14 January 1992, p. B4; "Florio Signs an Overhaul of Welfare," *The New York Times,* 22 January 1992, p. B1, 4.

64. "To Counter Tax Cynics, Florio's Party Tries Ads," *The New York Times,* 7 August 1991, p. B2.

65. The new budget included layoffs affecting up to 3,000 state workers, cut most agency budgets by 8%, froze state aid to college students, for the fourth year in a row included no increase in welfare benefits to keep up with inflation, and sliced $4 million in job-training programs for the working poor. Yet for all the cuts aimed at the lower classes, overall state spending went up, with nearly $2 billion slotted for middle-income property tax relief, which one Florio advisor called the "heart and soul" of the budget. "Second Florio Budget Is Study in Survival," *The New York Times,* 8 July 1991, p. B2.

66. Led by the Communications Workers of America, the coalition also included the American Federation of State, County and Federal Employees, the Service Employees International Union, the Amalgamated Transit Union, the International Federation of Professional and Technical Engineers, the American Federation of Teachers, and the State Policemen's Benevolent Association. "Old Friends Break Up: Trenton Democrats and Angry Unions," *The New York Times,* 7 May 1991, p. B1.
67. Quoted in "To Counter Tax Cynics," *The New York Times,* p. B2.
68. The state Republican Party chair, Robert D. Franks, urged voters to take heart from the fact that Republicans did deliver on two promises, the sales tax rollback and big state spending cuts. As for direct democracy, the equations of power in the state simply favored corporations and other interest groups: "The interests of State Street [location of the state capital and many lobby offices]," he explained, "triumphed over the interests of Main Street," but then, "Two out of three isn't bad." "Defeat of Citizen-Lawmaking Bills Leaves G.O.P. With Credibility Problem," *The New York Times,* 22 July 1992, p. B5.
69. *The New York Times,* 3 November 1992.

Chapter Seven

1. C. Wright Mills, *The Power Elite* (New York: Oxford University Press, 1956), p. 155.
2. *Empire State Report,* 1982.
3. This is not to suggest that large business interests had never done this before. U.S. political history is replete with tales of corporate political abuse. The most recent reassertion of business political power came when corporate interests recognized that their structural power was insufficient to bring the number and kinds of political victories needed. They also had before them, as discussed in the text below, the experience of public-interest groups who had gained some measure of success in the late 1960s and early 1970s. The strategies and tactics of these public-interest groups provided the model eventually pursued by the business sector.
4. See Thomas B. Edsall, *The New Politics of Inequality* (New York: W.W. Norton, 1984); Thomas Ferguson and Joel Rogers, *Right Turn: The Decline of the Democrats and the Future of American Politics* (New York: Hill and Wang, 1986); David Vogel, *Fluctuating Fortunes: The Power of Business in America* (New York: Basic Books, 1989). An excellent criticism of the thesis of the political re-emergence of business is found in G. William Domhoff's *The Power Elite and the State* (New York: Aldine De Gruyter, 1990), pp. 257-285.
5. Bennett Harrison and Barry Bluestone, *The Great U-Turn: Corporate Restructuring and the Polarization of America* (New York: Basic Books, 1986); *The New York Times,* 9 October 1983, p. A31.
6. In February 1978, Mayor Koch presented a four-year plan before the Assembly Ways and Means Committee and the Senate Finance Committee. The Koch plan called for a 10% reduction of the city's workforce—a loss of 20,000 employees—over a four-year period. See "Testimony of Edward I. Koch,

Before a Joint Fiscal Committee, Assembly Ways and Means Committee and Senate Finance Committee," Legislative Office Building, Albany, New York, 16 February 1978. Located in AFSCME New York District, Box 1, file New York State Budget and Financial Information, Walter P. Reuther Library, Wayne State University, Detroit, Michigan.

7. Just days prior to the election, every major poll showed Koch winning by a large margin. One poll even had the mayor leading by eighteen percentage points. See "None of the Polls Showed Cuomo Leading," *The New York Times,* 25 September 1982, p. 31.

8. See " Emotional Appeals Are Made Directly," *The New York Times,* 31 October 1982, sec. IV, p. 6E.

9. *Ibid.*

10. William E. Scheuerman, "Fragmented Politics and De-Industrialization: The Case of Bethelem Steel," *Teaching Politics,* Fall 1984; also reprinted in *The American Way: Government and Politics in the U.S.A.* (New York: Longmans, 1985).

11. Walter Goldstein, "Rx For New York's Economy: More World Trade, Less Welfare," *Empire State Report,* October 1983, pp. 7-14.

12. Joseph Laura, "Capital's Point Man," *Empire State Report,* September 1986, p. 11.

13. Robert Goodman, *The Last Entrepreneurs: America's Regional Wars for Jobs and Dollars* (Boston: South End Press, 1979).

14. Roy Bahl and Larry Schroeder, "Two Steps Forward, One Step Backward, and Some Tough Decisions for the New Governor," *Empire State Report,* January 1983, pp.18-19.

15. Michael B. Sawicky, *The Roots of the Public Sector Fiscal Crisis* (Washington, D.C.: The Economic Policy Institute, 1991), p. 6.

16. Paul D. Moore, "Ready or Not (And Like It or Not) The Action Is Shifting to Albany," *Empire State Report,* July 1983, pp. 12-14.

17. All groups, of course, are not organized, and resources are not evenly distributed, making for great inequities in the process even during "normal," wealthier times. This is complicated by the structural power of capital. See Domhoff, 1990.

18. Goldstein, 1983, p. 3.

19. Robert S. McElvaine, *Mario Cuomo: A Biography* (New York: Charles Scribner's Sons, 1988), p. 312.

20. McElvaine, 1988.

21. Michael Lipsky, *Street-Level Bureaucracy: Dilemmas of the Individual in Public Service* (New York: Russell Sage Foundation, 1980), p. 7.

22. Edward A. Gargen, "Unionist Tells Cuomo Early Retirements Can End Need for Layoffs," *The New York Times,* 7 March 1983, p. B2.

23. Michael Orestes, "New York State to Cut Many From Payroll," *The New York Times,* 6 May 1983, II, I: 6.

24. See *The New York Times,* 20 June, sec. II, p. 5.

25. Democratic Staff Study of the Joint Economic Committee, Congress of the United States, *Falling Behind: The Growing Income Gap in America,* n.d.

26. See *The New York Times,* 8 August 1984, p. B2.

27. Judy Watson, "A Good Year in Albany," *Empire State Report,* September, 1985, p. 18.
28. Frank Lynn, "Unions Lead Donors Aiding Cuomo Over Four Years," *The New York Times,* 28 October 1986, II, 1:5.
29. The exception to this was in 1988 when the governor, responding to the Feerick Commission's report on campaign finances by statewide office holders, temporarily placed a voluntary ceiling of $8,000 on contributions.
30. New York State Commission on Government Integrity, *The Midas Touch,* June 1988, p. 31.
31. "Cuomo Seeks Big Donations Despite Panel," *The New York Times,* 26 February 1990, p. B1.
32. Mary Hedglon, "Striking a Balance," *Empire State Report,* September 1988, pp. 38-42.
33. Daniel Wash, "A Taxing Situation," *Empire State Report,* March 1990.
34. Jan Sorensen, "A Banner Year for Business," *Empire State Report,* September 1987, pp. 12-13.
35. Terry Golway, "The Tax Cut Fiasco," *Empire State Report,* January 1990, p. 21.
36. Fiscal Policy Institute, *The Fair Tax Guide for New York,* November 1991.
37. American Economics Group, Inc., prepared for the New York State United Teachers, *New York's 16 Billion Dollar Dilemma* (Washington, D.C., 1992).
38. "Why Corporate America Moves Where," *Fortune* (New York: Time, Inc., 1982).
39. In 1988, for instance, corporate profits jumped some 15%, but corporations paid 10% less in taxes than in the previous year. This trend has persisted over time when profitability and taxes are contrasted. Profits for the 1988-89 fiscal year were 22% greater than the 1984-85 fiscal year, but corporations paid almost 20% less in taxes.
40. New York State AFL-CIO, *UNITY,* vol. 6, iss. 1, January 1989, p. 2.
41. Letter to Editor, *The New York Times,* 25 February 1989, p. 28.
42. Anthony Howard, "SCAA: Start Cutting Corporate Welfare," *Legislative Gazette,* 6 January 1992, p. 3.
43. Assemblyman Francis J. Pordum, Press Conference on IDA Reform, 23 March 1992, Albany, New York.
44. For a discussion, see Fiscal Policy Institute, *High on the Hog in New York's Corporate Boardrooms: A Study of Executive Compensation and Tax Avoidance in New York State* (Albany, 1991).
45. *The Midas Touch,* p. 34.
46. During 1990 and 1991, the New York State United Teachers spent $1,766,831.10, the Civil Service Employees Association spent $1,139,791.80, and the Public Employees Federation invested $879,392.27. See New York Public Interest Research Group, Inc. and New York State Common Cause, *Influence Peddling in New York: Albany's Fat Cats: 1990-1991,* 25 June 1992.
47. *The Midas Touch,* pp. 35-36.
48. Ken Goldfarb, "Look for the Union Label," *Empire State Report,* October 1989, pp. 31-33.

49. Meeting with Governor Cuomo on the occasion of the signing of legislation sponsored by UUP, Albany, NY, 26 August 1992.

50. The Public Policy Institute, *The Zero Option,* (Albany, N.Y., 1990).

51. Nancy Meyer, "Is Your Job Safe?," *Empire State Report,* March 1991, p. 12.

52. Although the legislature and the governor continued to dismantle the public sector, there was a minor change in the state's personal income tax, thanks to the work of the Fiscal Policy Institute. "The Tax Table Benefit Recapture," passed as part of the budget agreement, meant that people with adjusted gross incomes over $150,000 would pay the top tax rate on their entire income rather than first going through the graduated rates. This would increase state income taxes by $717.50 for about 225,000 taxpayers. (Fiscal Policy Institute, *Economic Advisory Bulletin,* July 1991).

53. See *The New York Times,* 15 January 1992, p. 20:1.

54. Lipsky, p. 9.

55. Senator Marino made these comments publicly on 1 September 1992 at the New York State AFL-CIO convention held at the Concord Hotel, Lake Kiamisha, New York.

Chapter Eight

1. Michael Goldfield, *The Decline of Organized Labor in the United States* (Chicago and London: University of Chicago Press, 1987); Bennett Harrison and Barry Bluestone, *The Great U-Turn* (New York : Basic Books, Inc., 1988); Thomas Geoghegan, *Which Side Are You On?* (New York: Farrar, Straus & Giroux, 1991); AFL-CIO Committee on the Evolution of Work, *The Changing Situation of Workers and Their Unions* (Washington, D.C.: AFL-CIO, 1985).

2. Gerald Silverman, "Labor's Agenda," *Empire State Report,* October 1990, pp. 13, 14, 18.

3. Barry Bluestone & Bennett Harrison, *The Deindustrialization of America* (New York: Basic Books, Inc., 1982); Robert Reich, *The Work of Nations* (New York: Alfred A. Knopf, 1991).

4. John McDermott, *The Crisis in the Working Class & Some Arguments for a New Labor Movement* (Boston: South End Press, 1980).

5. Mike Davis, *Prisoners of the American Dream* (London: New Left Books, 1986); Ira Katznelson, *City Trenches: Urban Politic and the Patterning of Class in the United States* (Chicago and London: University of Chicago Press, 1981).

6. Stanley Aronowitz, *Working Class Hero: A New Strategy for Labor* (New York: Adama Books, 1983); Martin Oppenheimer, *White Collar Politics* (New York: Monthly Review Press, 1985).

7. G. William Domhoff, 1990.

8. Ken Goldfarb, "Look for the Union Label," *Empire State Report,* October 1989, p. 32.

9. The Fiscal Policy Institute, "The Right Choice for New York," 1992.

10. "Reverse the Slide," *New York Teacher,* Vol. XXXIV, No. 13, 22 March 1993, p. 3.

11. *Empire State Report,* August 1992.

12. Nancy Meyer, "Is Your Job Safe?," *Empire State Report,* March 1991, pp. 12-17.

13. Andre Gorz, *Critique of Economic Reason* (London and New York: Verso, 1990), p. 143.

14. Alison Mitchell, "Posing as Welfare Recipient, Agency Head Finds Indignity," *The New York Times,* 2 February 1993, p. A1.

15. Jon Sorenson, "Workers of New York...UNITE!," *Empire State Report,* March 1992, pp. 29-30.

16. New York State AFL-CIO, "Taxes We Can Live With," March 1991.

17. Public labor unions have spent a good deal of time either fighting each other or resisting jurisdictional raids from private-sector unions. In fact, at the very juncture at which the major unions were uniting against layoffs, lock-outs, and other attacks, CSEA backed legislation that would take UUP members out of their bargaining unit and put them into CSEA. For a short journalistic account of jurisdictional battles within the state's public sector, see Michael P. Moran, "CSEA: A 75 Year Retrospective," *Empire State Report,* October 1985, pp. 9-13.

18. New York State United Teachers, "Tracking of Public Attitudes Toward Education," 20 February 1992.

19. James O'Connor, *The Fiscal Crisis of the State* (New York: St. Martin's Press, 1973); Martin Carnoy, *The State and Political Theory* (Princeton: Princeton University Press, 1984).

20. Gabriel Kolko, *The Triumph of Conservatism: A Reinterpretation of American History, 1900-1916* (New York: The Free Press, 1963); James Weinstein, *The Corporate Ideal in the Liberal State* (Boston: Beacon Press, 1968).

21. Paul A. Baron and Paul M. Sweezy, *Monopoly Capital: An Essay on the American Economic and Social Order* (New York and London: Monthly Review Press, 1966).

22. Nicos Poulantzas, *Political Power and Social Classes* (London: New Left Books, 1974).

23. Baron and Sweezy, *Monopoly Capital,* 1966.

24. O'Connor, 1973; Claus Offe, *Contradictions of the Welfare State,* ed. John Kean (Cambridge: MIT Press, 1985).

25. American Economic Group Inc., *New York's 16 Billion Dollar Dilemma: Consequences of Our State's Well-Intentioned Tax Cuts—and a Plan to Solve Our Revenue Crisis* (Washington, D.C., 1991), prepared for the New York State United Teachers.

26. Fiscal Policy Institute, "The Right Choice for New York," March 1991, p. 11; Testimony of M. Martin, executive director, Fiscal Policy Institute, before the Joint Senate and Assembly Fiscal Committees on the governor's proposed budget, 28 January 1992.

27. Selig Perlman, *A Theory of the Labor Movement* (New York: MacMillan, 1928).

28. Franz Neumann, "The Concept of Political Freedom," *The Democratic and Authoritarian State* (New York: Free Press, 1964).

29. Paul Johnson, "The Promise of Public Sector Unionism," *Monthly Review,* 1978, pp. 1-17.

30. William E. Scheuerman, "Politics and the Public Sector: Strategies for Public-Sector Unions," *Policy Studies Journal,* vol. 18, no. 2, Winter 1989-90, pp. 433-442.

31. Ralph Miliband, *Divided Societies: Class Struggle in Contemporary Capitalism* (New York: Oxford University Press, 1989); Brecher, 1984.

32. PERB, "What is the Taylor Law?," 1985; Michael P. Moran, "CSEA: A 75 Year Retrospective," *Empire State Report,* pp. 9-14.

33. Charles W. de Seve, *Taxes We Can Live With: Designing a System to Meet Future Needs,* prepared for the New York State AFL-CIO, March 1991, p. 4.

34. Government Employee Relations Report, vol. 29, 26 August 1991, p. 1068.

35. CSEA's grabbing for its own at the expense of union solidarity is seen in other ways too. As noted earlier, at the same time, for instance, that the statewide unions were promoting solidarity, CSEA managed to get a bill introduced in the legislature that would shift some UUP members into the CSEA bargaining unit.

36. Kim Moody, *An Injury to All: The Decline of American Unionism* (London and New York: Verso, 1988); O'Connor, *Fiscal Crisis of the State,* 1973.

37. Moody, 1988.

38. Nick Salvatore, "The Decline of Labor," *Dissent,* Winter 1992, pp. 86-92.

39. Robert S. Lynd, *Knowledge for What: The Place of Social Science in American Culture* (Princeton: Princeton University Press, 1967).

Chapter Nine

1. Samuel P. Huntington, *American Politics: The Promise of Disharmony* (Cambridge: Harvard University Press, 1981), p. 75.

2. Fredric Jameson, *Postmodernism, or The Cultural Logic of Late Capitalism* (Durham: Duke University Press, 1991), p. 273.

3. Obviously, as his surprisingly narrow third-term victory margin suggests, Cuomo's ability to marry a pro-business tax policy with a pro-social policy reputation declined as the evidence of hard times was too clear for most people to miss. By the time the 1992 presidential sweepstakes rolled around, "Impeach Cuomo" bumper stickers were familiar sights on the state's highways, especially in the suburbs of New York City and upstate. And according to Cuomo himself, it was a looming fiscal crisis that kept him from making his long-awaited bid for the White House. Yet Cuomo backers might note that the Clinton Administration includes an array of faces who would have likely been featured in a Cuomo White House, too. Such figures include Roger Altman, vice-chair of the Blackstone Group, who is the number-two person at the Treasury Department, and Robert Rubin of Goldman Sachs, who heads Clinton's economic council in the White House. Altman and Rubin each served on Cuomo's Commission on Trade and Competitiveness.

4. Francis Fox Piven and Richard Cloward, *The New Class War: Reagan's Attack on the Welfare State and Its Consequences* (New York: Pantheon, 1982).

5. Kevin Phillips, *Boiling Point: Democrats, Republicans, and the Decline of Middle-Class Prosperity* (New York: Random House, 1993), pp. 31, 3.

6. *Ibid.,* p. 62.

7. Jameson, *Postmodernism,* p. 265.

8. Bertram Gross, *Friendly Fascism: The New Face of Power in America* (Boston: South End Press, 1980); Andre Gorz, *Paths to Paradise: On the Liberation from Work* (Boston: South End Press, 1985), p. 39; Alain Touraine, *Return of the Actor: Social Theory in Postindustrial Society* (Minneapolis: University of Minnesota Press).

9. Richard Flacks, *Making History: The American Left and the American Mind* (New York: Columbia University Press, 1988), pp. 225-226.

10. Carl Boggs, "Rethinking the Sixties Legacy: From New Left to New Social Movements," in *Breaking Chains, Social Movements and Collective Action, Comparative Urban and Community Research,* vol. 3, ed. Michael Peter Smith (New Brunswick, N.J.: Transaction, 1991), p. 64.

11. Francis Fox Piven and Richard A. Cloward, *Poor Peoples Movements, Why They Succeed, How They Fail* (New York: Random House, 1979), ch. 1.

12. Touraine, *Return of the Actor,* p. 121.

13. Gorz, *Paths to Paradise,* p. 36.

14. Manning Marable, *The Crisis of Color and Democracy: Essays on Race, Class, and Power* (Monroe, ME: Common Courage, 1992), pp. 9-10, as quoted in Cathy J. Cohen and Michael C. Dawson, "Neighborhood Poverty and African-American Politics," *American Political Science Review,* No. 87, June 1993, p. 290.

15. Flacks, *Making History,* p. 261.

16. Jurgen Habermas, *Legitimation Crisis* (Boston: Beacon, 1973), p. 40.

17. David P. Calleo, *The Bankrupting of America: How the Federal Deficit is Impoverishing the Nation* (New York: Avon, 1992), p. 13.

18. C. Wright Mills, *The Power Elite* (New York: Oxford University Press, 1956), p. 267; Theodore J. Lowi, *The End of Liberalism, The Second Republic of the United States,* 2nd ed. (New York: Norton, 1979).

19. Phillips, *Boiling Point,* p. 78.

20. Donald Kettl, *Deficit Politics: Public Budgeting in Its Institutional and Historical Context* (New York: Macmillan, 1992), pp. 166-167; Calleo, *The Bankruptcy of America,* p. 174.

21. Benjamin Friedman, *Day of Reckoning: The Consequences of American Economic Policy* (New York: Random House, 1989), pp. 285-286.

22. Robert S. Lynd, "Power in American Society as Resource and Problem," in Arthur Kornhauser, ed., *Problems of Power in American Democracy* (Detroit: Wayne State University Press, 1957), p. 26.

23. Lynd, "Power in American Society," p. 22.

24. "Opinion Outlook," *National Journal,* 13 June 1992, p. 1434; Kettering Foundation, *Citizens and Politics: A View from Main Street America* (Dayton, Ohio: Kettering, 1991), p. 5.

25. Joseph M. Kling and Prudence S. Posner, "Class and Community in an Era of Urban Transformation," in Kling and Posner, eds., *Dilemmas of Activism, Class, Community, and the Politics of Local Mobilization* (Philadelphia: Temple University Press, 1990), pp. 23-45. Their work on publics draws heavily on the ideas of John Dewey, *The Public and Its Problems* (New York: Henry

Holt, 1927) and C. Wright Mills, *The Sociological Imagination* (New York: Oxford University Press, 1959).

26. *Ibid.,* p. 40.
27. *Ibid.,* p. 41.
28. *Ibid.,* p. 41.
29. See, e.g., Manning Marable, *Race, Reform and Rebellion: The Second Reconstruction in Black America, 1945-1982* (Jackson: University of Mississippi Press, 1984).
30. Lowi, *End of Liberalism,* p. 67.
31. *Ibid.*
32. Franz Neumann, "The Concept of Political Freedom," in *The Democratic and the Authoritarian State,* ed. Herbert Marcuse (New York: Free Press, 1957), p. 193.
33. The proposal presented here is borrowed from Paul E. Peterson, *City Limits* (Chicago: University of Chicago Press, 1980), pp. 218-219.
34. Steven J. Rosenstone, "Electoral Myths, Political Realities," *Boston Review,* XVIII, January/February 1993, p. 5.
35. Gorz, *Pathways to Paradise,* p. 76.
36. Neumann, "The Concept of Political Freedom," p. 193.
37. Gorz, *Pathways to Paradise,* p. 39.

Index

About South End Press

South End Press is a nonprofit, collectively run book publisher with over 175 titles in print. Since our founding in 1977, we have tried to meet the needs of readers who are exploring, or are already committed to, the politics of radical social change.

Our goal is to publish books that encourage critical thinking and constructive action on the key political, cultural, social, economic, and ecological issues shaping life in the United States and in the world. In this way, we hope to give expression to a wide diversity of democratic social movements and to provide an alternative to the products of corporate publishing.

If you would like a free catalog of South End Press books or information about our membership program—which offers two free books and a 40% discount on all titles—please write us at South End Press, 116 Saint Botolph Street, Boston, MA 02115.

Other titles of interest from South End Press:

Hard Pressed in the Heartland:
The Hormel Strike and the Future of the Labor Movement
Peter Rachleff

Mask of Democracy:
Labor Suppression in Mexico Today
Dan LaBotz

Workers of the World Undermined:
American Labor's Role in U.S. Foreign Policy
Beth Sims

The New Resource Wars:
Native and Environmental Struggles Against Multinational Corporations
Al Gedicks

Confronting Environmental Racism:
Voices from the Grassroots
Edited by Robert Bullard